Studies in Talmudic Logic

Volume 16

O'Kheiluf!

The Rabbinic Struggle
with the Contrapositive

Studies in Talmudic Logic Series Editors
Michael Abraham, Dov Gabbay and Uri Schild   dov.gabbay@kcl.ac.uk

O'Kheiluf!

The Rabbinic Struggle
with the Contrapositive

Amelia Spivak

ISBN 978-1-84890-432-3

College Publications
Scientific Director: Dov Gabbay
Managing Director: Jane Spurr

http://www.collegepublications.co.uk

Original cover design by Laraine Welch

לזכר נשמת אמי מורתי

לונה בת ר׳ משה ,ע״ה

CONTENTS

Preface and Acknowledgements

I would like to explain how I came to discover a previously unrecognized tannaitic form of argument that was already lost during the amoraic period and remained lost until this work. While the answer ultimately is luck, as Louis Pasteur said, "Luck favors the prepared mind," and my mind was prepared in a Haredi girls' yeshiva.

The Midrash Halakhah is a subject that has been, throughout my life, in the words of Harold Bloom, "an inescapable interest."[1] Tanakh and the medieval commentators were the major focus of my elementary, high school, and seminary education. The Midrash Halakhah is endlessly fascinating to me because it is one of the primary answers to a question that was on my mind throughout my yeshiva education: what is the source of Rashi's material — the explanations and stories in his commentary on the Humash? The dismissive answer girls invariably received to this question was *ruakh hakodesh*, or divine inspiration.

In Spring 2010, I came across an argument from the Mekhilta that contained the phrase *o'kheiluf*. I was immediately struck by the logical form of the expressions that preceded and followed the phrase, recognizing its relationship to the contrapositive. I wondered whether it was possible that *o'kheiluf* was a technical phrase and always indicated this same particular type of logical operation.

I set out to find all the occurrences of the phrase *o'kheiluf* and other phrases based on the root, פ,ל,ח. Using Bar Ilan's Responsa Project, I

---

[1] "Upfront: Harold Bloom", New York Times, May 7, 2010. Bloom is quoted: "Antisemitism is an inescapable interest, though I never suffered it personally."

slowly amassed all such occurrences (along with occurrences of other roots like ה,פ,כ). At the time, Menahem Kahana's critical edition of the Sifre Bamidbar with comments was not yet available and so I was looking at all of this with fresh unbiased eyes. By 2012, I had determined that *o'kheiluf* was indeed the precise technical term I had originally guessed it might be.

I wanted to compare what I had learned about the logical attempts of the Tannaim to what was known about Stoic logic and the role that logic played in Stoic philosophy. I was very fortunate to be able to just show up at the door of the eminent Stoic scholar, Anthony A. Long. Professor Long was happy to look at what I had and to advise me on his scholarship and also that of Suzanne Bobzien to whom he introduced me. In 2011, when I showed Tony one of the *o'kheiluf* arguments carved up into labeled propositions, as I do in the book, he immediately saw the logic I was trying to expose and was clearly charmed by it. He was the first person with whom I shared any of these arguments and his reaction encouraged me.

I did not have the opportunity to study Talmud in the traditional manner until I moved to the Bay area and was introduced to Reb Henry Falkenberg. Reb Henry, of blessed memory, was the long-time leader of Congregation Keneseth Israel of San Francisco. Trained in the Volozhin tradition, his vast erudition was a treasure to this Jewish community. Reb Henry studied Talmud all day long. In addition to running a small, full-time bais medrash, he was available and able to learn with whoever was interested, whatever they were interested in. I owe my Gemara skills and my entire approach to the *daf* to the more than five years I studied with Reb Henry.

Besides rabbinics, this work also draws on another intellectual interest: I could not have engaged in this work without some training in philosophy. I had the great fortune to study under a number of leading philosophers, including Alan Code, Dorothea Frede, Hannah Ginsborg, David Malament, John Searle, Daniel Warren and the late Barry Stroud. Professor Searle introduced me to professional philosophizing. He convinced me that it was what I was already doing and that I should do more of it. I will always be grateful for his generous mentorship. I am also thankful to David Malament and the Department of Logic and Philosophy of Science for very kind hospitality during my stay in Irvine. This book has especially benefited from Dorothea Frede's superb courses on Plato and Aristotle.

The third ingredient I needed to carry out this work is, what I would describe as, logical attentiveness. Much of the logic needed to understand this book involves no more than what undergraduate philosophy students generally learn. Yet I have taken great pains to make this book readable to a general audience interested in rabbinic discussions and arguments. The professional logician or student of mathematical logic will hopefully appreciate the light hand I have exerted in all things logical. I have endeavored to give only as much background as is necessary to understand the subject of this book and nothing more, while a few footnotes direct the reader to more technical background or ramifications. I have avoided introducing technical terminology not absolutely necessary for understanding the content of this book, but my choice of words will at times ring bells in the mind of the professional logician.

Perhaps nothing has shaped my mind as much as the idea of systems of axioms and proofs from those axioms that I first encountered in high school geometry. Indeed, basic logic has been second nature to me for as long as I can remember and while my doctoral dissertation and my published research has been in mathematical physics and differential geometry, I also trained at the graduate level in mathematical logic. The late Jack Silver had a great influence on me professionally and personally. I deeply miss his friendship.

The findings in this book point to a further moral. Talmudic literature consists of rabbinic arguments, and therefore whatever it is that interests the Talmud student, he or she must grapple with rabbinic reasoning. Many academic papers in Judaic studies make this or that claim of how to understand a particular piece of rabbinic reasoning without distilling the reasoning from the content of the passage.

Philosophers since Aristotle have recognized logic as a major tool with which to investigate reasoning. I hope this book demonstrates to the reader that it is just as true today that basic contemporary formal logic is a very useful tool for examining the *pshat* of rabbinic reasoning. In this book, logic has been used to lay bare how at least two important and popular passages, one in the Mishnah and the other in the Yerushalmi, have been seriously misunderstood.

My home library throughout this work has been the Doe Library of the University of California at Berkeley. I thank the Judaica librarian Dr. Ruth Haber for her cheerful assistance on a number of occasions. I am grateful to two library staff members, Diego A. Holguin and Javier Rodriguez, who went well beyond the extra mile helping me track down hard to find documents and mysteriously missing library volumes.

Some of the research for this book was done at the National Library of Israel in the summer of 2018 and in March 2019. I want to especially thank Dr. Ezra Chwat of The Institute of Microfilmed Hebrew Manuscripts for generously lending me his expertise in manuscript research. I also want to thank Reference Librarian Galia Richler-Grebler for the great kindness she showed me, pulling some strings so that I could get everything I needed under a tight travel schedule.

By 2019, working on it during my spare time, I had turned my notes and charts into a manuscript that would become the first six chapters and Appendix I of this book. I approached Professor David Biale who was very encouraging of this interdisciplinary work, and he suggested that his former student Azzan Yadin would be the perfect person to read and comment on it. It was really thrilling to get a chance to finally meet Professor Yadin-Israel whose work I have admired for many years. I am very grateful to Azzan for reading that early draft and meeting with me to go over it. He made important suggestions on how to make the exposition clearer. He also impressed upon me the significance of my findings that the Tannaim had no Greek word for *o'kheiluf*.

My publishers Dov Gabbay and Jane Spurr at College Publications have been wonderful to work with. I am grateful to Ms. Spurr and to Dr. Michael Gabbay for their skillful guidance in preparing this manuscript. Having my work recognized by a logician of Professor Dov Gabbay's legendary stature is a tremendous honor. It is almost impossible to be a student of philosophy or logic or computer science and never to have learned of Dov Gabbay's work or used his books and papers. Being invited to join the ranks of such first-rate logicians and Talmud scholars that are the editors of the series Studies in Talmudic Logic and having my book join volumes that represent recent path-breaking work in the long history of attempts at logical analysis of talmudic hermeneutics, is really a dream come true for this yeshiva girl.

On a more personal note, this book would never have been written if not for my husband Joshua's encouragement and enthusiasm. His readiness to serve as a sounding board enabled me to make my points sharper. He also read through each draft of each section and his suggestions on how to make my arguments clearer are evidenced on almost each page. He is also responsible for putting together the index. Our sons, now teen-aged, have been the source of my inspiration. They impress me each day with their grace, courage and loyalty to each other.

I did not grow up in a community that encouraged girls to be ambitious outside of the home. My drive, my accomplishments, and my education are, to a large extent, the result of my mother's influence. My mother was independent minded, wildly talented, and broadly very intellectually curious. Unfortunately, illness of many years halted her hectic pace. I discussed with her some of the findings in this book, and I remember how, on one particular night, she became very stimulated over the ideas, briefly appearing roused out of her illness. I had been looking forward to giving her a copy of this book. I miss her so much. I dedicate this book to her memory.

Translations, Abbreviations and Notation

Translations of biblical verses are based on the Jewish Publication Society translation.

Passages from the Midrash Halakhah are quoted according to the following critical editions: Horovitz's edition of the Sifre Numbers, the Horowitz-Rabin edition of the Mekhilta (of R. Ishmael), the Finkelstein edition of the Sifre Deuteronomy. For the Sifra, the Weiss edition is used. Reference is made to Menahem Kahana's critical edition of the Sifre Numbers where it disagrees with the Horovitz edition.

The translations into English that accompany the quoted passages are my own unless stated otherwise. I have used Jacob Lauterbach's translation of the Mekhilta. I cite translations from Jacob Neusner's Sifre Numbers to point out that my own translation of the relevant passage corrects his, and I do the same with one passage from Reuven Hammer's translation of the Sifre Deuteronomy. I also weigh in on Sefaria's online translation (www.sefaria.org) of certain phrases.

Citations and quotations are from the standard editions of the Mishnah and of the Talmud Bavli. I have examined the other manuscripts in the Lieberman Database but only point out significant variants of a passage. I have used both the Vilna and Venice editions of the Talmud Yerushalmi; with regard to the passages I cite, the two editions are in agreement.

The translations into English that accompany cited or quoted passages from the Mishnah and the Talmuds are my own. Other translations of particular passages are cited, for example from the ArtScroll Talmud as well as from Herbert Danby's Mishnah, to critique them.

Abbreviations:

Standard abbreviations of biblical works have been used throughout:
Exod. for Exodus or Shemot.
Lev.   for Leviticus or Vayikra
Num. for Numbers or Bamidbar
Deut. for Deuteronomy or Devarim.

The full names have been used for the works of Midrash Halakhah, with the exception of the Mekhilta de-Rabbi Ishmael, which has been at times referred to simply as the Mekhilta.

The following abbreviations are used followed by the tractate name:

M. = Mishnah
T. = Tosefta
B. = Talmud Bavli
Y. = Talmud Yerushalmi

'Mishnayot' is the plural of enumerated passages in the Mishnah.
'Derashot' is the plural of 'derash' i.e. interpretations.
'Baraitot', is the plural of 'baraita', i.e. tannatic traditions that were not incorporated into the Mishnah.

Capitals are used when referring to the entire work of Mishnah or Talmud, or when referring to a particular tractate of either. When referring to a particular passage of the Mishnah or of the Gemara on the Mishnah that has been cited earlier, lower case is used in the expression. For example, "the mishnah should be understood to mean..," or "the gemara is taking up the question of ..."

Throughout the book letters are used to refer to entire propositions. For example, the following proposition, it is prohibited to derive benefit from the stoned ox, is represented by the letter Q as follows:

Q = 'It is prohibited to derive benefit from the stoned ox.'
The reason for the quotes around the statement of the proposition, is in order to make it clear that it is the entire proposition that is being set equal to the letter Q. The letter Q is then shorthand for the entire proposition. Another convention I used throughout the book to indicate the scope of the expression set equal to a letter symbol, is to italicize the entire intended expression.

INTRODUCTION: On Recovering a Lost Type of Tannaitic Argument

The subject of this book is a type of argument original to the Tannaim that appears to have gone unrecognized by traditional as well as modern scholars.[1] Tannaitic argumentation has been subjected to exhaustive analysis since the talmudic era, yet this type of argument has remained unidentified. The recovery of this argument form requires no modern techniques. Rather, the exposition is along lines that could have been familiar to the Tannaim or their contemporaries.

The type of argument identified in this book is signaled by the phrase או חילוף (transliterated, *o'kheiluf*) which I recover as uniquely tannaitic logical terminology. The phrase and the argument it accompanies occurs 16 times in tannaitic literature: 15 times in the different works of Midrash Halakhah and once in the Mishnah, in an often-cited passage.[2] The presence of this argument form, across so many

---

[1] The rabbinic sages in the Land of Israel from the time of the destruction of the temple until roughly 220 C.E. are referred to as the Tannaim (sing.Tanna). They composed the Mishnah, the Tosefta, and the different works of Midrash Halakhah. (The consensus view of the Midrash Halakhah is that it consists of mostly tannaitic material that underwent a redactional process that probably began in the second century B.C. and concluded in the third century. See the references cited and discussion in H.L.Strack and G. Stemberger, *Introduction to the Talmud and Midrash* (Minneapolis: Fortress Press), 1996, 247-75.)

[2] There is another occurrence of the phrase *o'kheiluf* in the Sifre Deuteronomy, piska 260. In the Addendum to Chapter Two I argue that the occurrence of the phrase in this text was likely a later addition and I show that it does not signify an *o'kheiluf* argument. (For one thing the 'o' means 'and' in piska 260 while in the other 15 occurrences it means 'or' and the argument consists of a systematic choosing between two options rather than the adding of two possibilities together in piska 260 to create a full picture.) There is also another occurrence of the phrase in Chapter 23 of the Midrash Tannaim and the phrase there does represent an *o'kheiluf* argument. However between the set up of that last argument and its resolution there are several missing lines of text and for this reason the argument is not

1

different tannaitic works by different schools, speaks to the likelihood that it was indeed a popular type of tannaitic argument. There are examples of this type of argument also in the Talmuds, some lifted from tannaitic sources and others of amoraic origin.

What I will refer to as the o'kheiluf argument is actually structured as a meta-argument. It consists of two arguments, usually (but not always) qal v'homer or a fortiori arguments sandwiching the phrase או חילוף, followed by a determination of which of the two a fortiori arguments is correct. The meta-argument ends with a formula, almost identical everywhere it occurs, employing uniform terminology to sum up all of the logical steps of the analysis and its results. This is followed by a repetition of the qal v'homer argument that in the analysis was determined to be the correct choice. Other times it is pointed out that there is no way to decide between the two qal v'homer arguments and that some other method is needed to decide the point at issue.

In claiming to recover this argument form, I am certainly not denying that the sixteen tannaitic arguments were studied individually. The one from Mishnah Pesahim, was studied extensively by the Talmuds and one from the Midrash Halakhah, from the Sifra, was copied into and commented upon in the Talmud Bavli. In each case from the Midrash Halakhah, medieval commentators sought to make clear the meaning of the relevant passage. Much later, the Vilna Gaon's copy of the Sifre Bamidbar and Devarim incorporated clarifying emendations.[3] However, commentary on any of these arguments has

---

considered in this work. Those missing lines in the Midrash Tannaim also known as the Mekhilta on Deuteronomy, are perhaps not a surprise as the work is a reconstruction by David Hoffmann from fragments preserved in the Midrash HaGadol (composed in the 14th Century). For more on the Midrash Tannaim and Hoffmann's work, see Michael Tilly, Burton L. Visotzky, *Judaism II: Literature* (Kohlhammer 2021).

[3] *Sifre: Bamidbar, Devarim, im perush ha-meyuhas leha-Rabad* (and with the Vilna Gaon's text version of the Sifre). The recently recovered commentary attributed to the Rabad, Abraham ben David, of Posquières, approximately 1125-1198, was edited by Ralbag, Eli'ezer Dan Ben Aryeh Leyb, Israel: Mechon Sofrim, 2009.

tended to focus on the content rather than the underlying form. None of these arguments has ever been seen as having a certain special form or structure. No commentary has seen these different arguments as related or even similar to one another.

A full appreciation of the underlying structure of this type of argument requires ancient Greek logic. After the closing of the Babylonian Talmud and later during the Medieval and Early Modern eras, prominent Talmud scholars wrote explicitly on Greek logic. For example, in the 1700's the Ramkhal's work taught students how to use Western logic to better understand talmudic arguments.[4] Yet he too makes no mention of this argument form and its associated terminology which I identify in this work as logical terminology.

O'Kheiluf is Not a Vague Context-Dependent Phrase

The signaling phrase או חילוף, transliterated *o'kheiluf*, did not seem to alert scholars that an argument of a precise form was being introduced. The word 'או', means 'or' and the root of the word חילוף, is ח,ל,פ, which means to exchange or to switch. The latter is certainly a common root that shows up in many noun, verb and adjective forms in the Tanakh and in rabbinic works. The noun חילוף (or חלוף) though is not very common and the noun phrase או חילוף arises precisely 17 times in tannaitic literature. Informed by the root ח,ל,פ, the phrase או חילוף has typically been translated 'or the reverse,' i.e. the phrase has been understood to be referring to the second *a fortiori* vaguely as 'the reverse' of the first *a fortiori* argument.

The phrase 'the reverse' is an everyday expression with a context-dependent meaning: what the 'reverse' of something is depends on

---

[4] *Derekh Tevunot* and *Sefer HaHigayon*, both by Rabbi Moshe Hayyim Luzzatto,1742. Some of the topics he discusses are subject and predicate of a statement, *hekesh* which seems to refers to the categorical syllogism, and *hekesh hatina-ee-yee* (הקש התנאי) which seems to refers to *modus ponens*.

the matter being discussed. The phrase *o'kheiluf* did not appear to be a very precise expression in tannaitic literature. Instead its meaning was believed to vary depending on the context of its use. This book will show that 'or the reverse' is not a fair translation of the phrase *o'kheiluf*. The two *a fortiori* arguments are in fact related to one another in a very precise and uniform way which is hardly captured by translating the phrase *o'kheiluf* by the context-dependent phrase 'or the reverse' and thereby describing the second qal v'homer argument vaguely as 'the reverse' of the first one.

The Midrash Halakhah contains many passages where one qal v'homer is pitted against another or one qal v'homer is critiqued and a different hermeneutical technique is applied in its place. The way traditional and modern scholars have typically studied these arguments is by examining their content and not seeing their structural form. Thus in the sea of argument and counterargument that makes up so much of the Midrash Halakhah, a certain way of countering one qal v'homer with another, announced with a seemingly everyday expression, 'or the reverse', eluded critical examination.

The Need for Symbolic Representation

To describe this argument form with some precision it is necessary to give the correct definition of the phrase *o'kheiluf*. But there is no word in English that can serve as a proper translation of the phrase nor is there any word for it in ancient Greek. This is because the Greeks did not have the concept of *o'kheiluf*. Since the concept has no Western counterpart, it will not be possible to give a definition in one sentence.

The *o'kheiluf* will be shown to be a logical and linguistic technical term. It will be shown that it refers to an argument, usually (but not always) a qal v'homer argument, that results from taking a particular sort of qal v'homer and exchanging its parts in a completely specifiable way. There is no word in English, nor was there in Greek, for such changes to the parts of a statement.

4

However, the idea of defining a term to describe a particular change to the form of a sentence is not unusual. We have Western concepts and therefore English words for certain types of changes to a sentence. Defining such terms is always clearest when symbols are used.

For example, defining the *converse* of a statement as a new statement formed by exchanging the positions of the two halves of the original 'If,then' sentence, is vague and hard to follow. Adding more words to accurately identify the two halves to be exchanged, makes it even more complicated to follow. In contrast, symbolic definition is both precise and unambiguous. The *converse* of a statement of the form 'If P then Q', where P and Q are symbols representing specific statements, is defined as 'If Q then P'. Given a particular statement there is in general little ambiguity about how to use this definition to form its converse. For example, 'If he will study then he will learn' becomes 'If he will learn then he will study'. Greek philosophers studied the converse and noted that the converse of a true statement, depending on the particular statement, is often not a true statement.

Other words in English used to indicate a sentence arrived at by making certain precise changes to a particular sentence are *inverse* and *contrapositive*. The *kheiluf* is none of these. It refers to a new qal v'homer formed by rearranging the parts of a first qal v'homer in a way that cannot be specified as the reverse or the converse or the contrapositive or the negation of the original. We have no concept for the change the *kheiluf* is describing, because the Greeks from whom we inherited these logical, philosophical and linguistic concepts, had no such concept either.

Chapter One calls on a symbolic representation of the qal v'homer defended in depth in Appendix I. Building on this formula, I present a symbolic definition of the phrase *o'kheiluf* and a symbolic representation of the *o'kheiluf* argument. It is then shown that this representation fits the example of the *o'kheiluf* argument from the Sifre Bamidbar examined earlier in the chapter. The discussion then turns to the function served by this form of argument and the unusual conditions under which it arose. The terminological role played by the phrase *o'kheiluf* in the argument is displayed.

Chapter Two presents each of the 15 *o'kheiluf* arguments in the Midrash Halakhah in detail in order to show that what was demonstrated in Chapter One for the one example from Sifre Bamidbar holds as well for each of the other *o'kheiluf* arguments: The phrase *o'kheiluf* has the same precise definition everywhere it occurs and every *o'kheiluf* argument fits the symbolic representation presented in Chapter One. The writing style in Chapter Two is less expository than in the other chapters, the pace is brisk with the goal of staying on point to prove this generalization. In Chapter Six the same is shown for the one *o'kheiluf* argument that occurs in the Mishnah. I thus establish that the phrase *o'kheiluf* is uniquely tannaitic logical terminology and that the *o'kheiluf* argument is a unique form of tannaitic argument which concludes with more uniquely tannaitic logical terminology. The perfectly identical meaning of this phrase throughout the works of the R. Ishmael and R. Akiva schools and the Mishnah suggests that this technical logico-linguistic terminology was widely applied in tannaitic discourse.

Chapter Three, points out that the noun *kheiluf* does arise in another tannaitic phrase besides *o'kheiluf*. That phrase is *kheiluf ha-devarim*. Examples of passages employing the phrase are discussed and the phrase is shown to have a very precise meaning, one that is clearly distinct from the meaning of *o'kheiluf*. The Tannaim are shown to have been attuned to the need for terminology to distinguish between different logical operations. A case of *o'kheiluf* was not to be confused with a case of *kheiluf ha-devarim*. This is further evidence that the phrase *o'kheiluf* functioned as technical terminology.

Chapter Four is a study comparing the *o'kheiluf* arguments of the school of R. Ishmael with those of the school of R. Akiva. Because these arguments number only 15 with six of them occurring in the school of R. Ishmael and nine occurring in the works of the school of R. Akiva, they present an opportunity for a thorough and in-depth comparative study of how the two schools employ a shared argument form or hermeneutical tool. Previously unrecognized and important differences between the analytical traits of the two schools are exposed.

The new findings from this comparative study contradict Menahem Kahana and the earlier scholarship he cites that the Mekhilta de-Miluim in the Sifra, specifically the passage containing the *o'kheiluf* argument I identify there, should be attributed to the school of R. Ishmael rather than to the school of R. Akiva.[5] Thus the *o'kheiluf* argument emerges as a concrete tool for determining school authorship for different passages in the Midrash Halakhah.

Chapter Five steps back to analyze the logical coherence of the *o'kheiluf* argument. Does it do what it claims to do and reasonably eliminate one of two possible arguments so that the correct answer remains? This question is explored and answered by the lights of the logicians and the rhetoricians of the age of the Tannaim, the Stoic philosophers. The *o'kheiluf* argument is seen to involve maneuvers that the Stoic philosopher would interpret as functioning to compensate for blanket ignorance of Greek logic. But as to the logical coherence of the argument, surprisingly different answers are reached for the R. Ishmael and R. Akiva schools that challenge conventional thinking about these two schools.

Chapter Six takes up the single *o'kheiluf* argument of the Mishnah. Although it is not presented in one voice but rather as a debate between two individuals, this *o'kheiluf* argument fits precisely the same symbolic form as do all the others of the different works of Midrash Halakhah. My demonstration that the phrase *o'kheiluf* is precise, uniquely tannaitic terminology wherever it is found, is thus complete.

---

[5] Menahem Kahana, "The Halakhic Midrashim," in *The Literature of the Jewish People in the Period of the Second Temple and the Talmud. Volume III: The Literature of the Sages*, eds. Shmuel Safrai, Ze'ev Safrai, Joshua Schwartz, and Peter Thomson (New York: Brill Publications, 2006), 83-87.

The single *o'kheiluf* argument of the Mishnah which spans the first two mishnayot of tractate Pesahim, chapter 6, is a very famous argument in the Mishnah, quoted and cited widely. The mishnayot concern whether the Passover sacrifice may be brought on the Sabbath. This is clearly an important topic, but the Gemara on these mishnayot goes further and attaches paramount importance to this question: the Gemara there cites a baraita that tells the story of how, on the sole basis of Hillel's ability to answer this question, he was chosen to be *nasi* over Palestinian Jewry.[6]

The Bavli and the Yerushalmi are very much exercised by these mishnayot and especially by R. Akiva's strategy in the argument. They examine the content of the argument, and to whom the different statements are attributed, but they do not study its form. Consequently they do not come to a good understanding of the argument and of R. Akiva's impressive contribution. Neither the Bavli nor the Yerushalmi seems to be aware that the collection of arguments in the Midrash Halakhah bearing the phrase *o'kheiluf* have a particular form and function and that it would be useful to compare the argument in the Mishnah to those others in order to better understand the mishnaic argument.

Despite the popularity of these mishnayot, no traditional or scholarly commentary has brought any more clarity to the argument than the

---

[6] See B.Pesahim 66a. The *nasi* during the Second Temple Period was the leading member of the *Sanhedrin*, the highest court and assembly. The Roman government viewed the *nasi* as the Patriarch of the Jews and required all Jews to pay him a tax for the upkeep of his office. For more background see Lawrence H. Schiffman, *From Text to Tradition* (Hoboken: Ktav,1991).

The sages that followed the Tannaim (see footnote 1) are referred to as the Amoraim (sing., Amora). The Amoraim in the Land of Israel, active from 220 CE to about 400 CE, generated the Palestinian Talmud (i.e. the Yerushalmi) and the amoraic midrashim. The teachings of the Amoraim in Babylonia form the basis of the Babylonian Talmud (i.e. the Bavli) whose redaction was not completed until sometime into the seventh century. The Gemara is the component of the Talmud that consists of the rabbinic analysis and commentary on the Mishnah by the Amoraim and the rabbis that followed, up until the closing of the Talmud.

strained and cumbersome treatment in the Bavli. This is the first work to compare the argument in the Mishnah to all the other tannaitic arguments that contain the phrase *o'kheiluf*. It is a natural thing to do once it is recognized that *o'kheiluf* has a precise technical meaning in the Midrash Halakhah. Comparing the mishnaic argument to all the other tannaitic *o'kheiluf* arguments brings new illumination and clarification to the famous mishnaic argument and to R. Akiva's methodology.

Chapter Seven considers the *o'kheiluf* arguments in the Midrash Halakhah that were not incorporated as baraitot in the Talmuds and seeks to glean from the Talmuds' treatment of the topics involved, the reasons for which the Talmuds rejected this tannaitic material in favor of other material. I address the question of whether the absence of these arguments in the Talmuds can be taken to indicate that the Amoraim (and later the Savoraim) saw logical shortcomings in these arguments.

Chapter Eight studies the two *o'kheiluf* arguments that appear in the Bavli. One is found on B.Temurah 28b as a baraita and is a copy of an *o'kheiluf* argument from the Sifra. The other *o'kheiluf* argument on B. Avodah Zarah 46b is of amoraic origin, original to the Bavli. I find that the Amoraim used the phrase *o'kheiluf* exactly as the Tannaim did with the same exact meaning and that they were able to correctly set up the *kheiluf* argument. But in its analysis of the argument from the Sifra, the Bavli reads its own objectives into the passage in a manner that exposes serious ignorance of the structure and function of the tannaitic *o'kheiluf* argument. The *o'kheiluf* argument in Avodah Zarah, leads Rava to formulate a principle that would put an end to amoraic *o'kheiluf* arguments. My analysis makes sense of this development, which the Tosafists did not understand properly, and leads to a theory of why the *o'kheiluf* argument died out. These reasons are very different from those given for the demise of different hermeneutical techniques in the talmudic era.

Chapter Nine examines the two amoraic *o'kheiluf* arguments identified in the Yerushalmi. These display the same expertise at forming the negation of a complex claim and they use the phrase *o'kheiluf* exactly as do the Tannaim in the Midrash Halakhah and the Mishnah and as the Amoraim later in the Bavli. But unlike those other *o'kheiluf* arguments, after setting up the two possibilities, the original and the *kheiluf*, the Yerushalmi does not pursue determining which of the two is correct. The chapter examines each one in turn to discover why this is the case.

The understanding of the *o'kheiluf* argument developed in this book illuminates a popular and widely quoted but seriously misinterpreted statement that appears on Y. Sanhedrin 4:1, 21a and is paralleled on B. Sanhedrin 17a: Only one who is able to prove, in one hundred ways, from the Torah, that a *sheretz* is pure and in another one hundred ways that the *sheretz* is impure, may judge capital cases. (The *sheretz* there refers to one of the eight impure reptiles listed in Lev.11:29-30.)

Chapter Ten briefly summarizes the conclusions found in each of the earlier chapters and draws several of them together for some further meta-conclusions and suggestions. Aside from rabbinic culture, attention is drawn to the contribution this book makes to the study of the history of logic.

Appendix I develops and defends a simple symbolic representation of the tannaitic qal v'homer argument useful for the project of Chapter One, i.e. describing what this book identifies as an *o'kheiluf* argument. In particular, it is the first step for clarifying the difference between a typical qal v'homer and one that occurs as part of an *o'kheiluf* argument.

Appendix II considers to what extent the Tannaim and later the Amoraim can be said to have argued in the manner of *reductio ad absurdum*. This is relevant to the subject of this book, as the Stoic philosophers formalized this ancient way of arguing with (what is commonly referred to as) *modus tollens*. An argument in the Bavli reflecting *modus tollens* reasoning is presented.

CHAPTER ONE: Definition and Function of *O'Kheiluf*

Introduction

The subject of this book is a type of tannaitic argument that appears to have gone unrecognized by traditional as well as modern scholars. I will refer to it as the *o'kheiluf*, as each argument of this form can be identified by the presence of the phrase "או חילוף", pronounced *o'kheiluf*. The word *o'* (the transliteration of או) means 'or' and the root of the word *kheiluf* (חילוף) is ח,ל,פ which means to exchange or to switch. Although this root is not uncommon, the particular phrase "או חילוף" arises precisely 16 times in tannaitic sources: 15 times in the different works of Midrash Halakhah and once in the Mishnah.[7] Each of those 16 occurrences is in exactly one *o'kheiluf* argument.

It will be shown that the phrase *o'kheiluf* was used intentionally to mark the argument as an example of one particular form. The presence of this argument form, across so many different tannaitic works, speaks to the likelihood that it was indeed a popular and clearly defined type of tannaitic argument.

What will be referred to as the *o'kheiluf* argument is structured as a tannaitic meta-argument. It consists of two arguments usually qal v'homer or *a fortiori* arguments sandwiching the phrase או חילוף, and followed by a determination of which of the two arguments is correct.[8]

---

[7] See footnote 2.

[8] Except in one case, Sifre Bamidbar, piska 155, on Parshat Matot, (and one case in the Talmud Yerushalmi) where the two arguments that sandwich the phrase או חילוף are just-as arguments rather than *a fortiori* argument.
See Chapter Two, #6, for the text. This important example is examined in Chapter Five.
An *a fortiori* argument has a quality of how-much-more-so while what is being referred to here as a just-as argument has a quality of so-too.
An example of an *a fortiori* statement or argument:

Prior to this work, the phrase *o'kheiluf* has typically been translated 'or the reverse' i.e. it has been understood to be referring to the second *a fortiori* argument vaguely as 'the reverse' of the first *a fortiori* argument.[9] The reader will soon see that 'the reverse' is not a

---

If grammar school students can understand this book, most certainly a high school student will be able to understand it.

While a just-as argument would be:

A fifth grader Alan understands the book, so Bob who is also in the fifth grade should be able to understand the book.

[9] The single occurrence of the phrase *o'kheiluf* in the Mishnah is M.Pesahim 6:3. In the ArtScroll edition of the Bavli, folio Pesahim 66a[1], the phrase is translated 'Or [perhaps] the reverse [is true]'. There are no further comments in the Notes on bottom of the pages regarding the phrase or in the treatment of folio 69a where that part of the Mishnah is discussed. In the ArtScroll's Schotenstein edition of the Yerushalmi, folio Pesachim 48a[2], the phrase is translated 'or [perhaps say] the reverse'.There are no comments in the Notes at the bottom of the page taking up any further the meaning of this phrase. This is reflective of the fact that, as far as I can tell, no Medieval or Early Modern commentary, preserved in Hebrew, explains or describes this phrase in words other than the word *kheiluf*.

This holds as well for the occurrences of the phrase in the Midrash Halakhah and so the phrase has been similarly translated in those works:

i. On page 78 of volume III of the critical edition of Mekilta de-Rabbi Ishmael, with translation and notes by Jacob Z. Lauterbach, published by the Jewish Publication Society of America in 1976, the occurrence of the phrase in Tractate Nezikin, parsha 10, is translated 'Perhaps just the reverse!'. The online translation Sefaria also translates this occurrence as 'the reverse'.

ii. Azzan Yadin, *Logos as Scripture: Rabbi Ishmael and the Origins of Midrash* (Philadelphia: University of Pennsylvania Press, 2004),124. Yadin quotes there the same passage from the Mekhiltah cited in i above and presents Lauterbach's translation of the passage with the phrase או חילוף translated as 'or perhaps the reverse holds true'. Yadin writes of this passage, "[T]he reversal of the argument points to an inherent weakness of *din* – an arbitrariness inherent in the application of interpretive principles to Scripture" and that "ultimately it argues against the use of *din* independently of Scripture." The understanding of the *o'kheiluf* argument developed in Chapters One, Two and Five of this book, make clear that this is not the right way to understand the passage and its function. (This *o'kheiluf* argument from the Mekhilta is analyzed in Chapter Two of this work. The function of the phrase *o'kheiluf* in each of the arguments in which it appears is discussed in Chapter One.) Yadin quotes the passage along with others from the school of R. Ishmael to make the point that "*din* is not self-grounding." Yadin's point about *din* in general, outside of *din* contained in an *o'kheiluf* argument, is not directly addressed in this book. But from a reading

12

of Chapters One and Five, one may see that this is not the correct way to understand the components that make up a qal v'homer argument. His claims also do not take into account the inductive nature of qal v'homer reasoning. For treatment of Yadin's claims, see my paper "How are Scripture and Reason Related in the Midrash Halakhah? Refutation of Neusner's Influential View and its Serious Consequences," submitted for publication. Yadin's conclusions somewhat in support of Neusner, and his logically problematic manner of characterizing *din* as separate from Scripture, so that a contrast can be made between *din* and Scripture, are adopted and extended by Christine Hayes on pages 167-184 (especially 178-184) of her book, *What's Divine about Divine Law?: Early Perspectives* (Princeton: Princeton University Press, 2015).

Neusner's views referred to in this note are those expressed in his translations to the Sifre Numbers and Sifra and their respective introductions:

Jacob Neusner, *Sifre to Numbers: An American Translation*, 2 vols.(Atlanta: Scholars Press,1986).

Jacob Neusner, *Sifra: An Analytic Translation*, 3 vols. (Atlanta: Scholars Press,1988).

iii. In the new online translation by Sefaria, the occurrence of the phrase in Sifre Bamidbar, piska 155, is also translated 'or the reverse' and the occurrence of the phrase in Sifre Devarim, piska 249, is translated 'or conversely'.

iv. In his critical edition of the Sifre Bamidbar published by Magnus Press, 2015, Menahem Kahana points out in Part IV, page 919, in discussing piska 118, that the phrase *o'kheiluf* occurs as well in other passages in the Sifre Bamidbar. He does not however understand the phrase *o'kheiluf* or the argument in which it occurs to have a precise and interesting meaning and function.The only word he uses to describe *o'kheiluf*, או חילוף, is a word with the same root, חלופי, which translated in English, means 'alternative'. Kahana uses this word frequently throughout the work in other contexts; it is an everyday non-technical word to him and he incorrectly concludes that it was that way for the Tannaim as well.

v. On page 266 of his book, למשנה מדרש בין (Raanana: Open University, 2020), Ishay Rosen-Zvi cites Kahana's collection of various occurrences of the phrase חילוף או in Midrash Halakhah. Like Kahana, Rosen-Zvi does not recognize a single uniform and precise meaning for the phrase. Instead he writes that the phrase appears in different variations and like Kahana describes it tautologically as preceding, הלימוד החלופי שהובא בלשון 'או חילוף'. He continues, writing of the alternative teaching, that it is contradicted by a different *katuv*, textual phrase: נסתר על ידי כתוב אחר. But that is incorrect: it is contradicted by the original textual phrase that is the basis for the original teaching. Rosen-Zvi's misconstrual of *o'kheiluf* and its function is not very different from Yadin's (ii), he writes:

fair translation. The two *a fortiori* arguments are in fact related to one another in a very precise and uniform way which is hardly captured by translating the phrase "או חילוף," by the context-dependent phrase 'or the reverse' and thereby describing the second qal v'homer argument vaguely as 'the reverse' of the first.
'

It is because of this context-dependent and incorrect understanding of the phrase *o'kheiluf* that the *o'kheiluf* argument has never before been recognized as an argument form. The phrase *o'kheiluf* was seen by subsequent interpreters of tannaitic works as an everyday phrase and was not understood to have a context independent meaning.

Rather, the relevant passages were viewed as presenting one *a fortiori* argument and then suggesting that perhaps that one was wrong and another *a fortiori* argument instead was correct. It was thought that *o'kheiluf*, read as 'the reverse', meant something different depending on which *a fortiori* argument was being countered with another one. Since the countering of one possible *a fortiori* argument with another is not uncommon in tannaitic literature, not much attention was paid to uncovering the significance of the phrase *o'kheiluf* involved. It was not recognized that the specific instances involving the phrase *o'kheiluf*, represent a consistent and precise tannaitic argument form.

There is no Western concept and therefore no word in English that can capture the essence of the phrase *o'kheiluf*. The first objective of this chapter is to show that the phrase *o'kheiluf* is a technical term, a uniquely tannaitic logical and linguistic term having no parallel in Greek logic. The focus will then turn to the function this logical term serves as well as the role served by the entire *o'kheiluf* argument.

כלומר הדין לעצמו לא מספיק, שכן אפשר היה לדון גם ההפך (= 'או חילוף'), ולכן יש צורך
בכתוב שיכריע בין ההיסקים האפשריים השונים.

1.1: Symbolic Formulation of the *O'Kheiluf* Argument

The whole complex, the two *a fortiori* arguments (or the two just-as arguments) along with the phrase "אי חילוף" sandwiched between them, will be referred to as the first part of an *o'kheiluf* argument. What follows and the conclusion of the *o'kheiluf* argument, will be referred to as the second part of the argument. Since the *o'kheiluf* argument is built out of two arguments which are usually rabbinic *a fortiori* arguments, before presenting an example of the former it makes sense to pause to provide some pertinent background on the latter.

Following some brief remarks about the qal v'homer, a rough description of the format of the *o'kheiluf* argument will be given along with an example of one such argument. These will motivate the quest for a symbolic formulation of the *o'kheiluf*, by demonstrating the need for a clear context-independent understanding of this form of argument. To that end, a symbolic representation of the qal v'homer will be offered and defended. This symbolic representation will be reformulated into one that symbolizes propositions rather than terms. Building on careful analysis of the nature of the propositions that make up a typical qal v'homer argument, discussion will follow detailing how the qal v'homer arguments of the *o'kheiluf* argument are different from those typical ones. These points along with the second symbolic representation of the qal v'homer argument will be used to obtain a symbolic formulation of the (first half of the) *o'kheiluf* argument. The example given earlier of an *o'kheiluf* argument will then be put into this formulation. I claim that each tannaitic *o'kheiluf* argument may be represented with this same exact symbolic formulation. Later, in Chapter Two this claim will be verified for each of the *o'kheiluf* arguments of the Midrash Halakhah.

Some brief preliminary background on the rabbinic *a fortiori*

A *fortiori* arguments in rabbinic literature, and specifically in tannaitic literature, are usually referred to by the phrase *qal v'homer*, קל וחומר, or by the word *din*, דין as in 'אינו דין' or 'דין הוא' (and also sometimes by the phrase 'על אחת כמה וכמה').[10] *Qal v'homer* means [from the] light [to the] weighty while *din* usually means judgment. The qal v'homer is the first of Hillel's seven hermeneutical rules for interpreting the Torah listed in the Tosefta, Sanhedrin, 7. It also leads the list of 13 hermeneutical principles set forth in the Baraita of R. Ishmael found in the opening of the Sifra, the tannaitic commentary on Leviticus. For the purposes of this work, all rabbinic a fortiori arguments will be lumped together, whether they contain the word *din* or the phrase *qal v'homer*, or whether the argument is introduced as *qal v'homer* but contains the word *din*. Each such argument will be referred to as a qal v'homer argument.

In the Midrash Halakhah the qal v'homer is often used to derive laws from biblical verses. Sometimes this is achieved directly, that is, a certain claim is shown to be the conclusion of a qal v'homer argument that starts from a statement in a biblical verse. Because it is derived by compelling qal v'homer reasoning from a biblical law, the conclusion also has the status of a law. More often however, the qal v'homer serves indirectly in deriving new laws. A biblical verse is shown to be unnecessary for its simple meaning — and therefore available for a new teaching — because the teaching of the simple meaning is derivable by qal v'homer from another biblical phrase. The Mishnah uses the qal v'homer more commonly to test different rulings against each other than to derive new laws.

Although the qal v'homer has long been viewed as identical to the (non-Judaic) *a fortiori,* the presentations of the two are not always

---

[10] Appendix I contains several examples from the Mishnah and one from the Midrash Halakhah. For a defense of the rationality of such arguments see, Naomi Janowitz and Andrew Lazarus,"Rabbinic Methods of Inference and the Rationality Debate," *The Journal of Religion*, vol 72, no.4, (Oct. 1992): 491-511.

identical. Aristotle is one of the ancient writers, for example, who discusses a *fortiori* argumentation. He refers to it by the phrase 'from the more and the less' and describes it as a well established form of reasoning; he gives some examples in his Topics.[11] Each of Aristotle's examples is expressed as a declarative statement while the rabbinic a *fortiori*, on the other hand, whether or not introduced with the phrase *qal v'homer*, is more often presented as a rhetorical question.[12] As will soon be seen, the latter is the case with the qal v'homer arguments that occur in the *o'kheiluf* argument.

A quick example of a tannaitic qal v'homer that takes the form of a rhetorical question rather than a statement is Example ii below, which is taken up for analysis a bit later in this section:

ספרי דברים, פרשת ראה, פיסקא עו :

רבי אליעזר אומר:

ומה פסח שאין חייבים על בשולו, חייבים על אכילתו, בשר בחלב שחייבים על בשולו

אינו דין שחייבים על אכילתו !?

Sifre Deuteronomy, Parshat Ri-ay, piska 76:
Rabbi Eliezer says:
Since [in the case of] the Paschal lamb where there is no stated law not to cook it, there is a prohibition against eating it if cooked, [with regard to the case of] meat with milk [together], where there is an explicit prohibition against cooking it, must it not follow that it be prohibited to be eaten if cooked ?![13]

---

[11] William and Martha Kneale, *The Development of Logic* (Oxford: Oxford University Press, 1962), 42-43. The footnote at the bottom of page 42 gives many references in Aristotle's *Topica*: ii. 10 (114^{b}37); iii. 6 (119^{b}17); iv. 5 (127^{b}18); v. 8 (137^{b}14); vi. 7 (145^{b}34); vii. I (152^{b}6); vii. 3 (154^{b}4).

[12] See Appendix I.

[13] The commentary continues with a refutation of this qal v'homer argument. The phrase "you will not eat it" in Deut.12:25 is upheld as necessary to serve as the source for the law that eating meat and milk together is forbidden. The end of Chapter Five discusses the logic involved in refuting a qal v'homer argument.

The Rough Format of the *O'Kheiluf* Argument

Having provided above some brief background on the qal v'homer, it is now possible to give a rough outline of (what has been named in this work) the *o'kheiluf* argument:

(1) The *o'kheiluf* argument begins with what seems like an ordinary qal v'homer argument.

(2) This qal v'homer argument is apparently not viewed as completely convincing as it is immediately attacked with the words או חילוף, *o'kheiluf*, usually translated 'or perhaps [the correct argument should be] the 'reverse'.

(3) The *kheiluf* argument is then presented. The *kheiluf* is a different qal v'homer argument related to the original one. To date the relationship between the two arguments has been understood as dependent on the details and context of the particular example. The *kheiluf* has not been recognized as a technical term and it has correspondingly been translated by the everyday vague and context dependent expressions 'the reverse' or 'the alternative'.

(4) In the second part of the successful *o'kheiluf* argument, one of the two qal v'homer arguments (i.e. the argument positioned to be the second argument) is invalidated by a biblical proof text and the other argument is then by default declared correct. While in other cases, which can be described as unsuccessful, it is shown that there is no way to choose which one of the two contradictory qal v'homer arguments is correct. (Chapter Four takes up the latter situation when it considers arguments of the school of R. Akiva.)

A quick example, streamlined a bit, will clarify the above description of the first half of an *o'kheiluf* argument. The example is from the Sifre Numbers, piska 123 which deals with Num.19:2. The full argument is taken up later in this chapter and subjected to extensive analysis.

Here only a sketch is presented, sufficient to identify in the example, features 1-3 above.

The *O'Kheiluf* Argument, Example i:

Numbers, Chapter 19, deals with the purification rite involving the ashes of a red heifer. Verse 2 spells out the requirements that the animal chosen for this rite must satisfy:

זאת חקת התורה אשר צוה ה' לאמר, דבר אל בני ישראל ויקחו אליך פרה אדומה תמימה אשר אין בה מום אשר לא עלה עליה על.

This is the decree of the Torah that the Lord commanded, saying:
Speak to the children of Israel, and they shall take to you a pure[ly] red heifer which is without blemish, upon which no yoke was mounted.

In examining this verse the Sifre analyzes the function of the phrase "upon which no yoke was mounted." The Sifre seeks to answer the question of whether the words "no yoke" in the verse mean to include any work as disqualifying the red heifer from serving in the rite, whether or not it involved the wearing of a yoke.

The Sifre seeks an answer by relating the case of the red heifer to the case of the calf of the *eglah arufah* rite which has much in common with the former. With regard to the calf of the *eglah arufah* rite the verse does not say anything about being blemish-free but it does stipulate that it be a calf "that was not made to work, that did not draw with a yoke" (Deut. 25:3).

Sifre Bamidbar, piska 123:

Since a <u>calf</u>, which is not disqualified by a blemish <u>is disqualified [from serving as the eglah arufah] by work done [even] without a yoke</u>, then with regard to a <u>red heifer</u>, which is disqualified by a blemish [from serving], must-it-not-follow that it too should be <u>disqualified [from serving] by work done [even] without a yoke</u>?!

19

O'kheiluf

Since a <u>red heifer</u>, which is disqualified by a blemish,<u> is not disqualified for work done without a yoke</u>, then with regard to the <u>calf</u>, which isn't disqualified by a blemish, must-it-not-follow that it too <u>is not disqualified for work done without a yoke</u> ?!

The symbol '?!' is used to denote a rhetorical question. The beginnings and the endings of each of the two qal v'homer arguments in the *o'kheiluf* argument above have been underlined. Referring to the beginning of the first argument, by 'Beginning 1' and the beginning of the second argument, by 'Beginning 2', and likewise for the endings, the following identifications can be made:

'Beginning 1'	= 'The calf is disqualified by work done without a yoke.'
'Ending 1'	= 'The red heifer is disqualified for work done without a yoke.'
'Beginning 2'	= 'The red heifer is not disqualified for work done without a yoke.'
'Ending 2'	= 'The calf is not disqualified for work done without a yoke.'

Note that the statement labeled 'Beginning 2' is the negation of the statement labeled 'Ending 1'. That is, 'Beginning 2' is precisely the statement that 'Ending 1' is not true. Likewise, 'Ending 2' is the negation of 'Beginning 1'.

'Beginning 2' = 'negation of Ending 1'
'Ending 2' = 'negation of Beginning 1'

Thus the first qal v'homer argument begins with 'Beginning 1' and ends with 'Ending 1', and it is easy to see that the qal v'homer that follows the phrase *o'kheiluf* begins with the negation of 'Ending 1' and ends with the negation of 'Beginning 1'.

For rabbinic qal v'homer arguments like the ones above, words like 'Beginning' and 'Ending' are too vague to identify the intended propositions, and this is why underlines were needed to direct the reader to which propositions are to be isolated and labeled as 'Beginning' and 'Ending' of each argument.

It would be desirable to obtain instead very clear criteria for 'Beginning' and 'Ending' which can be applied consistently to each qal v'homer argument in each *o'kheiluf* argument. With such clear criteria, it will then be possible to show that indeed the second or *kheiluf* qal v'homer argument is related to the first in a perfectly precise way, only vaguely referred to above by 'Beginning 2' = 'negation of Ending 1' and 'Ending 2' = 'negation of Beginning 1'. To this end, a symbolic representation will be needed, one that will reveal the logical structure of each *o'kheiluf* argument. And for this, a symbolic representation that characterizes qal v'homer arguments will be needed first.

The first step towards a precise and accurate characterization of the *o'kheiluf*:

The symbolic formulation of the qal v'homer argument[14]

---

[14] *In Rabbinic Interpretation of Scripture in the Mishnah,* chapter 7, pages 178-179, Alexander Samely puts forward a symbolic formulation of the mishnaic qal v'homer argument that attempts to fill in the implicit reasoning that bridges the premises and the conclusion. His work has merits but I do not use his formulation as it is unnecessarily complex and detailed. The far simpler formulation (1) is more suitable for my purposes in this book. I take the position that the qal v'homer is a valid form of reasoning that we today use all the time. My project here is to use (1), offered as a general enough description of the qal v'homer's apparent form, to arrive at the first symbolic

The tannaitic *a fortiori* or qal v'homer can be put into the following symbolic form.[15]

Since R which *lacks* X has Y must-it-not-follow-that S which *has* X certainly has Y ?!   (1)

where R and S represent nouns and X and Y represent properties and the symbol '?!' indicates a rhetorical question, one that

---

characterization of what I have identified as an argument form and named 'the o'kheiluf argument'.

[15] There are those qal v'homer arguments that are better symbolized by:
Since R which has X' has Y must-it-not-follow-that S which lacks X' certainly has Y ?! (1').
But in claiming considerable generality for (1), my idea is that a qal v'homer argument of form (1') can, although somewhat cumbersomely, also be put into the form (1), by having X' represent "a lacking of X." Each of the tannaitic qal v'homer arguments that sandwich occurrences of the phrase אנ היליו tabulated in Appendix II, can be put into form (1) or (1'). In the interests of space, it is left to the reader to use pen and paper to convince herself of this. Samely, however, points out that (1) is not sufficiently general to capture the logical structure of all qal v'homer arguments because sometimes rather than 'R lacks X' and 'S has X' the structure is more correctly described by R and S having X to varying degrees as in the case of M.Yevamot 8:3. Again, with some effort one can usually force this sort of example into form (1) as well, but indeed Samely is correct in that capturing the varying degrees makes for a more natural symbolic characterization. Though for the purposes of this book the most general expression of a qal v'homer that reveals its logical structure, is not needed. This is because here I am not analyzing what makes a qal v'homer a reasonable argument. I am taking for granted that in general qal v'homer arguments are reasonable. My position is that *a fortiori* reasoning is very natural and we even today use it all the time and most qal v'homer arguments are roughly bona fide examples of reasonable *a fortiori* reasoning. What we do have in (1) is a logical expression that characterizes many qal v'homer arguments and that is all that is needed for the purposes here. Taking into account more than that I fear would make the work here unnecessarily more difficult for the reader to follow and obscure my process and results.

anticipates the response, "yes, of course." [16][17]

In (1), three propositions 'R lacks X', 'R has Y', and 'S has X', are used to draw the conclusion 'S has Y' by a *fortiori* reasoning. This aspect of the structure of the formulation (1), that three stated propositions are used to yield a conclusion a *fortiori,* is a key feature of the vast number of rabbinic qal v'homer arguments. It is one of the most important aspects of (1) that this work focuses on. Other aspects of (1) that are also most common amongst rabbinic qal v'homer arguments are discussed a bit further along.

The symbolic formulation of the qal v'homer laid out in (1) was arrived at by making one very important correction to the formulation first presented by Louis Jacobs in his 1953 paper the *Aristotelean*

---

[16] As argued in Appendix I, to impress upon the listener that the conclusion of the qal v'homer forces itself upon him with logical force, there is often a change of tense within the argument, using the past or present tense on the earlier part of the argument so as to emphasize that those statements are facts well known to the listener and these taken together make it the case that the conclusion will have to be true and so the conclusion is in the future tense. For these numerous tannaitic qal v'homer arguments, (1) fits better if adjusted as follows:
Since R which *lacks* X has Y, must-it-not-follow-that S which *has* X will certainly have Y ?!

[17] This symbolic formulation is a general description that characterizes most qal v'homer arguments. It is not an expression of the qal v'homer's most general logical structure. Although there have been many attempts in the past at uncovering the logic of the qal v'homer argument, this goal has only been achieved by M. Abraham, Dov Gabbay and Uri Schild in chapter two of their *Studies in Talmudic Logic*. Volume 10, College Publications, 2013. They put forward a new form of induction, matrix abduction, which they are able to demonstrate successfully models the qal v'homer argument, even the especially complex one found on B. Kiddushin 5a-5b. See also their companion paper in Hebrew which offers more analysis of the qal v'homer and, in particular, of the argument on Kiddushin 5a-5b:
מידות הדרש ההגיוניות כאבני הבסיס להיסקים לא דדוקטיביים: מודל לוגי לקל וחומר בניין
אב והצד השווה, בתוך: בד"ד 23 (תשע)
For some further refinements, see also Dov Gabbay and Karl Schlechta, *A New Perspective on Nonmonotonic Logics* (Switzerland: Springer International Publishing, 2016), chap.12.

Syllogism and the Qal Wa-Homer.[18][19] In the interest of getting to our subject with as few preliminaries as possible, justification for the symbolic formulation (1), was relegated to Appendix I. In particular, a detailed explanation is included of why Jacobs is incorrect in characterizing the qal v'homer as a conditional and why it is therefore misleading to put an 'if' at the beginning of the symbolic formulation. It is shown that doing so is not only misleading but totally incorrect when characterizing, as Jacobs does, those qal v'homer arguments that do not end in a rhetorical question but instead are read as declarative statements.[20]

One qualifying remark about formulation (1) needs to be made. In most examples of the qal v'homer, as in Example ii below, the phrase that corresponds to 'S has X' actually precedes the phrase translated as 'must-it-not-follow-that'. The ordering in (1) was chosen deliberately for rhetorical reasons. Namely, for emphasizing to the

---

[18]Louis Jacobs,"The Aristotelean Syllogism and the Qal Wa-Homer,"*The Journal of Jewish Studies*, Vol IV, No 4 (1953):154-157.
Jacobs' focus in the paper was on refuting Adolf Schwarz's claim and showing that in fact the qal v'homer is not at all similar or related to Aristotle's categorical syllogism. The paper begins by distinguishing between what Jacobs calls the simple and complex qal v'homer and giving a symbolic representation for each of the two.

[19] Jacobs' symbolic formulation is just a general description of the qal v'homer. For the only successful work to date modeling the logic of the qal v'homer argument see Michael Abraham, Dov Gabbay, and Uri Schild, *Studies in Talmudic Logic*, Vol.10, (London: College Publications, 2013) chapter two. See also their companion paper in Hebrew which offers more analysis of the qal v'homer and, in particular, of the argument on Kiddushin 5a-5b:

מיכאל אברהם, דב גבאי, אורי שילד, מידות הדרש ההגיוניות כאבני הבסיס להיסקים לא דדוקטיביים: מודל לוגי לקל וחומר, בניין אב והצד השווה, בתוך: בד"ד 23 (תשע)

For some further refinements, see also Dov Gabbay and Karl Schlechta, *A New Perspective on Nonmonotonic Logics*.

[20] The many works that reference Jacobs' work, present without criticism his formulations of the biblical and rabbinic qal v'homer arguments as conditional statements. Even Samely whose work on spelling out the nature of qal v'homer reasoning in *Rabbinic Interpretation of Scripture in the Mishnah* has many merits, presents his own formulation of the qal v'homer on p.178, as a conditional or 'If,then' statement.

listener the list of things she already knows to be true and how those things compel the conclusion the speaker is urging. In the symbolic formulation (1), the changed order was chosen over the more literally accurate order, for the reason that in the English language the latter sounds far less natural: 'Since R which lacks X has Y, S which has X, must-it-not-follow-that it has Y ?!'.

(In any case, this small deviation from literal accuracy will be corrected in (2), the further symbolization to which (1) is subjected.)

Looking now at a random example of a tannaitic qal v'homer argument, it is easy to confirm that it can indeed be represented by (1).[21]

A Qal V'Homer Argument, Example ii:

ספרי דברים, פרשת ראה, פיסקא עו :

רבי אליעזר אומר:

ומה פסח שאין חייבים על בשולו, חייבים על אכילתו, בשר בחלב שחייבים על בשולו

אינו דין שחייבים על אכילתו ?!

Sifre Deuteronomy, Parshat Ri-ay, Piska 76:
Rabbi Eliezer says:
Since [in the case of] the paschal lamb where there is no stated law not to cook it, there is a prohibition against eating it if cooked, [with regard to the case of] meat with milk [together], where there is an explicit prohibition

---

[21] For an example that fits more naturally into form (1'), see Eduyot 6:2.
Given that the living [person] which is pure (i.e. does not pollute others), a limb that separates from it is impure, a human corpse which is impure [i.e. pollutes others] does it not follow that a limb that separates from it, is impure?!
It is easily put into form (1') by making the substitutions
'R has X' = 'The living has the property of being pure.'
'R has Y' = 'The living has the property that a limb that separates from it is impure'.
S = 'a human corpse'
'S lacks X' = 'S is impure' = 'S does not have the property of being pure.'

against cooking it, must it not follow that it be prohibited to be eaten if cooked ?!²²

Justifying that the word ומה at the start of the passage is correctly translated as 'Since', is put off for now. It will later be done by demonstrating that everything after the word ומה and before אינו דין (or 'must it not follow') are facts to the Tannaim rather than suppositions. This is more succinctly handled after the next symbolization, (2), is introduced.

With the exception of the justification for using the word 'since', it is clear that the example from Sifre Deuteronomy can be expressed by (1), once the following substitutions are made:

R = 'the Paschal lamb'
X = 'the property that cooking it is prohibited'
Y = 'the property that eating it cooked is prohibited'
S = 'meat with milk'

With these substitutions the expressions on the left in the table below represent the statements on the right,

---

²² The commentary continues with a refutation of this qal v'homer argument. The phrase "you will not eat it" in Deut.12:25 is upheld as necessary for serving as the source for the law that eating meat and milk together is forbidden. The end of Chapter Five discusses the logic involved in refuting a qal v'homer argument.

'R lacks X'	= 'The Paschal lamb lacks the property that it is forbidden to cook it.' = 'There is no prohibition forbidding cooking the paschal lamb.'
'R has Y'	= 'The Paschal lamb has the property that it is forbidden to eat it cooked.' = 'Eating the cooked Paschal lamb is prohibited.'
'S has X'	= 'Meat and milk together has the property that it is forbidden to cook it.' = 'It is forbidden to cook meat and milk together.'
'S should have Y'	='Meat and milk together should have the property that it is forbidden to eat it cooked.' ='It should be forbidden to eat meat and milk that has been cooked together.'

With the substitutions made above, and because as we will show shortly 'R lacks X', 'R has Y' and 'R has Y' are facts to the Tannaim, Example ii can be symbolized as follows:

Since R which *lacks* X has Y, S which *has* X must-it-not-follow-that it certainly has Y ?! (1'')

It is clear then that this symbolization does accurately represent Example ii. As explained earlier, although (1'') accurately represents most qal v'homer arguments, for reasons of readability in English, we reorder (1'') as follows, thereby obtaining (1):

Since R which *lacks* X has Y must-it-not-follow-that S which *has* X certainly has Y ?!

The first objective of this chapter is to give a simple symbolic characterization of the first part of the *o'kheiluf* argument. (Analysis of the second half of the *o'kheiluf* argument, which is the conclusion of the argument, will be taken up later.) Towards that end, a more succinct symbolic formulation of the qal v'homer argument than (1) will be presented next. This new formulation will facilitate easy comparison of the two qal v'homer arguments that sandwich the phrase אי חילוף. Unfortunately this ease is bought at the expense of obscuring the *a fortiori* aspect which is indicated in (1). Therefore when referring to (2) one will have to keep in mind that indeed it represents a qal v'homer argument.

New symbolic reformulation of (1):

The symbolic representation of the qal v'homer (1) can be re-expressed as follows:

Since **A**, **P** & **B** must-it-not-follow-that **Q** ?! (2),

where **A** is substituted for 'R lacks X', which will be denoted by **A** = 'R lacks X', and likewise, **P** = 'R has Y', **B** = 'S has X', and **Q** = 'S has Y'.

Notice that the new symbols, **A**, **B**, **P** and **Q** represent propositions[23], expressions that could stand alone as sentences, while the symbols they contain, the symbols used in (1) represent nouns or properties.

Consider again the previous example of a particular qal v'homer argument, Example ii. The use of 'Since' has not yet been justified,

---

[23] To use the language from the history of logic, (1) is an expression in term logic and (2) is an expression in propositional logic. The logic of the Peripatetics, the school that derived from Aristotle, was a term logic while the logic of the Stoics was a propositional logic. A person trained in Stoic logic interested in representing the qal v'homer symbolically would therefore be far more likely to choose (2) over (1). In the Hellenistic world in which the Tannaim lived, philosophy was very popular and especially Stoic philosophy of which logic was a central part. These points are taken up in Chapter Five.

but as for the rest of the general symbolic representation of a qal v'homer argument, (1), the earlier discussion confirmed that it does represent Example ii. It is easy to see that with the following substitutions, Example ii can be represented also by the symbolic form (2):

A = 'There is no prohibition forbidding cooking the Paschal lamb.'
P = 'Eating the Paschal lamb cooked is prohibited.'
B = 'It is forbidden to cook meat and milk together.'
Q = 'It should be forbidden to eat meat and milk that has been cooked together.'

The Sources for the Claims made in the Qal V'homer as represented by Symbolic formulation (2):

We return now to justifying the 'Since' at the start of both (1) and (2), by showing that **A**, **B**, and **P** are facts to the Tannaim. This qal v'homer argument, as is the case in the vast majority of qal v'homer arguments, is not a hypothetical argument arguing that if **A**, **B** and **P**, are true then it would follow that **Q** obtains.[24]

In the vast majority of rabbinic qal v'homer arguments, the statements represented in (2) by **A**, **B**, and **P** are facts that the author(s) of the argument is (are) certain the audience accepts as true. It is from these facts that the listener is urged to see that **Q** follows *a fortiori*. To be more precise, **A** and **B** are facts that justify the claim that the fact **P** implies **Q**. Sources for statements represented by **A** and **B** are often unmentioned in the argument.

In the qal v'homer arguments of the Midrash Halakhah, as will be shown for Example ii, the sources for the facts represented by **A** and **B**, although often unmentioned, are usually biblical. In the midrash of the school of Rabbi Ishmael, the Mekhilta and the Sifre Bamidbar, the facts represented by **A** and **B** usually express the contents of biblical

---

[24] See Appendix I for a demonstration of these general points.

29

verses and other times they express well-known cultural or common sense facts.[25] The same is true of the midrash of the school of Rabbi Akiva, but sometimes, especially in the Sifra, the fact that **A** or **B** represents might not be quite the content of a biblical verse but rather a reasonable conclusion from a biblical statement.

In the qal v'homer arguments of the Mishnah, in addition to the above sources, the facts represented by **A** and **B** could also be known from other lines of Mishnah (exterior to the qal v'homer argument itself). Having a biblical source would give a statement the status of a fact to the audience of the qal v'homer, and for a qal v'homer in the Mishnah the same is true also for a mishnaic source for a statement.

In the Midrash Halakhah, which is commentary to the Pentateuch that follows the order of verses as they occur in the Torah[26], the statement represented by **P** is often a restatement of part of the very biblical verse which originally prompted the qal v'homer argument in the commentary. Other times **P** represents a verse that occurs elsewhere in the Pentateuch and the concluding **Q** represents part of the biblical verse being glossed by the commentary. In the Mishnah[27], the unmentioned source for **P** might instead be a line in the very Mishnah containing the qal v'homer which follows or it might be in the preceding Mishnah. In the Midrash Halakhah of the school of Rabbi Akiva, although rarely in that of the school of Rabbi Ishmael, the source of **P** might sometimes be a midrash derived from a biblical verse.

---

[25] For example, in the Mekhilta's comment on Exod. 12:9, a qal v'homer argument is applied to the phrase "cooked in water" to derive that since the Paschal lamb may not be cooked in water it certainly may not be cooked in anything else. In that argument, **A** and **B** are the well-known facts from everyday experience, respectively, that water has no taste to impart to whatever is cooked in it and other liquids do impart their flavor to the food cooked in the liquid.

[26] Although there does not exist commentary on every verse.

[27] This is the case for the M. Zevahim 12:3 examined in Appendix I; the source for claim P is a line from the very mishnah that precedes it, M. Zev. 12:2.

In the Midrash Halakhah the sources for the statements represented by **A**, **B** and **P**, are often referenced neither in the qal v'homer argument itself nor in the midrashic passage in which the argument occurs. One could argue that this is because indeed the Tannaim were so extremely well-versed in the Torah that they thought the biblical sources of those statements in their qal v'homer arguments would certainly be known and therefore did not need to be cited. Also, the statements represented by **A** and **B** tend to have their source in more than one verse of the Torah and sometimes in many verses and to therefore be especially well-known. Other times they have their source in the very biblical verse that the qal v'homer argument is commenting upon, so one does not have to look very far in such cases for the sources of the claims made in **A** and **B**. (The Midrash following the Pentateuch in a line-by-line manner would likely be studied together with the biblical book, hard copy or perhaps mental version, it is meant to accompany.) As mentioned above, this is very often the case with the biblical source of **P** in the Midrash Halakhah. In the mishnaic qal v'homer argument as well, the source for **P** also tends to be close by at hand, often in a line from the very same mishnaic verse.

Of the different reasons why the sources for claims **A**, **B** and **P** in a qal v'homer argument are often not cited in the argument, perhaps most relevant is that the qal v'homer is a rhetorical argument. The first half, everything before must-it-not-follow-that, needs to consist of things that the listener would completely agree with and are collected together so that the conclusion forces itself upon the listener; hence the expression used in (2), 'must-it-not-follow'. If each of **A**, **B** and **P** were true because of some obscure verse, rather than because of well-known verses and everyday facts, the momentum of the argument would be lost and the reader would not feel the push of must-it-not-follow. The way the whole argument is structured so as to be expressible in one long breath, rather than broken up into separate propositions, lends to this momentum so that the reader or listener feels the logical push.

We turn now to verify the claims just made about the sources of the statements that correspond to **A**, **B** and **P**, for the particular example of a tannaitic qal v'homer argument, Example ii from Sifre Devarim.

In Example ii,

A='R lacks X'	= 'The Paschal lamb lacks the property that it is forbidden to cook it.' = 'There is no prohibition forbidding cooking the Paschal lamb.'

A is known from Exod. 12:8, 9, the source of the topic of the Paschal lamb. Verse 9 forbids specifically eating the Paschal lamb cooked, it does not forbid cooking it.

B='S has X'	='Meat and milk together has the property that it is forbidden to cook it.' ='It is forbidden to cook meat and milk together.'

The source for **B** is the explicit injunction in Exod. 23:19.

Thus the propositions represented by **A** and **B** have their sources in the Torah (the source for **A** being complete absence[28] from the Torah) and are therefore incontrovertible.

P ='R has Y'	='The Paschal lamb has the property that it is forbidden to eat it cooked.' = 'Eating cooked Paschal lamb is forbidden.'

The source for **P** is the explicit verse Exod.12:9.

---

[28] Recognizing that proof by even seemingly expressive absence is not the strongest sort of proof, the Midrash Halakhah will sometimes provide an additional proof. See for example Sifre Bamidbar, piska 123, the derivation that the calf used for the *eglah arufah* need not be blemish-free.

The claims made above about qal v'homer arguments have thus been verified for the particular example, Example ii. In particular it was shown that the argument in Example ii, can be described symbolically by the form (2) where **A**, **B** and **P** are facts, as they represent propositions expressing statements in the Torah.[29] The sources for the propositions represented by **A**, **B** and **P**, are not mentioned in the argument.

The Qal V'Homer Arguments in the *O'Kheiluf* Argument of the Midrash Halakhah

The qal v'homer arguments in the Midrash Halakhah that sandwich the phrase או חילוף (*o'kheiluf*) are however very different from what we have been describing as typical of the vast majority of tannaitic qal v'homer arguments. Using the language of formulation (2), these have the very unusual property that while **A** and **B** do represent facts as described above, **P** is a proposition in which the author has some but not full confidence. The author views the evidence for **P** as insufficiently strong to be conclusive. (In some of the *o'kheiluf* arguments of the school or Rabbi Akiva, specifically in the Sifra, there is no apparent evidence for or against **P** even according to the tannaitic authors.)

These very unusual qal v'homer arguments are also represented by (2) beginning with the word 'Since.' They cannot be correctly represented using Jacobs' symbolic formulation beginning with an 'if' because, as will be shown from examples, **P** is taken or assumed to be true (in the first qal v'homer). These qal v'homer arguments although different were still qal v'homer arguments to the Tannaim and in particular were therefore not meant to be understood as saying that *if* **P** is true then because of **A** and **B**, it would follow that **Q** is true. Rather, the evidence and the degree of confidence in the truth of **P**

---

[29] In this example, the source for **A** is what we referred to earlier as "(not quite the content of scriptural verses but rather) reasonable implications of scriptural statements."

was kept in mind by the Tanna while the truth of **P** was accepted and relied upon in making a standard qal v'homer argument : 'Since **A & P & B** must-it-not-follow that **Q** ?!'. The Tannaim did not mean their argument to be deviating from the qal v'homer format and expressing a conditional, where the truth of **P** is not assumed. This distinction will become clear by looking at examples beginning shortly with a deeper study of Example ii.

The authors of such qal v'homer arguments kept in mind that the evidence for **P** was not conclusive and they were therefore not fully confident in the conclusion **Q** obtained from it. They were therefore able to entertain the possibility that the contradiction -**Q** was true and propose the *kheiluf* qal v'homer which takes -**Q** to be true. (The question as to how such arguments arose will be taken up in Section 1.3.)

To emphasize that this is the type of very unusual qal v'homer arguments involved in *o'kheiluf* i.e. arguments represented by (2) for which **A** and **B** are known to be facts but **P** is a proposition for which there is some confidence but not complete confidence in its truth, we rearrange (2) so that the facts, **A** and **B**, are grouped together separate from **P**. Rewriting (2) in the resulting equivalent form (in terms of content) yields:

Since **A, B & P** must-it-not-follow-that **Q** ?!   (2')

With (2') in hand it will now be possible to describe the first half of the *o'kheiluf* argument in two different ways:

<u>The first way</u> describes what it seems, from considering the full *o'kheiluf* arguments, the Tannaim themselves had in mind when they used the phrase או חילוף.

<u>The second way</u> is the result of our analysis and makes clear the full structure of the *o'kheiluf* argument introduced with the phrase או חילוף.

The First Way: the Tanna's View of what he is doing

The Tanna introduced a qal v'homer argument represented by (2').

What is meant by this is not that the Tanna used symbols to represent propositions but rather, as emphasized in (2'), the Tanna saw his argument as drawing by qal v'homer a conclusion from three known propositions, in one of which he did not have full confidence. To indicate this differentiation the Tanna's understanding of (2') will be referred to by (2')*.

When the Tanna said או חילוף, meaning 'or perhaps [instead] the *kheiluf*' and then presented the *kheiluf,* what he was saying was, "perhaps instead of the preceding qal v'homer, the correct argument is the following qal v'homer that begins from the opposite of the conclusion of the first qal v'homer argument." In every one of the *o'kheiluf* arguments, this opposite of the conclusion of the first qal v'homer argument, is actually what we would call the negation of the conclusion of the first qal v'homer argument.

A Tanna used the phrase 'או חילוף' when presenting such a qal v'homer related to the previous qal v'homer, as has just been described, and the way he saw the start of his *o'kheiluf* argument could be put by us into the following symbolic form:

Since **A & B & P** must-it-not-follow-that **Q** ?!   (2')*

או חילוף

Another qal v'homer argument beginning from -**Q**

where **A & B** are facts and **P** is a proposition in which the Tanna has some but not complete confidence. (As is the case with any qal v'homer argument, to the Tanna the Torah appears silent on whether or not **Q** is true.)

35

The first part of the *o'kheiluf* argument begins with a qal v'homer argument represented by (2'):

Since **A**, **B** & **P** must-it-not-follow-that **Q** ?!   (2')

It is followed by the phrase חילוף או, which introduces another qal v'homer argument related to (2') as follows:

Since **A**, **B** & -**Q** must-it-not-follow-that -**P** ?!   (3')

The Symbolic Representation of the *O'Kheiluf* Reveals its Structure

Putting (2') and (3') together to obtain a symbolic representation of (the first part of) the *o'kheiluf* argument as follows:

Since **A**, **B** & **P** must-it-not-follows-that **Q** ?!

או חילוף

Since **A**, **B** & -**Q** must-it-not-follow-that -**P** ?!   (4'),

where **A** and **B** represent facts while **P** represents a proposition for which the evidence is not sufficiently compelling. The author has no evidence regarding the content of **Q**, supporting or refuting it. (-**Q** denotes the negation of **Q**, i.e. -**Q** is the statement 'It is not true that **Q**' and likewise for -**P**.) Further, each of the two rhetorical questions sandwiching the phrase או חילוף represents a qal v'homer argument.

In the Midrash Halakhah, the facts that **A** and **B** represent have their sources in the Torah or in common sense. In the midrash of the R. Akiva school, especially in the Sifra, the statement that **A** or **B** represents might sometimes be, not quite the explicit content of a biblical verse but rather, a reasonable conclusion from a biblical statement. In the Midrash Halakhah, the evidence for **P**, if it exists, is biblical.[30] In all of the arguments of the R' Ishmael school there is some biblical evidence for **P**. In several of those and in several of the arguments in Sifre Devarim, the biblical evidence for **P** is in fact fairly suggestive but does not meet the high standards of the authors for evidence or proof.[31]

_____

I claim that the first part of each and every one of the 16 tannaitic *o'kheiluf* arguments has the precise form prescribed by (4'). The second or concluding part of the argument will be dealt with later. It will be seen then that the different examples show uniformity (with uniform terminology) in the second parts as well. Demonstration of the above claims will establish that these 16 tannaitic arguments are a unique form of argument indicated with the phrase *o'kheiluf* whose precise context-independent definition is given by (4').

This chapter along with Chapters Two and Six will verify the claim that the first part of each of the 16 tannaitic *o'kheiluf* arguments has the precise form described by (4'). This chapter demonstrates this for Example i, from Sifre Bamidbar, piska 123 which is considered in detail. In Chapter Two it is shown that in fact each and every one of the 15 *o'kheiluf* arguments in the Midrash Halakhah has the exact form (4'). Chapter Six will confirm the claim for the single *o'kheiluf* argument in the Mishnah, showing that it too has the form given by (4').

By going through the example in this chapter and in Chapter Two, dealing with each of the other 15 examples of *o'kheiluf* in tannaitic

_____

[30] The five *o'kheiluf* arguments of the Sifra, are launched from propositions P for which the authors have no biblical evidence. For these, P is just a guess that is taken to be true in the first qal v'homer argument.
[31] See Chapter Two, # 3, 4, 5,12,13,14.

literature, it is shown that (the first part of the) argument in which each occurrence of the phrase is embedded, has the exact form (4'). In this way it is established that the phrase או היפוך is technical tannaitic linguistic terminology. Later in this chapter it will be shown that the phrase actually functioned as terminology.

By demonstrating in this chapter, and in Chapter Two and Chapter Six on the Mishnah, that all the *o'kheiluf* arguments in tannaic literature do in fact have the precise form of (4'), I am not suggesting that the Tannaim who authored these arguments were aware of this form (4') that the arguments take, that is, of <u>The Second View</u>. To the contrary, as will be seen in this work, the full *o'kheiluf* arguments themselves suggest that the Tannaim had the content of <u>The First View</u>. They had an argument form that they recognized as an argument form, what we would describe by <u>The First View</u>, which they referred to as *o'kheiluf*. They were unaware that the *o'kheiluf* arguments all had the form (4'). This may seem like a strange assertion. How could the Tannaim have authored 16 arguments following a highly precise form without having been aware of this form?

The authors of each of the *o'kheiluf* arguments introduced, with the phrase *o'kheiluf,* a new qal v'homer argument. As described in <u>The First View,</u> they intentionally introduced the new argument with, what is the negation of the conclusion of the original qal v'homer. By the *o'kheiluf* they meant a qal v'homer that begins with, what we would call the negation of the conclusion i.e. with what is **-Q** of the original qal v'homer, 'Since **A**, **B** & **P** must-it-not-follow that **Q**'.

I do not mean that they were able to put the qal v'homer into symbolic form. What I do mean is that they kept clear in their minds which details were the facts, what I have labeled **A** and **B**, and which was the claim for which there was only weak evidence, what I have labeled **P**, and which was the conclusion, what I have labeled **Q**. In intending to start a new argument from what they meant as the opposite of the conclusion they always picked out what we label **Q**, and they never failed to take precisely, what we would describe as, the negation of **Q** and start the *o'kheiluf*-introduced argument, the *kheiluf*, with the negation of **Q**.

From the statement that corresponds to -**Q**, keeping carefully in mind which were the facts, **A** and **B**, and which was the claim for which they only had weak evidence, **P**, they thought through the issues to construct a qal v'homer argument. That such an argument beginning with, what is precisely, the negation of the conclusion would lead them by reasoning to conclude with -**P** regardless as to the particular content of (what we label) **P**, is not something they ever entertained. This point will be taken up in depth in Chapter Five.

To leave exactly the factual claims unchanged in forming the *kheiluf* qal v'homer from the original qal v'homer, the authors had to keep distinct in their minds the facts from the somewhat speculative claims. They also had to correctly form negations of statements. Some of the *o'kheiluf* arguments are very tricky[32] and all of this was therefore indeed an impressive feat.[33] They correctly constructed the *kheiluf* qal v'homer from the original qal v'homer in each case such that the *kheiluf* was coherent and related to the original as described by (2') and (3').

Chapter Five argues that if the Tannaim had had more than The First View and realized that the arguments take the form (4'), that is, had they realized that the qal v'homer that started from -**Q** must conclude with -**P**, the second halves of the *o'kheiluf* arguments would have looked very different from what they are.

Despite not recognizing a form that all the *o'kheiluf* arguments took, the Tannaim in each case consistently constructed the *kheiluf* qal v'homer argument from the original qal v'homer argument so that the

---

[32] See in Chapter Two especially the *o'kheiluf* argument in the Sifra commenting on Parashat Shemini, Lev. 9: 22, 23.

[33] This author needed to use paper and pencil to draw diagrams to keep all this straight in her mind.

two are related to each other as described by (4'). The *o'kheiluf* is truly a piece of tannaitic technical linguistic terminology and the terminological role it played will soon be made clear.

1.2: Verified for Example i: Sifre Bamidbar, piska 123

The *O'kheiluf* Argument in Example i can indeed be represented by (4')

We take up our earlier example of an *o'kheiluf* argument,
Example i, to confirm that it indeed fits into the form claimed here for all *o'kheiluf* arguments, (4'). This time it is presented without underlines and both the form and the content of the argument are considered.

The Sifre Bamidbar, piska 123, comments on Numbers 19:2,

Numbers 19:2, 3:
"This is the law of the Torah that the Lord commanded, saying:
Speak to the children of Israel, [say] take to yourselves a pure red heifer that has no blemish, upon which no yoke was placed. Give it to Elazar the priest and he will take it outside the camp and slaughter it in front of him."

Commentary on this verse from the **Sifre Bamidbar, piska 123**:

From where do we know to equate other labors with [the bearing of] a yoke [i.e. that they disqualify the cow from serving as the red heifer in purification rites]? You say it is [known by a] qal v'homer:

And since [regarding] the calf which is not disqualified by a blemish [from serving as the eglah arufah], other labors are equated with [the drawing of] a yoke; with regard to the [red] heifer which is disqualified

40

by a blemish [from serving in rites], does it not certainly follow that we should equate other labors with [the bearing of] a yoke?!

Or the kheiluf

And since [regarding] the [red] heifer which is disqualified by a blemish, other labors are not equated with [the bearing of] a yoke; with regard to the eglah which is not disqualified by a blemish, must it not certainly follow that we should not equate other labors with [the drawing of] a yoke?!

The biblical verse in Bamidbar quoted above in translation which is the prompt for the comment in this passage in the Sifre Bamidbar, discusses the commandment to set aside a red heifer with the particular qualities that it be blemish-free and that no yoke had ever been laid on it. Verses that follow discuss the purification rites for which this heifer is needed. The Sifre Bamidbar in commenting on this verse seeks to understand the requirement that the cow chosen should never have worn a yoke.[34] The Sifre wants to know whether this restriction is specifically about a yoke or whether it includes any type of work, even work that does not involve drawing a yoke. In the latter case, the mention of the wearing of a yoke to include any type of work, would make sense because most work done by a cow involves drawing a yoke.

To answer this question the Sifre considers the calf in the rite of the *eglah arufah* discussed in chapter 21 of Deuteronomy. This rite is enacted, as stated in verse 1 there, when a slain person is found and the perpetrator is unknown. Verse 3 orders that the elders of the city closest to the corpse are to *take a calf with which work has never*

---

[34] Prior to the quoted passage, the Sifre establishes by qal v'homer from the *eglah arufah* that the cow for the red heifer rite is likewise disqualified if it bore a yoke while working. Why then does the verse Num.19:2 need to state this explicitly if it could be derived by qal v'homer? The Sifre explains that in the verse the words 'upon which no yoke was mounted' is referring to the wearing of a yoke even while not working, that it would disqualify the cow as well (as bearing a yoke during the course of work).

been done, that has never drawn a yoke. This verse may be interpreted as restricting the calf chosen for the rite to be one that has never done any work at all, even work that does not involve wearing a yoke. However this is not particularly clear from the verse for which other interpretations are possible, such as that only work involving a yoke would disqualify a calf. Furthermore, there are no other verses that address and clarify this issue further.

Nowhere in the entire description of the rite of the *eglah arufah* is anything said about the calf having or not having a blemish. Thus the presumption[35] is that unlike for the red heifer, being blemish-free is not a requirement on the calf for the *eglah arufah*. A comparison between the two seemingly related topics, the red heifer and the calf for the *eglah arufah*, is to be set up along the axis of (having or not having) the requirement to be blemish-free.

Summarizing and labeling the statements in the argument is next. From the verses dealing with the *eglah arufah* the Sifre knows (from absence[36]) that for this rite the calf need not be blemish-free. Keeping in mind the notation in formulation (2'), this fact should be symbolized by the letter **A**.

The restriction that the calf chosen for the *eglah arufah* rite may not have done even other types of work that do not involve wearing a yoke is not stated clearly in the Torah. This restriction can only be justified as a reasonable interpretation of the Deut 21:3, "to take a calf with which work has never been done, that has never drawn a yoke."

---

[35] Besides the argument from expressive absence there is also a derivation that indeed the calf chosen for the *eglah arufah* rite need not be blemish-free: A few lines above the quoted passage, the Sifre argues that to keep one from drawing a qal v'homer from sacrificial offerings to *eglah arufah* to derive that the calf in the *eglah arufah* rite must be blemish-free, the verse states by the red heifer, what is also derivable by *a fortiori* reasoning from sacrifices, that **it** need be blemish-free. The explicit statement is needed, even though it is derivable by a fortiori reasoning from sacrifices, in order to make the point that this one, the red heifer, must be blemish-free and not so the other, the *eglah arufah*.

[36] Ibid.

(Other readings are possible such as that only an animal that worked and that wore a yoke to do the work, may not be used. So that yoke-wearing that had nothing to do with work does not disqualify the calf from serving in the *eglah arufah* rite.) Yet this verse, because of the extra first clause, is more suggestive that the calf must not have done any kind of work, than is Num.19:2, about the heifer chosen for the red heifer rite, that it may not have been put to work that does not entail a yoke. Again in keeping with the earlier notation, this claim will be symbolized by the letter **P**.

The verse quoted above about the red heifer which is the subject of the Sifre's commentary, Num 19:2, states clearly that it must not have a blemish. This therefore has the status of a fact. Again, in keeping with the notation we established in (2'), this fact will be represented with the symbol **B**.

The passage from the Sifre above consists of an *o'kheiluf* argument where the first qal v'homer argument uses the two facts, **A** and **B** and the claim **P** for which the evidence is not conclusive, to argue that from these three, it follows by *a fortiori* reasoning, that for the red heifer, other work disqualifies the heifer just as does wearing the yoke. This last claim will be symbolized by **Q**, again in keeping with the notation in (2'). Attaching all the symbols to their respective statements in the argument to obtain:

And since, with regard to
A = the eglah [young calf] which is not disqualified by a blemish [from serving as the eglah arufah]
P = other labors are equated with a yoke,
with regard to
B = the [red] heifer which is disqualified by a blemish [from serving in rites],
does it not certainly follow that
Q = other labors are to be equated with a yoke (i.e. having done work that does not involve wearing a yoke would also disqualify the calf from serving in the red heifer rite)

?!

This first qal v'homer argument in the passage is then followed by the phrase *o'kheiluf* which is then followed by the second qal v'homer argument. In this second argument, the Sifre again uses facts **A** and **B**, but this time additionally the claim **-Q**, to conclude by *a fortiori* reasoning that **-P** is the case:

And since, with regard to
B = *the [red] cow which is disqualified by a blemish,*
-Q= *other labors are not equated with a yoke (i.e. the Torah prohibited the calf that is to serve as a red heifer from ever having worn a yoke, but it did not prohibit it from having done any other work)*
with regard to
A = *the eglah which isn't disqualified by a blemish,*
must it not certainly follow that

-P= *other labors are not to be equated with a yoke*
?!

The contents of the two arguments in the passage in Sifre Bamidbar, make clear that they are indeed qal v'homer or *a fortiori* arguments. As laid out above, with **A** and **B** symbolizing factual propositions in the first qal v'homer argument, and with **P** representing the claim in the argument whose supporting evidence is not tight shut, the *o'kheiluf* argument in the passage above from the Sifre Bamidbar consists of two qal v'homer arguments that sandwich the phrase אן חילוף and can be symbolized as in (4'):

Since **A**, **B** & **P** must-it-not-follow-that **Q** ?!

או חילוף

Since **A**, **B** & **-Q** must-it-not-follow-that **-P** ?!

where **A**, **B** represent biblical or common sense facts, **P** represents a proposition for which there is some biblical evidence but not what the author sees as compelling evidence. There is no biblical expression that addresses the issue of **Q**, supporting or refuting it. **-Q** is the negation of **Q** and likewise for **P**. (Thus, for example, **-P** is the statement 'It is not true that **P**'.)

Hence it has been shown that indeed for this example from the Sifre Bamidbar of an argument which contains the phrase אוֹ חִילוּף, the phrase is sandwiched between two qal v'homer arguments and the whole complex can be described symbolically by the form (4') which exposes its structure.

Confirmation that every other *o'kheiluf* argument can be described by (4')

Every other occurrence of the phrase *o'kheiluf* in tannaitic literature, regardless of source, has this exact meaning, i.e. the argument it is centered in has the symbolic form (4'); this is shown in Chapter Two for all other occurrences in the Midrash Halakhah and in Chapter Six for Mishnah. Thus the word *kheiluf* when preceded by the word *o'* which means 'or' in English, has the status of linguistic terminology of the Tannaim. Section 3 will investigate why it was useful for the Tannaim to have a term that refers to the *kheiluf* of an argument, that is, how the phrase *o'kheiluf* truly functioned as terminology.

As pointed out earlier, the formulation (4') also gives very clear criteria for how the *kheiluf* qal v'homer is constructed from the original qal v'homer. The *kheiluf* is revealed to specify something that is far more precise than is suggested by the current translation, 'the reverse'. Referring to the original quick treatment of this *o'kheiluf* argument given at the start of this section, Example i, it should be apparent that with formulation (4') the vague label 'The Beginning' is replaced with the very precise **P**, and 'The Ending', with **Q**; the negation of 'The Beginning' is now referred to as **-P**. (**A** and **B** are facts and therefore remain unaltered.)

45

All 15 occurrences of the phrase או חילוף in the Midrash Halakhah are tabulated in Chapter Two. The one example in the Mishnah was left for Chapter Six. It is demonstrated that indeed every occurrence of the phrase *o'kheiluf* shares the same precise meaning captured by (4'). In each case it is pointed out which propositions would be represented by each of **A, B, P, Q, -P, -Q**. In each case the qal v'homer nature of each of the two arguments is made clear. When it is not perfectly obvious, it is shown how the proposition represented by **-P** is indeed the negation of the proposition represented by **P**, and the same is done with **Q**. The sources for **A** and **B** are given and the evidence for **P**, so that it is clear that labels have been correctly assigned to statements: **A** and **B** are labels given to facts and **P** is a label for a proposition taken to be true for which there is at most minor evidence.

With all this it should then be clear to the reader that for each of the 16 occurrences, regardless of the particular source, the *o'kheiluf* argument has the precise form (4') above. That is, in each of its occurrences, the phrase או חילוף, 'or the *kheiluf*', is sandwiched between two qal v'homer arguments, and it is the second qal v'homer argument which is referred to as the *kheiluf* of the first. The first qal v'homer argument uses facts **A** and **B** and the claim **P**, to conclude **Q**. The second qal v'homer, the *kheiluf* of the first, uses facts **A** and **B** and the claim **-Q** to conclude **-P**.

1.3: How are *O'Kheiluf* and the Contrapositive Related?

Expression (4') defines precisely what the *kheiluf* actually refers to in the phrase *o'kheiluf*, i.e. 'or [perhaps instead] the *kheiluf*; 'o' in the Hebrew meaning 'or'. In English there is certainly no term for taking a sentence that can be symbolized by the first line of (4') and turning it into a sentence that can be symbolized by the second line of (4'). But there is a common logical term for switching and changing parts of a statement in certain ways (to arrive at another statement) which bears

46

resemblance to the *kheiluf* in the phrase *o'kheiluf*. This will now be described and the resemblance shown as will all be important for the analysis in Chapter Five.

This very precise relationship described by expression (4') between the two qal v'homer arguments in the *o'kheiluf* argument bears similarity to the relationship that exists between two conditional, i.e. 'If,then' statements where one is the contrapositive of the other. This resemblance is despite the fact, justified at length in Appendix I, that the qal v'homer cannot be correctly expressed as a conditional statement.

Let us pause to explain the common terms from elementary logic and philosophy used in the last paragraph.

A conditional statement has the form 'If p then q' where p and q represent propositions.
Here is an example: If she has milk in her breasts then she has conceived.[37]

In this example,
p= 'she has milk in her breasts', and q='she has conceived'.

It is called a conditional statement, because it begins with a conditional rather than a fact. The conditional is, 'if she has milk in her breasts'. Another way to put this is that the statement draws a conclusion from a hypothesis: from the hypothesis that she has milk in her breasts, it follows that she has conceived.

The contrapositive is always the contrapositive of a conditional statement. It is another conditional statement related to the original conditional statement as follows:

---

[37] Taken from a Stoic example (of a true and demonstrative argument) discussed in the classic by Benson Mates, *Stoic Logic* (Berkeley: University of California Press,1953), 63.

If a conditional statement is symbolized as above by 'If P then Q',
then the contrapositive conditional is symbolized by 'If -Q then -P'.

In the definition given for the contrapositive, P and Q represent any
propositions or statements. -P refers to the negation of whatever
statement is referred to by P and likewise for -Q. Note that P does not
refer back to boldface **P** given in (4') and likewise for Q as compared
to **Q**. The choice to make use of the same letters as in (4') is intended
to be suggestive: in the definition (4') of *o'kheiluf*, the **P** and the **Q**
represent the propositions that are not held fixed but are negated in
the *kheiluf* qal v'homer.

In the above example, the contrapositive of the conditional,
'If she has milk in her breasts then she has conceived', is
'If she has not conceived then she does not have milk in her breasts'.
For this example, the P in the definition of the contrapositive refers to
the proposition or statement, 'she has milk in her breasts', while the Q
refers to, 'she has conceived'.

Lining up the *o'kheiluf* and the contrapositive makes their
resemblance to one another apparent:

Conditional statement:| If P then Q.
Contrapositive: | If -Q then -P.

Qal v'homer argument:| Since **A&B** & **P**, must-it-not-follow-that **Q** ?!
Kheiluf of qal v'homer: | Since **A&B** & **-Q**, must-it-not-follow-that **-P** ?!

Notice that the contrapositive of a conditional statement is another
conditional statement. Similarly, the *kheiluf* of a qal v'homer argument
must be another argument. (In fact according to the definition (4'), in
the *o'kheiluf* argument the *kheiluf* is another qal v'homer argument.
This can only be confirmed from a consideration of the particular
values **A, B, P, Q, -P** and **-Q** in (4'), take on. Being a qal v'homer is a
semantic not a syntactic property. So verifying that the argument that
follows the phrase אי היילף is indeed a qal v'homer argument is not

analogous to determining whether some conditional statement is the contrapositive of another conditional statement. For the latter is determined from syntax alone.)

How does one obtain the contrapositive of a conditional statement? Referring to everything after 'if' and before 'then' the first part of the conditional statement and calling everything after 'then' the second half one gets the contrapositive by switching the first and second halves of the conditional and replacing them with their negations. Exchanging the places of P and Q, the conditional becomes 'If Q then P' and then replacing the two halves with their negations, one obtains finally, 'If -Q then -P'.

Divide the two halves of the original qal v'homer argument similarly: everything before 'must-it-not-follow-that' being the first half, everything after it being the second half. Recall that **A** and **B** are facts, while **P** is either a guess or something for which there exists only minor evidence. Since **A**, **B** and **P** together imply **Q**, and since the evidence for **P** is not conclusive, one cannot be certain of **Q** either.

To arrive at the *kheiluf*, one does the same thing as one does to obtain the contrapositive of a conditional statement, except one needs to hold the facts **A** and **B** aside. With regard to the remainder, positions are switched, first half to second half and vice versa. Finally, each half must be replaced with its negation.[38]

If the qal v'homer argument is reorganized as follows,

---

[38] We keep **A** and **B** aside so as not to apply the switching to {**A&B&P**} and **Q**, for then the negation of the switch would be '-**Q**, therefore -(**A&B&P**)' and that is not the *kheiluf* qal v'homer. The latter is '**A&B & -Q** therefore -**P**'. The negation of {**A&B&P**} denoted -(**A&B&P**) above, must be {**A&B&-P**}. This is because, since **A** and **B** are known to be facts while **P** is not, the other two possibilities for the negation of {**A&B&P**}, {-**A&B&P**} and {**A&-B&P**}, are known to be false.

49

'**P**, must-it-not-follow-that **Q**, by *a fortiori* reasoning using facts **A** and **B** ?!'

then the *kheiluf* argument is

'**-Q**, must-it-not-follow-that **-P**, by *a fortiori* reasoning using facts **A** and **B** ?!'

In the first qal v'homer of the pair, facts **A** and **B** function to justify the truth of '**P** must-it-not-follow-that *a fortiori* **Q** ?!'.

In the *kheiluf* qal v'homer likewise, facts **A** and **B** are used to argue for the truth of '**-Q**, must-it-not-follow-that *a fortiori* **-P**?!'.

If the facts **A** and **B**, i.e. the evidence in support of the qal v'homer arguments, are left out and only the claims are kept, the pair of arguments become,

'**P**, must-it-not-follow-that *a fortiori* **Q** ?!'
'**-Q**, must-it-not-follow-that *a fortiori* **-P** ?!'.

Now if the rhetorically questioning aspect of the arguments is left out and those rhetorical questions are instead expressed as assertions, the pair of arguments become,

'**P**, *a fortiori* **Q**'
'**-Q**, *a fortiori* **-P**'.

This last pair exhibits a relationship very similar to that which exists between a conditional statement and its contrapositive, with two differences: in the last pair, implication is restricted to *a fortiori* and the statements are not conditional statements. Examining the two pairs side by side will make this all clear:

	Omitting Evidence **A** & **B**:
Conditional: If P then Q	qal v'homer: P, *a fortiori* Q
Contrapositive: If -Q then -P	*kheiluf* qal v'homer: -Q, *a fortiori* -P

50

There is one example[39] in the Midrash Halakhah, in the Sifre Bamidbar, Parshat Matot, piska 155 [40] of an *o'kheiluf* argument that consists not of a pair of qal v'homer arguments but instead consists of a pair of 'just as' arguments sandwiching the phrase או חילוף , i.e.

A & B; just as **P** so-too **Q**.

או חילוף

A & B; just as **-Q** so-too **-P**.   (5')

A 'just as' statement is a more specific implication than a general 'then' or 'therefore' as in 'P therefore Q'. For such an *o'kheiluf* argument the resemblance to the contrapositive is even stronger than it is for the *o'kheiluf* argument composed of qal v'homer arguments:

Omitting Evidence **A** & **B**:

Conditional: If P then Q	'Just as': P so-too Q
Contrapositive: If -Q then –P	*kheiluf* 'Just as': -Q so-too -P

Earlier it was shown for Example ii and the reader was directed to Chapter Two for verification for the other 14 examples in the Midrash Halakhah, that expression (4') gives a precise definition of *o'kheiluf*. The prevailing translation 'or the reverse' is thus shown to be incorrect most importantly because it implies that the phrase *o'kheiluf* does not have a precise meaning but rather a vague meaning and that it is only the details of the contents of the specific two qal v'homer arguments and not the phrase *o'kheiluf* that can meaningfully inform as to how the two qal v'homer arguments are related to one another.

---

[39] There is another example in the Talmud Yerushalmi, Y. Bava Batra 22a.
[40] See Chapter Two, #6.

But what phrase captures the meaning of (4') and could be used as an English translation of the phrase o'kheiluf? In English (and in Greek for that matter[41]) there is no concept of and therefore no term for taking a sentence that can be symbolized by the first line of (4') and turning it into a sentence that can be symbolized by the second line of (4'). However, the contrapositive was introduced as a common logical concept and term for switching and changing parts of a sentence in specified ways and it was shown by lining it up with the o'kheiluf that the two do bear some resemblance to one another.

As argued earlier and at length in Appendix I, it is incorrect to view the qal v'homer as expressing a conditional statement. It is for this reason that the resemblance between the contrapositive and the o'kheiluf is only partial. Otherwise, the o'kheiluf would be very close to the contrapositive (with implication limited to by a fortiori or by 'just as' instead of allowing any sort of implication as is indicated with the word 'then'). The above two charts would instead be the following:

	Omitting Evidence A & B:
Conditional: If P then Q	qal v'homer: If P, a fortiori Q
Contrapositive: If -Q then -P	kheiluf qal v'homer: If -Q, a fortiori -P

	Omitting Evidence A & B:
Conditional: If P then Q	'Just as': If P so too Q
Contrapositive: If -Q then -P	kheiluf 'Just as': If -Q so too -P

In summary, the o'kheiluf argument of the Tannaim, in each of its occurrences, may be symbolized by the form (4'). There is no western concept for (4') and therefore no English word that expresses the o'kheiluf. It was shown however that the o'kheiluf shares some

---

[41] This point is taken up in Chapter Five of this work.

resemblance to the contrapositive. Chapter Five takes up the significance for the *o'kheiluf* of its difference from the contrapositive.

The contrapositive was well-known and analyzed by the Stoics. It appears though that neither the Stoics nor any other thinkers had a term for the *o'kheiluf* or for its essential feature, i.e. a term for how '-Q, therefore -P' relates to 'P, therefore Q.' Thus the *o'kheiluf* is uniquely tannaitic terminology. Next we take up the function of the argument and the terminological function of the phrase *o'kheiluf*.

1.4: Unraveling the Function of the *O'Kheiluf* Argument

As discussed earlier and in depth in Appendix I and confirmed above for Example ii, for the vast majority of tannaitic qal v'homer arguments, the propositions labeled **A**, **B** and **P** in formulation (2) represent facts. In the arguments of the Midrash Halakhah the sources for these facts are usually biblical verses or everyday experience; in the cases found in the Mishnah another possible source for **P** may be another line of Mishnah. In all of these arguments **Q** is derived by *a fortiori* reasoning from facts **A**, **B**, and **P**.

The relatively small collection of *o'kheiluf* arguments is an exception to this picture. As indicated in the symbolic definition (4') and discussed in the paragraphs that lead up to (4'), in the first qal v'homer argument of the *o'kheiluf* argument the proposition labeled **P** is not an incontrovertible fact. Rather **P** is a claim supported by, what the author considers to be, insufficiently strong evidence. (This was shown earlier for Example i from the Sifre Bamidbar and the reader was directed to Chapters Two and Six for demonstration of this in all the other tannaitic occurrences of the *o'kheiluf* argument.) Because **P** is not a fact, the conclusion **Q** drawn from **P** and from facts **A** and **B**, cannot be known with certainty to be true. The authors of these arguments recognized this and they also recognized that it is therefore possible, for exactly such arguments, to entertain the possibility that the negation of the proposition symbolized by **Q**, i.e. the proposition represented by **-Q**, is a true statement.

The qal v'homer they entertain which begins with **-Q** is introduced with the phrase *o'kheiluf,* translated, 'or [perhaps] the *kheiluf* [is the truth]'. **-Q** whose truth is possible but not certain can then be used along with facts **A** and **B** to argue by qal v'homer that **-P** follows. This argument is the second qal v'homer argument in the *o'kheiluf* argument. Thus it is only because **Q** is not a certainty that an *o'kheiluf* argument is possible and the uncertainty in **Q** comes about because of the uncertainty in **P**.[42]

Indeed as discussed earlier and as seen in Example i, the first part of the *o'kheiluf* argument is a presentation of two possible qal v'homer arguments that are mutually exclusive, if one is true the other must be false. From the above discussion, the formulation (4') may be rearranged (and restyled to omit the rhetorically questioning aspect) so that the first qal v'homer can be represented by '**P**, *a fortiori* **Q**, by virtue of facts **A** and **B**'. In reference to this representation, the second or *kheiluf* qal v'homer argument can be represented by '**-Q**, *a fortiori* **-P**, by virtue of facts **A** and **B**'.

The second part of the *o'kheiluf* argument analyzes whether one of the two qal v'homer arguments can be disproved. If that is possible, the other argument is declared correct. It is not apparent why this should be the case. (To clarify the problem, finding Q to be false is the usual way for the author of a qal v'homer to disprove 'A & B & P must-it-not-follow-that Q?!'. But in a typical qal v'homer, P is known with certainty to be true, so the disproof of Q, means that {P & -Q} is true. In the qal v'homer of the *o'kheiluf,* P is not known with certainty to be true; there is only some degree of confidence in its truth. Therefore the disproof of Q implies only that -Q is true and {P&Q} is false. This does not imply that {-P & -Q} is true (nor does it imply that

---

[42] See the Addendum at the end of Chapter Five for discussion of other types of tannaitic arguments, different from the *o'kheiluf,* that attack garden-variety qal v'homer arguments in the usual case where **P** is a fact.

-P and -Q can be related by qal v'homer). So it does not seem to necessarily follow that the disproof of the first qal v'homer argument implies that 'A & B & -Q must-it-not-follow-that -P ?!' must be true.)

This question of why it is that the disproof of one of the two arguments implies that the other argument is true will be taken up later in this section. Here the focus will be on characterizing the circumstances under which the o'kheiluf argument arises. To that end the earlier example from Sifre Bamidbar is examined again, this time considering the entire argument including the second half.

Considering Example i in its entirety

In commenting on Num. 19:3, which states that the heifer chosen to serve as the red heifer must be one "upon which no yoke was placed," the Sifre Bamidbar asks:

מנין לעשות שאר עבודה כעול

From where do we know to equate other labors with the bearing of a yoke [i.e. that they disqualify the cow from serving as the red heifer in purification rites]?

As discussed earlier, the reason for the commentator's question is that the verse does not say anything about work that does not involve wearing a yoke; in fact no verse addresses this. The commentator in searching for an answer to the question looks to the somewhat related case of the calf in the *eglah arufah* rite. Both the red heifer and the *eglah arufah* serve in rites that atone for the sins of people. And for both, the animals have to meet qualifications that include not having worn a yoke. Because of all this, the commentator believes that in the absence of any direct biblical instructions about the matter, the laws regarding the red heifer and the *eglah arufah* should inform one another, so that whatever the law is for one, about whether or not it may have done other types of work and still qualify to serve in the rite, the law should be the same for the other.

The problem is though that the law in question is not clearly stated in the Torah for either case, the red heifer or the calf of the *eglah arufah* rite. But for the latter case there is some biblical evidence as to what the law is. It is precisely this situation which gives rise to the *o'kheiluf*: the law in question is not known for the subject of discussion as well as for the topic of comparison, however there is possibly some evidence for the law in one of the two cases.

Had the Torah been explicit about the law in the case of the *eglah arufah*, there would have been no *o'kheiluf*. Instead the argument would have consisted of one qal v'homer argument, argued from the *eglah arufah* to the red heifer, and ended with the conclusion of the first qal v'homer argument, that the case for the red heifer follows from that of the *eglah arufah*.

Here again is the first qal v'homer argument of the *o'kheiluf* argument:

You say it's [known by a] qal v'homer:

And since [regarding] the calf which is not disqualified by a blemish [from serving as the eglah arufah], other labors are equated with [the drawing of] a yoke; with regard to the [red] heifer which is disqualified by a blemish [from serving in rites], does it not certainly follow that we should equate other labors with [the bearing of] a yoke?!

In the earlier section the propositions of this argument were labeled as follows:

And since, with regard to
A = *the eglah [young calf] which is not disqualified by a blemish [from serving as the eglah arufah]*
P = *other labors are equated with a yoke*
with regard to
B = *the [red] heifer which is disqualified by a blemish [from serving in rites],*
does it not certainly follow that

56

Q = *other labors are to be equated with a yoke (i.e. having done work that does not involve wearing a yoke would also disqualify the cow from serving in the red heifer rite)*
?!

In the Midrash Halakhah, after presenting such an argument, the author would often come to a stop, having argued a qal v'homer showing that any kind of work disqualifies the animal from serving as a red heifer. But as described above, in this case - unlike in Example ii of a typical qal v'homer argument - there is uncertainty about and lack of confidence in the proposition labeled **P,** the law in the case of the *eglah arufah.*

The verse that discusses the *eglah arufah* rite, Deut. 21:3, says that the elders of the city closest to the corpse are to *take a calf with which work has never been done, that has never drawn a yoke.* This verse, because it says *with which work has never been done,* may be interpreted as restricting the calf chosen for the rite to be one that has never done any work at all, even work that does not involve wearing a yoke. However this is not explicit in the verse (which might be interpreted as all about the next clause, work drawing a yoke).

Because of lack of confidence in the truth of the claim labeled **P,** the conclusion of the *a fortiori* argument based on **P,** the proposition labeled **Q,** is also not fully convincing and can therefore be doubted. Because the conclusion **Q** may be doubted, the author continues and considers the following possibility:

O'kheiluf
Or perhaps the *kheiluf* [argument]

And the author follows with the *kheiluf* qal v'homer argument:

And since [regarding] the [red] heifer which is disqualified by a blemish, other labors are not equated with [the bearing of] a yoke; with regard to the eglah which isn't disqualified by a blemish, must it not certainly follow that we should not equate other labors with [the drawing of] a yoke?!

Earlier, the propositions contained in this argument were labeled as follows, in keeping with the labeling established for the first qal v'homer argument:

And since,
B = *the [red] heifer which is disqualified by a blemish,*
-Q= *other labors are not equated with a yoke (i.e. the Torah prohibited the calf that is to serve as a red heifer from ever having worn a yoke, but it did not prohibit it from having done any other unrelated work);*
with regard to
A = *the eglah which isn't disqualified by a blemish,*
 must it not certainly follow that
-P = *other labors are not to be equated with a yoke*
?!

The second or the *kheiluf* qal v'homer argument reaches the conclusion represented by **-P**, namely, that a calf is disqualified from serving in the *eglah arufah* rite only by work involved in wearing a yoke and not by any other work.

The *o'kheiluf* argument continues with its second or concluding part. It answers the rhetorical question ending the last qal v'homer argument, 'shouldn't we rule that work other than that done wearing a yoke does not disqualify the calf?' with an implicit, 'No!' and a prooftext: Deut. 21:3 says about the *eglah arufah, "which has never been worked with."* It is being argued that it is therefore not possible to say that only work involving wearing a yoke disqualifies the calf.

תלמוד לומר: 'אשר לא עבד בה'.

The conclusion of the *kheiluf* qal v'homer argument, it is declared[43], contradicts the evidence that exists for **P** on the basis of which the original qal v'homer was launched. The verse in Deuteronomy says about the calf to be used in the *eglah arufah* rite that it be one, "that has never been worked with, that has never drawn a yoke."The phrase "that has never been worked with" is the weak evidence for **P** on the basis of which the original qal v'homer was launched. It is weak, because it is not explicit due to the clause that follows about the yoke. The second o*r kheiluf* qal v'homer concludes with the ruling that only work with a yoke would disqualify a calf, contradicting **P**. But this cannot be correct, the argument goes, as the verse says "that has never been worked with.*"*

Thus although the author was uncomfortable launching a qal v'homer argument on the basis of weak evidence, he did feel that the evidence has some weight and he was never prepared to just dismiss it. The author did not anticipate that the *kheiluf* qal v'homer would conclude by negating his weak evidence for **P**.

The midrashist attacked the conclusion of the second qal v'homer argument with the phrase *talmud lomar,* i.e. the Torah stated these extra words to prevent that conclusion, that is, to extend the class of disqualifying work to not just work with a yoke but to any other kind of

---

[43] Answers to the question of why it is that in a qal v'homer argument in the Midrash Halakhah, the evidence for **P** (and also **A**, and **B**) is not presented in the argument, were given earlier. But in the *o'kheiluf* argument where the biblical evidence for **P** exists but is weak and is only cited in the *Talmud lomar* when the *kheiluf* qal v'homer concludes with **-P**, can we be confident that the Tanna considered that biblical evidence at the start when he launched his original qal v'homer argument? That is, can we be confident that the entire *o'kheiluf* argument is not a fishing expedition that elicits the weak evidence for **P**? Yes to both. Five of the eight *o' kheiluf* arguments with some evidence for **P** make this clear because the original qal v'homer is a comment on the very biblical verse that contains the weak evidence, i.e. the qal v'homer is launched from the evidence in the verse being commented upon, so it is clear that the Tanna is looking and thinking about that weak evidence. See especially Sifre Bamidba, piska 125, and piska 126 in Chapter Two.

work. (Perhaps he is suggesting that the verse from Deuteronomy be read as, 'that has never been worked with, **for example**, that has never drawn a yoke.')[44] [45]

Since the conclusion of the qal v'homer is found to be false, that whole qal v'homer argument is therefore rejected, leaving only the first qal v'homer argument.

The commentator continues through to a final conclusion to the whole o'kheiluf argument, using a formula that is word-for-word almost identical in each of the o'kheiluf cases in tannaitic literature that reach a conclusion (8 in total), regardless of whether the argument occurs in a work of the school of R. Akiva or of the school of R. Ishmael:

דנתי, וחלפתי, בטל או חילוף וזכיתי לדון כבתחילה

I executed a qal v'homer argument (read: *danti* , from the root *din*; literally, I judged), *I switched it around* (read : *kheilafti*, same root as *kheiluf*), *the 'o'kheiluf' was invalidated, and I* [therefore] *merited to execute a qal v'homer argument* (read: *ladun*, from the root *din*; literally, to judge) *as in the beginning.*

The author starts off this statement by reviewing what he has already done. In '*I executed a qal v'homer argument*' he is referring to the first

---

[44] The school of R. Ishmael to which the Sifre Bamidbar commentary belongs, follows some principle of biblical parsimony whereby seemingly redundant words in the Torah need to be justified even if only at times to declare that the Torah speaks in the language of people and a certain redundancy is just how people phrase things. R. Akiva's school holds to this principle more strictly and does not explain any biblical redundancy as simply imitative of human speech.

[45] Since the Sifre Devarim interprets "that has never been worked with" just as the Sifre Bamidbar does in our passage, the former finds the phrase "that has never drawn a yoke" to be adding nothing whatsoever to the verse if it means a yoke for work. The Sifre Devarim therefore interprets the phrase about the *eglah arufah* "that has never drawn a yoke" to be speaking of a yoke that is not for work. Regarding the red heifer, the Sifre Bamidbar interprets the phrase "upon which no yoke was mounted," in the same way.

qal v'homer argument he presented. Then he says 'I switched it around' or exchanged it or reversed it, there he is referring to the second or *kheiluf* qal v'homer argument presented. Thus, at that point, the author had presented two different qal v'homer arguments for consideration. Then he continues with *batail o'kheiluf,* meaning, the qal v'homer argument referred to by the phrase *o'kheiluf,* was invalidated. The author is referring to the *talmud lomar,* the proof text he presented, to disprove the conclusion of the second qal v'homer argument. He is arguing that the biblical phrase he presented, served to invalidate the *o'kheiluf* qal v'homer argument by invalidating its conclusion. Therefore since two different possible qal v'homer arguments were presented and one was invalidated, there is only one viable qal v'homer argument left.

The midrashist continues with '*and* [therefore] *I merited ladun,* to execute a qal v'homer *like in the beginning.*' The author is saying that as a result of the elimination of the second possible qal v'homer, only the first qal v'homer remains. And therefore it must be correct. This appears to be the conclusion of a proof by elimination, or by default, that the first qal v'homer argument is correct.

The midrashist now reinforces this point by repeating the first qal v'homer argument, but this time he has removed the rhetorically questioning elements from its expression. In this way he is suggesting that there is no longer any doubt about it and therefore he is no longer trying to convince. He therefore expresses that first qal v'homer argument, in the repetition, assertively, as a declaration and not as a rhetorical question. The questioning phrase אינו דין, in the first qal v'homer argument, (literally, 'is it not *din'* [46]) which throughout this work has been translated as 'must-it-not-follow' is now in the repetition replaced with the non-questioning assertive phrase דין הוא, translated 'it is *din'* or 'it-must-follow':

---

[46] Refer to Appendix I for elaboration.

ומה עגלה שאין המום פוסל בה, עשה בה שאר מלאכה כעול, פרה שהמום פוסל
בה דין הוא שנעשה בה שאר מלאכה כעול.

The first qal v'homer argument is asserted to be correct, and its conclusion provides the answer to the original question,

From where do we know to equate other labors with the bearing of a yoke [i.e. that they disqualify the cow from serving as the red heifer in purification rites]?

The answer being, it is true that the heifer that serves in the rite of the red heifer may not have been worked with, even if that work was without a yoke, and it is known from the following qal v'homer argument which was shown to be correct:

And since [regarding] the calf which is not disqualified by a blemish [from serving as the eglah arufah], other labors are equated with [the drawing of] a yoke; with regard to the [red] heifer which is disqualified by a blemish [from serving in rites], it certainly follows that we should equate other labors with [the bearing of] a yoke!

The phrase *o'kheiluf* actively functions as terminology

The function of the logico-linguistic terminology *o'kheiluf* in Example i is not difficult to discern. The meta-argument considered the two qal v'homer arguments presented as possibilities and decided between them, the first one referred to by *danti,* meaning 'I [originally] drew a qal v'homer' and *batail o'kheiluf,* meaning 'the *o'kheiluf* was invalidated' and so only the original qal v'homer argument remained. Referring to the qal v'homer arrived at from the original by beginning with the negation of the conclusion of the original, i.e. the *kheiluf* qal v'homer, as the *o'kheiluf*, rather than repeating the entire qal v'homer argument brings clarity to the organization of the meta-argument. The alternative of writing out the entire *kheiluf* qal v'homer argument would make it hard to follow the structure of the meta-argument (what in this work is referred to as the *o'kheiluf* argument). Referring in the meta-argument to the specific qal v'homer related to the original by 'or the *kheiluf*, is truly making use of technical terminology.

In Example i from the Sifre Bamidbar which was considered at length, the author sought to answer a question prompted by the biblical verse under study. The answer was not something that was given plainly anywhere in the Torah but the author saw a possible analogy with the same issue of law regarding a different rite elsewhere in the Torah. However, with regard to that other rite, the Torah was also not explicit on the matter of this law and therefore the author could not conclude from one rite to the other using qal v'homer reasoning or some other hermeneutical rule. Such circumstances where the commentator had a hunch that the law in two different topics should relate to each other but where he had no clear knowledge of the law in either case, led him to engage in an *o'kheiluf* argument. In all of the 16 tannaitic[47] *o'kheiluf* arguments, the argument arises precisely because of this same set of circumstances.

Through the *o'kheiluf* argument, the author of Example i from Sifre Bamidbar sought to determine which of two qal v'homer arguments that connect the two rites and which are related to one another as indicated in The First Way, contains the correct answer to the original question. In each of the other cases of the *o'kheiluf* argument the argument proceeds in the same way to decide between the two qal v'homer arguments that are related as symbolized in the formulation of the *o'kheiluf*, (4').

The technical phrase *o'kheiluf* only appears when terminology is truly needed

In fact when the term *o'kheiluf* is not needed to act as terminology, it is not included. If two qal v'homer arguments related by (4') are presented but not followed by comparison of the two arguments, that

---

[47] The 15 cases from the Midrash Halakhah are laid out in Chapter Two and the unique case from the Mishnah is the subject of Chapter Five.

is, if there is no need to refer to each of the two arguments as wholes, then there may be no need for the text to use the *o'kheiluf* terminology to refer to one argument as *o'kheiluf* of the other. Such an example can be seen in M.Sotah 6:3. (The *o'kheiluf* phrase and argument that occur in the Mishnah is the subject of Chapter Six, but because the discussion here is focused on how the phrase *o'kheiluf* functions as terminology, this evidence from absence in the Mishnah is described briefly here.)

Two statements in M. Sotah 6: 1, 2, appeared to the Tannaim to be contradictory.[48] They were therefore followed with justifying

---

[48] The two situations that lead the husband to be suspicious of his wife's faithfulness, the first עדות ראשונה, is understood to require two witnesses to establish and the second, עדות אחרונה, is understood from the Mishnah to require only one witness.

P = 'עדות ראשונה,אינה מתקיימת בפחות משנים'
Q= 'עדות אחרונה, לא תתקיים בפחות משנים'
A = '[עדות ראשונה] אין אוסרתה אסור עולם'
B= '[עדות אחרונה] אוסרתה אסור עולם'
Q-= 'עדות אחרונה, מתקיימת בעד אחד'
P-= 'עדות ראשונה, תתקיים בעד אחד'

First qal v'homer:

ומה אם עדות ראשונה שאינה אוסרתה אסור עולם, אינה מתקימת בפחות משנים
עדות אחרונה שאוסרתה אסור עולם, אינו דין שלא תתקים בפחות משנים ?!

In symbols: A, B & P must-it-not-follow-that Q ?!

This qal v'homer is followed by the phrase *talmud lomar*, and a biblical proof text for, what is, -Q, thereby refuting the conclusion, Q, and the qal v'homer argument.

The second qal v'homer argument follows:

ומה אם עדות אחרונה שאוסרתה אסור עולם, הרי היא מתקימת בעד אחד
עדות הראשונה שאינה אוסרתה אסור עולם, אינו דין שתתקים בעד אחד ?!

In symboles: A,B & - Q must-it-not-follow-that -P ?!

The qal v'homer argument is followed by the phrase *talmud lomar* and two biblical prooftexts that are used together to demonstrate, what is, P and thereby refute the conclusion, i.e. -P, and the qal v'homer argument.

64

arguments. Referring suggestively to the two statements as **P** and **-Q,** there did not appear to be compelling evidence for or against these statements. After stating them the Mishnah says, the rulings on these matters seemed at first to logically be derived as follows by qal v'homer from two facts **A** and **B**: 'A,B and P must-it-not-follow-that Q ?!' But that was not possible, the Mishnah states, because of a biblical verse which could be seen as implying **-Q.**[49] But then it is argued by qal v'homer that from **-Q** one may conclude **-P**: 'A, B and **-Q** must-it-not-follow-that **-P** ?!'. But that was not possible, the Mishnah states, because of a different verse which (together with another biblical verse) could be seen as implying **P.**[50] These two arguments are the *kheiluf* of one another. Since the Mishnah can resolve each qal v'homer separately, because there is some biblical evidence for both **P** and **-Q** (and none for **-P** and **Q**), the Mishnah has no need to compare the two arguments and therefore no need for names to refer to the two different arguments. This Mishnah therefore has no need for the phrase *o'kheiluf* which accordingly it does not contain.

Answering a remaining question about the conclusion of *o'kheiluf* in Example i

There is a question posed earlier that still remains. In Example i from Sifre Bamidbar, in the *o'kheiluf* argument, the midrashist presents two different qal v'homer arguments, then eliminates one on the basis of a proof text, and then announces the remaining qal v'homer argument, apparently by default, to be correct. Why does he presume that one of the two qal v'homer arguments must be correct?

It is worth considering the situation as the midrashist would see it. He wants to know what the law is regarding other work for disqualifying

---

[49] Num. 5:13 states "and there be no witness against her," implying that only one witness would be needed against the wife, refuting **Q** which says that at least two witnesses are required.
[50] Deut.24:1 and Deut.19:5.

the heifer from serving as a red heifer. The verses on the red heifer are silent on this practical point of law. The Midrash Halakhah operates under the assumption that ideally any law, civic or cultic, addressed in the Torah, finds its complete treatment there as well.[51] That is, if the detailing of a certain law in the Torah leaves some question unanswered, the answer can be derived from verses in the Torah by one of the accepted modes of derivation.

Of the different possibilities of where to look to derive an answer to his question, the author imagines that his best bet is the *eglah arufah*. As mentioned earlier the rite of the red heifer and that of the *eglah arufah* have much in common. Both are rites that serve to achieve atonement for people for their sins. Related to this holy purpose, there are restrictions placed on the animals used for both. So the author's impression is that the law for one rite should inform the law for the other. Then because one animal needs to be blemish-free and the other animal for the other ritual does not, the author sees the possibility of relating the two situations by qal v'homer reasoning.

Of all the hermeneutical rules available to the Tannaim qal v'homer is viewed as the most natural, the one that is most like ordinary reasoning. It is for this reason that it is often referred to as *din*, judgment. The sense in the word *din* is that the conclusion forces itself upon us as a judgment, with logical force. The midrashist however has two contradictory possibilities for qal v'homer arguments between the two subjects on the point of law about the disqualifying work; the invalidation of one of them leaves him with a unique answer. Thus the midrashist has shown that exactly one qal v'homer argument exists that can address and answer the question. Since a derivation by qal v'homer is the most compelling derivation as

---

[51] In Azzan Yadin-Israel, *Scripture and Tradition:The Triumph of Midrash* (Philadelphia: University of Pennsylvania Press, 2015), the author argues that for the later anonymous Sifra this is very much a pretended assumption.Yadin-Israel argues that in many of these passages the Sifra "engages in a hermeneutic of camouflage, producing a veneer of midrashic rhetoric" of what are really oral teachings.

compared to the other hermeneutical methods and rules[52] and since some derivation of an answer from the Torah is sought, the commentator believes he has arrived at the answer and he stops there.

1.5: Conclusions

Prior to this work, no special attention was paid to the phrase 'או חילוף' in tannaitic literature (or in the Talmuds). The phrase was not recognized as having a technical meaning or even a very precise meaning and therefore no attempt was made to collect its occurrences. When it was translated, it was translated incorrectly by the vague phrase 'or the reverse'.

This chapter recovered the phrase 'או חילוף' as tannaitic technical terminology which occurs 16 times in tannaitic literature. It was shown that for Example i from the Sifre the phrase refers to the second in a pair of qal v'homer arguments that are related to one another precisely as described by (4').[53] Chapters Two and Six show that this is true for all other 15 tannaitic occurrences of the phrase או חילוף.

Since **A, B &** **P** must-it-not-follows-that **Q** ?!

או חילוף

---

[52] See Chapter Four (especially the section on *o'kheiluf* arguments in the Sifra) for further defense of this position in the Midrash Halakhah which is at variance with the position of the Mishnah on this matter. (The Mishnah views *gezerah shavah* as preferable to qal v'homer as a rule for deriving laws; see M.Sotah 6:3.)

[53] One of them does not involve qal v'homer arguments but instead just-as arguments and is therefore accordingly described by the related expression:

A & B; just as **P** so-too **Q**.
או חילוף
A & B; just as **-Q** so-too **-P**.   (5')

Since **A, B & -Q** must-it-not-follow-that -**P** ?!   (4')

where **A** and **B** represent propositions known with certainty to be true, while **P** represents a proposition for which the evidence is not (viewed by the author as) compelling. There is no evidence supporting or refuting **Q**. (-**Q** denotes the negation of **Q**; -**Q** is the statement 'It is not true that **Q**' and likewise for -**P**.) Further, each of the two rhetorical questions sandwiching the phrase או חילוף represents a qal v'homer argument.

In the Midrash Halakhah, the facts that **A** and **B** represent have their sources in the Torah or in common sense. In the midrash of the R. Akiva school, especially in the Sifra, the statement that **A** or **B** represents might sometimes be, not quite the explicit content of a biblical verse but rather, a reasonable conclusion from a biblical statement. In the Midrash Halakhah, the evidence for **P**, if it exists, is biblical.[54] In all of the arguments of the R. Ishmael school there is some biblical evidence for **P**. In several of those and in several of the arguments in Sifre Devarim, the biblical evidence for **P** is in fact fairly suggestive but does not meet the high standards of the authors for evidence or proof.[55]

In uttering the phrase o'kheiluf, the Tanna very likely did not have in mind, for the two topics he was comparing, all of what (4') symbolizes about them. The author very likely meant just this part of it: 'or perhaps instead [of the preceding qal v'homer] the argument should be the qal v'homer that begins from the opposite of the conclusion of the last [qal v'homer] statement', where by 'the opposite' the Tanna meant, what actually is the negation. In each case it is only by thinking about the particulars of the original qal v'homer, i.e. the facts that could be correctly labeled **A** and **B**, and through reasoning by qal

---

[54] The five o'kheiluf arguments of the Sifra, are launched from propositions P for which the authors have no biblical evidence. For these, P is just a guess that is taken to be true in the first qal v'homer argument.
[55] See Chapter Two, cases 3, 4, 5,12,13,14.

v'homer that the authors succeeded in reaching a conclusion that was in fact always the negation of **P**.

There is no word or phrase in English for changing the parts of a statement as described in (4') or (5') because no such concept exists in Western culture. That is, there is no word in English that describes the relationship between the two (non-conditional) statements 'P therefore **Q**' and '-**Q** therefore -**P**'. The Greeks had neither these concepts nor terminology for these concepts; Chapter Five takes up how a Stoic philosopher would have critiqued a comparison (as in the o'kheiluf argument) made between the two statements.

What has been identified and named in this work the o'kheiluf argument arises in the very unusual situation where the launching premise of the original qal v'homer argument, **P**, is one for which there is insufficient evidence. The typical qal v'homer argument on the other hand begins from facts and draws a conclusion from them. The o'kheiluf meta-argument begins with one qal v'homer argument and is then followed by the phrase 'or perhaps [instead] the kheiluf [argument]' which then introduces a new qal v'homer argument related to the first precisely by (4'). The meta-argument continues and tries to decide between the two qal v'homer arguments which one is the correct one. The meta-argument goes about this with a procedure and an analysis with descriptive formulas that are virtually identical in all 16 tannaitic o'kheiluf meta-arguments.

When deemed successful the meta-argument concludes with a determination of which of the two qal v'homer arguments gives the correct conclusions. Chapter Five analyzes this technique for reaching a conclusion as to which of the two arguments is correct.

After its first occurrence in the meta-argument where it is used to refer to the qal v'homer argument that it introduces, the phrase o'kheiluf indeed functions as technical terminology: the phrase is used as a stand-in for the whole long kheiluf qal v'homer argument whose repeated explicit inclusion in the meta-argument would obscure the logic of the whole argument.

Chapter Three analyzes the other phrase found in tannaitic literature which contains the noun *kheiluf*, חילוף הדברים. Our discussion there will provide further evidence that the phrase או חילוף, *o'kheiluf*, was intended as logico-linguistic terminology. Not only did the phrase identify an argument as the special *o'kheiluf* argument, where the negation of the conclusion of a prior qal v'homer argument is used to launch an alternative qal v'homer argument, but it also marked the argument as distinct from a case of חילוף הדברים, the *kheiluf* of the matters.

CHAPTER TWO: *O'Kheiluf* is Consistent Logico-linguistic Terminology in the Midrash Halakhah

This chapter presents each of the 15 passages containing the phrase או חילוף in the Midrash Halakhah. In each occurrence the phrase is shown to signify an *o'kheiluf* argument.[56]

For each passage, the first half of the *o'kheiluf* argument is quoted, that is, the two qal v'homer arguments and the phrase או חילוף sandwiched between them. It will be seen that in each passage the argument has the same form shown for the one example analyzed in Chapter One, from the Sifre Bamidbar:[57]

Since **A,B** & **P** must-it-not-follow-that **Q** ?!

או חילוף

Since **A,B** & **-Q** must-it-not-follow-that **-P** ?!　　　　　　(*)

where **A** and **B** represent propositions that are facts, and **P** represents a proposition for which there is less than completely convincing evidence, and in the second argument **-Q** is not known to be false. The ending '?!' is used to indicate that the expression is a rhetorically-questioning qal v'homer argument.

---

[56] There is a 16th: Sifre Devarim, piska 260, discussed at the end of this chapter. I have not included it in the sum because, as I argue, the occurrence of the phrase in this text was likely a later addition and I show that it does not signify an *o'kheiluf* argument. For one thing the *'o'* means 'and' in piska 260 while in the other 15 occurrences it means 'or' and the argument consists of a systematic choosing between two options rather than the adding of two possibilities together in piska 260 to create a full picture.

[57] #6 though involves two just-as arguments rather than two qal v'homer arguments. It has the same symbolic form (*), with the same requirements on A, B, P, and Q, but with 'just-as' and 'so too' replacing 'must-it-not -follow-that.'

It is shown that the argument in each of the passages has this form, by indicating, for each argument, the phrases that correspond to each of **A, B, P, Q, -P, -Q**. Also, when it is not perfectly obvious, it is shown that the phrase associated to **-P** is indeed the negation of the phrase associated with **P**, and the same is done for **Q**. Afterwards, the sources for the statements represented by **A** and **B** are given as well as the source of the inconclusive evidence for **P**.

For the *o'kheiluf* arguments of the Midrash Halakhah, it is seen that the facts that **A** and **B** represent have their sources in the Torah or in common sense. Though in the midrash of the R. Akiva school, especially in the Sifra, the statement that **A** or **B** represents is sometimes not quite the explicit content of a biblical verse but rather a reasonable conclusion from a biblical statement.

In the Midrash Halakhah, the inconclusive evidence for **P**, when it exists, is biblical. It is pointed out that for each case in the Sifra, all attributed to the school of R. Akiva, **P** is just a guess. But in all of the other arguments, those of the R. Ishmael school as well as those of the Sifre Devarim of the R. Akiva school, there is some biblical evidence for **P**. In fact in several of the arguments in the Sifre Bamidbar and in several in the Sifre Devarim, the biblical evidence for **P** would seem fairly strong, but it does not meet the high standards of the authors for conclusive evidence or proof.[58]

Although as discussed in Chapter One, the representing form (*) does not make it easy to see that indeed each of the two arguments that end with '?!' is a qal v'homer argument, each passage has been labeled in this chapter in such a way that the qal v'homer property can easily be assessed for the particular argument. Each of the two arguments separated by the phrase 'או חילוף', is broken up into a vertical list of four lines and each line is labeled with a symbol. If for example, the listed lines are labeled in order, R,S,T,U, then the qal v'homer argument represented is the following, and in each case the

---

[58] See in this chapter, # 3, 4, 5, 12, 13 and 14.

content of the lines the symbols represent, make clear that the argument is indeed a qal v'homer argument:

> R, also S. Therefore,
> Since T, must-it-not-follow-that U ?!

Thus if the lines are labeled, in (the usual[59]) order, A, P, B, Q, then the qal v'homer argument represented is,

> A, also P. Therefore,
> Since B, must-it-not-follow-that Q ?!

While if the lines are labeled, in (the less common[60]) order, A, B, P, Q, then the qal v'homer argument represented is,

> A, also B. Therefore,
> Regarding P, must-it-not-follow-that Q ?!

But in representing both of these qal v'homer arguments as in (*),

Since A, B & P must-it-not-follow-that Q ?!,

the difference between the two qal v'homer arguments is suppressed in order to highlight that in both, it is from A,B & P being the case that it is argued that Q should also be true. (The listed lines A, P, B are represented as A, B & P in (*), because facts are represented by the letters A and B and the somewhat speculative assertion is

---

[59] Seen in the o'kheiluf arguments of the R. Ishmael school #1-6 and in those in the Sifre Devarim #12-15.

[60] Seen in Sifra #7, #9. Sifra #11 has a uniquely unusual ordering:

> Regarding P, it is seen that A. Therefore,
> Regarding B, must-it-not-follow-that Q ?!
>   O'kheiluf
> Regarding -Q, it is seen that B. Therefore,
> Regarding A, must-it-not-follow-that -P ?!

represented by P and clarity is the goal in maintaining a distinction between the two categories of propositions.)

For each *o'kheiluf* argument, the second part and the concluding elements of the argument are briefly discussed. All of the *o'kheiluf* arguments of the school of R. Ishmael are deemed successful by their authors. That is, each refutes one of the two possibilities presented in the argument and declares the remaining possible qal v'homer to be correct. In contrast, this is the case for only two out of the nine *o'kheiluf* arguments of the school of R. Akiva.

All eight successful *o'kheiluf* arguments, whether of the school of R. Ishmael or of R. Akiva, employ an almost uniform formula to summarize the steps of the whole argument (and another for the ending that asserts the correct conclusion). With small grammatical variations the concluding formula in all 8 o'kheiluf arguments is as follows or very close to it:

דנתי חלפתי בטל או חילוף וזכיתי לדון כבתחילה

This will be discussed in each case.

Each passage will be presented line-by-line on the right-hand side of a table. The left column for each row will contain the statement portion of the corresponding right-hand entry, along with the appropriate label, as described above, assigned to that statement. My translation into English will follow immediately after.

2.1: Mekhilta de-Rabbi Ishmael

1. <u>מכילתא דרבי ישמעאל:</u>
<u>משפטים -מסכתא דנזיקין, פרשה י':</u>

ומה עגלה ערופה שהיא מכפרת על שפיכות דמים	A= 'עגלה ערופה מכפרת על שפיכות דמים'
הרי היא אסורה בהנאה	P= 'עגלה ערופה אסורה בהנאה'
שור הנסקל שהוא שופך דמים	B= 'שור הנסקל הוא שופך דמים'
אינו דין שיהא אסור בהנאה?!	Q= 'שור הנסקל אסור בהנאה'
או חילוף	
ומה שור הנסקל שהוא שופך דמים	B= 'שור הנסקל הוא שופך דמים'
הרי הוא מותר בהנאה	Q- = 'שור הנסקל מותר בהנאה'
עגלה ערופה שהיא מכפרת על שפיכות דמים	A= 'עגלה ערופה מכפרת על שפיכות דמים'
אינו דין שתהא מותרת בהנאה?!	P- = 'עגלה ערופה מותרת בהנאה'

Translation:

A = 'The *eglah arufah* atones for spilt blood',
yet
P = 'It is prohibited to derive benefit from the *eglah arufah*'.
75

Therefore,
Since
B = 'The stoned ox was a killer'
must-it-not-follow-that
Q = 'It is prohibited to derive benefit for the stoned ox'
?!

O'kheiluf

B = 'The stoned ox was a killer'
yet
-Q = 'It is permitted to derive benefit from the stoned ox'.
Therefore,
Since
A = 'The *eglah arufah* atones for spilt blood,
must-it-not-follow-that
-P = 'It is permitted to derive benefit from the *eglah arufah*'
?!

With the above symbols the argument can be represented as follows:

Since A, B & P must-it-not-follow-that Q ?!
אֹו חילוף
Since A, B & -Q must-it -not-follow-that -P ?![61]   (*)

---

[61] Following the argument closely, it is more accurately symbolized as
A & P & B must-it-not-follow-that Q ?!
          o'kheiluf
B & -Q & A must-it-not-follow-that -P ?!

As explained in Chapter One, in order to keep the facts and the somewhat speculative claims separate, we reorder A & P & B as the logically equivalent A, B & P. For easy comparison with the first qal v'homer, we reorder B, A &-Q as the equivalent A,B & -Q.

The qal v'homer nature of the arguments is made clear by following the ordering and deployment of the premises in the two arguments. This aspect can be represented as follows:

Regarding A, it is seen that P. Therefore,

To show that this *o'kheiluf* argument may indeed be symbolically represented by (*) it remains to show the following: A and B have the status of facts, P is a claim for which there is only weak evidence, there is no evidence for or against Q and the phrase *o'kheiluf* sandwiches two qal v'homer arguments. This is the goal of the immediately following exposition.

This passage is commentary to Exod. 21:28:

וכי יגח שור את איש או את אשה ומת, סקול יסקל השור ולא יאכל את בשרו ובעל השור נקי.

And if an ox shall gore a man or a woman and he dies, the ox shall be stoned; its flesh may not be eaten, and the owner of the ox is innocent.

Pointing out that the verse commands that the meat of the stoned ox may not be eaten, the Sifre asks, "From where do we know that it is also forbidden to have any benefit [at all from the condemned ox]?" To answer this question the Sifre looks to the calf in the *eglah arufah* rite which is also killed (by breaking its neck).

The *eglah arufah* rite is performed when a slain person is found in a field and it is not known who killed him (Deut. 21:1-9). The elders of the neighboring cities measure the distance from the corpse to their cities to determine which is closest. The elders of the closest city then perform the *eglah arufah* rite. They obtain a calf that has never worked, that has never drawn a yoke. They lower the calf into a wadi, which cannot be worked and cannot be sown, and there they break the calf's neck. The elders of the city wash their hands over the calf that was axed in the valley and they say, "Our hands have not spilled

---

Regarding B, must-it-not-follow-that Q ?!
    O'kheiluf
Regarding B, it is seen that -Q. Therefore,
Regarding A, must-it-not-follow-that -P ?!

this blood, and our eyes did not see." And they beseech the Lord for atonement.

The verses in Deut. 21 do not explicitly say that no benefit may be derived from this killed calf, but there is some evidence. The whole detailed ritual performed in a harsh, barren valley to which the calf is brought, suggests that the calf is also buried there. (The R. Ishmael school may have had such a comment in their midrash to Deuteronomy which is no longer extant. Or like the Sifre Devarim, piska 207 they may have derived that the calf is buried there from the phrase וערפו שם, meaning "they break its neck there".) If, as assumed, the calf is buried right there in the wadi at the close of the ceremony, then it would follow that no personal benefit may be obtained from its remains.

The phrase in Deut. 21:4, "and you will break the heifer's neck there in the wadi" and the ceremony that follows with the elders washing their hands over the killed calf and seeking atonement, is (not explicit evidence but only) mild evidence for claim P that no benefit may be derived from the calf of the *eglah arufah* rite. Because the evidence is mild an *o'kheiluf* argument (rather than a single determining qal v'homer) is set up. The stoned ox and calf of the *eglah arufah* rite are compared along the axis running from having committed murder to not just not having committed murder but actually, atoning for the shedding of blood. A and B are well-known from the Torah to be true, A from Deuteronomy, chapter 21 and B from Exodus, chapter 21. Thus the demonstration that the *o'kheiluf* argument may be symbolically represented by (*) is complete.

The *kheiluf* qal v'homer argument ends with must-it-not-follow-that-P, i.e. with the claim that the remains of the calf of the *eglah arufah* rite are permitted to be used for personal benefit. The argument continues with a refutation of this conclusion, *talmud lomar,* followed by the biblical phrase "and you must ax its neck there in the wadi," i.e. the mild evidence supporting P, implying with the rest of the

78

community ceremony that follows, that the calf is buried there in the wadi and therefore cannot be used for personal benefit.

The argument continues with a standard formulation summing up what was done: first one qal v'homer then the *kheiluf* argument which was then found to be invalid. The first qal v'homer is then declared (by elimination) to be correct:

דנתי וחלפתי בטל החלוף וזכיתי בדין מתחילה

A restatement of the first qal v'homer follows but this time the rhetorical elements seeking to convince, are replaced with declarations: הרי הוא (translated, indeed she is [forbidden for personal benefit]) replaces the prefix ש (meaning, that), and דין הוא (it does follow) replaces אינו דין (must-it-not-follow?!).

2.2: Sifre Numbers

<u>2.   ספרי במדבר:</u>
<u>פיסקא קיח (פרשת קרח, פרק יח, פסוק יז):</u>

<u>Piska 118:</u>

'במקום (בשלמים) ריבה בחלבין= A	מה אם במקום שריבה בחלבין
'P= (בשלמים) מיעט בדמים'	מיעט בדמים
'כאן (בבכור) מיעט בחלבין= B	כאן שמיעט בחלבין
'Q= (בבכור) למעט בדמים'	אינו דין שנמעט בדמים!?
	או חלוף
'במקום (בבכור) שמיעט בחלבין= B	ומה אם במקום שמיעט בחלבין
'Q -= (בבכור) ריבה בדמים'	ריבה בדמים
'כאן (בשלמים) ריבה בחלבין= A	כאן שריבה בחלבין
'P -= (בשלמים) לרבות בדמים'	אינו דין שנרבה בדמים !?

79

<u>Translation:</u>

A = 'In the place [i.e. by the Shelamim sacrifices] where abundant fat offerings are made',
P = 'The blood offerings [by the Shelamim sacrifices] are minimized.'
Therefore since,
B= 'Here [by the firstborn animal] where fat offerings are minimized'
must-it-not-follow-that
Q = 'The blood offerings [by the firstborn animal] are to be minimized'
?!

O'kheiluf

B = 'In the place [i.e. the firstborn animal offering] where fat offerings are minimized',
yet
-Q = 'Abundant blood offerings are made [by the firstborn animal offering]'
Therefore, since
A = 'Here [i.e. by the Shelamim sacrifices] where abundant fat offerings are made'
must-it-not-follow-that
-P = 'Abundant blood offerings are to be made [by the Shelamim sacrifices]'
?!

With this notation the argument may be symbolized as,

Since A, B & P must-it-not-follow-that Q ?!
        או חילוף
Since A, B & -Q must-it-not-follow-that -P ?!.

To show that this *o'kheiluf* argument may be symbolically represented by (*) it remains now to show the following: A and B have the status of facts, P is a claim for which there is only weak evidence, there is no evidence for or against Q, the phrase *o'kheiluf* sandwiches two qal v'homer arguments.

This passage in the Sifre Bamidbar is focused on Num.18:17. In verses 15-19, the Lord tells Aaron that every first born in Israel will belong to him and his sons. However, the first born of people and the first born of impure animals are to be redeemed. Verse 17: "The first born of an ox or a sheep or a goat you shall not redeem, they are holy. You shall throw their blood onto the altar and their fat you shall burn, a pleasing aroma for the Lord."

The Sifre asks, 'Where the verse says, את דמם תזרק על המזבח, "you shall throw their blood onto the altar," is it instructing on one dashing of blood or two?' (The Sifre comments,"את דמם תזרק על המזבח, one dashing, but perhaps it is two dashings?") The plural, דמם, leaves open a reading that two dashings are to be thrown. The assumption perhaps is that if more than two dashings were intended the verse would have specified that. So the question is, are they to throw one or two dashes. The verse is unclear and therefore the Sifre looks to the Shelamim sacrifice where throwing blood on to the altar is also mentioned, Lev. 3:3. But by the Shelamim the verse is also unclear about how many dashings of blood are required. Because of the absence of specification and the plural action and the requirement that the blood get all around the altar, the verse is reasonably understood to require two dashings (each one hitting two corners). Thus an *o'kheiluf* argument is set up.

The או חילוף argument that ensues to answer this question is unusual in that pronouns are used to describe the subjects instead of proper nouns: מקום, meaning place, and כאן, meaning here, refer to the proper nouns, Shelamim sacrifices and firstborn animal. Because pronouns are used and the two qal v'homer arguments are described as 'you start there and you end over here,' with the first going from P to Q and the second going from -Q to -P, 'here' and 'place\there' switch references in the two qal v'homer arguments. This is indeed how people argue especially while pointing with a finger.[62]

A = 'By the Shelamim sacrifices, the fat offerings are abundant.' The sources for A are Lev. 3:3-4. These verses describe all the fat from many parts of the animal that must be removed and offered on the altar. B = 'By the sacrifice of the first animal offspring, the fat offerings are minimized.' The source for B is the verse under discussion in the Sifre Bamidbar, Num.18:17. There it says that "their fat you should burn [on the altar]" of the firstborn of an ox, sheep or goat; it does not say 'all their fat...' Also the lack of elaboration as compared to the verse from Leviticus cited above makes the verse in Numbers the source for B.

P= 'By the Shelamim sacrifice the blood offerings are minimized.' The evidence for P is Lev. 3:3 where it says regarding the Shelamim sacrifice "and the children of Aaron will throw the blood on the altar around," וזרקו בני אהרן את דמו על המזבח סביב. The altar has four corners so to get the blood 'around' the altar would take at least two applications, one on the sides right by one corner and the other by the sides on the diagonal corner. Also, וזרקו, meaning, and they will throw, speaking of the children of Aaron, implies that there must be

---

[62] Menahem Kahana in Part IV of his critical edition of the Sifre Bamidbar , ספרי במדבר: מהדורה מבוארת, Magnus Press, 2015, page 920, is disturbed by the Sifre's unusual use of pronouns in this passage and in such a way that 'here' changes reference in the two parts of the argument, and the same for 'the place' functioning as 'there'. Kahana has found this odd and problematic because he is unaware of the logical structure and hermeneutical function of arguments containing the phrase o'kheiluf (או חילוף). For starters, he has not recognized how the Tanna has to carefully think through, while keeping track of the facts and taking the negation only of the speculative claims, going first in the direction from P to Q and then in the direction starting from -Q. P starts by considering the situation 'there'. Reasoning carefully takes the author to 'here', which is what the Sifre was after and which is why it is the 'here', i.e. the law about the first born. It is reached with Q. In the kheiluf the starting position is likewise referred to by 'there' and what is reached is 'here'. Lacking insight into the meaning of או חילוף, Kahana is not impressed by this consistency and is instead troubled by what he mistakes as the switching of references.

more than one dashing of blood. The plural action and the need to get the blood around the altar eliminate one dashing as a possibility leaving two as the minimum. Since the verse does not specify a number of dashings, the minimum is to be understood and that is two. (This is how the Sifra also understands Lev. 3:3.) This is how the phrase מיעט בדמים with regard to במקום, i.e. the Shelamim, in the first qal v'homer should be understood, that the verse requires this minimum possibility.

Q= 'For the sacrifice of the firstborn offspring, the blood offerings are to be minimized.' The conclusion Q that with regard to the firstborn נמעט בדמים, means that in the instruction about the blood dashing requirement for the first born of the ox, sheep or goat, the phrase should be interpreted minimally as well. The instructional phrase is את דמם תזרק על המזבח, translated as, "their blood you (singular) should throw upon the altar." Since תזרק, "you (singular) should throw," is singular yet דמם, "their blood," is plural, it is possible to understand the phrase as requiring either one or two dashings. More than that is not possible because if more was intended the verse would have had to specify a number. Since this verse can be read as requiring either one or two dashings, the qal v'homer conclusion, נמעט בדמים, means to uphold the minimal interpretation, and that would be of the two possibilities, one dashing.

Likewise in the *kheiluf* qal v'homer, -Q = 'ריבה בדמים with regard to the firstborn,' means taking a maximum interpretation of the relevant verse. Thus as explained above, the verse would be interpreted as requiring two dashings. -P = 'ריבה בדמים with regard to the Shelamim sacrifice,' means interpreting the relevant verse maximally. The possibility of such a conclusion is refuted by *talmud lomar*, followed by repeating the evidence for P which is, וזרקו בני אהרן את דמו על המזבח סביב. Because there really is no possibility of maximizing the blood offered, the minimal interpretation and the maximal implied in the verse are the same: In the absence of specification, the plural actions and the need to get the blood around the altar, imply only one minimal interpretation and so there is no maximal interpretation justified by the phrase.

Kahana finds the changing references of במקום, in the place, and כאן, here, bewildering. He points out that this absence of clarity as to what topics these words refer caused the commentators on the Sifre great difficulty and led them to offer various different suggestions for the reference of במקום.[63] My exposition above does away with these problems: A clear understanding of o'kheiluf as laid out in this work is shown to be key. Also, ריבה and מיעט must be understood as relative terms, minimal and maximal, to be determined by context. (Note that the argument does not adhere to the tannaitic principle of dayo, דיו לבא מן הדין להיות כנידון.[64])

---

[63] See Kahana, page 918, footnotes 102 and 103:

102. ראה למשל דברי הנצי"ב בפתיחת פירושו 'ברייתא זו סתומה מאוד וצריכא רבא לגלות מצפוניו'. או דברי רד"ף בחתימת פירושו: 'ואיברא דכל ב' הפירושים דחוקים אבל אין בידי לפרש בדרך יותר מרווחי'.

Trying to clarify the reference of 'מקום', commentaries on the Sifre made various suggestions noted in 103. See footnote 62 above.

103. 'בשאר קדשים כגון עולה או שלמים' (ר"ה), שלמים (אחת מהצעותיו של הורוביץ), חטאת פנימיות (המיוחס לראב"ד), פר כהן המשיח (הנצי"ב).

[64] This is the dayo principle that in a qal v'homer, P therefore must-it-not-certainly be the case Q (by virtue of properties A and B), the degree of Q not exceed that of P. The expression of the rule appears in the baraita of the 13 hermeneutical principles of R. Ishmael that precedes the Sifre. The first rule listed is qal v'homer followed by an example of how the Torah uses this rule. In Num.12:14, God explains to Moses after he entreats Him on behalf of his sister Miriam: If her father had spat in her face would she not hide herself for a week?! Let her seclude herself outside the camp for a week and then she will be collected. The baraita continues on explaining that by qal v'homer Miriam should seclude herself for two weeks because it is God who spat in her face (that is, who she offended) and a week is how long she would seclude herself if it was only her father who had spat in her face. But (by the principle) דיו לבא מן הדין להיות כנידון, she should only seclude herself seven days outside the camp. The word דיו (dayo) means 'it is enough'; the translation of the whole principle is roughly, 'it is enough that what derives from the din be like the given premise of the din.'

This principle appears once in the Mekhilta, once in the Sifre Bamidbar, and three places in the Sifra. In the Mishnah: Bava Kamma 2:5, Niddah 4:6. (In the Bavli the expression of the principle appears 20 times.)

For more on the dayo principle see for example,

After the *talmud lomar* and the proof text refuting the second qal v'homer, the first qal v'homer remains as the correct answer. In line with all of the other *o'kheiluf* arguments in the R. Ishmael midrash (and the two in the R. Akiva midrash where *o'kheiluf* succeeds) the argument should conclude with:

דנתי חלפתי בטל החלוף וזכיתי לדון כבתחילה

Followed by an expression of the first qal v'homer argument this time in a declarative manner:

ומה במקום שריבה בחלבים מיעט בדמים כאן שמיעט בחלבים אינו דין שנמעט בדמים.

This is absent, likely lost from an earlier manuscript. Meir Friedmann (1831-1908) in his edition and commentary to Sifre Bambar, מאיר עין, adds these words in brackets to the text and comments that those words appear in the hand-written manuscript he has and in the Yalkut Shimoni.

After the above standard formulation, Friedmann following the Yalkut Shimoni, adds the following additional words most likely for clarity because מיעט and ריבה, minimal and maximal, are relative terms:

ומה תלמוד לומר את דמם תזרוק על המזבח, מתנה אחת

Concluding that with regard to the firstborn, one dashing of blood is required.

Hyam Maccoby, *Early Rabbinic Writings* Cambridge: Cambridge University Press, 1988); Alexander Samely, *Rabbinic Interpretation of Scripture in the Mishnah* (Oxford: Oxford University Press, 2002); See also Allen Wiseman's 2010 Ph.D. thesis and references therein, *A Contemporary Examination of the A Fortiori Argument Involving Jewish Traditions*, Waterloo, Ontario, Canada.

A= 'עגלה, אין המום פוסל בה'	ומה עגלה שאין המום פוסל בה
P= 'עשה בה (בעגלה) שאר מלאכה כעול'	עשה בה שאר מלאכה כעול
B= 'פרה, המום פוסל בה'	פרה שהמום פוסל בה
Q= 'נעשה בה (בפרה) שאר מלאכה כעול'	אינו דין שנעשה בה שאר מלאכה כעול !?
	או חילוף[65]
B= 'פרה, המום פוסל בה'	ומה פרה שהמום פוסל בה
Q-= 'לא עשה בה (בפרה) שאר מלאכה כעול'	לא עשה בה שאר מלאכה כעול
A= 'עגלה, אין המום פוסל בה'	עגלה שאין המום פוסל בה
P-= 'לא נעשה בה [בעגלה] שאר מלאכה כעול'	אינו דין שלא נעשה בה שאר מלאכה כעול !?

---

[65] I have veered away from Horovitz's edition here using instead the version in Menahem Kahana's critical edition as the latter corrects previous versions including Horovitz's that contain the phrase או חילוף הן הדברים by removing the last two words and leaving only או חילוף. In those other versions as well, the conclusion uses the phrase או חילוף and not או חילוף הן הדברים. This is one clue that in the set-up of the argument as well, the extra phrase הן הדברים does not belong. Basing my reasoning also on all of the other o'kheiluf arguments of the Midrash Halakhah, not even just those in the Sifre Bamidbar, I am in agreement with Kahana's emendation and would suggest that the words הן הדברים are a later extraneous insertion.

86

Using the above notation the argument may be represented as,

Since A,B & P must-it-not-follow-that Q ?!

או חילוף

Since A,B & -Q must-it-not-follow-that -P ?!

To show that this *o'kheiluf* argument may be symbolically represented by (*), the following must also be shown: that A and B have the status of facts, P is a claim for which there is only weak evidence, there is no evidence for or against Q, the phrase *o'kheiluf* sandwiches two qal v'homer arguments. All of this was done in Chapter One where the passage was examined in depth. For convenience, substantiation of all but the last points is repeated in what follows immediately.

Deut. 21:3 discusses the requirements on the calf to be used in the rite of the *eglah arufah*. No mention is made there of not having a blemish, while it is mentioned by sacrifices and by the red heifer. The marked absence of this requirement in the biblical verses concerning the calf of the *eglah arufah* is the source for claim A. (In addition to the evidence from absence, the Sifre gives positive evidence a few lines earlier; see section 1.2, footnote 35.) A = 'The calf is not disqualified by a blemish [from serving in the *eglah arufah* rite].' The source for B is the explicit phrase in Num.19:3. B = 'The heifer is disqualified by a blemish [from serving in the rite of the red heifer].'

P = 'The calf is disqualified [from serving in the *eglah arufah* rite] by other types of work not involving a yoke.'

One possible reading of Deut. 21:3, provides the evidence for P. The verse says that the elders of the city should take the calf "that wasn't worked with, that didn't draw a yoke." It is possible to understand the phrase "that didn't draw a yoke" as an example of what is required in the preceding phrase "that wasn't worked with."

87

Q = 'The red heifer is disqualified by other types of work not involving a yoke.'

The *kheiluf* qal v'homer concludes that a calf is not invalidated for serving in the *eglah arufah* rite by work that does not involve wearing a yoke. This conclusion is followed by *talmud lomar* and a prooftext that refutes this conclusion. That prooftext is the biblical evidence that exists for P (on the basis of which the first qal v'homer was launched), Deut. 21:3:

אשר לא עבד בה

With the result of the *kheiluf* qal v'homer refuted, that whole qal v'homer is refuted. The Sifre in a standard formulation reviews what was done and declares the remaining qal v'homer argument, the first qal v'homer argument correct. The first qal v'homer is then repeated, this time the rhetorically-questioning elements are replaced with assertive expressions:

דנתי וחלפתי בטל או חילוף זכיתי כבתחילה:

ומה עגלה, שאין המום פוסל בה, עשה בה שאר מלאכות כעול; פרה, שהמום פוסל בה, דין הוא שנעשה בה שאר מלאכה כעול.

<u>Piska 125:</u>

'מת, חמור [מטמא]' = A	מת חמור
'(איש) מת אינו מטמא עד שעה שימות' = P	אינו מטמא עד שעה שימות
'שרץ, קל' =B	שרץ הקל
'(שרץ) לא יטמא עד שימות' =Q	אינו דין שלא יטמא עד שימות ?!
	או חלוף
'שרץ, קל' =B	מה שרץ הקל
'(שרץ) מטמא כשהוא מפרפר' =Q-	הרי הוא מטמא כשהוא מפרפר
'מת, חמור ' =A	מת החמור
'(מת) יטמא אפילו (כשהוא) מפרפר' =P-	אינו דין שיטמא אפילו מפרפר ?!

<u>Translation:</u>

A = 'The human corpse is grave'

yet

P = 'A dying person does not confer *tumah*, i.e. ritual contamination, until he actually dies'.

Therefore,

Since

B = 'The *sheretz* is light [by comparison]'

must-it-not-follow-that

Q = 'The dying *sheretz* confers *tumah* only once it (actually) dies'

?!

O'kheiluf

B = 'The *sheretz* is light [by comparison]'
yet
-Q = 'The dying *sheretz* confers *tumah* [before it dies], from when it is convulsing [in the throes of death]'
Therefore,
Since
A = 'The dead human body is grave'
must-it-not-follow-that
-P = 'A dying person confers *tumah* [even before he dies], from when he is convulsing [in the throes of death]'
?!

With these symbols the argument can be represented as,

Since A,B & P must-it-not-follow-that Q ?!

או חילוף

Since A,B & -Q must-it-not-follow-that -P ?!   (*)

To show that this *o'kheiluf* argument may be symbolically represented by (*) it remains now to show the following: A and B have the status of facts, P is a claim for which there is only weak evidence, there is no evidence for or against Q, -P is the negation of P and likewise for -Q, the phrase *o'kheiluf* sandwiches two qal v'homer arguments.

This argument is found in the Sifre's commentary to Num.19:13 which states that anyone who touches, "a dead body of a human being who will have died," and does not undergo a purification process, that person will be cut off from Israel.

The Sifre points out that since the verse says "who will have died," אשר ימות, this does suggest that a human body does not convey *tumah*, i.e. ritual impurity, unless it is dead when touched. The Sifre goes on and says that one can conclude, about a *sheretz* (a small reptile or insect of any of 8 species in Lev. 11:29-30 declared ritually

90

impure) that it too does not convey *tumah* unless it is dead. Leviticus is silent on this point about the *sheretz*, whether or not it need be dead, and therefore the Sifre seeks a determination by a promising-looking qal v'homer. But the premise of the first qal v'homer was not actually stated in the Torah, specifically that a human body does not convey ritual impurity when touched while in the throes of death. Thus the law is not known for the *sheretz* nor for the topic of comparison, the dying human. (This is the usual situation in which the *o'kheiluf* argument arises.) The premise for the first qal v'homer, was only an interpretation of the otherwise redundant phrase אשר ימות regarding the human body. Therefore the conclusion of the qal v'homer argument can be doubted and it is possible to consider the *kheiluf* qal v'homer.

The evidence for P is the extra language in the verse under examination by the Sifre, Num. 19:13 that can be read as emphatic, that only once the body is dead does it convey *tumah*: כל הנוגע במת בנפש האדם אשר ימות.

Num.19:11, 13 are the sources for A. They tell us that a corpse defiles a person, in fact for seven days before a purification process is completed. Lev.11:24, 25, 31 state that touching a dead (non-kosher) *sheretz* conveys ritual impurity to the person until the evening. Those verses are the sources for premise B. Comparison of these two sets of verses justifies the claims in A & B that the human corpse is a more serious case than that of the dead insect.

Thus the demonstration that the *o'kheiluf* argument may be symbolically represented by (*) is complete.

The *kheiluf* qal v'homer concludes with -P. The Sifre continues with *talmud lomar* and the biblical evidence that contradicts -P, i.e. the evidence that exists for P on the basis of which the first qal v'homer was launched. But that contradicts the evidence that exists for P: כל בנפש האדם אשר ימות הנוגע במת. The Sifre elaborates that (the extra words) אשר ימות implies that the dying person does not convey *tumah* before he dies.

The Sifre continues with the usual formula summing up what has been done, that the *kheiluf* qal v'homer was refuted leaving only the first qal v'homer which the Sifre declares true (by elimination):

דנתי וחילפתי , בטל או חלוף, זכיתי לדין כבתחילה

The Sifre repeats the first qal v'homer argument but this time in a declarative manner, replacing the rhetorically questioning elements of the expression with assertions:

מה מת חמור, אין מטמא עד שעה שימות, שרץ הקל, דין הוא שלא יטמא עד שעה שימות.

5. ספרי במדבר, פיסקא קכו (פרשת חקת, פרק יט, פסוק יד):

Piska 126:

A= 'אהל מקבל טומאה'	מה אהל שהוא מקבל טומאה
P= אהל אינו מטמא מכל צדדיו כשהוא פתוח	אין מטמא מכל צדדיו כשהוא פתוח
B= 'קבר אינו מקבל טומאה'	קבר שאין מקבל טומאה
Q= קבר לא יטמא מכל צדדיו כשהוא פתוח	אינו דין שלא יטמא מכל צדדיו כשהוא פתוח !?
	או חילוף
B= 'קבר אינו מקבל טומאה'	מה קבר שאינו מקבל טומאה
Q-= קבר מטמא מכל צדדיו כשהוא פתוח	הרי הוא מטמא מכל צדדיו כשהוא פתוח
A= 'אהל מקבל טומאה'	אהל שהוא מקבל טומאה
P-= אהל יטמא מכל צדדיו כשהוא פתוח	אינו דין שיטמא מכל צדדיו כשהוא פתוח !?

Translation:

A = 'A tent can become *tameh*, i.e. ritually polluted'
yet
P = 'When a tent is open it does not impart *tumah*, i.e. ritual pollution,
through its sides'.
Therefore,
Since
B = 'A grave does not become *tameh*'
must-it-not-follow-that
Q = 'When a grave is open it would not impart *tumah* through its
sides'
?!

O'kheiluf

B = 'A grave does not become *tameh*'
yet
-Q = 'When a grave is open it imparts *tumah* through its sides'.
Therefore,
Since
A = 'A tent can become *tameh*'
must-it-not-follow-that
-P = 'When a tent is open it imparts *tumah* through its sides'
?!

With the above notation the argument can be represented as,

Since A,B & P must-it-not-follow-that Q ?!

או חילוף

Since A,B & -Q must-it-not-follow-that -P ?!   (*)

93

To show that this *o'kheiluf* argument may be symbolically represented by (*) it remains now to show the following: A and B have the status of facts, P is a claim for which there is only weak evidence, there is no evidence for or against Q, the phrase *o'kheiluf* sandwiches two qal v'homer arguments.

The verse under examination in this passage of the Sifre is Num. 19:14 which states that if someone dies in a tent, then all those who come into the tent and everything that is in the tent will be *tameh*, ritually impure, for seven days. The Sifre posits that the phrase "all those who come into the tent" must be referring to the normal way of entering a tent, through its entrance. From this the Sifre shows by qal v'homer from a tent, that it can be concluded likewise that an open grave only conveys *tumah* to those who enter it through its official entrance. Since the premise of the qal v'homer was only a plausible interpretation and not stated explicitly in the verse, the Sifre recognizes that the conclusion may be wrong and that the *kheiluf* qal v'homer could be true. *O'kheiluf* ensues.

The source for A, the claim that a tent may receive *tumah*, i.e. may become defiled, is the verse under study, Num.19:14. The verse plainly says that if someone dies in a tent, anyone who comes into the tent and anything in the tent will be *tameh*, i.e ritually contaminated, for seven days. The source for B seems to be the very well-known belief that soil cannot receive *tumah*. (From a practical point of view this has to be so because otherwise it would be impossible to purify without creating sources of defilement.)

The evidence for P are the words in the above verse "anyone who comes into the tent" where "comes into" is interpreted to mean in a normal way, in the way 'comes into a tent' brings to mind. The evidence is not strong, because the verse does not explicitly say that only if someone 'comes in' in the normal way, through the entrance, does he become defiled, that if he comes in from any of its other sides he does not become defiled.

The *kheiluf* qal v'homer concludes with -P, that a person becomes *tameh* by entering an open tent through any of its sides. The confirmation that the *o'kheiluf* argument may be symbolically represented by (*) is now complete.

The Sifre continues with *talmud lomar* and a biblical proof text as refutation of this conclusion, the very same verse that is the evidence for P, on the basis of which the first qal v'homer was launched:

כל הבא אל האהל

Without more detail in the verse, the phrase does seem to imply, entering the normal way one enters a tent.

The Sifre continues with the standard summary formula of the *o'kheiluf* argument, declaring the *kheiluf* qal v'homer refuted and announcing that the remaining qal v'homer, the first one, is (by the process of elimination) correct:

דנתי, וחילפתי, בטל או חילוף, זכיתי לדון כבתחילה.

The Sifre follows with a repetition of the first qal v'homer but this time expressed assertively, with the rhetorically-questioning elements replaced with assertions:

מה אהל שהוא מקבל טומאה אין מטמא מכל צדדיו כשהוא פתוח, קבר שאין מקבל טומאה דין הוא שלא יטמא מכל צדדיו כשהוא פתוח.

6. ספרי במדבר, פיסקא קנה (פרשת מטות, פרק ל, פטוק יד):

Piska 155:

A= 'הבעל מפר'	הואיל והבעל מפר
B= 'והאב מפר'	והאב מפר
P= הבעל אינו מיפר אלא נדרין שבינו לבינה ונדרין שיש בהן עינוי נפש	מה הבעל אינו מיפר אלא נדרין שבינו לבינה ונדרין שיש בהן עינוי נפש
Q= האב לא יפר אלא נדרין שבינו לבינה ונדרין שיש בהן עינוי נפש	אף האב לא יפר אלא נדרין שבינו לבינה ונדרין שיש בהן עינוי נפש
	או חלוף
B= 'האב מפר'	הואיל והאב מפר
A= 'הבעל מיפר'	והבעל מיפר
-Q= 'האב מפר כל נדר'	מה האב מפר כל נדר
-P= 'הבעל מיפר כל נדר'	אף הבעל מיפר כל נדר

Translation:

A = 'The husband annuls vows'
B = 'The father annuls vows [that his daughter makes]'
Just-as
P = 'The husband may annul only those vows concerning matters between the two of them and those vows she makes to afflict herself'
So-too
Q = 'The father may annul only those vows concerning matters between the two of them and those the daughter makes to afflict herself'.

96

O'kheiluf
B = 'The father annuls vows [that his daughter makes]'
A = 'The husband annuls vows'
Just-as
-Q = 'The father may annul any vows his daughter makes'
So-too
-P = 'The husband may annul any vows she makes'

Notice that in this passage the two arguments that sandwich the phrase או חילוף are not qal v'homer or *a fortiori* arguments as is usual, but rather just-as arguments. This example is discussed at length in Chapter Five: Stoic Analysis.

With the above notation this argument can be represented as,

A,B & just-as P so too Q
או חלוף
A,B & just-as -Q so too -P.

It remains now to show the following: A and B have the status of facts, P is a claim for which there is only weak evidence, there is no evidence for or against Q, -P is the negation of P and likewise for Q, and the phrase *o'kheiluf* sandwiches two qal v'homer arguments.

In the same passage right before the *o'kheiluf* argument, the Sifre establishes on the basis of Num. 30: 9, 14, 17 that the husband may annul any vow that his wife makes that will cause herself harm or that involves matters between the two of them. 30:14: כל נדר וכל שבועה אסר לענות נפש, אישה יקימנו ואישה יפרנו.

30:17 אלה החקים ......בין איש, לאשתו
P is the claim that these are the *only* vows that the husband may annul. The biblical evidence that it is only these the husband may annul is that the cited verses above, 30:14, 17, specify precisely the vows to which 30:9 refers. With no other biblical verse to expand on the vows referred to by 30:14, 17, the author surmises that those are

all the vows the husband may annul. But the Torah does not explicitly express this limiting claim, and so the claim P, may be doubted.

There is no verse like 30:14 concerning the husband that specifies of the father that he may annul any vow his daughter makes that would cause her to suffer. The phrase "between a man and his wife" in 30:17 suggests that the husband may annul vows his wife takes regarding matters between the two of them. The phrase "between a father and his daughter [in her maidenhood, in her father's house]" in the same verse, would suggest the same for the father. But with the exception of this phrase in 30:17, the verses 30:4-6 concerning the father's right to annul his daughter's vows are very general, perhaps giving the impression that the father may annul any vow his daughter makes.

The author with reasonable evidence for P, that the husband's right to annul his wife's vows are only for the limited classes mentioned above, seeks to derive whether that is also the situation for the father.

Q= 'The father annuls only her vows that relate to matters between her and him and her vows that would cause her to suffer.'

This is equivalent to the following:

Q= {The father annuls her vows that relate to matters between her and him and her vows that cause her to suffer} & {The father does not annul any vows other than those}. This expression will be referred to by Q = {first} & {second}. There are three different propositions that logically could be described as the negation of Q: 1) -{first} & {second}, 2) {first} & -{second}, 3) -{first} & -{second}. Num. 30:17 is evidence for the first part of {first}, i.e. the father annuls vows on matters between himself and his daughter. The author seems to assume that the father also annuls vows that would cause her to suffer. The author's evidence for the latter is likely that since the father may annul at least certain of the daughter's vows, as per 30:4-6,17, that class would be very strange indeed if it did not include that the father may annul vows the daughter takes that may put her in harm's way. Since the father (as does the husband) annuls these two sets of vows, -{first} cannot be true. Thus the only possibility for the negation of Q that is not certainly false is 2).

In the *o'kheiluf* argument the author is not interested in presenting a *kheiluf* qal v'homer that starts from a patently false assertion so that the *kheiluf* must also be false. The author here chooses 2) for -Q, from all the possibilities for the negation of Q; it alone is not known to be false. That is, the author launches the *kheiluf* qal v'homer from 2). (Note: -{second} = {The father does annul (some) vows his daughter makes other than those that concern matters between him and her or vows that would cause her to suffer}.)

This -Q is chosen by the author as a real possibility for a true proposition. Since the Torah does not say anything about any other sorts of vows, it is hard to attribute to the Torah the position that it is only certain additional vows, along with the other two classes, that the father may not annul. Therefore for the -Q chosen, i.e. for 2), to possibly be true and not be refuted by (meaningful absence of details in) the Torah, 'some' in the expression for -{second} above, must be 'all'.

Thus, out of the logical possibilities, the negation of Q chosen by the author is,
-Q= {first} & {The father may annul all other vows} = {The father may annul all vows his daughter makes}.

Turning now to P,
P= 'The husband annuls only her vows that relate to matters between her and him and her vows that cause her to suffer.'

This is equivalent to the following:

P = [{The husband annuls her vows that relate to matters between

99

her and him and her vows that cause her to suffer} & {The husband does not annul any vows other than those.}.]

This last expression will be referred to by P= '{first} & {second}.'

There are similarly three possibilities for what -P can be:

-P = [-{first} and {second}] or [{first} and -{second}] or [-{first} and -{second}].

[-{first} and {second}] would mean that the husband annuls no vows.

This we know is false because of the fact A whose sources are verses 9-14. [-{first} and-{second}] would mean that the husband annuls some vows but not those that relate to him or involve the wife's suffering. This contradicts the biblical evidence for {first}, 30:14,17, which the author does not doubt at all. Thus these two possibilities for -P are known by the author to be false.

The remaining possibility, [{first} and-{second}], would mean that the husband annuls vows between him and his wife and vows that cause her to suffer and (some) other vows. Again, since the Torah does not even hint about any other specific sorts of vows, in order for [{first} and -{second}] to possibly be true of the Torah, it must be interpreted to mean that the husband could annul all other vows. Thus of all the logical possibilities for the negation of P, the only one that is not definitely false and is therefore possibly true is -P = {husband annuls all of wife's vows}. This choice for –P, is the conclusion of the *kheiluf* qal v'homer.

A and B are facts: B is stated explicitly in Num. 30:4-6 and A is stated explicitly in 30:7-9. Thus this *o'kheiluf* argument is confirmed to have the symbolic form corresponding to (*):
A,B & just-as **P** so too **Q**

או חילוף

A,B & just-as **-Q** so too **-P**

100

where **A** and **B** represent propositions that are facts, and **P** represents a proposition for which there is less than completely convincing evidence, and in the second argument -**Q** is not known to be false, and -**P** is the negation of **P** and likewise for **Q**. The phrase *o'kheiluf* separates two just-as arguments.

The *kheiluf* qal v'homer concludes with -P = {the husband may annul all of his wife's vows}. But this conclusion is refuted by Num. 30:14 which describes the specific type of vow that a husband may annul, a vow a wife takes to cause herself harm. This is stated explicitly, there is no room for doubt. So while the possibility remains that there are more types of vows the husband might annul, the verse does imply that he cannot possibly annul all vows.

The argument should then continue with, *talmud lomar,* followed by Num. 30:14, which specifies that the husband may annul any vow his wife takes that may cause her harm, thereby refuting -P, the conclusion of the *kheiluf.*

Instead the argument stops to consider the possibility that the refuting evidence, the contents of Num. 30:14 was not originally interpreted correctly. A derash found in piska 153 is then applied to rule out this possibility:

"But then [with the -P conclusion] how do I not face contradicting [Num. 30:14], 'any oath that she takes to cause herself suffering [the husband may annul]'? Perhap this should be understood as referring to a wife who is a mature woman (one who is in the days of *bagrut*) while for a younger wife, one who is a *naarah*, the husband may annul all and any vows she makes. *Talmud lomar,* בנעוריה בית אביה. This interpretation is not possible because a husband's rights are not with regard to whether the wife is a *naarah* or older, a girl's status as a *naarah* is only stated in regards to her relationship with her father." *Talmud lomar* is followed by the evidence for this, the phrase from Num. 30:17, בנעוריה בית אביה.

Thus it is not possible to understand Num.30:14 as referring to only when the wife is a mature woman. (Sifre, piska 153 describes a *naarah* as a female who is no longer a *kitanah*, a little one. A *naarah* is at least 12 years and a day old, but not yet in the state of *beger*, in the Bavli referred to as being a *bogeret*. B. Ketubot 39a specifies that a *bogeret* is a female who is at least 12 and one half years old.)

Here is the derash in piska 153 on the phrase בנעוריה בית אביה from Num 30: 17:

תלמוד לומר בנעוריה בית אביה, שכל נעוריה בבית אביה אמרתי, ולא נעוריה בבית הבעל. להוציא את שנתארמלה או נתגרשה מן האירוסין.

Note almost the exact same wording of the derash on that phrase in piska 155 in the *o'kheiluf* argument under discussion:

ת"ל בנעוריה בית אביה. נעורים בבית אביה אמרתי, ולא נעורים בבית הבעל.

The same derash with the same wording also in piska 156:

בנעוריה בית אביה – נעוריה בבית אביה אמרתי, ולא נעוריה בבית הבעל. ר' ישמעאל אומר: בנעוריה בבית אביה – בנערה המאורסה הכתוב מדבר, שיהיו אביה ובעלה מפירים נדריה.

Kahana, in his treatment of piska 155, points out that this derash was taken from piska 153 and piska 156 and brought into the argument in piska 155 under discussion here.

Further suggesting that this derash is a later interpolation, is that the author(s) of the original *o'kheiluf* argument would not have considered this derash as a way to interrogate whether or not the biblical evidence does indeed refute -P and thereby as a way to decide which qal v'homer, the original or the *kheiluf* is correct. The possible bifurcation of the husband's rights depending on the wife's status as a *naarah* or a *bogeret* is a critique of the *o'kheiluf* argument taken as a whole. It suggests that both qal v'homer arguments understood in the right context are true and together yield a complete description of the rights of the father and husband. This critique undermines the assumptions implicit in the original set-up of the *o'kheiluf* argument relating the father's and husband's rights.

Originally, with the *kheiluf* qal v'homer concluding with -P the argument continued -–with no insertion of the derash from piska 153– in the manner of all of the other o'kheiluf arguments of the R. Ishmael school. It is pointed out that Num. 30:14 which specifies that the husband may annul any vow his wife takes that may cause her harm, refutes -P, the conclusion of the *kheiluf*.

The Sifre continues with the standard formula summing up what was done, that the *kheiluf* was found to be invalid, and declaring that the remaining qal v'homer argument, the first, is correct:

דנתי וחלפתי בטל החילוף וזכיתי לדין כבתחילה

The Sifre then repeats the first just-as argument.

The author is now convinced that indeed the vows mentioned in 30:14,17 which the husband may annul are indeed the only vows that the husband may annul. And that it follows from this, by a just-as argument, that the rights of the father are limited in the same way.

2.3: Sifra

דבורא דנדבה, פרשה ב (ויקרא, פרק א, פסוק ב):

Dibbura de-Nedavah, parsha 2:

A= 'אתנן ומחיר [כלב] צפוייהן מותרין'	'ומה אם אתנן ומחיר שצפוייהן מותרין
B= 'אתנן ומחיר [כלב] פסולין מעל גבי המזבח'	פסולין מעל גבי המזבח
P= 'נעבד, צפויו אסורין'	נעבד שצפוייו איסורין
Q='נעבד יפסל מעל גבי המזבח'	אינו דין שיפסל מעל גבי המזבח ?!
	או חילוף
B= 'אתנן ומחיר [כלב] אסורין על גבי מזבח'	ומה אתנן ומחיר שהן אסורין על גבי מזבח
A= 'אתנן ומחיר [כלב] צפוייהן מותרין'	צפוייהן מותרין
Q-= 'נעבד מותר [לקרבן] על מזבח'	נעבד שהוא מותר
P-= 'צפויי [נעבד] מותרים'	אינו דין שיהיו צפוייו מותרים ?!

Translation:

While

A = 'The coverings of the gift given to a prostitute and the price paid for a dog are permitted [to be used]',

B = 'The gift given to a prostitute and the price paid for a dog are prohibited on the altar [as a sacrifice]'.

Therefore,

Since

P = 'The coverings of a worshiped animal are not permitted [to be used]'

must-it-not-follow-that
Q = 'A worshiped animal may not be put on the altar [as a sacrifice]'
?!

O'kheiluf

While
B = 'The gift given to a prostitute and the price paid for a dog are prohibited on the altar [as a sacrifice]',
A = 'The coverings of the gift given to a prostitute and the price paid for a dog are permitted [to be used]'.
Therefore,
Since
-Q = 'A worshiped animal may be offered as a sacrifice on the altar'
must-it-not-follow-that
-P = 'The coverings of a worshiped animal are permitted [to be used]'
?!

Using the above symbolization the argument can be represented a

Since A, B & P must-it-not-therefore-follow-that Q ?!
או חילוף
Since A, B & -Q must-it-not-therefore-follow-that -P ?!

The qal v'homer arguments are made by deploying the premises in the following less common ordering:

A, also B.   Therefore,
Since P, must-it-not-follow-that Q ?!

o'kheiluf

B, also A.   Therefore,
Since -Q, must it not follow-that -P ?!

105

To confirm that this *o'kheiluf* argument may be symbolically represented by (*) it remains to show the following: A and B have the status of facts, P is a claim for which there is only weak evidence, there is no evidence for or against Q, the phrase *o'kheiluf* sandwiches two qal v'homer arguments.

This passage arises in the Sifra's analysis of Lev.1:2: "Speak to the children of Israel and say to them: 'When a man among you brings an offering to the Lord, from the cattle or from the flock shall you bring your offering'." The Sifra which is midrash of the school of R. Akiva sees the word 'from' as (in general, throughout the Pentateuch) extraneous for its plain sense and based on their extreme principle of biblical parsimony, present in the text in order to limit. Thus instead of 'cattle' the verse says "from the cattle," meaning not any animal that is cattle but excluding certain animals. The Sifra claims that in this verse "from the cattle," means to exclude worshiped animals. They may not be brought as sacrifices. The Sifra continues, but perhaps the 'from' is not a cue to exclude worshiped animals because no such cue is needed because excluding worshiped animals can be arrived at through qal v'homer reasoning from other laws. Attempts at qal v'homer through *o'kheiluf* all fail, demonstrating that the law to exclude worshiped animals cannot be derived from any obvious qal v'homer argument. Thus the derivation of this law from the words 'from the cattle' is upheld. For more extended analysis see Chapter Four.

The whole *o'kheiluf* argument from the Sifra appears as a baraita on B.Temurah 28b. The Bavli's treatment of this baraita is taken up in Chapter Eight.

The source for fact B is the plain meaning of verse Deut. 23:19. Fact A is a reasonable conclusion from the last two words of that verse, "the two of them." That phrase is understood as limiting precisely to those two things, the gift given to a prostitute and the sale money of a dog, precisely those two, may not be brought to "the House of the Lord, your God, for any promise." Therefore, the coverings of those gifts are permitted to be brought to be of use in the House (as for example metal strips for the altar according to Rashi on B. Temurah 28b.) And since they are permitted for sacred purposes they are certainly also permitted for secular use. As mentioned at the start of this chapter, in the Sifra of the school of R. Akiva, the content of one of A & B may be a bit of a derash. While in the midrash of the R. Ishmael school and in the Sifre Devarim, A & B almost always represent the explicit content of biblical verses and therefore their truth is more certain.

There is no evidence at all for either P (or -P) or Q (or -Q). The Sifra quotes Deut. 7:25, and points out how although it at first seems to be evidence for premise P, it in fact is not because the idols it refers to are not live animals.

The confirmation that the *o'kheiluf* argument may be symbolically represented by (*) is now complete.

The Sifra continues with the phrase *talmud lomar*, followed by the phrase 'from the cattle' and a repetition of the derash it gave on these words at the start of the passage: '[these words are meant] *to exclude any worshiped animal.*' Thus Q is the law, it is the answer to the motivating question. (Nothing is concluded about whether P or -P is correct.[66])

Since neither the *kheiluf* qal v'homer nor the first qal v'homer argument can be refuted, the *o'kheiluf* argument has provided two possible contradictory qal v'homer arguments and no way to decide between them. Thus there is no obvious way to derive by qal v'homer reasoning that a worshiped animal may not serve as a sacrifice to the Lord. Hence the possible derivation of this law from the biblical phrase "*from* the cattle," introduced at the start of the passage. is upheld.

---

[66] B.Temurah 28b and Rashi and Tosafot there, take up those issues.

8-10. ספרא, דבורא דחובה, פרשתא יב (ויקרא, פרק ה, פסוק יז):

Dibbura de-Khova, parshata 12:

.8

'הודע [של קלות] פטור [מן האשם] =P	אם את הודע שלהם פטרתי
'נפטר את לא הודע [של קלות] מן האשם' =Q	אינו דין שנפטר את לא הודע ?!
	או חילוף
'לא הודע של קלות חייבתי [באשם]' =Q-	אם את לא הודע שלהם חייבתי
'נתחייב את הודע [של קלות באשם]'=P-	אינו דין שנתחייב את הודע ?!

Translation:
Since,
P = 'A minor sin that one knows he has committed does not require a guilt offering [i.e. an *asham*, for atonement]'
must-it-not-follow that
Q = 'A minor sin that one does not know he committed does not require a guilt offering [for atonement]'
?!

O'kheiluf

Since,
-Q = 'A minor sin that one does not know he committed does require a guilt offering [for atonement]'
must-it-not-follow-that
-P = 'A minor sin that one knows he has committed requires a guilt offering [for atonement].'
?!

Lev. 5:17-18 describes the *asham* offering as a sacrifice that must be brought as atonement for unknowingly committing a forbidden act, a

108

lo taaseh. The Sifra reasonably interprets these verses to be referring to the graver sins, the *khamurot*. The Sifra then wants to know whether the instructions to bring an *asham* offering also apply to the lesser sins, the *kalot*. To that end the Sifra tries deriving this law by qal v'homer but since the qal v'homer is launched from a guess the conclusion may be doubted and *o'kheiluf* is possible. Since there is no evidence for P or -Q (and therefore for -P or Q), neither of the two qal v'homers can be eliminated as possibilities.

Using the labels above the argument can be symbolically represented as,

P must-it-not-follow-that Q ?!

או חילוף

-Q must-it-not-follow-that -P ?!

Since there is no evidence for P or -Q (and therefore for -P or Q), neither of the two qal v'homers can be eliminated as possibilities. (In this argument, the A and the B are empty of additional content and so are not included.)

.9

The Sifra then tries another *o'kheiluf* argument to derive whether one must bring an *asham* offering for unknowingly violating a prohibition, i.e. a *lo ta'aseh*, of one of the lesser sins. P and Q are the same as in the preceding *o'kheiluf* argument. Separate facts A and B are used and the argument fits the symbolic form (*),

Since A,B & P must-it-not-follow-that Q ?!

או חילוף

Since A,B & -Q must-it-not-follow-that -P ?!

Notice also from the passage how the qal v'homer is argued.
The ordering (and respective functions) of the propositions in the qal v'homer arguments is as follows:

A, also B.   Therefore,
Since P, must-it-not-follow-that Q ?!
             o'kheiluf
B, also A.   Therefore,
Since -Q, must it not follow-that –P ?!

A= 'חייב את הודע של חמורות חטאת'	ומה אם במקום שחייב את הודע של חמורות חטאת
B= 'פטר את לא הודע של חמורות מן החטאת'	פטר את לא הודע שלהם מן החטאת
P= 'פטר את הודע של קלות מן האשם'	מקום שפטר את הודע של קלות מן האשם
Q= ' נפטור את לא הודע של קלות מן האשם'	אינו דין שנפטור את לא הודע שלהם מן האשם !?
	או חילוף
B= 'פטר את לא הודע של חמורות מן החטאת'	ומה אם במקום שפטר את לא הודע של חמורות
A= 'חייב את הודע של חמורות, חטאת'	חייב את הודע שלהם חטאת
-Q= 'חייב את לא הודע של קלות, אשם'	מקום שחייב את לא הודע של קלות אשם
-P= נחייב את הודע של קלות אשם	אינו דין שנחייב את הודע שלהם אשם !?

Translation:

While

A = 'A major sin that one knows he committed requires [one to bring] a sin offering',

B = 'A major sin that one does not know he committed does not require [one to bring] a sin offering'.

Therefore,

Since

P = 'A minor sin that one knows he committed does not require a guilt offering [for atonement]'

must-it-not-also-follow-that

Q = 'A minor sin that one does not know he has committed does not require a guilt offering [for atonement]'

?!

O'kheiluf

While

B = 'A major sin that one does not know he committed does not require [one to bring] a sin offering',

A = 'A major sin that one knows he committed requires [one to bring] a sin offering'.

Therefore,

Since

-Q = 'A minor sin that one does not know he has committed does require a guilt offering [for atonement]'

must-it-not-follow-that

-P = 'A minor sin that one knows he committed does require a guilt offering [for atonement]'

?!

Note that P and Q are the same as in the last set of qal v'homer arguments. The source for the part of A and B that says that the sin offering, the חטאת, is only for grave sins committed, the חמורות, is the Sifra's derash on Lev.4:2 (on the words אשר לא תעשינה). The source in A and B that the sin must be known to him in order for him to be obligated in the sin offering, is Lev. 4:28.

Again, neither qal v'homer may be eliminated. There is no biblical evidence for any of P, -Q, -P or Q to be used to rule out either qal v'homer argument.

The confirmation that the *o'kheiluf* argument may be symbolically represented by (*) is now complete.

Since the two qal v'homer arguments contradict one another and neither can be eliminated, the Sifra has not reached an answer.

10.

The Sifra tries a third *o'kheiluf* argument. P and Q are the same and so are A and B. But this time A and B are positioned and deployed in the argument in the usual way:

A, also P. Therefore,
Since B, must-it-not-follow-that Q ?!

o'kheiluf

B, also -Q. Therefore,
Since A, must it not follow-that -P ?!

The argument takes the form (*)

Since A, B & P must-it-not-follow-that Q ?!
או חילוף
Since A, B & -Q must-it-not-follow-that -P ?!,

where A and B as shown earlier are facts, P is not backed by strong evidence, there is no evidence for or against Q, and the rhetorical questions are qal v'homer.

112

A= 'חייב את הודע של חמורות חטאת'	ומה אם במקום שחייב את הודע של חמורות חטאת
P= 'פטר את הודע של קלות מן האשם'	פטר את הודע של קלות מן האשם
B= 'פטר את לא הודע של חמורות מן החטאת'	מקום שפטר את לא הודע של חמורות מן החטאת
Q= 'נפטור את לא הודע של קלות מן האשם'	אינו דין שנפטור את לא הודע של קלות מן האשם ?!
	או חילוף
B= 'פטר את לא הודע של חמורות מן החטאת'	ומה אם במקום שפטר את לא הודע של חמורות מן החטאת
-Q= 'חייב את לא הודע של קלות אשם'	חייב לא הודע של קלות אשם
A= 'חייב את הודע של חמורות חטאת'	מקום שחייב את הודע של חמורת חטאת
-P= 'נחייב את הודע של קלות אשם'	אינו דין שנחייב את הודע של קלות אשם ?!

There is no way to eliminate between these qal v'homer arguments either.

Translation:

While
A = 'A major sin that one knows he committed requires [one to bring] a sin offering',
P= 'A minor sin that one knows he committed does not require a guilt offering [for atonement]'
Therefore,

113

Since

B= 'A major sin that one does not know he committed does not require [one to bring] a sin offering'

Must-it-not-follow-that

Q= 'A minor sin that one does not know he has committed does not require a guilt offering [for atonement]'

?!

O'kheiluf

While

B = 'A major sin that one does not know he committed does not require [one to bring] a sin offering',

-Q = 'A minor sin that one does not know he has committed does require a guilt offering [for atonement]'

Therefore,

Since

A = 'A major sin that one knows he committed requires [one to bring] a sin offering'

Must-it-not-follow-that

-P = 'A minor sin that one knows he committed does require a guilt offering [for atonement]'

?!

The Sifra concludes by implying that since the answer to the question sought could not be arrived at by any qal v'homer argument (that the Sifra could think of) — and the Sifra tried three *o'kheiluf* arguments and therefore 6 different qal v'homer arguments — the Torah provided the hermeneutical cue to the answer.

The Sifra continues with *talmud lomar*, i.e it is for this reason that the Torah states *asham, asham*, the same word in two different places, so that a *gezerah shavah* can be applied from one context to the other, to answer the question: Chapter four of Leviticus, with regard to a prohibition via apparently a derash[67] on Num.15:29, refers to a matter whose intentional violation is punishable by extirpation and whose unintentional violation requires a sin offering and whose doubtful violation requires an *asham* offering, so too the word *v'ashaim* in the verse under study, Lev. 5:17, must be referring to a matter whose intentional violation is punishable by extirpation and whose unintentional violation requires a sin offering and whose doubtful violation requires an *asham* offering. Thus the *asham* is not to be offered for the doubtful violation of one of the lesser sins (nor is it offered for the unintentional violation of one of the lesser sins; i.e. both Q and also P are true).[68]

This example is discussed in more detail in Chapter Four.

---

[67] The Sifre Bamidbar has precisely this derash on Num. 15:29. Either the Sifra is referring to this derash of the R. Ishmael school or perhaps it is referring to a lost book of midrash on Numbers of the R. Akiva school which has essentially this same derash as the Sifre Bamidbar on the verse.

[68] In volume one of his translation to Sifra, Chapter Sixty-Five, Neusner translates this set of three arguments that we have numbered # 8, 9, 10. He translates the first occurrence of the phrase *o'kheiluf* (in #8) as 'Or to the contrary', the second occurrence (in #9) as 'Or perhaps the opposite conclusion should be drawn' and the third occurrence (in #10) as 'Another logical argument entirely'. Neusner does not understand the phrase *o'kheiluf* correctly and therefore the structure of these arguments signaled by the phrase. Admitting as much, he writes on page 326, "The details of this somewhat complex argument are not entirely clear." Neusner is mistaken; as our work shows, with a proper understanding of the *o'kheiluf* argument form, these three arguments are rendered perfectly clear (and coherent).

11. ספרא, מכילתא דמילואים (פרשת שמיני, פרק ט, פסוקים כב-כג):

Mekhilta de-Miluim, part 2, Shemini, commenting on Lev.9:23:

P= ' יציאה [מאהל מועד] אינה טעונה רחיצה'	ומה אם יציאה שאינה טעונה רחיצה
A= 'יציאה [מאהל מועד] טעונה ברכה'	טעונה ברכה
B= 'ביאה [לאהל מועד] טעונה רחיצה'	ביאה שטעונה רחיצה
Q= 'ביאה [לאהל מועד] טעונה ברכה'	אינו דין שטעונה ברכה !?
	או חילוף
Q-= [ביאה [לאהל מועד' אינה טעונה ברכה'	ומה אם ביאה שאינה טעונה ברכה
B= 'ביאה [לאהל מועד] טעונה רחיצה'	טעונה רחיצה
A= 'יציאה [מאהל מועד] טעונה ברכה'	יציאה שטעונה ברכה
P-= 'יציאה [מאהל מועד] טעונה רחיצה'	אינו דין שטעון רחיצה !?

Translation:

While
P = 'Leaving [the Tent of Meeting] does not require washing up',
A = '[Leaving the Tent of Meeting] does require [making a] blessing'.
Therefore,
Since
B = 'Coming [to the Tent of Meeting] requires washing up'
must-it-not-follow-that
Q = '[Coming to the Tent of Meeting] requires [making] a blessing'
?!

O'kheiluf

116

While

-Q = 'Coming [to the Tent of Meeting] does not require [making a] blessing',

B = '[Coming to the Tent of Meeting] requires washing up'.

Therefore,

Since

A = 'Leaving [the Tent of Meeting] does require [making a] blessing'

must-it-not-follow-that

-P = '[Leaving the Tent of Meeting] does require washing up'

?!

Using the above symbolization this argument can be represented as,

Since A,B & P must-it-not-follow-that Q ?!

או חילוף

Since A,B & -Q must-it-not-follow-that -P ?!

Notice that the qal v'homer arguments are made by organizing the premises in the following very unusually clever order:

P, also A. Therefore,
Since B, must-it-not-follow-that Q ?!
         O'kheiluf
-Q, also B. Therefore,
Since A, must-it-not-follow-that -P ?!

The source for fact B is the explicit statement in Exod. 30:20 after the statement in 19 that Aaron and his sons washed their hands and feet, "[W]hen they will come to the Tent of Meeting they will wash with water so that they will not die, or when they approach the altar to serve, to turn into smoke an offering by fire to the Lord [they shall wash their hands and feet so that they do not die]."

The source for fact A is the verse under study by the Sifra, Lev. 9:23. It plainly says that Moses and Aaron came to the Tent of Meeting, they went out and they blessed the nation. This is not quite a command that other priests should do the same. It can be said that A is a reasonable conclusion from verse 23 and it is viewed by the author of the midrash as a fact. There is no biblical evidence for P or -Q (or for Q, or -P).

Thus it is confirmed that the o'kheiluf argument can be represented symbolically by (*).

Because there is no biblical proof text in support of or contradicting either of P or -Q, the Sifra has no way to distinguish between the two possible qal v'homer arguments in the o'kheiluf argument and therefore no way to answer the question that prompted the Sifra to engage in o'kheiluf. In its discussion of Lev. 9:23, which says that Moses and Aaron went out and blessed the nation, the Sifra asks whether also on arriving at the Tent of Meeting it is necessary to bless the nation.

But the Sifra recognizes that the conclusion of the kheiluf qal v'homer, -P = {leaving the Tent of Meeting requires washing}, makes no sense. Hand and feet washing is meant to purify the priest to work in the sacred place, and this is why on arrival to the Tent of Meeting Aaron and his sons washed their hands. But washing hands, when leaving a sacred place, serves no function and so is not required. By refuting -P based on everyday knowledge of societal aspects of the holy versus the profane, the Sifra is able to refute the kheiluf qal v'homer and therefore eliminate it as a possibility.

The Sifra continues with much of the formulation that was seen to be standard in the) R. Ishmael o'kheiluf arguments (which all succeeded in arriving at a conclusion). The Sifra leaves out the danti, kheilafti, but goes on as is standard in the R. Ishmael examples, declaring the kheiluf qal v'homer refuted and announcing that the first qal v'homer is (by elimination) correct. (It leaves out, מתחילה, 'from the beginning'.) Continuing on, the Sifra repeats as in the R. Ishmael examples the first qal v'homer with all rhetorically-questioning elements such as אינו דין replaced with assertive elements:

בטל החילוף! וחזרנו לדין: ירידה טעונה ברכה, וביאה טעונה ברכה, מה ירידה מעין עבודה, אף ביאה מעין עבודה.

The Sifra is known to be a work of the school of R. Akiva. Menahem Kahana in his 2006 paper "The Halakhic Midrashim" suggests, in line with earlier scholarship, that although this is in general true, there are portions such as Mekhilta de-Miluim (covering Lev. 8:1-10:7) which betray signs of authorship by the school of R. Ishmael.[69] The passage cited and analyzed above falls in that section. It is outside the scope of this study to deal with Kahana's claim regarding the entire Mekhilta de-Miluim. But as regards the passage cited here, the particular details of this o'kheiluf argument speak overwhelmingly to its origin in the R. Akiva midrash.

In this o'kheiluf argument, like the other 4 o'kheiluf arguments in the Sifra, there is absolutely no evidence for the launching premise, P, (and for -Q); this o'kheiluf argument cannot therefore be resolved by a prooftext. This is the signature of the R. Akiva o'kheiluf argument which is generally not presented with the intention that it will succeed. On the other hand, every single o'kheiluf argument of the R. Ishmael school is launched from a premise, P, for which there is biblical evidence but not a fully explicit proof text to meet the high standards for certitude of the R. Ishmael school. There is no o'kheiluf argument of the R. Ishmael school like this one in the Sifra launched from a premise for which there is absolutely no biblical evidence. On the other hand, this o'kheiluf argument is very much like the other o'kheiluf arguments of the school of R. Akiva, especially all of the other ones in the Sifra.

---

[69] See, Menahem Kahana, "Halakhic Midrashim" in *The Literature of the Jewish People in the Period of the Second Temple and the Talmud*, Volume III: *The Literature of the Sages* (NewYork: Brill, 2006): 83-87. See there, citations to Epstein's *Prolegomena*, Goldberg's *Dual Exegesis* and others.

Also very importantly, unlike in the qal v'homer arguments and *o'kheiluf* arguments of the R. Ishmael school where facts A & B are known to be true because they express biblical statements or everyday common facts, the sources for the facts A & B in the R. Akiva qal v'homer arguments and *o'kheiluf* arguments are often some derash of that school. In this *o'kheiluf* argument, A is a bit of a derash, a reasonable conclusion from Lev. 9:23. Indeed this is not uncommon in the R. Akiva *o'kheiluf* arguments but completely absent in the R. Ishmael midrash.

Lastly, as for the wording of the closing, it is very similar to the variant found in the R. Akiva *o'kheiluf*, rather than the full formula with *danti, kheilafti,* found in each of the R. Ishmael *o'kheiluf* arguments.

Chapter Four is devoted to a full discussion of the differences in the *o'kheiluf* arguments of the two schools.

2.4: Sifre Deuteronomy

<u>פיסקא רמד (פרשת כי תצא, פרק כב, פסוק כח):</u>

<u>Piska 244:</u>

12.

A= 'אונס חמור'	ומה אונס חמור
P= [אונס] אינו חייב אלא על בתולה	אינו חייב אלא על בתולה
B= 'מפתה, קל'	מפתה הקל
Q= [מפתה]' לא יהיה חייב אלא על בתולה'	אינו דין שלא יהיה חייב אלא על בתולה !?
	או חילוף
B= 'מפתה, קל'	אם מפתה הקל
Q-= [מפתה]' חייב על בתולה ועל שאינה בתולה'	הרי הוא חייב על בתולה ועל שאינה בתולה
A= 'אונס חמור '	אונס חמור
P-= [אונס]' יהא חייב על בתולה ועל שאינה בתולה'	אינו דין שיהא חייב על בתולה ועל שאינה בתולה ?!

<u>Translation:</u>
While
A = 'The sin of the rapist is grave',
P = 'The rapist is only liable when his victim is a virgin'.
Therefore,
Since

B = 'The sin of the seducer is light [by comparison to the rapist]'
must-it-not-follow-that
Q = 'The seducer should only be liable when his victim is a virgin'
?!

O'kheiluf

While
B= 'The sin of the seducer is light',
-Q ='The seducer is liable whether or not his victim is a virgin'.
Therefore,
Since
A = 'The sin of the rapist is grave'
must-it-not-follow-that
-P = 'The rapist is liable whether or not his victim is a virgin'
?!

With this symbolization, the argument can be represented as,

Since A,B & P must-it-not-follow-that Q ?!

או חילוף

Since A,B & -Q must-it-not-follow-that -P ?!

The qal v'homer arguments, in this *o'kheiluf* as well as all the others in Sifre Devarim, #13, #14, and #15, are composed by ordering the premises in the most usual way:

A, and P. Therefore,
Since B, must-it-not-follow-that Q ?!
        O'kheiluf
B, and -Q. Therefore,
Since A, must-it-not-follow-that -P ?!

122

To confirm that this *o'kheiluf* argument may be described symbolically by (*) it remains to show the following: A and B have the status of facts, P is a claim for which there is at most weak evidence, there is no evidence for or against Q, the phrase *o'kheiluf* sandwiches two qal v'homer arguments.

The purpose of this *o'kheiluf* argument, unlike all the others discussed up to this point, is not to discover the law by choosing between two possible qal v'homer arguments or to show that qal v'homer will not work and another hermeneutical technique is needed to answer the question at issue. Its purpose here rather is to show why a certain word or phrase which appears redundant is not redundant but in fact necessary.

Given that Deut. 22:28 specifies *betulah,* the mention of *betulah* in Exod. 22:15 seems redundant to the Sifre Devarim, as it seems that it could be derived from the presence in the former. To discover the need for the word *betulah* in Exodus and to show that it is indeed not superfluous, the Sifre engages in a thought experiment.

The Sifre Devarim imagines, contrary to fact, that the word *betulah,* meaning virgin, does not appear in the case of the seducer in Exod. 22:15. Thus in this imagined situation there is no direct evidence for Q. The evidence for P is the verse under study, Deut. 22:28, where it says, "[I]f a man finds a *naarah, betulah* who is not betrothed and he grabs her and he lies with her, and they are discovered."The next verse 22:29 says that the man must then give the father fifty silver *shekel* and the girl will become his wife and he may never send her away. In specifying a *betulah* the verse is implying that the girl being a *betulah* is one of the conditions for which the rapist must make the reparation described in 29.

The first qal v'homer starting from P, that if the victim of the rapist is a *betulah* or virgin then he must pay the father and marry the girl, infers that since the rapist is only punished in this way if the girl is a virgin, it follows that for the comparatively minor transgression of the seducer, the punitive measures taken against him are also only imposed if the girl is a virgin. (Thus *betulah* need not be said with regard to the crime of the seducer since it can be derived by qal v'homer.)

The evidence for P from the presence of the word *betulah* in Deut. 22:28 is apparently not viewed by the author as strong evidence and therefore he does not affirm Q, the result of the first qal v'homer launched from P.

Instead he continues, *"or* [perhaps] the *kheiluf,"* launching a qal v'homer from -Q. Because the word *betulah* is imagined to be removed from Exod. 22:15, -Q is a possible reading of the redacted verse. If the seducer is punished whether the girl is or is not a virgin then certainly it must follow that for the far more serious crime, the rapist is also punished regardless as to whether the girl is or is not a virgin.

But then the Sifre points out, *talmud lomar*, that the conclusion of the *kheiluf* qal v'homer (i.e. -P) contradicts (the evidence that exists for P,) Deut. 22:28:

ומה תלמוד לומר ייבתולהיי באונס?

Before concluding as the R. Ishmael *o'kheiluf* arguments do, that since the conclusion of the *kheiluf* contradicts the biblical evidence (for launching the first qal v'homer) it is false and therefore the entire *kheiluf* qal v'homer argument is wrong, the Sifre Devarim stops to see if that evidence could be interpreted differently:

The Sifre speculates, perhaps the *betulah* in Deut. 22:28 about the rapist, is not meant to be a condition for imposing the penalty on the rapist cited in 29, but maybe its reference is to the recipient of the coins in 29, that the rapist gives the silver coins to the father (and not the girl herself) when she is a *betulah*. The verse allows this reading which contradicts the reading supporting P. Since P and -P are each possible, neither qal v'homer argument may be eliminated and the *o'kheiluf* fails to provide an answer to the question originally posed.

The thought experiment has thus concluded showing that indeed the word *betulah* needed to be included in Exod. 22:15. For if it were excluded it would not be possible by qal v'homer to know that the seducer is only liable for the stated punishment when the girl is a *betulah* (but not when she is a *bi'ulah)* and the same for the rapist.

The sources for the fact A are the verses being commented upon, Deut. 22: 28, 29. The source for the fact B is Exod. 22: 15, 16. (Comparing these verses, we do see indeed that more is required in restitution from the rapist than from the seducer. The seducer's victim is the girl's father, the rapist's victims are the girl and her father and it is for this reason according to the Sifre Devarim, that raping is more serious a crime than seducing.)

The verification that the *o'kheiluf* argument can be represented symbolically by (*) is complete.

A= 'אונס חמור'	מה אונס חמור
P= [אונס]' אינו חייב אלא על הנערה'	אינו חייב אלא על הנערה
B= 'מפותה הקל'	מפותה הקל
Q= [מפותה]' לא יהא חייב אלא על הנערה'	אינו דין שלא יהא חייב אלא על הנערה !?
	או חילוף
B= 'מפתה הקל'	ומה מפותה הקל
-Q= [מפותה]' חייב על נערה ועל שאינה נערה'	הרי הוא חייב על נערה ועל שאינה נערה
A= 'אונס חמור'	אונס חמור
-P= [אונס]' יהא חייב על נערה ועל שאינה נערה'	אינו דין שיהא חייב על נערה ועל שאינה נערה?!

Translation:

While
A = 'The sin of the rapist is grave',
P = 'The rapist is only liable when his victim is a young woman [a naarah]'.
Therefore,
Since
B = 'The sin of the seducer is light [by comparison to the rapist]'
must-it-not-follow-that
Q = 'The seducer should only be liable when his victim is a young woman'
?!

O'kheiluf

126

While

B= 'The sin of the seducer is light',

-Q ='The seducer is liable whether or not his victim is a young woman'.

Therefore,

Since

A = 'The sin of the rapist is grave'

must-it-not-follow-that

-P = 'The rapist is liable whether or not his victim is a young woman'

?!

With the above labeling, the argument can be represented as,

Since A,B &   P must-it-not-follow-that Q ?!

או חילוף

Since A,B & -Q must-it-not-follow-that -P ?!

To confirm that this *o'kheiluf* argument may be described symbolically by (*) it will remain to verify the following: A and B have the status of facts, P is a claim for which there is at most weak evidence, there is no evidence for or against Q, the phrase *o'kheiluf* sandwiches two qal v'homer arguments.

This *o'kheiluf* argument is prompted by the same verse under study, Deut. 22:28, as was the last one. By again relating this verse about a rapist to Exod. 22:15 which discusses the law for the seducer, the Sifre Devarim this time is involved in the usual *o'kheiluf* program of seeking to conclude about the law for the latter from the former. Deut. 22:28 explicitly mentions a *naarah*, "[I]f a man finds a *naarah*, a *betulah* who is not betrothed and he grabs her and lies with her..," and so seems to limit imposing the prescribed punishment on the rapist to the case where his victim is a *naarah*. This possible reading of Deut. 22:28 is the evidence in support of P.

What is labeled -P is indeed the negation of P, likewise for Q. A & B are the same facts as in the last *o'kheiluf* argument, and they are known to be true from the verses cited in the above discussion.

It is thus verified that this *o'kheiluf* argument can indeed be represented symbolically by (*).

Exod. 22:15 does not specify that the victim of the seducer is a *naarah*. The Sifre Devarim tries to derive by qal v'homer from P, that since the prescribed penalties on the rapist refer to when his victim was a *naarah,* the same must be so for the less serious transgression of the seducer. Since the evidence for P is not explicitly stated in the verse but is only a possible reading of the verse, the Sifre is not confident about the conclusion of the qal v'homer and the author therefore attempts *o'kheiluf*. Since no age specification is made with respect to the victim of the seducer on Exod. 22:15, the verse could be read as applying to a *naarah* or to an older woman. Well, if the seducer is so punished regardless of the age of the woman, the *kheiluf* qal v'homer concludes that the same must be the case for the more serious transgression of rape. But that would contradict Deut. 22:15 that specifically mentions a *naarah*, "[I]f a man finds a *naarah*..."

Unlike in the R. Ishmael *o'kheiluf* arguments the author does not rush to conclude that the *kheiluf* qal v'homer is refuted by the latter verse and therefore the first qal v'homer must be right. Instead the author argues, similar to how he argues in the last *o'kheiluf*, perhaps the function of the *naarah* in the verse is to serve as a reference to the father, that only if the woman is a *naarah* (and not older) are the silver coins paid to him (rather than her). [70]

---

[70] This difference between the *o'kheiluf* arguments of the two schools is discussed further in Chapter Four.

But unlike in the last argument this possibility is eliminated because 29, the verse about the payment states, "[T]he man who laid with her will give the father of the *naarah*, fifty silver coins..." Since *naarah* is mentioned in this verse in reference to the father (and in this spot would best serve the suggested function of stipulating that the rapist gives the coins to the father only when his victim is a *naarah*) there is no need for another statement of *naarah* to refer to the father. And since *naarah* does not have this other function, its function must be the first assumed, to limit the prescribed punishments of the rapist to the case where his victim is a *naarah*. Thus the *kheiluf* conclusion, -P, is contradicted by Deut. 22:28.

The author concludes, refuting the *kheiluf* qal v'homer:

להחליף את הדין אי אתה יכול שכבר נאמר 'נערה', 'נערה' שני פעמים.

Since 'it is not possible to להחליף the *din*' i.e to do *o'kheiluf*, only the first qal v'homer is possible and the implication is that it is correct. Thus the prescribed penalties are imposed on the rapist only if his victim is a *naareh* and therefore by qal v'homer the same follows for the less egregious case of the seducer.

(A mangled version of this same argument, with the phrase לחלף את הדין אי אתה יכול, appears in Epstein's reconstruction of the lost Mekhilta de Rabbi Shimon bar Yohai, which is midrash on Exodus attributed to the R. Akiva school, in commenting on Exod. 22:15.)

A= 'אונס חמור'	מה אונס חמור
P= [אונס]' / 'אינו חייב על שנתארסה ונתגרשה	אינו חייב על שנתארסה ונתגרשה
B= 'מפותה הקל'	מפותה הקל
Q= [מפותה]' / 'לא יהא חייב על שנתארסה ונתגרשה	אינו דין שלא יהא חייב על שנתארסה ונתגרשה ?!
	או חילוף
B= 'מפותה הקל'	מה אם מפותה הקל
-Q= [מפותה]' / 'חייב על שנתארסה ונתגרשה	הרי הוא חייב על שנתארסה ונתגרשה
A= 'אונס חמור'	אונס חמור
-P= [אונס]' / 'יהא חייב על שנתארסה ונתגרשה	אינו דין שיהא חייב על שנתארסה ונתגרשה ?!

Translation:

While
A = 'The sin of the rapist is grave',
P ='The rapist is not liable if his victim was betrothed and then divorced'.
Therefore,
Since
B = 'The sin of the seducer is light [by comparison to the rapist]'
must-it-not-follow-that
Q = 'The seducer should not be liable if his victim was one who was betrothed and divorced'
?!

O'kheiluf

While

B= 'The sin of the seducer is light',

-Q ='The seducer is [also] liable if the woman was betrothed and divorced'.

Therefore,

Since

A = 'The sin of the rapist is grave'

must-it-not-follow-that

-P = The rapist is [also] liable if his victim was betrothed and divorced'

?!

With the above labels the argument can be described as,

Since A,B & P must-it-not-follow-that Q   ?!

או חילוף

Since A,B & -Q must-it-not-follow-that -P ?!

To complete the demonstration that this *o'kheiluf* argument has the form (*), all of the following will be shown further along: A and B represent facts, the evidence for P is at most weak, there is no evidence for or against Q, and each ?! comes at the end of a qal v'homer argument.

This *o'kheiluf* argument is just like #12 above prompted by the same verse. The argument aims to show that the words לא אורשה are in fact needed in Exod. 22:15 about the seducer. To do so, just as in #12, the author engages in a thought experiment where he pretends that the phrase whose necessity he is questioning is not present in the verse. In this case that phrase is לא אורשה.

Deut. 22:28 states, "[I]f a man finds a *naarah*, a virgin that was not betrothed and he grabs her and lies with her and they are found" and the next verse 29 deals with the penalties that are then imposed on the rapist. What about the case where the victim was betrothed? That was dealt with earlier in 22: 25-26. In this more serious case (as the woman's husband is also a victim) the rapist is killed, but the woman because she was a victim is not killed. Two verses later, 22:28, the text deals with the case where the rape victim was not betrothed. It appears that the phrase "not betrothed" is meant to distinguish this case from the more egregious crime described earlier in the text, in 25-26.

But it seems like the Sifre Devarim does not see it this way. With the principle of extreme biblical parsimony characteristic of the R. Akiva school, the author of this passage seems to be of the opinion that the words "not betrothed" are not needed in Deut. 22:28 because it is understood to be such a case, since the other case specifically about the rape of a betrothed woman was dealt with just a few verses before. Finishing with that, the Torah moves on from that special case to the more general case where the girl is not betrothed.

To save the words "not betrothed", לא אורשה, from seeming redundant, the author seeks to re-interpret these words as reasonably as he can so that they do not mean simply 'she isn't betrothed.' He re-interprets the phrase as 'she was never betrothed' i.e. she was not betrothed and then divorced[71]. This is a status, with possible legal ramifications, distinct from the status of being a virgin and the status of no longer being a virgin or being married.

With this understanding of the phrase, Deut. 22:28-29 is the biblical evidence for P = 'The rapist is not liable if his victim was betrothed (more precisely, went through *erusin*) and then divorced.' The verses

---

[71] The author is referring to the two components of effecting a marriage: אירוסין, נישואין. Breaking off of the first component, the *erusin*, also required a *get*, or divorce papers. To indicate that a woman went through *erusin* that were subsequently broken off, we refer to her as divorced.

are thus understood to be saying, 'if the man raped a *naarah*, a virgin, one who was not betrothed and then divorced, and he is found the following penalties are imposed on him.' The verses are further understood to imply that this specification represents a necessary condition. That is, if the victim had been betrothed and then divorced then the penalties prescribed in verse 29 are not to be imposed on the rapist.

Facts A and B are as in the last two *o'kheiluf* arguments, #12 and #13. The source for the fact A are the verses being commented upon, Deut. 22-28, 29. The source for fact B is Exod. 22:15, 16. (Comparing these verses one does indeed see that more is required in restitution from the rapist than from the seducer. The seducer's victim is the girl's father, the rapist's victims are the girl and her father and it is for this reason that raping is more serious a crime than seducing.)

Recall that the author is pretending that the phrase "not betrothed" is not found in Exod. 22:15. Supposing the phrase is not there, the author draws a qal v'homer from P, that since the rapist who has committed a far more serious crime is not subject to the prescribed penalties if his victim had been betrothed and subsequently divorced then certainly the seducer whose crime is not as serious is also not subject to the prescribed penalties for the seducer (in Exod. 22:15, 17) if his victim had been betrothed and subsequently divorced. Since the evidence for P is not explicitly in the Torah (but only perhaps suggestive) the conclusion of the qal v'homer, Q, may be doubted and *o'kheiluf* ensues.

Thus the confirmation that this *o'kheiluf* argument may be represented symbolically by (*) is complete.

The *kheiluf* qal v'homer argues from -Q, that since the seducer does face the prescribed penalties whether or not the woman was betrothed and subsequently divorced certainly the same holds for the far more egregious crime of rape. But this, i.e. -P, cannot be right because the verse says about the victim of the rapist "who is not betrothed," the evidence for P. This is how the R. Ishmael *o'kheiluf* would proceed to declare the *kheiluf* qal v'homer refuted and it would go on to assert the first qal v'homer to be correct by default.

But instead this midrash of the R. Akiva school proceeds as did #12, also of the R. Akiva school. When the *kheiluf* qal v'homer concludes with -P contradicting the evidence for P suggested by Deut. 22:28, the author considers whether this reading of the verse is correct. The author considers, similarly to what was conjectured in #12, perhaps the phrase "who is not betrothed" in 22:28 still understood as 'who was not betrothed and subsequently divorced' is referring not to the condition under which the prescribed penalties are imposed on the rapist, but instead refers to the conditions in 22:29 under which the fifty silver coins are given to the girl's father (as opposed to the girl herself). To make clear the reasonableness of this reading, 22:28-29 are presented together here:

28. "If a man finds a young woman (a *naarah*), a virgin, who was not betrothed and subsequently divorced, and he grabs her and lies with her and they are found
29. then the man who laid with her shall give to the father of the young woman 50 silver coins and she will be his wife; he will not be permitted to send her away for all of his life."

Thus the *kheiluf* qal v'homer is a possibility that cannot be refuted. Therefore, the author continues, in order to make it clear that the rapist is only liable in the case that the girl had not been betrothed the phrase לא ארשה must also appear in the case of the seducer. Thus the thought experiment has succeeded: the phrase אשר לא אורשה in Exod. 22:15 is shown to be needed and not derivable from the case of the rapist.

Piska 249:

A= ' ממזר, לא נאמר בו "עד עולם"'	ומה ממזר שלא נאמר בו 'עד עולם'
P= '[ממזר] עשה בו נשים כאנשים אסר גם על הנשים מלבוא בקהל'	עשה בו נשים כאנשים
B= 'עמונים ומואבים נאמר בהם "עד עולם"'	עמונים ומואבים שנאמר בהם 'עד עולמי
Q= '[עמונים ומואבים] נעשה נשים כאנשים [לאסר גם את הנשים]'	אינו דין שנעשה נשים כאנשים ?!
	או חילוף
B= 'עמונים ומואבים, נאמר בהם "עד עולם"'	ומה עמונים ומואבים שנאמר בהם 'עד עולמי
-Q = '[עמונים ומואבים] לא נעשה בהם נשים כאנשים [לאסר את הנשים]'	לא עשה בהם נשים כאנשים
A= 'ממזר, לא נאמר בו "עד עולם"'	ממזר שלא נאמר בהם 'עד עולם'
-P= '[ממזר] לא נעשה בו נשים כאנשים [לאסר את הנשים]'	אינו דין שלא נעשה בו נשים כאנשים ?!

Translation:

While

A = 'About the *mamzer* it is not said [that he may not be admitted into the congregation of the Lord is] *ad olam*, i.e. forever',

135

P = 'Women are ruled upon as men, [i.e. a female *mamzer* may not be admitted into the congregation of the Lord]'
Therefore,
Since
B = 'About Ammonites and Moabites it is said *ad olam* [meaning forever, that they may not be admitted into the congregation of the Lord]'
must-it-not-follow-that
Q = 'Women Ammonites and Moabites are to be ruled upon as are the men [i.e. they should also be prohibited from admission into the congregation of the Lord]
?!

O'kheiluf

While
B = 'About Ammonites and Moabites it is said *ad olam* [meaning forever, that they may not be admitted into the congregation of the Lord]',
-Q = 'Women Ammonites and Moabites are not ruled upon as are the men [i.e., they are not prohibited from joining the congregation of the Lord].
Therefore,
Since
A = 'About the *mamzer* it is not said [that he may not be admitted into the congregation of the Lord] *ad olam*, i.e. forever'
must-it-not-follow-that
-P = 'Women should not be ruled upon as men, [i.e. a female *mamzer* may be admitted into the congregation of the Lord]'
?!

With the above labels the argument can be represented as,

Since A,B & P must-it-not-follow-that Q ?!

או חילוף

136

Since A,B & -Q must-it-not-follow-that -P ?!

To confirm that this *o'kheiluf* argument may be described symbolically by (*) it remains to show all of the following: A and B have the status of facts, P is a claim for which there is at most weak evidence, there is no evidence for or against Q, the phrase *o'kheiluf* sandwiches two qal v'homer arguments.

The source for fact A is the verse that immediately precedes the verses being commented upon, Deut. 23:3. The source for fact B is the verses that are being commented upon, verses 4 & 5 of the same chapter.

Prior to the *o'kheiluf* argument, the Sifre Devarim on verse 3 states the content of what is (later in the *o'kheiluf* argument) P and gives as proof of the claim, that ממזר means מום זר and thus does not refer to a gender but to all who have this *mum zar,* i.e. foreign defect. In its comment on the next verse the Sifre derives the content of -Q from the fact that the verse uses עמוני and מואבי, grammatically a male Ammonite and a male Moabite. In the school of R. Akiva, a derash in which they have confidence has the status of a fact, like a verse in the Torah. The particular two derashot, one on verse 3 and one on verse 4 are not farfetched. They are based on close and careful attention to the grammar of the expressions involved.

The first purpose of this *o'kheiluf* argument seems to be to demonstrate that the conclusion of neither one of the two derashot (without also excluding the other derash) could have been arrived at instead by qal v'homer reasoning. (Specifically, in each qal v'homer argument the derash in support of the launching premise is the derash that is suppressed so that the qal v'homer may be described as launched from a questionable premise. The derash that is not in support of the launching premise is not suppressed and is used to refute the conclusion of the qal v'homer argument after the *o'kheiluf* is presented.)

Putting aside the derash of מום זר (and of עמוני מואבי) there is certainly no strong evidence for P and therefore the conclusion of the first qal v'homer argument may be doubted. The author may therefore consider the possibility of -Q being true (but again because the derash on עמוני מואבי has been put aside, -Q is not known through strong evidence to be true) and engage in o'kheiluf. The kheiluf qal v'homer concludes with -P, that the law regarding the mamzer does not apply to women as it does to men.

The verification that this o'kheiluf argument can be represented symbolically by (*) is complete.

The author refutes the conclusion of the kheiluf qal v'homer with talmud lomar, followed by the prooftext לא יבא ממזר and likely the content of the earlier derash that was set aside, 'anyone who has מום זר'. The kheiluf qal v'homer is thus refuted.

Turning then to the qal v'homer that remains, the first one, the author refutes its conclusion with talmud lomar and the prooftext עמוני followed by the derash ולא עמונית, that the masculine singular tense was used to exclude the female.

The author continues on to the second purpose of his o'kheiluf argument. In the o'kheiluf argument, each of its two qal v'homers was argued with respect to whether the prohibition was expressed as עד עולם, i.e. forever, or not. But since the o'kheiluf failed, the phrase עד עולם is shown to not have been placed in the Torah for the purpose of deriving either of the two qal v'homer arguments. But without this special purpose, the phrases "forever" and "until the tenth generation" taken together appear at best redundant. Given that the Torah puts in the restriction to last "forever" why must it also state "until the tenth generation"?

The phrase "forever" now that it has been shown to not be needed to derive a qal v'homer is present in the verse in order to serve in its literal sense. The phrase "until the tenth generation" is therefore not needed for its literal meaning and is therefore 'freed up' to serve the hermeneutical function of drawing a *gezerah shavah*:

ואם נאמר 'עד עולם' למה נאמר 'דור עשירי' ?
אלא מופנה להקיש ולדון גזירה שוה:
נאמר כאן 'דור עשירי' ונאמר להלן. מה דור עשירי האמור כאן 'עד עולם' אף 'דור
עשירי' האמור להלן 'עד עולם'.

See Chapter Four for further discussion.

2.5: Conclusion

This concludes the examination of the 15 occurrences of the phrase או חילוף in the Midrash Halakhah of both the R. Ishmael and R. Akiva schools. The key point established is that the phrase או חילוף has precisely the same meaning everywhere it occurs:

Since **A,B** & **P** must-it-not-follow-that **Q** ?!

או חילוף

Since **A,B** & **-Q** must-it-not-follow-that **-P** ?!   (*)

where **A** and **B** represent propositions that are facts, and **P** represents a proposition for which there is less than completely convincing evidence, and in the second argument **-Q** is not known to be false. The ending '?!' is used to indicate that the expression is a rhetorical-questioning qal v'homer argument.

2.6: Addendum: A Corrupted Later Addition

There is one exception. There is one occurrence of the phrase *o'kheiluf* in the Midrash Halakhah, which unlike the other 15 occurrences, does not satisfy all features of definition (*). Unlike all of the other occurrences of the word *kheiluf* in the Midrash Halakhah of the R. Akiva school, but in keeping with all of the occurrences in the Mishnah, this expression (following the Finkelstein edition) has no *yud*, i.e. it appears as או חלוף. I suspect that this phrase was added into the argument by a later editor. The exclusive 'or' in the phrase *o'kheiluf*, i.e. 'or the *kheiluf*', so critical to all of the other *o'kheiluf* arguments in rabbinic literature, makes no sense for this argument. Rather, what was intended was 'and', as the results of the two qal v'homer arguments are added together to establish the claim that the word *kadaish*, male cultic prostitute, appears to be unnecessary in the verse. With an intended 'and' instead of an 'or' the entire argument has a different structure than the *o'kheiluf* argument.

ספרי דברים: פרשת כי תצא, פיסקא רס:

The passage in Sifre Deuteronomy, piska 260, comments on the laws in Deut. 23:18, לא תהיה קדשה מבנות ישראל ולא יהיה קדש מבני ישראל. This verse warns against allowing there to be any female cultic prostitutes amongst the daughters of Israel or any male cultic prostitutes among the children of Israel. The derash on these words explains the specification to Israelites, as disallowing cultic prostitutes among the Israelites but not warning against allowing there to be Caananite cultic prostitutes. This is arrived at --- the author uses the phrase 'שהיה בדין' — by qal v'homer on a biblical text where the admonition against the *kadaish* is imagined to be omitted from the verse, Deut 23:18. This strategy of the Sifre Devarim was seen earlier in *o'kheiluf* arguments from piska 244, #12-14 discussed in this chapter.

The first qal v'homer argument, starting from the first part of verse Deut. 23:18, the warning regarding female cultic prostitutes among the Israelites, derives the same restriction on male Israelite cultic prostitutes:

Since

A ='male prostitution [presumably because it involves male sodomy] is a most serious sin' while

B= 'female prostitution is a sin of lesser seriousness'

And since

P= 'there may be no female cultic prostitute from the daughters of Israel'

must-it-not-follow that

Q= 'there may be no male cultic prostitute amongst the Children of Israel'

?!

Thus it is shown that from the law warning against allowing female cultic prostitutes amongst the daughters of Israel, it may be derived by qal v'homer that there may be no male cultic prostitutes amongst the children of Israel. Therefore there would seem to be no need for the phrase in the verse that makes the latter warning explicit.

With the phrase o'kheiluf the author then introduces another qal v'homer argument this time starting from the imagined-to-be-absent-and-therefore-blank second and concluding part of Deut. 23:18, which just like the words imagined absent, issues no warning regarding male cultic prostitutes amongst the Caananites. By qal v'homer there can therefore be no such warning with regard to Caananite female cultic prostitutes:

A ='male prostitution [presumably because it involves male sodomy] is a most serious sin' while

B= 'female prostitution is a sin of lesser seriousness'

And since

*Q ='there is no law stated [nor by the first qal v'homer was there implied any] warning against a male cultic prostitute amongst the nations'

must-it-not-follow-that

*P = 'there is no warning that there may be no female cultic prostitute amongst the nations'

?!

Thus from the first warning in Deut. 23:18 with regard to female cultic prostitutes amongst the Israelites and the fact that the verse includes no warning regarding male cultic prostitutes amongst the Caananites, the entire content of the initial derash was obtained. That is, it was derived by qal v'homer that there may not be Israelite male cultic prostitutes and it was concluded from the absence of a warning against male prostitutes among the Caananites that there is also no admonition against (allowing) female cultic prostitutes among the Caananites.

This leads to the question posed in the passage, why then was it necessary for the verse to include the warning regarding the male cultic prostitutes, seeing as all of the above teachings could be derived without the expression of this warning. The answer the author gives is that had it not been included, one would have argued by qal v'homer from the first law regarding female prostitutes among the Israelites that since the male prostitute is more abominable than the female prostitute, it should entail even more restrictions than the former. (This would then be an instance where the Sifre Devarim is not in keeping with the principle דיו לבוא מן הדין להיות כנידון. Similarly, #2, as in the discussion there, is an example where the Sifre Numbers does not adhere to the *dayo* principle.)

This pair of qal v'homer arguments separated by the phrase או חלוף, is not what we have been referring to as an *o'kheiluf* argument. There is no exclusionary 'or', no choosing between contradictory qal v'homer arguments. The contents of both qal v'homer arguments are collected and together they include all of the midrash at the beginning of piska 260, thus making the point that it was not necessary for the Torah to state the warning regarding the male prostitute. There is therefore no typical second part of an *o'kheiluf* argument where the two contradictory qal v'homer arguments are evaluated with the goal of refuting one and declaring the other correct by default. Instead, the conclusions from each of the two qal v'homer arguments are added together.

One can see why an editor might have wanted to refer to the second qal v'homer argument as some kind of switch or exchange and would want to express that through the root נ, ל, פ. The second qal v'homer is a switch of the first qal v'homer argument in the sense that the direction of the qal v'homer argument is changed: while the first qal v'homer argument goes from the statement of law concerning a female cultic prostitute to conclude something about a male cultic prostitute the second qal v'homer goes from the absence of a consideration concerning the male prostitute to conclude something about the law regarding a female prostitute.

None of the translations of the Sifre Deuteronomy into English seem to pick up that the exclusive 'or' is odd, given that the argument is making the point that it is the results of both qal v'homer arguments taken together which make the inclusion in the Torah of the admonition against the male cultic prostitute unnecessary. While Neusner's translation does recognize that the argument is making the latter point, Reuven Hammer in his translation does not. His translation of the argument is somewhat problematic, especially his translation of the second qal v'homer argument, the one that follows the phrase o'kheiluf. Hammer's note 1 is simply incorrect: he explains the argument as making the point that one might reason that either one of the two admonitions, the one against male prostitutes or the one against female prostitutes, might have been omitted from the biblical verse. Omitting the admonition against female prostitutes is not something that the argument considers possible. (In the Vilna Gaon's version of piska 260, which is not the standard version that Hammer translates, there is an additional argument that does explicitly consider this possibility. It points out that if the admonition against a female cultic prostitute amongst the Israelites had been left out of the verse, one would conclude that the admonition against male cultic prostitutes was made because this sin is so much graver than that involving female prostitutes, and therefore that there is no reason to think that the admonition extends to female prostitutes.)

CHAPTER THREE: A Tannaitic Logic Term Distinguished from *O'kheiluf*

The root ח, ל, פ is very common in Tanakh and in rabbinic literature. As a verb חלף primarily means to exchange. Other related meanings that derive from to exchange (perhaps viewed in the context of a cycle) include to grow back, to move past, to die, to refresh oneself. In Tanakh, the plural noun חלפות or חליפות refers to a change of clothing[72], חלף עבודתם in Bamidbar[73] means 'in exchange for their work'. In tannaitic literature as well חלף means a physical exchange. Sometimes the noun חליף, in a related fashion, refers to a shoot (i.e. a part of vegetation that undergoes changeover in the cycle of life).

The use of the root ח, ל, פ to mean a more abstract exchange like the exchange of parts of a statement or the exchanging of two rulings or the exchange of situations, unsurprisingly only first appears in rabbinic literature. In tannaitic literature such types of exchange are exclusively indicated with the word חילוף or חלוף and not with any of the other myriad grammatical manifestations of the root.[74]

---

[72] See Genesis 25:22, Kings II, 5:22 & 23.

[73] See Num.18:21.

[74] The verb מחליף, meaning, he exchanges, shares the same root ח,ל,פ. It appears in tannaitic literature referring to composing a חילוף הדברים, in baraitot on B.Yevamot 20a, B.Pesahim 53a. While the Mishnah says, "Rabbi X says, 'the matters are exchanged'" and therefore uses the phrase חילוף הדברים the baraitot cited say, 'Rabbi X exchanges [the matters]' and therefore uses the verb, מחליף.

But in other tannaitic sources the word מחליף is used to refer to a physical exchange or giving in exchange: M. Pe'ah 3:2, in a baraita on B. Moed Katan 24a.

In the Bavli, the word מחליף shows up in 7 Amoraic expressions as well. In 6 of these it refers to a physical action. The word appears in the phrase גזעו מחליף mean it ['s trunk] is regenerated in B. Niddah 55a, B. Eruvin 100b, B.Sanhedrin 105b, B. Taanit 20a, B. Ketubot 79a. In B.Niddah 47a the phrase refers to switching physical objects, i.e. women (in a disturbing passage). More abstractly, מחליף refers to exchanging names in B.Gittin 11a. In the Amoraic expressions in the Bavli the word מחליף does not refer to exchanging parts of a statement. The word is not used to refer to a

The occurrence of the noun חילוף (or חלוף) in the phrase או חילוף (or או חלוף) and how this phrase או חלוף always means precisely the same thing wherever it occurs, was already discussed in Chapter One. Formulation (4') expressing the precise meaning is recopied here for convenience:

Since **A**, **B** & **P** must-it-not-follows-that **Q** ?!

או חילוף

Since **A**, **B** & **-Q** must-it-not-follow-that **-P** ?!   (4')

where **A** and **B** represent biblical or common sense facts, while **P** represents a proposition for which there is some biblical evidence but not what the author sees as compelling evidence.[75] There is no biblical expression that addresses the issue of **Q**, supporting or refuting it. (**-Q** denotes the negation of **Q**, i.e. **-Q** is the statement 'It is not true that **Q**' and likewise for **-P**.) Further, each of the two rhetorical questions sandwiching the phrase או חילוף represents a qal v'homer argument.

The noun חלוף shows up in one other tannaitic phrase, *kheiluf ha-devarim*, חלוף הדברים (or חילוף הדברים), where it represents a different

---

חילוף הדברים. There is one exception, on B.Shavuot 19a, described below.
When the Amoraim engage in what in this chapter is shown to be the definition of the tannaitic חילוף הדברים, the Bavli refers to it with the Aramaic phrase איפוך אנא (*eepukh ana*) which is only used for this purpose: B. Ketubot 103b, B. Shavuot 26a, B. Shavuot 34a, B. Yevamot 8b, B. Yevamot 97a, B. Bekhorot 26b.
There is one exception: On B. Shavuot 19a, Rav Sheshet is exchanging the attributions of two statements made by Tannaim, one is attributed to R. Akiva and the other to R. Eliezer. The verb used is מחליף, as in all the tannaitic cases listed above where Tannaim express a חילוף הדברים.
[75] The 5 o'kheiluf arguments of the Sifra, are launched from propositions P for which the authors have no biblical evidence. For these, P is just a guess that is taken to be true in the first qal v'homer argument.

sort of exchange of sentence parts or parts of rulings. We turn to this phrase now.

3.1: *Kheiluf ha-Devarim*

The phrase חלוף הדברים occurs in 6 places in the Mishnah in reporting rules (or oral traditions)[76]; the phrase חלוף היו הדברים occurs once[77]. Two of the Mishnayot containing the phrase חלוף הדברים appear almost verbatim in the Sifra with the spelling חילוף הדברים.[78] Sifre Devarim has one[79] original occurrence of חילוף הם הדברים, which does not appear in the Mishnah. The Tosefta contains 8 occurrences of חלוף הדברים (or with the spelling חילוף הדברים) 3 of which are in Mishnah as well; 2 occurrences of חלוף הן הדברים one of which also occurs in the Yerushalmi; and 3 occurrences of חלוף היו הדברים , one of which also occurs in the same passage found in Mishnah.[80] Adding these up, in the Tosefta there are a total of 14 unique tannaitic occurrences of חלוף or חילוף along with הדברים. All three of these expressions have the same exact single meaning in all of their occurrences, loosely 'the switch of the matters'. But I will describe this meaning more precisely; all three of these slight variations of חלוף הדברים share the same exact meaning and therefore constitute one technical term.

---

[76] Here is the list: M.Bava Batra 5:10 (also appears in Sifra on Kedoshim, parsha 3, beginning of chapter 8); M. Shevi'it 4:2 (also appears in Sifra on Behar, parsha 1, beginning of chapter 1); M. Gittin 5:4; M. Kelim, 26:8; M. Mikvaot 6:9 (also appears in Tosefta Mikvaot 5:6); M. Eduyot 7:8 (also in Tosefta Eduyot 3:1); M. Yevamot 10:3 (also in Tosefta Yevamot 11:8). There are 9 occurrences in the Tosefta that are not also in the Mishnah: Eduyot, chapter 3, halakha 4; Pesahim 3:8; Kelim Metzia 4:15, 11:3; Kelim Kamma 2:3; Shabbat 2:21; Sukkah 2:6 where the expression is חלוף דברים; twice in Yevamot 11:8.

[77] M. Yevamot 10:3 which also occurs with the phrase in Tosefta, chapter 11, halakha 8.

[78] There is also one occurrence of חלוף הדברים in Sifre Zuta 19:11.

[79] Sifre Devarim on Parashat Ri-ey, piska 66.

[80] Two occurrences of חלוף היו הדברים in Tosefta Yevamot 11:8, which do not occur in Mishnah.

Here is an example from M. Bava Batra 5:10 which is also found (with slight syntactic variations) in the Sifra on Kedoshim, parsha 3, chapter 8:7:

בבא בתרא, פרק ה, משנה י :

הסיטון מקנח מדותיו אחת לשלשים יום ובעל הבית אחת לשנים עשר חודש.

רבן שמעון בן גמליאל אומר <u>חלוף הדברים</u>.

חנוני מקנח מדותיו פעמים בשבת וממחה משקלותיו פעם אחת בשבת, ומקנח מאזנים על כל משקל ומשקל.

Translation of the first two lines that end with the phrase, חלוף הדברים follows. (The third line of the Mishnah presents a new case and is not included.)

A wholesale [provisions] dealer must clean his measures once in thirty days, and a producer once in twelve months.
Rabban Shimon ben Gamliel says 'the reversal of the matters'.
(M. Bava Batra 5:10)

Thus according to Rabban Shimon ben Gamliel, it is the producer who must clean his measures once in thirty days and the wholesale dealer must clean his measures once in twelve months. As is most usually the case, the elaboration is not presented in the Mishnah because it is seen as following obviously from the phrase חלוף הדברים, which I have translated roughly as 'the reversal of the matters'.[81] Let me spell out precisely what sort of reversal was inferred.

I use symbols A and B to represent objects and X and Y to represent properties that the objects A and B have.

---

[81]M. Kelim 26:8 is an example of the unusual case where the Mishnah follows the words חלוף דברים by elaborating what the חלוף דברים would be. It appears that it does so because the Mishnah consists of two different cases and it is the second case that is followed by the phrase חלוף דברים . The elaboration that follows makes clear that the case the phrase חלוף דברים refers to is the case that immediately follows the expression, the second case.

Let A = *a wholesale dealer*

   B = *a producer*

   X = *has the requirement that he must clean his measures every*
thirty days'

   Y= *has the requirement that he must clean his measures once in*
twelve months

Using these symbols we can schematize the Mishnah as follows:

A has property X

   &

B has property Y.

'The reversal of the matters' would refer to the following:
A has property Y &
B has property X.

This schematization characterizes all of the texts in which the phrase
חילוף הדברים arises as well as the incidence of חילוף הם הדברים in Sifre
Devarim, and also the one occurrence of חלוף היו הדברים in
M.Yevamot 10:3.[82]

Thus every time the author of a tannaitic statement uses חילוף הדברים
(or one of its slight variants above including both words) it is very
clear what sort of a switching around of matters from the preceding
statement, he is announcing. Further in choosing to indicate the
switch he has in mind with this phrase, the author avoids using the
phrase או חילוף, *o'kheiluf*. The latter phrase, *or perhaps the kheiluf*, is
exclusively used as described in Chapter One, to refer to an
argument, the *kheiluf*, (usually a qal v'homer argument) presented as

---

[82] In this last case if we let, X= 'died earlier', Y='died later', A= 'your
husband' and B= 'your son', then the start of the Mishnah may be
schematized as 'A has property X, B has property Y'. The 'matters were [as
described by] the reversal' is then shorthand for 'B has property X, A has
property Y'.

a counter to the preceding argument and which is related to the latter in the precise way described by (4').

Likewise, there is no qal v'homer argument related to another qal v'homer argument by the form (4'), which is described by the words חלוף הדברים. What all of the texts containing the two phrases tell us, is that the careful and consistent uses of the phrases חלוף הדברים and או חילוף to represent and distinguish between the two different distinct linguistic and logical formulations of statements or arguments, clearly constitute technical linguistic and logical terminology.

The following outlier is consistent with our claim of intentionality in the application of these two different terms. There is a unique case in a baraita quoted on B.Zevahim 11a, of a debate containing the phrase או חילוף הדברים. [83]

The phrase follows a qal v'homer argument and introduces another qal v'homer argument. The fact that they did not instead use the phrase או חילוף suggests that the authors or editors paid close attention to the form of the argument and were very clear on the general nature of the two different logical forms, the או חילוף and the חילוף הדברים. They realized that although the phrase followed a qal v'homer argument and preceded another qal v'homer argument just as is the case with the occurrences of the phrase או חילוף, the two qal v'homer arguments sandwiching או חילוף הדברים in the baraita are not related to one another by חילוף או. Rather, they realized, the two qal v'homer arguments are related to each other by an exchange of two parts of a proposition and are therefore instead a חילוף הדברים of one another. Because the baraita consists of a debate[84], the two qal

---

[83] This Baraita appears also in T. Pesahim 4:6, but without the phrase או חילוף הדברים.

[84] With regard to the slaughtering of the paschal sheep on the 14th of Nissan when the sheep that is over one year old, or other animals slaughtered on the 14th to serve as the paschal offering, R' Eliezer says these are invalid, while R. Yehoshua rules them valid. A debate between the two Tannaim, R. Yehoshua and R. Eliezer ensues where each tries to prove his position

v'homers are not simply two different declarations and so they indicated debate by preceding the חילוף הדברים with the word או, meaning 'or' i.e. *or [perhaps it is the] switch of the matters [that is the case].* Then because it is not clear from the first qal v'homer argument what precisely are the parts of the proposition that are to be exchanged, the phrase חילוף הדברים is followed with precisely what the חילוף הדברים is, i.e. the qal v'homer that results from making the switches to the original qal v'homer argument.

The two qal v'homer arguments in the baraita are related as follows:
A & P & B must-it-not-therefore-be-the-case-that Q ?!

או , חילוף הדברים

A & P' & B must-it-not-therefore-be-the-case-that Q' ?!

Where P and P' denote the following:

P: *On days other than Passover,*
   '*a different sacrifice' slaughtered to serve as 'the Passover sacrifice' is kosher.*

P': *On days other than Passover,*
   '*the Passover sacrifice' slaughtered to serve as 'a different sacrifice' is kosher.*

Similarly, Q and Q' are related as follows:

Q: *In its time,*
   '*a different sacrifice' slaughtered to serve as 'the Passover sacrifice' is kosher.*

Q': *In its time,*

---

correct or the other's position wrong. R.Yehoshua starts first, with an argument to prove his position.

'the Passover sacrifice' slaughtered to serve as 'a different sacrifice' is kosher.

P' is the switch of P, the positions of 'a different sacrifice' and 'Passover sacrifice' are switched.
The same is the case with Q and Q'.

This is unlike the examples of חלוף הדברים in that each of two statements undergoes a switching of its parts. Yet it is a simple switching, the places of 'a different sacrifice' and 'Passover sacrifice' are switched. The context of the argument makes it clear that the או, the 'or', is speculative or argumentative. The whole argument, the two qal v'homer arguments sandwiching the phrase, is nothing like an או חלוף argument even though the switching takes place within a proposition contained in a qal v'homer argument. Including the word הדברים suggests that the author recognized that the switching involved here is not an או חלוף but just a simple exchange similar to a חלוף הדברים and therefore introduced it with the phrase 'or [perhaps instead the] חלוף הדברים [is correct]!'

Thus although involved in comparing two different qal v'homer arguments, it was recognized that the two arguments are not related by או חילוף, but are rather two alternative arguments related by חילוף הדברים. The phrase by which the second argument is introduced should be parsed as 'או, חילוף הדברים' meaning, 'or perhaps instead the situation is חילוף הדברים'.

3.2: Conclusions

חילוף הדברים, the other tannaitic phrase that contains the noun חילוף (with or without a *yud* in the word *kheiluf*), was shown to have a precise meaning completely distinct from או חילוף. The two expressions were used carefully by the Tannaim, with the intention of distinguishing a passage as a case of the one from a case of the other.

CHAPTER FOUR: Comparing *O'Kheiluf* in the Two Schools

4.1: Overview

Chapter One arrived at a symbolic expression for the set-up of the *o'kheiluf* argument. This formulation was then verified for Example i from the Sifre Bamidbar. Chapter Two verified that each of the other 14 *o'kheiluf* arguments of the Midrash Halakhah is likewise representable with the same symbolic formulation. This formulation is presented here again for reference:

Since **A**, **B** & **P** must-it-not-follows-that **Q** ?!

או חילוף

Since **A**, **B** & **-Q** must-it-not-follow-that **-P** ?!   (*) ,

where **A** and **B** represent facts, and **P** represents a proposition for which the evidence is less than compelling. (The author has no evidence that supports or refutes **Q**.) **-Q** is the negation of **Q** and likewise for **P**. The ending '?!' is used to indicate that the expression is a rhetorically questioning qal v'homer argument.[85]

For the *o'kheiluf* arguments of the Midrash Halakhah, it was seen in Chapter Two that **A** and **B** represent biblical or common sense facts. In the midrash of the R. Ishmael school, the biblical facts express the contents of biblical verses. In the midrash of the R. Akiva school, especially in the Sifra, the statement that **A** or **B** represents is sometimes not quite the explicit content of a biblical verse but rather a

---

[85] In all but one of the *o'kheiluf* arguments, Sifre Bamidbar, piska 155, which involves a pair of just-as arguments rather than a pair of qal v'homer arguments; we study this case in detail in Chapter Five.

reasonable conclusion from a biblical statement. The inconclusive evidence for **P**, when it exists, is biblical. In all of the arguments of the R. Ishmael school as well as those of the Sifre Devarim of the R. Akiva school, there is some biblical evidence for **P**. In fact in several of the arguments in the Sifre Bamidbar and in several in the Sifre Devarim, the biblical evidence for **P** would seem fairly strong, but it does not meet the authors' high standards for conclusive evidence or proof.[86] The 5 o'kheiluf arguments of the Sifra, on the other hand, are launched from propositions **P** for which the authors have no biblical evidence. For these, **P** is just a guess that is taken to be true in the first qal v'homer argument. There is no biblical expression that addresses the issue of **Q**, supporting or refuting it.

The works of Midrash Halakhah are organized as running commentary to the Pentateuch. They consist of works attributed to the school of R. Ishmael and other works attributed to the school of R. Akiva. The Mekhilta on Exodus and the Sifre Bamidbar on Numbers are attributed to the school of R. Ishmael. The Sifra on Leviticus and the Sifre Devarim on Deuteronomy are attributed to the school of R. Akiva.[87] Six of the o'kheiluf arguments that occur in the Midrash Halakhah are in the works of the school of R. Ishmael. The other nine occur in the works of the school of R. Akiva.[88]

As shown at the end of Chapter One for Example i and demonstrated in Chapter Two for the others, all of the o'kheiluf arguments arise to answer a question of law prompted by the biblical verse under study where the topic of the verse is seen by the author of the midrash as

---

[86] See in this chapter, cases 3, 4, 5, 12, 13, 14.

[87] This was first demonstrated by David Hoffman in his *Zur Einleitung in die halachischen Midraschim* published in 1888, on the basis of the different terminology used by the two sets of works and the different rabbis cited in each. His results gained wide approval through their treatment in J. N. Epstein's *Progemena to Tannaitic Literature*, 1959.

[88] Three are in one passage in the Sifra (8, 9, 10 in Chapter Two) and three are in another passage in Sifre Devarim (piska 249; #12, 13, 14 in Chapter Two), so the nine occurrences range over midrash prompted by study of five different biblical verses.

analogous to a topic elsewhere in the Torah. It therefore seems that the law in question for one topic should inform the law on the other topic, however the law is not known for either topic. In the *o'kheiluf* arguments of the school of R. Ishmael, i.e. all those that occur in the Mekhilta and the Sifre Bamidbar, there is however some but not compelling biblical evidence for the law regarding one of the two topics.

4.2: *O'Kheiluf* Arguments of the R. Ishmael School

I will refer to the propositions contained in the *o'kheiluf* argument by their corresponding symbol in the symbolic formulation (*) copied above. All of the *o'kheiluf* arguments of the school of R. Ishmael, just as the particular Example i, proceed as follows.[89] To answer the question of law, the argument begins with a qal v'homer launched from a claim **P** about the law in question, regarding one of the two topics for which (as mentioned above) there is limited evidence regarding its truth. Concerned therefore about accepting the results of that qal v'homer argument, the author launches another qal v'homer from the negation of the conclusion of the first qal v'homer argument, i.e. from the claim labeled **-Q**. The qal v'homer launched from **-Q** leads to the conclusion **-P**.

---

[89] Two of the six *o'kheiluf* arguments of the Midrash Halakhah of the school of R. Ishmael (see Sifre Bamidbar, piska 125 & 126 in Chapter Two) differ from our example from the Sifre, on one small point. The question that is prompted by the verse being glossed is not a question about the topic of that verse but about the related law in the different topic discussed elsewhere in the Torah that the author finds analogous to the topic of the verse under discussion. In this type of case, the evidence for the claim labeled **P** is in the very verse under discussion, rather than in the text dealing with the analogous topic. In these cases, in fact, it is most clear that the author of the *o'kheiluf* argument views the words in the very verse under study as evidence for and as therefore the basis of his claim **P** in the first qal v'homer argument.

But the claim labeled -**P**, cannot possibly be true, the argument goes, because it contradicts the evidence, insufficient as it may be, that exists for claim **P**. The second qal v'homer argument is therefore rejected and the author expresses confidence that the first qal v'homer argument must be correct. This process of considering the second qal v'homer and then rejecting it has given the Tanna full confidence in the first qal v'homer which he originally lacked, again, because of the weakness he saw in the evidence for claim **P**. (In the next chapter, Chapter Five, I will subject these arguments to analysis and criticism from an imagined Stoic philosopher.) Thus the inconclusive evidence for **P** is now viewed as sufficient evidence and the qal v'homer launched from **P**, the first qal v'homer, and its conclusion are upheld.

The author sums up what has been argued: I executed a qal v'homer (*danti*), I switched it around (*kheilafti*), the *o'kheiluf* was found to be invalid, and I merited to derive by qal v'homer as in the beginning. The expression is the following or a slight grammatical variant of the following:

דנתי וחילפתי בטל החילוף וזכיתי לדון כבתחילה

4.3: *O'kheiluf* Arguments of the R. Akiva School

The *o'kheiluf* arguments of the school of R. Akiva arise under the same conditions as do those of the school of R. Ishmael and they too engage in comparing two possible qal v'homer arguments, from two seemingly related topics, which are related to each other symbolically as indicated in (*). However, the *o'kheiluf* arguments of the school of R. Akiva proceed very differently from those of R. Ishmael. That is, the second parts of the *o'kheiluf* arguments are very different for the two schools.

In the cases found in the Sifra there is absent even mild biblical evidence for proposition **P**. This is not so for the examples in Sifre Devarim, which like those of the R. Ishmael school are each launched from a **P** for which there is (albeit less than explicit) biblical evidence. Yet all but two of the arguments of the school of R. Akiva, do not reach a conclusion.[90] This is unlike the R. Ishmael cases, all of which do reach a conclusion.

Turning now to examine closely those *o'kheiluf* arguments of the school of R. Akiva, it will not be possible to give a general algorithm for how they proceed as was done for the cases of the school or R. Ishmael. Because of the great variation in the arguments of the school of R. Akiva, the treatment of these will of necessity be far more extensive. As will be seen, these arguments were engaged in with far more varied aims and with far more rhetorical inventiveness as well as analytical skill than those of the school of R. Ishmael.

4.4: Arguments of the R. Akiva School that Do Not Yield an Answer

FROM THE SIFRA

The focus will first be on those *o'kheiluf* arguments of the school of R. Akiva that do not reach a conclusion and the aim will be to seek reasons for why the arguments arose and what they were really meant to accomplish. Those in the Sifra will be examined first.

Sifra Dibbura de-Khova, Parshata 12:
Graver/lighter/known/unknown:
(In Chapter Two, # 8, 9, 10)

In the Sifra, Dibbura de-Khova, parshata 12, a set of three *o'kheiluf* arguments arises to answer a question prompted by the Sifra's

---

[90] For one argument in the Sifra (# 11 in Chapter Two) even though there is no biblical evidence for any of P, Q,-Q,-P, there is everyday evidence that is recognized as discrediting -P and thereby refuting the *kheiluf* qal v'homer. The first qal v'homer therefore remains as the only possibility and the author concludes that it is correct.

reasonable understanding of the biblical verse under examination. Leviticus 5:17-18 describes the *asham* offering as a sacrifice that must be brought as atonement for unknowingly committing a forbidden act, a *lo taaseh*. The Sifra reasonably interprets these verses to be referring to the graver sins, the *khamurot*. The Sifra then wants to know whether the instructions to bring an *asham* offering also apply to the lesser sins, the *kalot*.

Three different *o'kheiluf* arguments are presented in an effort to arrive at an answer. The **P** and **Q** are the same in all three arguments and so are the **A** and **B**. The different *a fortiori* arguments obtained from different arrangements of these four propositions account for the different *o'kheiluf* arguments (See Chapter Two for the full content of the arguments.) Unlike in all of the R. Ishmael arguments, there is no evidence for **P**, **Q**, **-P** or for **-Q** in these *o'kheiluf* arguments.

I.   P must-it-not-follow-that Q ?!

                        או חילוף

      -Q must-it-not-follow-that -P ?!

II.   A, also B. Therefore,

      Since P, must-it-not-follow-that Q ?!

                  o'kheiluf

      B, also A. Therefore,

      Since -Q, must it not follow-that -P ?!

III.   A, also P. Therefore,

      Since B, must-it-not-follow-that Q ?!

        o'kheiluf

      B, also -Q. Therefore,

      Since A, must it not follow-that -P ?!

P = 'A minor sin that one knows he has committed does not require a guilt (*asham*) offering [for atonement].'

Q = 'A minor sin that one does not know he has committed does not require a guilt (*asham*) offering [for atonement].'

A = 'A major sin that one knows he committed requires [one to bring] a sin offering.'

B= 'A major sin that one does not know he committed does not require [one to bring] a sin offering.'

The three *o'kheiluf* arguments fail in that they cannot decide between two competing qal v'homer arguments and this happens because in each argument there is no evidence for either **P** or **-Q**. Thus the *o'kheiluf* arguments are of no help in answering the question of whether the instructions to offer an *asham* sacrifice also apply to the lesser sins, the *kalot*. The author continues with,

תלמוד לומר 'ואשם' 'ואשם' לגזירה שוה,

meaning, *talmud lomar*[91], the Torah therefore states, instances of the word '*vi-ashaim*' here and in a related passage, Lev. 4: 27-28, for the

---

[91] In the R. Ishmael midrash the phrase *talmud lomar* often follows a qal v'homer argument and introduces a biblical phrase that contradicts the conclusion of the qal v'homer, thereby showing that the qal v'homer argument cannot be correct. *Talmud lomar* there means, 'therefore, in order to prevent the drawing of the just-mentioned conclusion, which one might be inclined to do, the Torah includes the following expression.' This sort of attack on a qal v'homer argument is discussed in the Addendum at the end of Chapter Five. In the case of the R. Ishmael *o'kheiluf* arguments, *talmud lomar* with the biblical phrase it introduces, follows the second (or *kheiluf*) qal v'homer and serves this function. It indicates that the conclusion of that second qal v'homer argument is incorrect and that the biblical phrase that follows was included in the Torah to prevent the drawing of that conclusion.

In some other passages of the R. Ishmael midrash (which do not contain any *o'kheiluf* arguments) *talmud lomar* has a different role. The phrase there follows a series of arguments aimed at answering a single question of law. The series starts off with a qal v'homer argument to answer the question, it is followed by a refutation of that argument followed by another attempt at qal purpose of drawing a *gezerah shavah*, an analogy between two topics established on the basis of a shared word in the biblical sources of the two different topics.[92] ('*Vi*' means 'and' and '*ashaim*' literally means 'he incurs guilt', refers to a guilt offering, as the root of '*ashaim*', ם‎,ש‎,א‎, means 'guilt'.) Just as the '*vi-ashaim*' which is stated

---

v'homer followed by a refutation of that argument. After several rounds of this, where the author has attempted via qal v'homer to compare the topic of the question at hand with every other topic he considers comparable, the author concludes that qal v'homer just won't yield the answer to the question. He continues with the phrase *talmud lomar* and a biblical proof text. In this sort of passage the *talmud lomar* means the following: It is because it was not possible to derive the answer to the question by (qal v'homer) reasoning from all the other seemingly related topics in the Torah, that the Torah needed to include an up-until-this-point seemingly redundant phrase as a the proof text. The latter phrase now appears to pointedly speak to the failed attempts, delivering an answer to the question. (For some examples of this type of series and this type function of the follow-up phrase *talmud lomar,* see Sifre Numbers 23, 25, 26, 29, 65, 110.)

In the R. Akiva *o'kheiluf* argument above, the phrase *talmud lomar* serves a role that is very similar to the second role described for it in the midrash of the R. Ishmael school unrelated to *o'kheiluf*. But with one important difference: in the R. Ishmael instances, all of the qal v'homer attempts in the series are launched from facts known about the other topics of comparison, they are not speculations about them, taken as assumptions. While in this argument of the school of R. Akiva, all of the qal v'homer attempts are launched from guesses.

The phrase *talmud lomar* in this passage from the Sifra follows a sequence of three contradictory pairs of inconclusive qal v'homer arguments launched from guesses. The phrase is most accurately translated as 'the Torah therefore states' that is, because it was not possible to decide between two different qal v'homer arguments in three different ways to frame the issue, the Torah included [these two instances of the word *vi-asham* so that they may be used to draw a *gezerah shavah* and in that way] decide the issue.' Through the *talmud lomar* followed by the biblical cues and the recommended technique, it is (again consistently) the second (or *kheiluf*) qal v'homer arguments that are shown to all be false.

[92] For more on this hermeneutical rule and technique see Azzan Yadin's *Scripture as Logos: Rabbi Ishmael and the Origins of Midrash*, 82-83. Also, although this derash does not include the phrase *mufneh lehakish (v'ladun gezerah shavah)*, it is clear from the texts in Leviticus that the word *v'asham* is indeed not needed in either text, i.e. the word does not add any content to either verse.

160

in Lev. 4:27-28 with regard to a prohibition, via apparently a derash[93] on Num.15:29, refers to a matter whose intentional violation is punishable by extirpation and whose unintentional violation requires a sin offering and whose doubtful violation requires an *asham* offering, so too the word *vi-ashaim* in the verse under study, Lev. l5:17, must be referring to a matter whose intentional violation is punishable by extirpation and whose unintentional violation requires a sin offering and whose doubtful violation requires an *asham* offering. Thus the *asham* is not to be offered for the unintentional violation of one of the lesser sins.

A *gezerah shavah* is understood to draw information known from the Torah about the topic where the word or phrase that is the basis of the *gezerah shavah* occurs, and to claim that this information is also true of the other topic where the word occurs. Note that here in the Sifra instead, the information drawn is not from the text of the Torah itself but from a bit of midrash on the text. In this way the Sifra is treating that midrash as if it were a biblical verse.[94]

---

[93] Sifre Bamidbar has precisely this comment on Num.15:29. Either the Sifra is referring to this derash of the R. Ishmael school or perhaps it is referring to a lost book of midrash on Numbers of the R. Akiva school which has essentially this same derash as the Sifre Bamidbar on the verse.

[94] This is not a surprising thing for the midrash of the R. Akiva school to be doing. The school of R. Akiva had a very ambitious program to derive as many laws as possible from the Torah. If the premises of any derivation they made had to be actual expressions in the Torah, there would be a limited number of laws they could derive from the Torah. Being able to use derived laws or facts as premises from which to derive new laws, would enable them to derive far more new laws.Thus the R. Akiva school did not endorse the R. Ishmael principle rejecting, למד מן הלמד (*lamed min ha-lamed*) i.e no new teaching should be derived from another derivation. In endorsing the deriving of new laws from previously derived laws, it is not surprising that the R. Akiva school would apply *gezerah shavah* as well, to the derivations from a shared biblical word or expression. (The R. Ishmael school held to this principle disallowing *lamed min ha-lamed* because their focus was the concern about the error incurred with the application of their imperfect hermeneutical rules, a derivation from a derivation has whatever that rate of error is, squared.)

Through this application of the method of gezerah shavah the Sifra obtains the answer to the question it originally posed, i.e. that indeed the asham sacrifice is not also offered for the lesser sins, the kalot. This is a reasonable (and practical) answer. Since the answer to the Sifra's question on the verse it was studying is arrived at by a gezerah shavah, what then was the need to first present o'kheiluf arguments consisting of three possible pairs of qal v'homer arguments, that all failed to provide an answer?

The o'kheiluf arguments of the R. Akiva school that are discussed further along suggest that considering qal v'homer possibilities that are launched from a guess was part of a casting about approach to see what ideas the author could hit on. There is nothing to criticize about such a mental activity; it is perfectly sensible to consider the question of what sort of things would follow if indeed some premise was true. The question though is why after coming to his correct solution via gezerah shavah, did the author feel the need to include these failed qal v'homer arguments that are launched from guesses, which make up these o'kheiluf arguments.

It seems that the author believed that his derivation of the law in question by means of gezerah shavah would be more readily accepted once the reader sees that it was preceded by serious attempts at proof by qal v'homer that failed. Perhaps the author felt that his gezerah shavah was not completely convincing as it drew what a midrash says, rather than what the Torah itself seems to say, about the one topic to apply it to the other topic where the word vi-asham also occurs. Or perhaps the author believed that proof by qal v'homer is more compelling than proof by gezerah shavah, the drawing of an analogy between two occurrences of the same word in the Torah.[95]

---

[95] This would be a very reasonable position; the Talmuds recognize that it is not the case that a valid analogy may be drawn between any two occurrences of the same word in the Torah. A person's sense may be relied upon to guide him in drawing a valid qal v'homer but may prove a poor guide in making a gezerah shavah. The Talmuds make this point in their respective treatments of M. Pesahim 6:1-2, the subject of Chapter Six of this book.

The author seems to imply by the whole sequence of three *o'kheiluf* arguments that it is precisely because qal v'homer could not give the answer to the question that the Torah provided other clues. Namely, we are to understand about the word *vi-ashaim* here, what we know about the word *vi-ashaim* in another place in Lev. 4: 27, and what we know about *vi-ashaim* in the latter, is from a derash. Thus the Torah foresaw and intended the derash on the word *vi-ashaim* that it included so that a *gezerah shavah* could be drawn, precisely because it knew that qal v'homer would not work. It is being argued that once the reader also sees that qal v'homer will not lead to an answer, careful scrutiny of the Torah for new clues makes the two instances of *vi-asham* stand out as the biblically intended source for deriving the law in question.

By including all of those failed qal v'homer attempts the author seems to be saying to the reader, 'I know what natural, compelling proof is, I have the same sensibilities as you, it is only when such methods proved impossible that I turned to a less obvious method to get the answer to the question. After all, the Torah must provide a source for each law including this one. These cues, the pair of two instances of ואשם, is the best available candidate for the source of the law in question, therefore it must have been intended by the Torah as the source for that law.'

Thus these three *o'kheiluf* arguments (and therefore six qal v'homer arguments) which fail to reach a conclusion because their **P** and **-Q** claims are total guesses that are not backed by any evidence, are included so that the author can convince the reader that qal v'homer cannot help answer the question asked and that therefore a less

---

B. Pesahim 66a: דאין אדם דן גזירה שוה מעצמו

Y. Pesahim 6:1, 39a: שאין אדם דן גזירה שוה מעצמו. רבי יוסי בירבי בון אמר בשם רבי אבא בר ממל, אם בא אדם לדון אחר גזירה שוה מעצמו עושה את השרץ מטמא באהל ואת המת מטמא בכעדשה   ....אדם דן קל וחומר לעצמו ואין אדם דן גזירה שוה לעצמו

ס

163

obvious method needs to be used. In this way the author is able to make an argument (that uses a version of *gezerah shavah* and so) that would be less compelling to his audience (than qal v'homer), more palatable.[96]The Sifra's recognition here that qal v'homer is the simpler or more natural method to try first, does indeed suggest that the reading sensibilities of the school of R. Akiva might not be unlike our own. This point will be returned to after the stronger evidence in the next *o'kheiluf* argument is presented.

Sifra, Dibbura de-Nedavah, Parsha 2: A gift given to a prostitute and the proceeds from the sale of a dog
(In Chapter Two, # 7)

Leviticus begins with the topic of sacrifices offered voluntarily. Lev 1:2 reads as follows: "Speak to the children of Israel, if a person amongst you brings a sacrifice to the Lord, from the domestic animals, from the cattle and from the sheep you should offer your sacrifices."

In studying this verse the Sifra interprets each "from" as serving to exclude something different. This is no surprise as the word *from* in a biblical phrase is a common hermeneutical marker of exclusion in the midrash of the R. Akiva school.[97]

The phrase "from the domestic animals" according to the Sifra, is to be understood as from amongst the domestic animals (one may bring a sacrifice) but not of all. The Sifra states that the *from* there excludes animals used for sodomy. That is, the Sifra's derash is that in order to make the point that animals used for sodomy are not permitted to be

---

[96] The Mishnah views *gezerah shavah* as preferable to qal v'homer as a rule for deriving laws. (See M.Sotah 6:3.) This point will not be pursued here. But this is not the case in the passage above from the Sifra which reflects our natural reading sensibilities (that an *a fortiori* argument is often more compelling than drawing an analogy between two uses of the same word in the Torah).

[97] J.N. Epstein in his 1957, *Prolegomena to Tannaitic Literature* included *min* as one of the hermeneutical cues characteristic of the school of R. Akiva.

brought as sacrifices, the Torah used the word *from* and the wordy phrase *from the domestic animals.* Thus animals to be sacrificed must be domestic animals but not any domestic animal may be sacrificed, specifically a domestic animal that was involved in sodomy may not be sacrificed. The Sifra then interrogates its derash.

The Sifra asks whether the word *from* is really needed to derive this law from the Torah. The Sifra asks, 'Doesn't it follow by *din* (i.e. qal v'homer reasoning)?' The Sifra then presents a qal v'homer to derive this law, starting from the well-known biblical law that an animal to be brought as a sacrifice must be without blemish (i.e., see Lev. 1:3,10; 3:6; 4:3; 4:23, 28, 32; 5:18,25).

Since an animal with [just] a blemish, which was not used to commit a transgression, is unfit for the altar, the animals that sodomized or were used to sodomize (a person) were clearly used to commit those transgressions, must-it-not-follow-that most certainly they are not fit for the altar?!

The Sifra responds with a counterexample that refutes this reasoning: In the case of the ox plowing together with an ass, the ox is used for this sin but it is kosher for the altar. But this counterexample is then refuted: The sin of putting an ox to plow together with an ass is not a [major] transgression for which the animal must be put to death as is the sin of sodomy where the animal used is put to death. With the counterexample refuted, the qal v'homer argument stands unrefuted and is accepted.

The qal v'homer derivation of the law is thus upheld, but the Sifra points out, the law holds for a case where the sin of sodomy is established, as is usual, through the testimony of two witnesses: An animal known by the testimony of two witnesses to have been used for sodomy may not serve as a sacrifice.

The Sifra then asks, "What about the case of an animal known to have been used for sodomy by the testimony of only one witness, or only the testimony of the owner, from where would we derive that it may not serve as a sacrifice?" R. Ishmael presents a derivation by qal v'homer. R. Akiva follows with a perspicacious refutation invalidating R. Ishmael's comparison of the sodomized animal with an animal that has a blemish, something that is visible on the animal. The sodomized animal would therefore appear to not be unfit for the altar. There is no apparent qal v'homer argument from which to derive the desired law in the case of only one witness.

The Sifra continues with *talmud lomar*, i.e. it is for this reason that the Torah employed the phrase, "from the domestic animals" to exclude animals used for sodomy. For otherwise, we would not know that of the domestic animals, those used for sodomy, even when there is only one witness to the sin, may not serve as a sacrifice.

What the Sifra has done is carefully refine its original question so that the refined question of law is one for which, as the Sifra shows, there is no obvious qal v'homer derivation possible. This law would therefore be one for which it would be expected of the Torah that it provide some hermeneutical key to its source. The Sifra declares this to be the function of the word *from* in the phrase "from the domestic animals."[98] It serves to restrict. Thus not all domestic animals may be brought as sacrifices, only those that were not used for the sin of sodomy, including when there is only one witness to the act of sodomy.

Thus the Sifra, by showing that the law in question cannot be derived by qal v'homer, makes the case that some textual element must serve this hermeneutical function. It is then declared that the word *from*, which is known to be a hermeneutical marker of exclusion, must be the source of the law. If the law could have been arrived at by qal v'homer the Torah would not have needed to encode this law into Scripture.

---

[98] See Yadin-Israel's discussion of what he terms 'hermeneutical markedness' in his two books *Scripture as Logos* and *Scripture and Tradition* cited above.

Had the Sfira instead left out all of these qal v'homer attempts and just glossed, 'in "from the domestic animals" the *from* serves to exclude those animals that were used for sodomy' the reader might have been less accepting of this derash. The reader might have rejected the interpretation saying, 'Aren't you reading too much into the word *from* and even if it does mean to exclude, how do you know it means to exclude that?' What the Sifra has done by including the qal v'homer attempts, is to also convey to the reader that it has the same reasoning sensibilities as the reader. It knows what a reasonable derivation is and therefore it starts with trying to establish such a derivation; qal v'homer reasoning is often compelling, using the sort of reasoning we use in everyday situations. It is only, after such reasoning is exhausted and fails as happens with the refined question that the Sifra then turns to a less commonplace method.

Between the lines of the passage is an appeal to the reader's understanding, 'We tried what is reasonable, it failed so then we tried the next best thing we could find.' The reader is less inclined to reject this seemingly honest argument. After all, there must be some way to derive the law from the Torah; does the reader have any better idea how to do this?![99] The Sifra's gloss on the next "from" in the verse will further support the reading I am suggesting.

The Sifra in Dibbura de-Nedavah, Parsha 2, turns to the next phrase in Lev. 1:2, "from the cattle" and tells us that this phrase is meant to exclude from the cattle those animals that were worshiped. Thus

---

[99] The Sifra does not seem in this passage to be deriving a law from the Torah but rather starting with a law accepted by oral tradition, and then seeking a biblical source so as to present the law in question as biblically derived. Whether the project of Midrash Halakhah was to derive law from the Torah or to give biblical support to oral traditions has been a matter of long standing debate. (See Yadin, *Logos as Scripture,* for discussion and references. He cites J.N. Epstein's *Prolegomena to Tannaitic Literature* as the most influential work arguing the latter position, that the oral traditions (as those cited in the Mishnah) came first and midrash arose to buttress those traditions).

sacrifices of cattle may be brought but not of cattle that was worshiped. The exclusionary "from" in the phrase is, according to the Sifra, the biblical source for the law that worshiped animals may not be sacrificed on the altar. The Sifra interrogates its derash, asking whether indeed the word "from", in the biblical verse needs to be used as a source for this law. Is it not possible to derive the law, the Sifra asks, by the following qal v'homer argument or its *kheiluf*:

Since the gift given to a prostitute and the proceeds from the sale of a dog, whose coverings are permitted (for ordinary usage), [they however] are prohibited as sacrifices, must-it-not-follow-that a worshiped animal whose coverings are prohibited (for ordinary usage), should be prohibited as a sacrifice?!

O'kheiluf

Since the gift given to a prostitute and the proceeds from the sale of a dog, which are prohibited as sacrifices, their coverings are permitted (for ordinary usage), must-it-not-follow-that a worshiped animal which is permitted as a sacrifice, its coverings should be permitted (for ordinary usage)?!

The argument as labeled in Chapter Two:

While
A = 'The coverings of the gift given to a prostitute and the price paid for a dog are permitted [to be used]',
B = 'The gift given to a prostitute and the price paid for a dog are prohibited on the altar [as a sacrifice]'.
Therefore,
Since
P = 'The coverings of a worshiped animal are not permitted [to be used]'
must-it-not-follow-that
Q = 'A worshiped animal may not be put on the altar [as a sacrifice]'
?!

168

While

B = 'The gift given to a prostitute and the price paid for a dog are prohibited on the altar [as a sacrifice]',

A = 'The coverings of the gift given to a prostitute and the price paid for a dog are permitted [to be used]'.

Therefore,

Since

-Q = 'A worshiped animal may be offered as a sacrifice on the altar'

must-it-not-follow-that

-P = 'The coverings of a worshiped animal are permitted [to be used]'

?!

As laid out in detail in Chapter Two, the problem with this *o'kheiluf* argument is that there is no evidence for the claim that corresponds to **P** or the claim that corresponds to **-Q** (in the symbolic formulation of the argument via (*)). The Sifra points out that Deut. 7:25 seems to contradict **-P** and therefore to support **P**. But further reflection shows that the verse in Deuteronomy is referring to a non-living worshiped object and therefore does not apply to the topics being compared here. With no evidence whatsoever for **P**, **Q**, or **-P** or **-Q**, it is impossible to choose between the original qal v'homer argument and the *kheiluf* argument. Since the two qal v'homer arguments contradict each other they cannot both be right, and so the *o'kheiluf* argument fails to arrive at a conclusion as to whether a worshiped animal may or may not serve as a sacrifice.

The evidence for fact **B** is a biblical verse, Deut. 23:19, but as with the last set of three *o'kheiluf* arguments in the Sifra, the evidence for fact **A** is a derash on the last two words of that verse. As pointed out already with regard to that set of three arguments, this is unlike the R. Ishmael school's *o'kheiluf* arguments where **A** (and **B**) are very well-known facts whose sources are usually explicit biblical verses. The lifting of a derash or a derivation to serve as a fact in another argument, as is the case with **A** serving as a fact in each of the two qal v'homer arguments of the *o'kheiluf* argument, is indeed a major difference between the schools of R. Ishmael and R. Akiva.[100]

The Sifra concludes that since it is not possible to decide between the original qal v'homer argument and the *kheiluf* argument, i.e. since it is not possible to derive from a qal v'homer that the worshiped animal is prohibited as a sacrifice, it was therefore necessary for the Torah to tells us, i.e *talmud lomar*, by inserting the exclusionary word *from* into the verse, that we are to exclude the worshiped animal. This entire passage from the Sifra is also quoted as a baraita in Talmud Bavli, on Temurah 28b.

Thus the Sifra seems to present this *o'kheiluf* argument just to show that qal v'homer does not provide an answer, and that it was therefore necessary for the Torah to use the phrase "*from* the cattle" the '*from*' serving to exclude worshiped animals from the cattle that may be sacrificed. As in the Sifra's gloss of the phrase *from the domestic animals,* the word *from* becomes a source for the law only because the law cannot be derived by qal v'homer.

There is an implicit principle of biblical parsimony here, in that there would be no textual hint planted in the Torah for deriving a law that could be derived without this encoded clue and just by reasoning from something else in Scripture as for example via a qal v'homer argument. And it is for this reason that qal v'homer needs to be eliminated as a possible way to obtain the law, before the proof from

---

[100] This is in line with criticism of *lamed min ha-lamed,* למד מן הלמד, which is found in the midrash of R. Ishmael's school but not recognized in the midrash of the R. Akiva school. The quoted rule means to imply that a new derivation may not be made which relies on the result of a prior derivation. See footnote 94 for my explanation of why the R. Akiva school was not interested in such a rule. For more on this principle in the R. Ishmael school see Yadin-Israel,*Scripture as Logos,* 88-93. See also Ishay Rosen-Zvi בין משנה למדרש: קריאה בספרות התנאית (Raanana: Open University), 2020, פרק 2, שער ב.

the exclusionary *from* rule can be applied as a source to learn out the law.

But this gloss, the gloss on "from the cattle," is different from the earlier gloss on "from the domestic animals," in that the qal v'homer arguments here that are initially tried, the two qal v'homer arguments of an *o'kheiluf* argument, are not bona fide qal v'homer arguments since they are not launched from known propositions. There is no evidence for or against claims **P** or **-Q**. The author is fishing for a qal v'homer argument that will connect two topics. And so the suggestion made above in the context of the gloss on "from the domestic animals," seems to apply here even more. The author, in first presenting an *o'kheiluf* argument, is appealing to the reader implying that he has the same concept of reasonable proof or justification as the reader. It is only because such reasonable derivation cannot be obtained that the author is reluctantly forced to identify some hermeneutical cues from which to derive the law from the Torah.

What we have learned from these last four *o'kheiluf* arguments of the Sifra that do not reach a conclusion

What we have seen in these last four *o'kheiluf* arguments from the Sifra, this last one and the previous set of three, demonstrates that the authors of these arguments did recognize qal v'homer reasoning as more obvious and natural than (at least certain applications of) the excluding *min* or a derivative *gezerah shavah*. These arguments suggest that when these authors offer more contrived derivations they do so out of commitment to finding some biblical source for the law in question after the most natural means have been exhausted.

In these arguments, there was no biblical evidence for any of the **P**, **Q**, **-P**, **-Q** claims; they were all guesses and therefore the *o'kheiluf* was unlikely to succeed. (In contrast, in a typical qal v'homer argument of either school, the Tanna sees the Torah as silent only on

171

whether the claim Q or -Q is true.) The author of the R. Akiva school may have engaged in these arguments despite the absence of any evidence upfront, as a sort of casting about approach. By engaging in *o'kheiluf* even without any biblical evidence in mind, the author is prompted to consider the claims **Q** and **-P** and whether either of them can be refuted in any way. In the Sifra one such argument [101]succeeds by recognizing, in the absence of any biblical evidence, an everyday fact that refutes **-P**.

But as to why the authors presented these ultimately unsuccessful *o'kheiluf* arguments that they first tried, the purpose seems to have been clearly rhetorical. The author was motivating a less compelling derivation of the law by first showing that more common methods failed. The authors thus demonstrate that they know what a reasonable derivation is and that they tried every possible qal v'homer argument they could think of before resorting to less obvious derivations of the law in question based on certain types of textual cues identified in the Torah.

Although few in number these arguments are fascinating, for one reason, because they are almost like journal entries by the authors describing their process of finding biblical proofs for laws they already know to be true and to which they are committed. The authors show that they are not only able to give coherent arguments but that they can distinguish between stronger and weaker arguments. The four passages suggest further that when these authors give arguments that are not as convincing it is only after trying and failing at more convincing avenues.

Now we turn to those *o'kheiluf* arguments of the Sfire Devarim, also of the school of R. Akiva, that likewise do not reach a conclusion.

---

[101] See Chapter Two, # 11.

FROM THE SIFRE DEVARIM:

Sifre Devarim, piska 244: Liability of the seducer if the victim is not a virgin or has previously been betrothed and subsequently divorced:
(In Chapter Two, # 12, 13, 14)

In the Sifre Devarim, piska 244, also of the school of R. Akiva, we find a set of three *o'kheiluf* arguments that arise in commenting upon Deut. 22:28 which deals with a man who rapes a young woman, a virgin, one who was not betrothed (*arusah*). In each of the three *o'kheiluf* arguments, phrases of the verse are analyzed with reference to the related verse in Exodus about the seducer of a young woman, a virgin who is not betrothed (22:15).

Unlike the previous *o'kheiluf* arguments discussed, the purpose of these is not to derive a law by choosing between two possible qal v'homer arguments or to show that qal v'homer will not work and another hermeneutical technique is needed to answer the question of law at issue. Rather, two of the *o'kheiluf* arguments here, #12 and #14 in Chapter Two, arise to show that a certain word in the verse about the seducer which might on first consideration be thought to be superfluous, is in fact needed. One argument shows this for the word 'virgin' and the other shows this for the phrase 'not betrothed'.

The Sifre begins each of the two derashot by asking whether a certain word is really necessary in the verse in Exodus. Could not the information it conveys, it asks, be learned out by qal v'homer reasoning from the related verse in Deuteronomy. To test this hypothesis the Sifre engages in a thought experiment whereby the word is omitted from the verse in Exodus. For example, in the first passage once the word "virgin" is removed from Exod. 22:15, the author can ask whether or not the verse, which discusses the reparation required of the seducer, applies whether or not his victim is a virgin. The altered verse and the verse in Deuteronomy allow a qal v'homer from the latter to the former but they also allow a qal v'homer in the other direction, and an *o'kheiluf* argument is set up to answer this question.

But the result of having removed the word from the verse from Exodus is that it is not possible to decide between the qal v'homer argument and its *kheiluf*. In other words, the *o'kheiluf* argument fails, leaving ambiguity about the law.[102] Once the omitted word is returned to the verse the ambiguity disappears. Thus the Sifre demonstrates that the word in question was not superfluous but was needed in the verse from Exodus and it is for this reason that the Torah included it. The Torah saw the confusion that could arise if that word was left out of the verse and therefore included it.

Unlike in the *o'kheiluf* arguments of the Sifra discussed above, the inability to decide between the first qal v'homer and the *kheiluf* does not arise because there is no evidence for either **P** or **-Q**. To the contrary, in each of the two *o'kheiluf* arguments, there is evidence for the claim **P**. **P**, in each case, is a reasonable reading of Deut. 22:28. While the verse provides evidence for **P** it is not an explicit statement of the contents of **P** and so **P** can be doubted. The conclusion of the first qal v'homer, **Q**, can therefore also be doubted. The *kheiluf* qal v'homer may thus be entertained and it concludes with **-P**.

At this point in the argument, after the set-up of the *o'kheiluf* argument,

Since **A**, **B** & **P** must-it-not-follows-that **Q** ?!

או חילוף

Since **A**, **B** & **-Q** must-it-not-follow-that **-P** ?!   (*) ,

each *o'kheiluf* argument of the R. Ishmael school continues by pointing out that **-P** contradicts the evidence that exists, inconclusive as it may be, for **P**. Since it contradicts this evidence, **-P** must be

---

[102] To follow the details see the argument as laid out in Chapter Two.

false. The *kheiluf* qal v'homer is therefore false and the remaining qal v'homer, the first qal v'homer, is the only viable possibility remaining and must therefore be true.

The two *o'kheiluf* arguments of the R. Akiva school in Sifre Devarim proceed differently. They engage in an expanded analysis as compared to the R. Ishmael arguments and as a result are not able to arrive at a unique conclusion. Specifically, upon reaching the conclusion **-P** in the *kheiluf* qal v'homer, the author pauses to consider whether there is another possible reading of Deut. 22:28 which supports **-P**. If such a reading is possible then **-P** does not contradict Deut. 22:28 and therefore **-P** cannot be declared false and the *kheiluf* qal v'homer is not refuted. The *kheiluf* then remains as a possibly valid qal v'homer argument. With two contradictory qal v'homer arguments as possibilities and no way to eliminate either, the *o'kheiluf* is unable to reach an answer.

In each of the two *o'kheiluf* arguments the author succeeds in finding another reasonable way to reinterpret Deut. 22:28 so that it does not contradict **-P**. Deut. 22:28 states, "[I]f a man finds a young woman, a virgin, who was not betrothed, and he grabs her and lays with her and they are found." The verse was first very reasonably understood by the author of the midrash as stipulating that only if the victim is a young woman and a virgin and is not betrothed are the penalties prescribed in the next verse, 29, imposed on the rapist. In the first *o'kheiluf* argument which focuses on the word *virgin*, **P** is the claim that the victim must have been a virgin in order for the penalties of verse 29 to be imposed on the rapist. When confronted with the conclusion **-P** of the *kheiluf* qal v'homer, that the victim need not have been a virgin in order for the penalties to be imposed on the rapist, the author suggests that perhaps the first interpretation of the function of the word "virgin" in Deut. 22:28 was incorrect and it should be interpreted instead as referring to the father in verse 29: "The man who lies with her shall give the father of the young woman fifty silver coins and she will be a wife to him, he may not ever send her away." That is, the specification "virgin" in 22:28 is not to be understood as a necessary condition for imposing on the rapist the penalties described in 29. But rather the word "virgin" in 28 refers to the father in 29, that only if the girl is a virgin is the payment made to the father, if the victim is not a virgin the payment is made directly to her. This possible reading is one that is in line with our modern reading sensibilities.

In the second *o'kheiluf* argument, where **P** is the claim that for the rapist to be liable (for the penalties described in 22:29) his victim may not have been previously betrothed and divorced, the author interprets the phrase "who was not betrothed" in Deut. 22:28 similarly to how the qualification "virgin" was interpreted for the previous *o'kheiluf* argument.[103] (See Chapter Two for full details.)

The remaining *o'kheiluf* argument of the three, #13 in Chapter Two, focuses on the word *naarah which* appears in Deut. 22:28, the case of the rapist, but not in Exod. 22:15, the case of the seducer. From the new claim **P**, that only if the victim was a *naarah* are the penalties of verse 29 imposed on the rapist, *o'kheiluf* seeks a conclusion about the seducer case. This *o'kheiluf* argument is very much like the other two with regard to the high level of analytical skill it demonstrates in seeking and finding a reinterpretation of Deut. 22:28 that could be consistent with the conclusion **-P** of the *kheiluf* qal v'homer.

Although a reasonable idea to try, the presence of the word *naarah* not just in 22:28 but also in 22:29 in reference to the father, "he shall give to the father of the young woman fifty silver coins," makes it difficult to interpret *naarah* in 22:28 as also referring to the father in 22:29. Thus the author concludes that the word functions in 22:28 as originally suggested by **P**, and that Deut. 22:28 therefore refutes **-P**. Hence unlike the other two *o'kheiluf* arguments, this one does reach a

___

[103] The phrase "who was not betrothed" is understood as meaning 'who wasn't betrothed and then divorced from the betrothal'. This interpretation is arrived at because the earlier verses 22:25-26 dealt with the rapist of a betrothed girl; he receives capital punishment. By considerations of biblical parsimony the phrase "who wasn't betrothed" cannot refer to that earlier case. See Chapter Two, #14 for fuller details.

conclusion. With -**P** refuted, the entire *kheiluf* is refuted. The first qal v'homer remains as the only viable possibility and the author declares it correct.

The consideration of another way to interpret the biblical evidence for **P** makes this *o'kheiluf* argument dialectically richer than the *o'kheiluf* arguments of the school of R. Ishmael all of which likewise reach a conclusion. It will be considered again later together with the one other *o'kheiluf* argument of the school of R. Akiva that does reach a conclusion. Most interesting is what all three of these arguments of the Sifre Devarim reveal about the exegetical style of the Sifre Devarim or perhaps of the school of R. Akiva more generally.

Sifre Devarim, piska 249: Mamzer/Ammoni & Moavi:
(In Chapter Two, #15)

There is a fourth *o'kheiluf* argument in the Sifre Devarim which also does not reach a conclusion, i.e. one qal v'homer argument cannot be chosen over the other. In fact both qal v'homer arguments are shown to be false. The proof texts used to refute the conclusion of each of the two qal v'homer arguments are not biblical expressions, but rather midrashim drawn from the grammar of biblical expressions. (There is no other more direct biblical evidence for the launching premises of the first qal v'homer or the *kheiluf* qal v'homer, i.e. for **P** or -**Q** than these midrashim.)

Focused on the prohibition in Deut. 23: 4-5, "[N]o Ammonite or Moabite shall be admitted into the congregation of the Lord; even the tenth generation shall never enter the congregation of the Lord," the passage in Sifre Devarim upholds midrashic proof that the restriction applies only to the males: The verse says *Ammoni* and *Moavi*, grammatically these are a male Ammonite and a male Moabite, respectively. The first qal v'homer in the *o'kheiluf* concludes that likewise the law restricting the *mamzer* refers only to males. This is refuted with the midrash that the word *mamzer*, is constructed from

177

mum zar, meaning foreign blemish and is thus gender neutral so as to apply to both genders.

The *o'kheiluf* fails and both qal v'homers are declared wrong because they contradict the midrashic answers to the question of which genders are intended in the Ammonite and Moabite restriction and which in the *mamzer* restriction. But both qal v'homer arguments in the *o'kheiluf* were drawn with respect to having or not having the property that the restriction under discussion is stated to be *ad olam*, meaning, forever.

Deut. 23:3 states, "A *mamzer* shall not enter the congregation of the Lord, even the tenth generation shall not enter the congregation of the Lord."

Deut 23:4 states, "An Ammonite or Moabite shall not enter the congregation of the Lord, even the tenth generation shall not enter the congregation of the Lord ever [*ad olam*]."

While
A = *About the mamzer it is not said [that he may not be admitted into the congregation of the Lord is] ad olam, i.e. forever,*
P = *Women are ruled upon as men, [i.e. a female mamzer may not be admitted into the congregation of the Lord]*
Therefore,
Since
B = *About Ammonites and Moabites it is said* ad olam *[meaning forever, that they may not be admitted into the congregation of the Lord]*
must-it-not-follow-that
Q = *Women Ammonites and Moabites are to be ruled upon as are the men [i.e. they should also be prohibited from admission into the congregation of the Lord]*
?!

O'kheiluf

178

While

B = *About Ammonites and Moabites it is said* <u>ad olam</u> *[meaning forever, that they may not be admitted into the congregation of the Lord]*,

-Q = *Women Ammonites and Moabites are not ruled upon as are the men [i.e., they are not prohibited from joining the congregation of the Lord].*

Therefore,

Since

A = *About the mamzer it is not said [that he may not be admitted into the congregation of the Lord is] ad olam, i.e. forever*

must-it-not-follow-that

-P = *Women are not to be ruled upon as men, [i.e. a female mamzer may be admitted into the congregation of the Lord]*

?!

With the failure of the *o'kheiluf* argument, the phrase *ad olam* in Deut. 23:4, no longer needed to drive a qal v'homer is left to serve the verse only with its plain meaning. The Sifra then sees the phrase "to the tenth generation" as unnecessary given the phrase *ad olam, forever,* in the verse. The presence of the latter in the verse makes the former unnecessary for its literal meaning, and therefore 'frees it up' in the language of the Sifra, *mufneh lehakish*, to execute a *gezerah shavah* which it goes on to describe.

The principle of *mufneh lehakish ladun gezerah shavah*, freed up to execute a *gezerah shavah*, is common in the midrash of the school of R. Ishmael where it serves the role of marking a word as not needed for the plain meaning of the text and therefore free or marked for a hermeneutic function, specifically to serve in a *gezerah shavah*.[104] In the midrash of the R. Akiva school the *mufneh lehakish* principle is only invoked twice.

---

[104] See Yadin, *Scripture and Logos*, 82-83.

In order for "to the tenth generation" to be *mufneh lehakish,* freed up of its function as contributing its plain meaning to the verse and able to serve another function, there must be another phrase in the verse that contributes the same information. The phrase *ad olam,* forever, certainly includes ten generations. But to the R. Akiva school the phrase *ad olam* can only free up the phrase "to the tenth generation" when the former serves no other function outside its plain meaning. (Otherwise both phrases would be needed, "to the tenth generation" for its plain meaning and "*ad olam*" for that other function.) This can only be true of the phrase *ad olam* once it is seen that it can no longer be considered the basis of a qal v'homer connecting the Ammonite and Moabite restriction to the restrictions on the *mamzer.*

The phrase "the tenth generation" is freed up to execute a *gezerah shavah*. The phrase is used with regard to the restriction on the Ammonite and the Moabite. (Deut. 23:4) and with regard to the *mamzer* (Deut. 23:3). Just as with regard to the former the verse says *ad alom*, meaning [the prohibition is] forever, so too the phrase "tenth generation" by the *mamzer* means *ad olam*, or forever.[105]

This *o'kheiluf* argument in the Sifre Devarim shows that the author is careful with the hermeneutical clues provided by the words of the Torah, careful not to waste any of them in order to derive as many laws as possible, and committed to the reading principle that one clue generates only one teaching.

---

[105] Notice that by thus establishing that the restrictions on the Ammonite and the Moabite and on the *mamzer* are to remain in force forever, the compelling logical force of qal v'homer in the *o'kheiluf* based on the fact that the phrase 'forever' as only mentioned for the Ammonite and Moabite is dissipated. That logic is no longer available to serve as a counter to the midrashic derivations of the gender restrictions on the two groups.

4.5: Two Arguments of the R. Akiva School that Do Yield an Answer

Earlier discussion concerned two of a set of three *o'kheiluf* arguments in the Sifre Devarim that occur in its analysis of Deut. 22:28. The remaining *o'kheiluf* argument of the three, #13 in Chapter Two, focuses on the word *naarah* and unlike the other two, it does reach a conclusion. This argument warrants a more careful examination as it is very different from the *o'kheiluf* arguments of the school of R. Ishmael all of which also reach a conclusion.

The word *naarah* appears in the verse from Deut. 22:28 about the victim of the rapist but does not appear in the verse from Exodus mentioned above (22:15) about the victim of the seducer. The Sifre Devarim asks, "How do we know that the passage about the seducer and his punishment only applies, as is the case with the rapist in Deuteronomy, when the victim is a young woman?" The Sifre first offers an *o'kheiluf* argument that begins with the following qal v'homer argument: Since the rapist, who has committed a far graver sin, is only liable if the victim is a young woman, as the verse says "young woman," must-it-not-follow *a fortiori* that the seducer should also only be liable if his victim is a young woman?!

Using the symbolization developed in Chapter One for the *o'kheiluf*, the propositions in the first qal v'homer argument may be labeled as follows:

While
A= 'Raping is a graver sin than seducing'
yet
P= 'The rapist is liable only if the woman is a young woman'.
Therefore,
Since
B= 'Seducing is not as grave a sin as raping' = **A**
must-it-not-follow-that
Q= 'The seducer is only liable when his victim is a young woman'

181

?!

A and **B**, which are identical, are known to be true.[106] There is biblical evidence for **P**, Deut. 22:28 specifically states "young woman." But the verse does not explicitly say 'the rapist only receives the punishment stated below if his victim is a young woman.'

Because the evidence for **P** does not meet the author's high standards, he is able to doubt the conclusion of the qal v'homer **Q** launched from **P**. He is therefore able to entertain a qal v'homer argument that begins with **-Q**. *O'kheiluf* ensues:

O'kheiluf

While
B = 'Seducing is not as grave a sin as raping'
yet
-Q = 'The seducer is liable whether or not his victim is a young woman'.
Therefore,
Since
A = 'The sin of the rapist is grave [as compared to the seducer]'
must-it-not-follow-that
-P = 'The rapist is liable whether or not his victim is a young woman'
?!

This author's standard of proof is very much comparable to that of half of the *o'kheiluf* arguments of the school of R. Ishmael: Sifre Bamidbar, piska 123, about work disqualifying a red heifer; piska 125, about the tent and the grave; and piska 126, about the dying person and the dying *sheretz*. In these three *o'kheiluf* arguments, there is

---

[106]There must have been a strong feeling that this is the case. The Sifre Devarim also gives a proof for **A** and **B**: the rapist sins against the girl's father and against the girl, while the seducer only sins against the girl's father.

reasonable biblical evidence for the respective claims **P** but not quite an explicit statement of the law.

The same high standard of proof is reflected in each of the other two *o'kheiluf* arguments on this verse in Sifre Devarim, piska 244. Those other two *o'kheiluf* arguments were engaged in order to show that a certain word was not superfluous in the Torah. For this third *o'kheiluf* argument on this verse (it is actually situated between the other two) the Sifre Devarim argues along the same lines as in the other two. Similarly to all of the *o'kheiluf* arguments of the R. Ishmael school, the Sifre Devarim proceeds to test conclusion **Q** with an *o'kheiluf* argument and the *kheiluf* qal v'homer concludes, as it must, with **-P**.

But this is where the similarity ends. In all of the cases of the school of R. Ishmael, the argument continues with what it sees as obvious: **-P** must be rejected because as stated earlier, there is some biblical evidence for claim **P** (on the basis of which the first qal v'homer was launched). Then since the *kheiluf* qal v'homer argument has thus failed, the first qal v'homer **Q**, by something like default, is declared true.[107]

In the case under study from the Sifre Devarim, the conclusion of the *kheiluf* qal v'homer is, **-P** = 'The rapist is liable whether the woman is a young woman or an older woman.' As with the cases mentioned above of the school of R. Ishmael, **-P** is viewed as a problematic conclusion because it contradicts evidence in the verse in support of **P** (which was the basis for the original qal v'homer argument). However, unlike the R. Ishmael cases, the Sifre Devarim does not then conclude that **-P** must be false because it contradicts the evidence that exists for **P** on the basis of which the original qal v'homer argument was launched. Instead it argues that perhaps the original thought that **P** is supported by the verse, was a result of misinterpreting the verse.

---

[107] Refer back to Chapter One for more patient explanation and especially for extensive analysis of the *o'kheiluf* argument in Example i.

The verse (Deut. 22:28) says, "[I]f a man finds a young woman, a virgin, one who was not betrothed, and grabs her and lies with her and they are found." But perhaps, the Sifre Devarim argues, the function of "young woman" in the verse is not to tell us that only if the victim of the rapist is a young woman besides also being a virgin and not betrothed, is the rapist liable for what follows in the next verse. Perhaps instead, the role of "young woman" in the verse is to indicate that the detail in the very next verse about the rapist's requirement to give to the victim's father fifty silver coins applies only if the victim is a young woman. That is, if the woman is older the rapist doesn't give the fifty coins to her father he gives them instead to her. The Sifre has found another reasonable interpretation for the detail "young woman" in the verse.[108]

This is something that the school of R. Ishmael does not seem to be able to do in the cases mentioned above (Sifre Bamidbar 123, 125, 126) or in any of the other o'kheiluf arguments. In general, it can be said that the R. Ishmael school would refrain from offering an alternate interpretation that relies on a reading of the Torah which is at variance with how people understand human speech. But this example from Sifre Devarim is not such a case. (The same can be said for the two other examples discussed earlier from Sifre Devarim, piska 244, based on the same verse.) The Sifre Devarim has offered an alternate understanding of the verse and of the verse that follows, that is in keeping with how people understand spoken language.

The Sifre Devarim then rejects this possible understanding of the function of "young woman" in the verse. It explains that the very next

---

[108] This is the same sort of argumentation that the Sifre Devarim applies in the two other o'kheiluf examples based on these two verses in Deuteronomy and Exodus discussed earlier. Namely, the argument that maybe the word virgin, or the phrase 'not betrothed' are in the verse concerning the rapist not to tell us that only in the case that the woman is a virgin and not betrothed is the rapist liable but to tell us that only in those cases that the woman is a virgin and not betrothed does the instruction in the verse that follows apply, i.e. that the rapist must give the fifty silver coins to her father (rather than to her).

verse, Deut. 22:29, says that the rapist "must give to the father of the young woman fifty silver coins." The words "young woman" in this last phrase serve that function: if the victim is a young woman the rapist should give the money to her father otherwise he must give it to the woman. Thus the phrase "young woman" in the prior verse 28 is not needed for providing this instruction and thus must retain the other simpler meaning.

Thus when the verse reads, "If a man finds a young woman....grabs her and lies with her," it is speaking only of a case when the act is committed against a young woman. This meaning contradicts -**P** and therefore -**P** must be false. Since the conclusion of the *kheiluf* qal v'homer is wrong, it is rejected and the original qal v'homer must be correct.[109] Just as in the cases of the R. Ishmael school, the *kheiluf* qal v'homer is rejected and the remaining qal v'homer argument, the original, is declared correct. The difference between this case from the Sifre Devarim and the cases of the school of R. Ishmael is the richer analytic treatment given to the *kheiluf* conclusion, -**P**, exhausting the possibilities that it may not be false.

What in fact all three *o'kheiluf* arguments from the Sifre Devarim, piska 244, also suggest is that unlike the school of R. Ishmael, these midrashists of the school of R. Akiva, are unlikely to draw conclusions in their *o'kheiluf* arguments. This is because, given their strong dialectical and analytical abilities, they may often find reasons why the claim -**P** need not be rejected. That is, they may find ways to reinterpret the verse that was earlier seen as biblical support for **P**.

---

[109] The concluding phrase in all the R. Ishmael *o'kheiluf* arguments which also appears in the other *o'kheiluf* argument of the school of R. Akiva which also reaches a conclusion, Sifra, on Lev.9:23, does not appear here. Instead of להחליף הדין אי אתה יכול, the expression used is דנתי חלפתי בטל או חילוף וזכיתי לדון כבתחילה.
The language is interesting, suggesting that the *kheiluf* was not just invalidated but realized to have been an error to even suggest because the evidence for claim P in light of the very next verse 29, as explained, was airtight and so the conclusion of a qal v'homer launched from it could not be attacked in this way.

They would then be without grounds to eliminate one of the two possible qal v'homer arguments in the *o'kheiluf* argument. In particular, it is not surprising that we do not see from the school of R. Akiva, *o'kheiluf* arguments like those mentioned above from the school of R. Ishmael, Sifre Bamidbar, piska 123, piska 125, piska 126.

The other *o'kheiluf* argument of the school of R. Akiva that also reaches a conclusion is from the Sifra, #11 in Chapter Two. Citing earlier scholarship by Jacob Nahum Epstein and others, Menahem Kahana in his 2006 paper "Halakhic Midrashim" claims that although the Sifra is known to be a work of the R. Akiva school, there are portions of the Sifra such as the Mekhilta de-Miluim (which covers Lev. 8:1- 10:7) which betray signs of authorship by the R. Ishmael school. In Chapter Two I argued against Kahana specifically for the *o'kheiluf* argument in the Mekhilta de-Miluim, Chapter Two #11. I showed that this argument has all of the signature marks of the *o'kheiluf* of the school of R. Akiva, distinguishing it from an *o'kheiluf* of the R. Ishmael corpus. (Specifically, there is no evidence at all for the launching claims of either qal v'homer, i.e. for either P or -Q. In addition, the source for fact A is not an explicit biblical expression or an everyday fact, instead it is a reasonable conclusion from Lev. 9:23. Lastly, the wording of the closing of the argument is very much like the other *o'kheiluf* arguments of the school of R. Akiva, distinct from the formula characterizing all those of the school of R. Ishmael.)

This *o'kheiluf* argument occurs in the Sifra's analysis of Lev. 9:23:

"And Moses and Aaron went into the Tent of Meeting, then they went out and blessed the people and the glory of the Lord appeared to all the people."

The verse makes clear that in leaving the Tent of Meeting, Moses and Aaron blessed the people. The Sifra understands and interprets this as a general rule, that whenever leaving the Tent of Meeting the priests must bless the people. This can be justified as the verse comes at the end of a seven-day ceremony inaugurating the priests over which Aaron presides as the senior priest.

The Sifra asks, "How do we know that arriving at the Tent of Meeting also requires [making] a blessing?"

The Sifra seeks to answer this question by drawing a qal v'homer from the claim that leaving requires washing the hands. But since there is no biblical evidence for this claim, the result of the qal v'homer can be doubted and the *kheiluf* qal v'homer can be entertained. To answer this question the Sifra engages in an *o'kheiluf* argument:

And it is din,
And since leaving which doesn't require washing requires blessing,
must-it-not-follow that coming which does require washing, requires blessing ?!

O'kheiluf

And since coming which doesn't require blessing requires washing,
must-it-not-follow that leaving which does require blessing, requires washing?

Presenting in translation, the labeling of the *o'kheiluf* argument as laid out in Chapter Two:

While
P = *Leaving [the Tent of Meeting] does not require washing up,*
A = *[Leaving the Tent of Meeting] does require [making a] blessing.*
Therefore,
Since
B = *Coming [to the Tent of Meeting] requires washing up*
must-it-not-follow-that
Q = *[Coming to the Tent of Meeting] requires [making] a blessing*
?!

O'kheiluf

While
-Q = *Coming [to the Tent of Meeting] does not require [making a] blessing,*
B = *[Coming to the Tent of Meeting] requires washing up.*
Therefore,
Since
A = *Leaving [the Tent of Meeting] does require [making a] blessing*
must-it-not-follow-that
-P = *[Leaving the Tent of Meeting] does require washing up*
?!

In this *o'kheiluf* argument, as is the case with all of the other *o'kheiluf* arguments of the Sifra (but never the case in any of the R. Ishmael *o'kheiluf* arguments) there is no biblical verse that can serve as evidence at all for any of the claims **P**, **Q**, **-P** or **-Q**. And therefore it would seem, as with the other *o'kheiluf* arguments of the Sifra, that the argument must fail: there is no biblical verse to refute either **Q** or **-P**.

When the *kheiluf* qal v'homer ends, as it must, with **-P** this conclusion cannot be refuted on the basis of biblical evidence for the launching premise **P** of the first qal v'homer. (Since there is no biblical evidence for **Q** or **-Q** the first qal v'homer also cannot be refuted with a biblical proof text.) With two contradictory qal v'homer arguments and no biblical evidence to refute either one of them, it is expected that the *o'kheiluf* argument would be unable to reach a conclusion and would therefore fail to answer the question of whether upon arriving at the Tent of Meeting it is necessary to bless the nation.

A and **B** represent facts, their sources are Lev. 9:23 and Exod. 30:19-20, respectively. (See Chapter Two, # 11, for more details.) Note how despite the unusual arrangement of the **P,Q**, **A** and **B**, in the argument, the Sifra had no trouble keeping track of which claims were which, that is, of which claims were the facts and which claims were the speculations and therefore to be negated in the *kheiluf* argument. This demonstrates understanding, great skill and experience in coming up with the *kheiluf* of an argument (which was shown in Chapter One to be related to the contrapositive).

Despite the absence of any biblical evidence for **P** or **Q** or **-P** or **-Q**, the *o'kheiluf* argument comes to a conclusion, as do all the other successful *o'kheiluf* arguments, by eliminating the *kheiluf* qal v'homer argument and thus leaving the original qal v'homer argument as the only possibility. But unlike all the other successful *o'kheiluf* arguments — all of the *o'kheiluf* arguments of the R. Ishmael school and the last *o'kheiluf* discussed of the R. Akiva school — this argument accomplishes this without a biblical proof text.

How does it eliminate the *kheiluf* qal v'homer without a solid proof text? This anonymous argument in the Sifra brilliantly steps outside the hermeneutical box in which it finds itself and considers the meaning of the different claims. (In Chapter Six, Rabbi Akiva is seen doing the same sort of thing but even more spectacularly in the single *o'kheiluf* argument found in the Mishnah.)

The *kheiluf* qal v'homer lands on the conclusion that 'leaving the Tent of Meeting requires washing up [hands and feet]'. Hand and feet washing is performed by priests to purify themselves to work in sacred space. This is why on arrival at the Tent of Meeting, Aaron and his sons wash their hands. But **-P** makes no sense because washing-up is a social/religious/cultic practice that is performed when going from secular space into holy space as preparation for entering holy space. Not vice versa. And therefore **-P** cannot be right and the *kheiluf* is rejected.

4.6: Conclusions: Disputing Heschel's Portrayal of the Two Schools

The first two chapters of this work demonstrated that *o'kheiluf* is a technical logico-linguistic expression whose meaning remains entirely consistent throughout its varied tannaitic sources.[110] In particular, it was shown that its meaning remains precisely the same throughout the works of the Midrash Halakhah regardless as to whether the work is one attributed to the school of R. Ishmael or to the school of R. Akiva.

Although the meaning of *o'kheiluf* and of the *o'kheiluf* argument is uniform everywhere it occurs, the uses to which it is put in the R. Akiva midrash are very different from its role in the R. Ishmael school.

The *o'kheiluf* arguments of the school of R. Ishmael all reach a conclusion. They are all honest attempts to derive the source of a law and they all follow the same format with no novelty at all. They are all also misguided. The authors engage in *o'kheiluf* because they are uncomfortable with the evidence for the premise from which the original qal v'homer argument is launched. The authors are then mistakenly reassured by the results of the *o'kheiluf,* that the premise, of which they were not originally confident, does merit stronger confidence. I analyze this faulty logic in the next chapter using Stoic logic.

---

[110] The one *o'kheiluf* argument to be found in the Mishnah is discussed in Chapter Six.

The *o'kheiluf* arguments of the school of R. Akiva on the other hand, are very different from this. Like those of the school of R. Ishmael these too are also anonymously authored. However, unlike the *o'kheiluf* arguments of the school of R. Ishmael, those of the Sifra have no evidence whatsoever for any of the claims that correspond to **P, Q, -P, -Q** in the symbolic formulation of the *o'kheiluf.*

For easy reference here again is the symbolic formulation of the *o'kheiluf* argument, (4') from Chapter One:

Since **A, B** & **P** must-it-not-follow-that **Q** ?!

או חילוף

Since **A, B** & **-Q** must-it-not-follow-that **-P** ?!   (4')

where **A, B** represent propositions known to be true, **P** represents a proposition whose truth is not established by strong biblical evidence. **-Q** is the negation of **Q** and likewise for **P.** [111]

Four out of the five arguments in the Sifra therefore fail to reach a conclusion and are followed by other derivations of the laws in question. This raises the question as to the author's purpose in including the failed arguments.

In the four *o'kheiluf* arguments in the Sifra, Dibbura de-Nedavah parsha 2 (Chapter Two #7) and Dibbura de-Khova, parshata 12 (Chapter Two #8, 9, 10) the authors are casting about looking for something that will prompt an answer to the question at issue. (They are thinking through the consequences that would follow if certain premises were in fact true.) As to why the failed *o'kheiluf* arguments are preserved and presented to the reader, the reason seems to be rhetorical, the author is trying to sell the reader on the successful derivation that follows. The author is beseeching the reader, 'I did not

---

[111] Thus for example **-P** is the statement 'It is not true that **P**'. Also, each of the two rhetorical questions sandwiching the phrase או חילוף represents a qal v'homer argument.

come up with this somewhat contrived derivation because I have no preference for a natural derivation. Quite the contrary, I first tried every reasonable derivation I could think of. Only when all those attempts failed did I locate clues in the Torah – placed there exactly because as I've shown a simple derivation was not possible – from which to derive the law.' Thus these *o'kheiluf* arguments are rather direct evidence that anonymous authors of this work of the R. Akiva school did indeed know what would constitute a reasonable derivation and could distinguish between convincing and less convincing midrash. Further, to the authors of the R. Akiva school, the failed qal v'homer arguments of the *o'kheiluf* arguments, are what justify their subsequent exploitation of hermeneutical cues to arrive at an answer to the question at issue.

In another *o'kheiluf* argument of the R. Akiva school from the Sifre Devarim, piska 249, this picture of desperately looking for hermeneutical clues to give biblical sources to as many laws as possible, is extended. The author wants to show himself to be not wasteful of these clues. He seems to hold the view that there are many laws for which to establish sources and perhaps limited hermeneutical markers in the Torah and therefore these markers should not be wasted on any derivation that does not require a marker. (This *o'kheiluf* argument uses the phrase *ad olam* as the basis of both qal v'homer arguments. Once the *o'kheiluf* argument fails it is therefore seen that this phrase is not needed to derive the law in question. Since it does not serve that function another function may be sought for it. Since its only meaning is therefore its literal meaning which makes another phrase in the verse superfluous, that other phrase is available to serve in a *gezerah shavah* establishing the source for another law.)

The *o'kheiluf* arguments of the school of R. Akiva in Sifre Devarim, especially the three in piska 244, demonstrate far more analytical acumen than we saw in the *o'kheiluf* arguments of the school or R. Ishmael. In each of the latter there is some evidence for claim **P**. When the *kheiluf* qal v'homer, as it must, results in **-P** which

192

contradicts the evidence for **P** with which the first qal v'homer began, the author of the R. Ishmael school folds, declaring that -**P** must be false. The school of R. Akiva does not conclude this way without first exhausting possibilities to reinterpret the evidence for **P** as evidence for something else instead.

In all but one case, these reinterpretations render -**P** plausible and not refutable and therefore the *o'kheiluf* cannot eliminate one of two possible but contradictory qal v'homer arguments. These explored possible reinterpretations are very plausibly in line with our own reading practices and they demonstrate further analytical skill than what we saw in the R. Ishmael *o'kheiluf* arguments.

In the one *o'kheiluf* argument (from piska 244) of Sifre Devarim where reinterpretation of the evidence for **P** does not succeed in rendering -**P** plausible, Chapter Two #13, the *kheiluf* qal v'homer argument is thereby refuted. The first qal v'homer is then by default declared correct. This *o'kheiluf* argument which does reach a conclusion does not suffer from the faulty logic, laid out in Chapter Five, found in all six *o'kheiluf* arguments of the R. Ishmael school that likewise reach a conclusion (by eliminating one of two possibilities.

The one other *o'kheiluf* argument of the school of R. Akiva that reaches a conclusion is from the Sifra, Mekhilta de-Miluim, #11 in Chapter Two. Like the other four *o'kheiluf* arguments in the Sifra, in this *o'kheiluf* argument there is no biblical evidence for any of the claims **P**, **Q**, -**P** or -**Q** of either qal v'homer argument. The argument manages to reach a conclusion by drawing evidence from outside the domain of biblical verses. By reflecting on the nature of the issue to be legislated, the author draws on a well-known fact from common religious practice. There is no similar *o'kheiluf* argument of the school of Rabbi Ishmael that succeeds by thinking outside the hermeneutical box. This *o'kheiluf* argument which reaches a conclusion does not suffer from the faulty logic that plagues the R. Ishmael *o'kheiluf* arguments each of which also reaches a conclusion. Specifically, the argument does achieve what it claims to achieve: it answers the question at issue with more justifiable confidence then the authors could claim for their originally posited qal v'homer solution.

Comparison of the 15 o'kheiluf arguments of the Midrash Halakhah has shown that those of the R. Akiva school demonstrate so much more analytical activity and ability than those of the R. Ishmael school. It is this richer and sharper analytic ability that accounts for why few of the o'kheiluf arguments of the R. Akiva school are able to eliminate one of the two possible qal v'homer arguments. Unable to do so, the o'kheiluf fails to reach a resolution on its own. In the Sifre Devarim the considered reinterpretations of biblical verses are in line with our own reading practices.

In the Sifra, more contrived proofs are offered only after all proof attempts by qal v'homer have been exhausted, thus demonstrating that the midrashists do share our sensibilities about proof and evidence and are led to less than perfectly convincing derivations of laws only after more common methods fail. The one argument in the Sifra where the o'kheiluf succeeds in yielding an answer to the question at issue shows impressive analytical creativity in thinking outside the set of possibly relevant biblical verses. There is no o'kheiluf argument of comparable cleverness and coherence in the Mekhilta or Sifre Bamidbar, both of the school of R. Ishmael.

At odds with Abraham Joshua Heschel's portrayal of the differences between the R. Ishmael and R. Akiva schools

Our careful study of the o'kheiluf arguments in the Midrash Halakhah has exposed important differences between those of the R. Ishmael and the R. Akiva schools. These differences are at odds with the picture Abraham Joshua Heschel painted of the two schools.[112]

---

[112]Abraham Joshua Heschel, *Heavenly Torah as Refracted through the Traditions*, translated by Gordon Tucker with Leonard Levin (New York: Continuum, 2007).

Heschel described the R. Ishmael school as being concerned with adhering to logic, while asserting that for the R. Akiva school adhering to logic was not a priority in interpreting the Torah.[113]

The *o'kheiluf* arguments do not bear out these characterizations.

First, as will be shown in Chapter Five the *o'kheiluf* arguments of the R. Akiva school are logically sound while those of the R. Ishmael school are not. The authors of the R. Akiva school are by far the better logicians. Second, contrary to Heschel's blanket assertions of flighty reading practices, the *o'kheiluf* arguments of the R. Akiva school demonstrate reading sensibilities that are very much like our own. (See especially the three in Sifre Devarim, piska 244.) The *o'kheiluf* arguments found in the Sifra preface derivations of the law in question by one of the formal hermeneutical cues of the R. Akiva school. These derivations were offered only after attempts by qal v'homer were exhausted. Those *o'kheiluf* arguments afford an opportunity to peer behind the curtain of the R. Akiva midrash machine. For the question of law they sought to answer, authors of the R. Akiva school first tried the most obvious and compelling method they could think of to derive an answer. Only after those attempts failed did they turn to a less natural and compelling method.

The forced derivations that Heschel writes of, not seen in the R. Ishmael midrash, do not expose a position of indifference to logic. Rather they are the result of a commitment, not shared by the R. Ishmael school, to obtain midrashic derivations for as many oral traditions as possible.[114] Since the R. Ishmael school is prepared to acknowledge that some oral traditions may not be biblically derived, they are not pressed to find the best possible derivation for an oral law when few options exist. Rather the R. Ishmael school only presents those derivations that they are able to make compelling.

---

[113] Ibid. pages 41, 44, 54, 57.

[114] See the early chapters of Yadin-Israel's *Scripture and Tradition* where he argues for a lot of anonymously authored midrash in the Sifra, that it represents "oral traditions camouflaged as midrash."

Is it simply a matter of philosophical taste that is at the root of why the R. Ishmael school is not engaged in the same project as the R. Akiva school? Can we completely chalk up the R. Ishmael school's abstention from this project to their distaste for the sometimes contrived derivation? It seems not. The o'kheiluf arguments suggest that the school of R. Ishmael simply did not have the analytical and logical chops of the school of R. Akiva.[115]

The o'kheiluf arguments in the Midrash Halakhah number only 15. This small number has allowed for close and complete analysis of the use of the same one type of argument in the two schools and thus for the appreciation of stark differences between the schools. Although small in number these arguments are close to equally divided between the works of the two schools. The type of thinking demanded in the o'kheiluf is amongst the logically most challenging to be found in the Midrash Halakhah and therefore should not be dismissed when taking a measure of the relative analytical and logical aptitudes of the two schools.

---

[115] From the analysis presented of the o'kheiluf arguments of the two schools, R. Akiva appears (if read as representing the works attributed to his school) as somewhat justified, even by our own lights, when he retaliates (Beraishit Rabbah 1:14) that it is not just a matter of taste that R. Ishmael does not derive all that he, R. Akiva, does: " 'It is not an empty thing for you' (Deut. 32:47) — meaning that if it is empty, it is because of *you*, because *you* do not know how to interpret it."

CHAPTER FIVE: Analysis of the *O'Kheiluf* Using Stoic Logic

In Chapter One after giving a precise definition of the phrase *o'kheiluf* and of the first part of the *o'kheiluf* argument, one complete *o'kheiluf* argument was carefully examined to discover what function it was meant to play in tannaitic literature. For this example from the R. Ishmael school and in Chapter Two, for all the other cases, it was seen that the law regarding a certain matter is sought and it is recognized that there is a different related topic but the law is not known regarding this topic either. However, the author's sense is that whatever the law is regarding one topic, the law should be the same for the other. The *o'kheiluf* argument attempts to determine between the two possible ways to decide the laws for the two related matters, which one is true, that is, which one is a correct derivation from the Torah. When the argument succeeds, it does so by eliminating one of the two possibilities as impossible and then by default declaring the other possibility as the correct derived law.

Chapter Four explored how the two schools, that of R. Ishmael and that of R. Akiva, use the argument. This chapter turns to analyze the logical coherence of the *o'kheiluf* argument. Does it do what it claims to do and reasonably eliminate one of two possible arguments so that the correct answer remains? This matter will be investigated and the question answered by the lights of the logicians and the rhetoricians of the age of the Tannaim, the Stoic philosophers. What is well known about the Stoics will be used to describe a conceivable conversation between a Stoic philosopher and a Tanna.

5.1: Analysis of Sifre Bamidbar, piska 123, using Stoic Logic

Suppose the Tannaim had presented to a Stoic philosopher the *o'kheiluf* argument from Sifre Bamidbar, piska 123, examined in depth

197

in Chapter One, Example i. Here is the beginning of it, the first qal v'homer argument, recopied with labels according to (4'), although the Tannaim had no such labels:

And since,
A *=the eglah [that is, a young calf] which is not disqualified by a blemish [from serving as the eglah arufah]*
P *= other labors are equated with a yoke [to disqualify the calf];*
with regard to
B *=the [red] heifer which is disqualified by a blemish [from serving in rites],*
does it not certainly follow that
Q *= other labors are to be equated with a yoke (i.e. having done work that does not involve wearing a yoke would also disqualify the calf from serving in the red heifer rite.)?!* **(1)**

It was shown (in fact in Chapter Two, for all the *o'kheiluf* arguments) that the author(s) of the *o'kheiluf* arguments were able to keep track in the two qal v'homer arguments of the claims, labeled in this work, **A**, **B**, **P** and **Q**, so that the established facts, labeled **A** and **B**, also appeared in the second or *kheiluf* qal v'homer argument while the less certain claims, labeled **P** and **Q**, were precisely the ones whose negations, **-P** and **-Q**, appeared in the *kheiluf* argument.

The Tannaim did not give the claims labels as I have done in this work, there is no such symbolizing in rabbinic literature. But they clearly kept these claims distinct in their minds and therefore when they formed the *kheiluf* argument, they succeeded in negating the correct claim. (See especially the discussion of the Sifra, on Lev. 9:23 in Chapter Four.) When they formed the *kheiluf,* they did so by starting from supposing the contradiction of the conclusion of the original qal v'homer, **-Q**, and arguing by qal v'homer reasoning. But they expressed surprise in each case, when the *kheiluf* qal v'homer argument was found to conclude with the proposition labeled here **-P**.

The framing of the *o'kheiluf* argument:

198

Qal v'homer I:

Chapter One confirmed for Example i, that the propositions labeled **A** and **B** are indeed facts; the Torah makes these statements explicitly. (Ashes of a burnt red heifer are sprinkled on a person as part of the ritual to purify him from the defilement he experienced through contact with a corpse.) It was also shown there that the proposition corresponding to **P** is not an expression of an explicit statement in the Torah. Rather, **P** expresses a possible reading of the biblical verse concerning the requirements on the calf taken to serve in the *eglah arufah* rite. (As discussed in Chapter One, this rite is so named because it involves breaking the neck of a calf and it is performed by the elders of the city in which the corpse of a murdered person is found but the identity of the murderer is unknown.) Thus the proposition in this example labeled **P** is indeed one for which there is some (inconclusive) biblical evidence but not proof or very strong evidence. It is for this reason that the Tanna engages in *o'kheiluf* and considers after the first qal v'homer concluding with **Q**, another qal v'homer, the *kheiluf* qal v'homer argument that starts off with the contrary as an assumption i.e that **-Q** is true. Along with the whole *o'kheiluf* example, the Tanna would have conveyed to the Stoic that he was certain of the truth of the propositions corresponding to **A** and **B** but only thought of **P** as possibly true.

An imagined Stoic philosopher analyzes the first qal v'homer argument in the *o'kheiluf* argument

Centuries earlier, in Athens, Stoic philosophers set their attention to analyze reasoning, particularly reasoning that drew consequences, i.e. reasoning that made use of the connectives 'if' and 'then'. Considering examples of everyday reasoning commonly believed to be sound, the Stoics set out to determine those features that these arguments have by virtue of which they were sound. Identifying these features led to a collection of forms that would characterize all valid arguments. Determining whether or not some new argument in question was valid then became a clearly defined program.

These logical discoveries retained a central place in Stoic philosophy for centuries. The Stoic philosopher in the days of the Tannaim, would have analyzed the argument the Tanna presented to him in the same way as he would analyze his own. He would set out to put the argument into the form of a syllogism.[116] Since every valid argument, according to the Stoics, can be put into the form of an inference schemata derived from the five indemonstrables, being able to do so for a specific argument is proof that it is a valid argument.[117]

The Stoic would say that the qal v'homer argument may be described as separable into two arguments, a rhetorical argument and a type 1 indemonstrable argument which is also known to us by the Latin name *modus ponens*. (It is not being claimed here that the Stoic would have imagined that the Tanna would have an easy time understanding this.)

A type 1 indemonstrable is one of the five basic valid arguments of the Stoics. It consists of three propositions, the first two of which are premises and the third is the conclusion; the first premise is a

---

[116] For the use of the word 'syllogism' and for more background see Suzanne Bobzien's entry "Ancient Logic" specifically the section "Stoic Syllogistic," in the *Stanford Encyclopedia of Philosophy*.
See also footnotes 227-229.

[117] The Greek Stoic philosopher Chrysippus (279-206 BC) viewed the following five valid inference schemata as basic or indemonstrable. 'First' and 'second' refer to propositions.
1. If the first, then the second; but the first; therefore, the second.
2. If the first, then the second; but not the second; therefore, not the first.
3. Not both the first and the second; but the first; therefore, not the second.
4. Either the first or the second; but the first; therefore, not the second.
5. Either the first or the second; but not the second; therefore, the first.
Using these five "indemonstrables" Chrysippus proved the validity of many inference schemata. The Stoics claimed that all valid inference schemata could be derived from the five indemonstrables.
See Benson Mates, *Stoic Logic*, (Berkeley: University of California Press, 1952) for more details and explanations.

conditional proposition. Using symbols to refer to propositions[118] the Stoics often represented the type 1 indemonstrable as follows, where the first two lines are premises and the last line is the conclusion:

If p then q

p

----

q

To say that a type 1 indemonstrable is a valid argument means the following. If an argument can be described as having two premises 'If p then q' and 'p', where p and q are shorthand for two specific propositions, then taking those two premises to be true would imply that it must be the case that 'q' is true.

Here is an actual Stoic example[119] discussed in Mates' *Stoic Logic*:

If it is day, then it is light. (the conditional)
It is day.   (its antecedent)
Therefore, it is light.   (its consequent)

Thus p is the proposition 'It is day' and q refers to the proposition 'It is light'.

The specific type 1 indemonstrable that the Stoic would be referring to in his analysis of the first qal v'homer argument above is the syllogism that follows below; note that indeed Premise 2 and the conclusion are contained in the qal v'homer argument. It is because this syllogism is a type 1 indemonstrable that the Stoic would be saying that it is a valid argument.

---

[118] This is expressed as the statement that the Stoics had a propositional logic rather than a term logic like Aristotle's logic. A proposition can be expressed as a sentence while a term is a noun or a predicate.
[119] See Benson Mates, *Stoic Logic*, 69. Sextus gives this example of a type 1 undemonstrated argument in Adv. Math. VII, 224.

Premise 1: If the *eglah* is disqualified by other types of work not involving a yoke, then the red heifer is disqualified by other types of work not involving a yoke.

Premise 2: The *eglah* is disqualified by other types of work not involving a yoke.

Conclusion: The red heifer is disqualified by other types of work not involving a yoke.

The rhetorical argument contained in the qal v'homer argument, the Stoic would tell the Tannaim, can be viewed as arguing for the acceptance of one of the premises that make up the above syllogism, Premise 1. In a syllogism all of the premises are accepted propositions, and from the premises the conclusion follows. That is, if the premises of a syllogism are true the conclusion must be true as well. Thus the rhetorical argument that argues for the acceptance of Premise 1 as a true proposition, is logically prior to the above syllogism. Once the rhetorical argument is accepted, Premise 1 is believed to be true. Then, Premise 1 taken together with Premise 2, which is asserted to be true in (1), yields via the syllogism, the conclusion that 'The red heifer is disqualified by work that does not involve a yoke'.

The rhetorical argument to show that 'If the *eglah* is disqualified by other types of work not involving a yoke, then the red heifer is disqualified by other types of work not involving a yoke', is based on qal v'homer or *a fortiori* reasoning that is advanced using the two other propositions contained in (1): 'The *eglah*.. is not disqualified by a blemish..' and 'The red heifer ..is disqualified by a blemish ..'. The listener is being urged to see that given that the *eglah* is not disqualified by a blemish while the red heifer is disqualified by a blemish, the disqualification of the *eglah* by work which does not involve a yoke would imply *a fortiori* that the red heifer is also disqualified by work which does not involve a yoke. Those two propositions in (1), 'the *eglah* is not disqualified by a blemish' and 'the red heifer is disqualified by a blemish', labeled as **A** and **B** respectively, have no place in the syllogism above: their only function is to support the acceptance of Premise 1 without whose acceptance there would be no syllogism. Once the rhetorical argument is accepted, the claim that 'if the *eglah* is disqualified by work which does not involve a yoke, then the red heifer is also disqualified by work which does not involve a yoke' loses the rhetorically questioning quality that it has in (1) and becomes the assertion, Premise 2.

Thus putting together all that is being argued in (1) as a Stoic would be imagined to see it, we have a valid syllogism (type 1 indemonstrable or *modus ponens*) along with a rhetorical argument arguing for the truth of Premise 1 of the syllogism:

Premise 1: If the eglah is disqualified by other types of work not involving a yoke, then the red heifer is disqualified by other types of work not involving a yoke.   ******

Premise 2:   The *eglah* is disqualified by other types of work not involving a yoke.

Conclusion: The red heifer is disqualified by other types of work not involving a yoke.

****** (Where Premise 1 is) argued by *a fortiori* reasoning to be true by virtue of the two facts (**A** and **B**):

> The *eglah* is not disqualified by a blemish.
> The red heifer is disqualified by a blemish.

The Tannaim might not have been at all interested in this imagined analysis of a qal v'homer argument by Stoic philosophers. To them the importance of the qal v'homer argument lies in the details of what has been described above as the rhetorical argument part and not in the syllogism part. The whole qal v'homer argument (unseparated into logical and rhetorical parts) (1), was organized so as to impress the listener with the logical force of the reasoning, and the Tannaim would likely have said that this form was just fine for analyzing just how good of a qal v'homer argument they had. The Tannaim are not known to have been interested in the study of logic proper and they would probably have said that for the types of arguments they are presented with and for those they come up with themselves, they can tell well enough whether the argument is fallacious or not without any Stoic or other formal logic.[120]

However, once the rest of the *o'kheiluf* argument is subjected to Stoic analysis, it will be seen that the Stoic logical analysis would have been very useful to the Tannaim for evaluating together the pair of qal v'homer arguments of the *o'kheiluf* argument.

Stoic analysis of the second (or *kheiluf*) qal v'homer argument

After the first qal v'homer, the *o'kheiluf* argument continues, introducing the second qal v'homer argument. As mentioned above,

---

[120] The type of fallacious arguments the Tannaim were confronted with were not intentionally deceitful, constructed to delude, as was the case with arguments presented by the Sophists to the ancient Greeks.
The rise of democracy in ancient Greece gave citizens the right to vote. Individuals who wanted to convince voters to vote a certain way might go so far as to employ Sophists to go around trying to convince people with their arguments. At times these Sophists would go to great lengths employing cunningly deceptive arguments in order to sway public opinion in a certain direction. It was therefore important to be able to distinguish between legitimate and invalid arguments presented, that is, to study logic. People therefore employed philosophers to teach their sons such things as the forms that logically valid arguments can take by virtue of which they are logically valid. For more background see, Michael Shenefelt and Heidi White, *If A, then B: How Logic Shaped the World* (New York: Columbia University Press, 2013):40-45.

the *kheiluf* begins by assuming the contradiction of the conclusion of the original qal v'homer argument:

Or [perhaps] the kheiluf,

And since the [red] heifer which is disqualified by a blemish, other labors are not equated with [the bearing of] a yoke; with regard to the eglah which is not disqualified by a blemish, must it not certainly follow that we should not equate other labors with [the drawing of] a yoke?!

As explained above with regard to the first qal v'homer argument, the Tannaim imagined the second qal v'homer as composed of distinct claims, as follows:

And since
the [red] heifer which is disqualified by a blemish,
other labors are not equated with [the bearing of] a yoke (i.e. the Torah prohibited the calf that is to serve as a red heifer from ever having drawn a yoke, but it did not prohibit it from having done any other work);

with regard to
the eglah which isn't disqualified by a blemish,
must it not certainly follow that
we should equate other labor with [the drawing of] a yoke ?!

Our Stoic philosopher would have analyzed the second qal v'homer argument as he did the first, putting it into the form of a type 1 indemonstrable syllogism (or as we would call it, *modus ponens*) along with a separate rhetorical part arguing for the truth of Premise 1':

Premise 1': If the red heifer is not disqualified by other types of work not involving a yoke then the *eglah* is not disqualified by other types of work not involving a yoke. ******

205

Premise 2': The red heifer is not disqualified by other types of work not involving a yoke.

Conclusion': The *eglah* is not disqualified by other types of work not involving a yoke.

****** (Where Premise 1' is) argued by *a fortiori* reasoning to be true by virtue of the facts: The *eglah* is not disqualified by a blemish.
                                    The red heifer is disqualified by a blemish.

Turning now to examine how the Stoic philosopher would relate his analyses of the two qal v'homer arguments in the *o'kheiluf*, to one another

To facilitate easy comparison, the Stoic analyses of the two, are presented again, one following the other:

Premise 1: If the *eglah* is disqualified by other types of work not involving a yoke then the red heifer is disqualified by other types of work not involving a yoke.   ******

Premise 2: The *eglah* is disqualified by other types of work not involving a yoke.

Conclusion: The red heifer is disqualified by other types of work not involving a yoke.

****** (Where Premise 2 is) argued by *a fortiori* reasoning to be true by virtue of the two facts: The *eglah* is not disqualified by a blemish.
                                    The red heifer is disqualified by a blemish.
Or [perhaps] the kheiluf

Premise 1': If the red heifer is not disqualified by other types of work not involving a yoke then the *eglah* is not disqualified by other types of work not involving a yoke. ******

206

Premise 2': The red heifer is not disqualified by other types of work not involving a yoke.

Conclusion': The *eglah* is not disqualified by other types of work not involving a yoke.

****** (Where Premise 2 is) argued by *a fortiori* reasoning to be true by virtue of the two facts: The *eglah* is not disqualified by a blemish.
The red heifer is disqualified by a blemish.

The Stoic would point out that Premise 1' is the contrapositive of Premise 1. That is, symbolizing Premise 1 by 'If **P** then **Q**', the symbolic representation of Premise 1' is then indeed 'If **-Q** then **-P**' where '-' means the negation or 'not'. (So that **-P** means 'not P'.) The Stoics also knew that the contrapositive of a conditional is equivalent to the original conditional. That is, a conditional statement is true, if and only if, its contrapositive is true. In symbols, 'If P then Q' is true, if and only if, 'If {not Q} then {not P}' is true.[121] Therefore our imagined Stoic would have said that the conditional statement Premise 1',

'If the red heifer is not disqualified by other types of work not involving a yoke, then the *eglah* is not disqualified by other types of work not involving a yoke'

is equivalent to the conditional statement Premise 1,

'If the *eglah* is disqualified by other types of work not involving a yoke, then the red heifer is disqualified by other types of work not involving a yoke.'

---

[121] For more details, see Suzanne Bobzien,"Logic" in *The Cambridge History of Hellenistic Philosophy,* ed. Kiempe Algra et al. (Cambridge: Cambridge University Press, 2006): 115; See also Suzanne Bobzien,"Logic," in *The Cambridge Companion to the Stoics,* edited by Brad Inwood (Cambridge: Cambridge University Press, 2006), 85-123.

I will refer to Premise 1 as being a qal v'homer conditional because it is a conditional statement whose truth is argued for by qal v'homer reasoning. If that reasoning is accepted, then Premise 1, the conditional, is considered true. If Premise 1 is a qal v'homer conditional, is Premise 1' also a qal v'homer conditional? Since Premise 1' is clearly a conditional statement, the focus of the last question is on the qal v'homer part, i.e. it is asking whether contraposition preserves the qal v'homer property of the original conditional. To put it in yet another way, if two conditionals are equivalent by virtue of one being the contrapositive of the other, and if one of the conditionals has the property of being a qal v'homer conditional, must the other conditional also be a qal v'homer conditional?

Our Stoic philosopher might have said that the Stoics had not formalized *a fortiori* reasoning so he cannot answer that question.[122] However, from the Stoic's above schematizations of the arguments separating the logical from the rhetorical arguments, one can see that in Premise 1 taken along with its rhetorical note on the right and in Premise 1' taken along likewise with its justification presented with an arrow, the same objects, the red heifer and the *eglah*, are being compared with respect to the same properties, the property of being disqualified by a blemish and the property of being disqualified by other types of work that do not involve a yoke. The Stoic would therefore recommend that attending to the particular objects and properties in a particular *o'kheiluf* argument, one verify that Premise

---

[122] His inclusion below of the phrase (translated) 'vice versa', means to this author that Cicero would have answered this question in the affirmative. Cicero discusses a norm (what we call *a fortiori*) which he calls *a minori ad maius*, in his Topics (4.23): 'What applies to the *maius* must apply also to the *minus* and vice versa.' For this translation see David Daube, "Rabbinic Methods of Interpretation and Hellenistic Rhetoric," *Hebrew Union College Annual* 22 (1949): 239-264, or Cicero's "Topica," ed.T. Reinhardt (Oxford: Oxford University Press, 2013).
Cicero (who lived before the Tannaim, 90 years before R. Ishmael, contemporaneous with Hillel the Elder) translated key philosophical terms from Greek into Latin and thus brought philosophy to the Romans. He wrote in Latin, some of his works were on Stoic logic.

1' with its justification presented with an arrow, is something he would indeed recognize as a qal v'homer conditional.

Thus Premise 1 and Premise 1' are equivalent conditionals, both are qal v'homer conditionals and the qal v'homer reasoning in both is based on the same two facts (indicated by respective arrows).

The *o'kheiluf* argument is thus not engaged in deciding between two different qal v'homer conditionals. The *o'kheiluf* argument is not an attack on the qal v'homer conditional of the qal v'homer it responds to. The *o'kheiluf* argument, in choosing between two qal v'homer arguments that contain the same qal v'homer conditional, is clearly committed to the single qal v'homer conditional.

Using symbols to represent propositions is logical technology of the Stoics that was useful for clarifying the structure of an argument. It is not a technology that the Tannaim had; when it was shown in Chapter One that the *o'kheiluf* could be represented symbolically by (4') everywhere it occurs, the point was made that the Tannaim could not do this. To clarify further the imagined Stoic's analysis, propositions in the above syllogisms will be replaced with symbols according to the symbolic representation of the *o'kheiluf*, (4'): **P** = 'The *eglah* is disqualified by other types of work not involving a yoke' and **Q** = 'The red heifer is disqualified by other types of work not involving a yoke'.
A = 'The *eglah* is not disqualified by a blemish [from serving in the *eglah arufah* rite]' and **B** = 'The red heifer is disqualified by a blemish [from serving in rites].'

Recall that with these symbols the first argument treated by the Stoic philosopher can according to (4') be symbolized by,

Since **A, B & P** must-it-not-therefore-follow-that **Q** ?!

where **A** and **B** are facts and **P** is a proposition for which there is some but not conclusive evidence, and ?! indicates that this is a rhetorical question. (i)

Or equivalently,

P, must-it-not-follow-that **Q**, by virtue of *a fortiori* reasoning using facts **A** and **B** ?! (ii)

The Stoic has just shown that for the particular example from the Sifre, (i) or (ii) can be formalized as a typical type 1 indemonstrable (or *modus ponens*) as follows on the left:

Premise 1: If **P** then **Q**.   argued by *a fortiori* reasoning to be

true by virtue of the two facts,

A = 'The *eglah* is not disqualified by a blemish'

B = 'The red heifer is disqualified by a blemish'

Premise 2: **P**

Conclusion: **Q**

Turning to the *kheiluf* qal v'homer argument, recall that according to (4') it can be symbolized by,

Since **A**, **B** & **-Q** must-it-not-follow-that **-P** ?!

where **A** and **B** are facts, and ?! indicates a rhetorical question (iii).

Or equivalently,

-Q, must-it-not-follow-that **-P**, by virtue of *a fortiori* reasoning using facts **A** and **B** ?! (iv).

The Stoic has also shown that for Example i from the Sifre, (iii) or (iv) can be formalized as the following type 1 indemonstrable i.e. *modus ponens* argument, on the left:

Premise 1': If -Q then –P   argued by *a fortiori* reasoning to be true by virtue of the facts **A** & **B** :

A = 'The *eglah* is not disqualified by a blemish.'

B = 'The red heifer is disqualified by a blemish.'

Premise 2': -Q

_____

Conclusion: -P

Recall the discussion in Chapter One of the resemblance between the *o'kheiluf* and the contrapositive. When put into syllogistic form as above, Premise 1 and Premise 1' make the point even sharper since one conditional statement is the contrapositive of the other.

As discussed above, the Stoic would say that Premise 1 is equivalent to Premise 1' because the contrapositive of a conditional statement is logically equivalent to the original conditional. (The contrapositive of a statement always has the same truth value as the original statement, i.e. one is true precisely if the other is true.) Therefore, he would say, Premise 1' may be replaced with the equivalent Premise 1 and hence the *kheiluf* qal v'homer argument may be formalized on the left by the following syllogism:

Premise 1: If **P** then **Q**   *a* argued by *a fortiori* reasoning to be

true by virtue of the facts:

A = 'The *eglah* is not disqualified by a blemish'

B = 'The red heifer is disqualified by a blemish'

Premise 2' **-Q**

Conclusion: **-P**

This last formalization of the second qal v'homer argument describes a type 2 indemonstrable argument, also known to us by the Latin name it was given in the Middle Ages, *modus tollens*.

The two arguments rewritten below side by side, with Premise 1' replaced with the equivalent Premise 1 and also referred to as the conditional premise, make what is going on in the *o'kheiluf* argument starkly clear; the *a fortiori* justification for the truth of the conditional premise noted on the right hand side of the last set of representations, is left out:

Syllogism part of qal v'homer Argument 1:	Syllogism part of qal v'homer Argument 2:
Type 1 indemonstrable (*modus ponens*)	Type 2 indemonstrable (*modus tollens*)
Premise 1: If P then Q.	Premise 1: If P then Q.
Premise 2: P	Premise 2: -Q
Conclusion: Q	Conclusion: -P

The *kheiluf* argument, represented by Argument 2, is a qal v'homer argument that starts from the negation of the conclusion of the original qal v'homer, **-Q**. The *kheiluf* was only entertained and considered possibly true by the Tannaim when they had less than complete confidence in premise **P** of the original qal v'homer argument. The biblical evidence for **P** was not quite explicit or complete. Because the Tanna was not certain of the truth of **P**, he was therefore uncertain of the conclusion to the argument, **Q**. And because he was uncertain of the truth of **Q**, he could entertain the possibility that **-Q** is true. The Stoic would say that this thinking was consistent with the syllogism, for in a syllogism the conclusion is only certain to be true when all of the premises are known to be true. The Stoic would say that since the truth of **Q** could be doubted, logic was not violated when the Tannaim began an alternative argument to Argument 1 beginning from the premise **-Q**.

Argument 1, is a type 1 indemonstrable argument (or an example of *modus ponens*) which represents the original qal v'homer in the *o'kheiluf* argument. Since a type 1 indemonstrable is one of the five fundamental valid arguments of the Stoics, our imagined Stoic recognized the syllogism of the original qal v'homer to be a valid argument. Likewise, because he considered the *kheiluf* argument to be correctly formalized by Argument 2 and because Argument 2 is a type 2 indemonstrable (or as we would say, an example of *modus tollens*) and therefore certainly a valid argument, the Stoic would have found the *kheiluf* to be a valid argument. Again, for an argument like *modus ponens* or *modus tollens* to be valid means that if the premises of the argument are true then so is the conclusion.

With the *o'kheiluf* argument the Tanna sought to determine which of the two qal v'homer arguments is true, i.e. consists entirely of true propositions. The arguments are attempts to answer a question of law on which the Torah is silent. The Tanna first constructed a qal v'homer argument to answer the question by relating the issue to another similar-appearing issue in the Torah. The Torah is also not

213

explicit on this point of law with regard to the other topic. The two topics, the red heifer and the *eglah arufah* and the requirements on the two, strike the Tanna as related. He therefore felt that the law about the type of work that would disqualify one should be the same for the other. Properties of the two subjects made the Tanna believe that the relationship establishing that the type of work should be the same for both is *a fortiori*.

The Tanna was uncertain of the truth of his first qal v'homer argument because he was uncertain of the truth of the premise **P**. There is biblical evidence for **P** but it is not quite explicit. This led him to consider another possible qal v'homer, the *kheiluf*. The original qal v'homer argument and the *kheiluf* qal v'homer seem to be the only cogent qal v'homer arguments the Tanna can think of that relate the relevant features of the two subjects, the *eglah arufah* and the red heifer. Therefore the Tanna wanted to decide which of the two arguments describes the truth.

The Stoic has shown that both Arguments 1 & 2, which represent the two qal v'homer arguments respectively, share the same conditional premise, Premise 1. Therefore the stipulation that one of the two arguments must be true, implies commitment to the truth of Premise 1. Hence the *o'kheiluf* argument cannot be seen as a challenge to the conditional premise, Premise 1, of the original qal v'homer argument. Because Argument 1 is a valid argument and Premise 1 is stipulated to be true, if **P** is true then **Q** must be true. The same point regarding Argument 2 holds: if **-Q** is true then **-P** must be true. The Stoic would say that Arguments 1 & 2 cannot both be true, i.e. contain only true propositions, because **P** & **Q** being true is inconsistent with **-Q** & **-P** being true.

Saying that the conditional premises of the two arguments, Argument 1 & 2, are contrapositives of one another and therefore equivalent, can be expressed in terms of the qal v'homer arguments, as saying that the two qal v'homer ideas are really the same. Specifically, the two qal v'homer arguments deal with the same subjects, the red heifer and the *eglah arufah* and the question of whether they are disqualified from serving in their respective rites by work other than the drawing of a yoke. The *a fortiori* drawn from one case to the other is with respect to the property that the red heifer has the added restriction that it need be blemish-free to qualify for serving in the rite, while the *eglah arufah* is not subject to this restriction.[123]

In considering the *kheiluf* argument as a candidate for the correct way to argue, the Tanna finds to his apparent surprise that it concludes with (what corresponds with) **-P**. The *o'kheiluf* argument continues, declaring that the *kheiluf* argument cannot be true because **-P** cannot be true as it contradicts the weak biblical evidence supporting **P** on the basis of which the original qal v'homer was launched. Since **-P** must be false the *kheiluf* argument must be rejected and the Tanna declares the remaining qal v'homer argument therefore to be true.

The Stoic in commenting on the Tanna's reasoning would say that if the Tanna accepts the evidence for **P**, believing it to be undeniable despite being weak evidence so that therefore in the absence of any additional evidence **-P** cannot be true, then he is correct in declaring the *kheiluf* qal v'homer to be false. And if the Tanna is committed to one of the two qal v'homer arguments being true, then as he declares, the remaining qal v'homer must be true. The Stoic would also point out that the reasoning that gave rise to the *o'kheiluf* was sound as well. Specifically, the Stoic would say that the Tanna's reasoning was in line with the syllogism, the valid Argument 1, that represents the qal v'homer argument. Because the Tanna was not certain of the truth of **P**, since the evidence supporting it was not strong enough, he was not obligated to accept the conclusion **Q** of the qal v'homer argument represented by Argument 1. In a valid argument or a syllogism the truth of the premises compels the conclusion, but if **P** which is Premise 2 is not certainly true then one cannot say that all the premises are true. The Tanna was therefore logically free, according to *modus ponens*, to entertain the possibility

---

[123] See Chapter One of this work for a fuller exposition and analysis of Example i.

that **-Q** was true and to launch a different argument from that possibility.

The Stoic would point out that although the Tanna was justified in attempting an argument that began with the premise **-Q**, in choosing that argument to be specifically the *kheiluf,* the Tanna unknowingly also assumed the same conditional premise as the original qal v'homer argument. As Argument 2 makes clear the *kheiluf* argument besides taking **-Q** as a premise, has the same conditional premise, Premise 1', as the original qal v'homer argument. Argument 2 is a type 2 indemonstrable or *modus tollens* argument, and from those two premises, '**-Q**' and 'If **P** then **Q**', the conclusion must always be -**P**. Thus if in the first qal v'homer, as is the case, the Tanna felt that the evidence backing **P** was insufficient but yet could not be dismissed, then regardless of the particular meanings that the particular example gives the symbols, the Tanna would have to reject the *kheiluf* qal v'homer as false since it must conclude with **-P**.

Thus the Stoic would say that when a Tanna constructs a qal v'homer argument from a premise **P** in whose truth he has some but only weak confidence, the Tanna must find the *kheiluf* qal v'homer to be false. This is regardless of the degree of confidence the Tanna has in **P**, as long as he feels that the confidence is undeniable. That is, the refutation of the *kheiluf* argument is because it must conclude with **-P** and has nothing to do with the particular evidence for the particular value of **P** in the example. The refutation of the *kheiluf* cannot be viewed as thereby strengthening the evidence in support of **P** and that is the Tanna's error.

The Tanna's Error

The Tanna thinks that by eliminating the *kheiluf,* what he sees as the other possible and relevant qal v'homer argument relating the red heifer and the *eglah arufah,* he has strengthened the case for the original qal v'homer argument. The premise **P**, in whose truth he lacked confidence because the biblical evidence supporting it is weak, made him hesitant about the original qal v'homer argument. Ruling out the *kheiluf* qal v'homer because it concludes with **-P**, and thus contradicts the weak biblical evidence for **P**, makes the Tanna confident about the truth of **P** and of the whole first qal v'homer argument. The Tanna concludes repeating the original qal v'homer argument this time as a declarative statement, without the original rhetorically-questioning elements in its expression. The Tanna no longer feels the need to convince, for he believes he has established the original qal v'homer as correct.

The Stoic would point this out as the Tanna's serious error. The elimination of the *kheiluf* should not have given the Tanna any increased confidence in the truth of **P**. This is because the *kheiluf* by virtue of the validity of *modus tollens* must result in **-P**. From *modus ponens* and *modus tollens*, Arguments 1 & 2 respectively, it is clear that whatever evidence exists for **P**, irrespective of its strength or weakness, is contradicted by **-P**. Thus the discrediting of the *kheiluf* qal v'homer because it concludes with **-P** does not give any more weight to the biblical evidence for **P**. Considering the *kheiluf* is irrelevant for the purpose of strengthening or weakening the case in favor of the original qal v'homer argument.

According to the Stoic philosopher, the result of this error is that the Tanna is led to have more confidence in the truth of **P** than he would otherwise have had. The Tanna concludes that his original qal v'homer is correct and he puts forth a law based on a biblical source which by his own lights he should have viewed as he originally did, as insufficient for establishing the law in question. Had the Tanna understood the Stoic's analysis, he would have sought some other source and method to establish the law in question.

5.2: Stoic Logical Analysis of the R. Ishmael School

Our imagined Stoic has analyzed only one *o'kheiluf* argument of the R. Ishmael school. All of the other five *o'kheiluf* arguments of the R. Ishmael school function similarly. They proceed because there is only weak biblical evidence for the launching premise of the original qal v'homer argument, the premise that the Stoic would label Premise 2. The result of considering the *kheiluf* qal v'homer argument is the realization that it concludes with the contradiction of the above mentioned evidence. It is therefore eliminated as a possibly true qal v'homer argument. Consequently only the original qal v'homer argument remains as a viable candidate. This gives the author sufficient confidence in the latter to declare it true.

The Stoic's analysis of these other *o'kheiluf* arguments and his remarks would therefore have been very similar to his treatment of the above example. The Stoic would report that in all six *o'kheiluf* arguments the authors were misled into endorsing sources for six different laws that by their own lights they would have viewed as insufficient and therefore sought other interpretive means by which to decide (or derive, depending on how we understand the author's project[124]) the laws in question.

---

[124] Whether the project of Midrash Halakhah was to derive law from the Torah or to give biblical support to oral traditions has been a matter of long standing debate. (See Yadin, *Logos as Scripture,* 1, for discussion and references. He cites J.N. Epstein's *Prolegomena to Tannaitic Literature* as the most influential work arguing the latter position, that the oral traditions (as those cited in the Mishnah) came first and midrash arose to buttress those traditions.)

Stoic analysis of an *o'kheiluf* argument of the Rabbi Ishmael school that does not involve qal v'homer reasoning

The Stoic's criticism of the Tannaim, is essentially that they did not know that what Argument 2 describes is a valid argument, i.e. that if one knows that 'P implies Q' and that -Q is true, then it must be the case that -P is true, regardless as to what propositions are assigned to the symbols P and Q. The reader may feel that this criticism is unfair, that perhaps the Tannaim did know this informally but only had trouble with this reasoning in the *o'kheiluf* situations because these situations are complicated by involving *a fortiori* reasoning as well. In other words, what the Tannaim did not recognize is that 'P, therefore is it not *a fortiori* Q?!' likely implies '-Q, therefore is it not *a fortiori* -P ?!'. The reader might suggest that we refrain from concluding from this that the Tannaim would not have recognized that 'P, therefore Q' implies '-Q, therefore -P'.

Additionally, and more fundamentally, a reader might be skeptical of the likelihood that our imagined Stoic would offer the analysis in the last section. She might argue that since the Stoics had not formalized *a fortiori* reasoning, our imagined Stoic would be unwilling to analyze an *o'kheiluf* presented to him by his friend the Tanna. This is certainly possible. But what is being tested here is the assumption that the Tanna was concerned about the legitimacy of the *o'kheiluf* argument, that he knew enough about the existence of Stoic logic to recognize that there were logical issues involved in the *o'kheiluf* argument and that it is for this reason that he would have sought out the Stoic philosopher. (Further, since the Tanna would have known that the phrase *o'kheiluf* introduced the *kheiluf* qal v'homer argument he would very likely have had a whole list of *o'kheiluf* arguments to show the Stoic.)

When the Stoic would have demurred because he did not want to hear about a qal v'homer argument, the Tanna might have pressed on with the following *o'kheiluf* argument because it does not involve any qal v'homer arguments and this argument the Stoic should have been willing to engage with. The Stoic analysis of the following *o'kheiluf* argument will address the two possible objections described above that might occur to our reader.

Sifre Bamidbar, piska 155, deals with Num. 30:14, which expresses that a husband may annul vows a wife takes that would cause her to suffer. (The midrash hashes out the range of what could be considered causing the wife suffering.) The Sifre also points out that Num. 30:17 on the same topic, implies by the phrase 'between a man and his wife' that the husband has rights specifically over vows on matters between the two of them. Since the verse also states "between a father and his daughter" the same is certainly true of the father's rights.

In the absence of any other biblical statements the Sifre surmises that Num. 30:14,17 are a full specification of the vows a husband may annul. With regard to the father's rights, the phrase in Num. 30:17 is the only biblical reference to a class of vows that the father may annul. The Sifre takes for granted that the father also may annul any vow his daughter takes that would cause her suffering. After all, it would be a very strange law indeed that would allow a father to annul some of the vows his daughter takes but not those that would cause her suffering.

But because the Torah does not spell out this right to annul any vow the daughter takes that would cause her to suffer, as it does for the husband, and since the Torah does not contain much more than a general statement that the father annuls vows, the Torah could be understood as broadly allowing the father to annul any vow his daughter makes. The Sifre wants to know whether, on the contrary, what it surmised about the husband is true about the father's rights also, namely, that those two classes of vows are the *only* vows the father may annul. An *o'kheiluf* argument ensues to answer this question:

We have that the husband may annul only the vows his wife makes that regard matters between the two of them or matters that would cause her to suffer. From whence do we know that the same applies to her father?

Behold, the husband annuls and the father annuls,
Just as the husband [may] only annul vows [his wife makes] that regard matters between the two of them or regard matters that would cause her to suffer so too the father [may] only annul vows between the two of them or regarding matters that would cause her to suffer.

Or [perhaps] the Kheiluf,

Behold, the father annuls and the husband annuls,
Just as the father [may] annul any vow [she makes] so too her husband [may] annul any vow she makes.

Our Stoic would analyze these arguments as follows:

Premise 1: If the husband annuls only the vows [of the wife] concerning matters between the two of them or matters that would cause her to suffer then the father may annul only her vows concerning matters between the two of them or matters that would cause her to suffer. ******
Premise 2: The husband annuls only the vows of the wife concerning matters between the two of them or matters that would cause her to suffer.

Conclusion: The father may annul only vows she makes concerning matters between the two of them or matters that would cause her to suffer.

****** This premise is argued to be true on the basis of the facts from the Torah: Both the husband and the father are said to annul vows the woman makes.

The *Kheiluf* argument:

Premise 1': If the father may annul any vow she makes then the husband may annul any vow she makes.   ******
Premise 2': The father may annul any vow she makes.

———————————————

Conclusion': The husband may annul any vow she [his wife] makes.

****** This premise is argued to be true on the basis of the biblical facts: Both the husband and the father may annul vows the woman makes.

Num. 30:17 is understood as saying that a father may annul any vow his daughter takes regarding matters between the two of them. Common sense dictates that since the father may annul (at least) some vows his daughter makes, these must certainly include those vows the daughter takes to cause herself suffering. Therefore the only negation of Conclusion that could possibly be true is Premise 2'. [125]

---

[125] As explained in Chapter Two, Conclusion = {The father annuls vows concerning matters between him and his daughter.} and {The father annuls vows the daughter takes that would cause her suffering.} and {There are no other vows the daughter takes that the father may annul.}. We can abbreviate this as,
Conclusion = {first} and {second} and {third}. There are a number of statements that can be described as the negation of Conclusion. They are any combination of the three assertions where at least one of the three is negated. But since {first} is true and {second} is true, any negation of Conclusion arrived at by negating either {first} or {second} or both, must be false. Thus the only negation of Conclusion that could possibly be true is the statement '{first} and {second} and not {three}'. This statement could be rephrased as 'The father annuls vows his daughter takes on matters between the two of them and vows that she takes that would cause her to
222

Premise 1' is the contrapositive of Premise 1.
Conclusion' negates or contradicts Premise 2.[126]

Assigning labels according to (4') in order to make the arguments clearer yields:

P= 'The husband annuls only the vows of the wife concerning matters between the two of them or matters that would cause her to suffer.'
And
Q= 'The father may annul only vows she makes concerning matters between the two of them or matters that would cause her to suffer.'

According to the Stoic the first argument may be represented by

Argument 1:
Premise 1: If **P** then **Q**
Premise 2: **P**
Conclusion: **Q**

And the *kheiluf* argument may be represented by

Argument 2:
Premise 1': If **-Q** then **-P**
Premise 2': **-Q**
Conclusion': **-P**

---

suffer and some other vows.' But without further biblical specification of what these 'some other vows' could be they must be interpreted as 'all vows'. Thus a possible negation of Conclusion (which could possibly be true) is 'The father may annul any and all vows his daughter takes.' This is precisely the content of Premise 2'.

[126] We continue along the lines in the last note. Because we know from Num.30: 9, 14, 17 that the husband may annul any vow his wife makes regarding matters between the two of them and any vow that would cause her suffering, and because these are the only biblical specifications of the vows the husband may annul, of all the possible negations of Conclusion' the only one that could possibly express a truth is Premise 2.

Because conditionals are subject to the law of contraposition, the Stoic would say that Premise 1 and Premise 1' are equivalent as conditionals. And since conditionals are all they are, they are equivalent. Period. (There is no issue here of Premise 1 being a qal v'homer conditional and therefore there is no question as to whether it follows necessarily that Premise 1' is also a qal v'homer conditional.) Thus Argument 2 can be expressed with Premise 1 replacing Premise 1'. The Stoic would point out that Argument 1 is a type 1 indemonstrable and that Argument 2, in this latter form, is a type 2 indemonstrable.

Presenting the arguments again with Premise 1' replaced with the equivalent Premise 1:

Argument 1:   Argument 2:

Premise 1: If **P** then **Q**   Premise 1: If **P** then **Q**

Premise 2: **P**   Premise 2': **-Q**

Conclusion: **Q**   Conclusion': **-P**

Using his Arguments 1 & 2, the Stoic could explain the essence of what the Tanna has done in the o'kheiluf argument, after presenting the kheiluf. The Tanna recognized that (what the Stoic has labeled) Conclusion' contradicts Premise 2 for which there is biblical evidence, albeit not explicit nor conclusive. Num. 30:14 specifies one class of vows the husband may annul and Num. 30:17 refers to a broad second such class. In the absence of any other biblical specifications these two classes would seem to define precisely which vows are referred to in Num. 30:9 where it says the husband may annul his wife's vows and describes the timetable for doing so. It is from this evidence for assessing completeness that the Tanna originally launched the first qal v'homer argument. The Tanna realized that Conclusion' must be false because it contradicts this assessment, and therefore the *kheiluf* argument is not true. Thus only Argument 1 remains as a possibly true argument. Argument 1 is then declared true.

The Stoic would explain to the Tanna, as follows:

'You started your first argument from a premise, Premise 2, of which you were not fully confident because the biblical instructions are not explicit. Therefore, you were correct in your concern about the truth of the conclusion of that argument. That is, when put into the form of Argument 1, you were not very confident of what is referred to there as Premise 2 and therefore you could not be certain of Conclusion. Argument 1 is a valid argument, but the Conclusion expresses a truth only if both of Premises 1 & 2 are known to be true.'

'Because Conclusion could not be known to be true, it was possible to entertain the possibility that a negation of Conclusion was true, specifically the **-Q** = {The father may annul any vow his daughter makes}. You were correct about that. And so you sought to launch a new argument starting from the possibility that **-Q** was true. That was also fine. But the new argument you constructed, the *kheiluf* argument, accurately represented by Argument 2, had the feature that {Premise 1'} = {Premise 1} because Premise 1' is the contrapositive of Premise 1 (and vice versa). This is something you did not recognize.'

'Thus correctly construed, in both the original and the *kheiluf* argument, you were committed to the same Premise 1. That is, given that you were taking the position from the start that one of these two arguments must be correct, and since both arguments had the same Premise 1, it follows that you were committed to Premise 1 being true. Another way to put this, the stipulation at the start that one of these two arguments must be correct can equivalently be framed as the stipulation that Premise 1 be true.'

'Thus in the final representations, Argument 1 and Argument 2, it is clear that if Premise 1 is by stipulation true, then if **P** is true it will follow that **Q** is true, but if **-Q** is true it will follow that **-P** is true. Also it should be clear that Argument 2 is in no way an evaluation of the evidence for Argument 1. That is, regardless of the strength of the evidence for **P**, if it is supposed that **P** is true then Argument 1 will conclude with **Q**, and Argument 2 will always conclude with **-P**. Thus Argument 2 concluding with **-Q** is in no way an affirmation of the evidence for **P**. Whatever evidence you had for **P** which was the basis for launching an argument from **P**, has not because of Argument 2 been affirmed to be any stronger than what you originally thought it to be.'

The Stoic would conclude, 'This is finally the biggest error in the *o'kheiluf* argument: your incorrect belief that you engaged in two different arguments and that the second or *kheiluf* argument, represented by Argument 2, in contradicting your original evidence for **P** strengthens the evidence you originally had for **P**. The truth is that your original argument is fine but if you were uncomfortable with the evidence for the claim from which it was launched, claim **P**, you cannot remove the basis for that discomfort. You have executed an argument based on a claim with weak scriptural support by your very own standards. If you insist on firmer scriptural support for ruling in favor of **Q**, you should seek a different derivation of **Q**.'

Thus the imagined Stoic in his analysis of this *o'kheiluf* argument which does not involve qal v'homer reasoning would lay bare the same shortcomings he was seen pointing out regarding the more typical *o'kheiluf* argument which does involve qal v'homer reasoning.

The Stoic views an *o'kheiluf* argument as essentially a comparison of the two statements 'P, therefore Q' and '-Q, therefore -P'. In his analysis, the Stoic philosopher replaces each of the two statements with a syllogism, two different *modus ponens* arguments. Making use of the law of contraposition, the Stoic philosopher shows through his analysis that the *o'kheiluf* does not present a choice between two different arguments but rather a choice between a *modus ponens* and a *modus tollens* that share the same conditional premise.

5.3: Stoic Logical Analysis of the R. Akiva School

As discussed earlier, the *o'kheiluf* arises in both schools under the same set of circumstances, namely, insufficient confidence in the truth of the launching premise of a qal v'homer (what below is Premise 2). The Tannaim did recognize that the conclusion of an argument could be no more reliable than the degree to which the premises of the argument were reliable. With insufficient confidence in a premise, they could not be confident of the truth of the conclusion of the argument.

The Stoic would say that like the *o'kheiluf* of the R. Ishmael school, the two qal v'homer arguments of the *o'kheiluf* of the R. Akiva school can each be described as a syllogism along with a rhetorical argument in support of the conditional premise. Like the R. Ishmael school, the R. Akiva school did not seem to know that a conditional statement and its contrapositive are equivalent (one is true if and only if the other is true) and that therefore the first qal v'homer argument and the *kheiluf* share the equivalent conditional premise.

Argument 1: First Qal V'homer	Argument 2: *Kheiluf* Qal V'homer
Type 1 indemonstrable (*modus ponens*)	
Premise 1: If P then Q ***	Premise 1: If -Q then -P ***
Premise 2: P	Premise 2: -Q
Conclusion: Q	Conclusion: -P

***argued by *a fortiori* to be true on the basis of facts A & B.

In either argument, if the two premises are true then so is the conclusion. In taking the position that one of the two arguments must be true, the author of the *o'kheiluf* is committed to the truth of the conditional premise, Premise 1. Thus Q is true precisely if P is true, and -P is true precisely if -Q is true. Therefore in deciding which one to uphold as true, the first qal v'homer or the *kheiluf*, all the author needs to consider is his evidence for P and his evidence for -Q.

Of the Sifra

In the five *o'kheiluf* arguments of the Sifra, there is no biblical evidence for (or against) P or -Q. Therefore it is not very surprising that four of them fail: the author cannot choose between the two contradictory arguments, the first and the *kheiluf*, which one of the two must be true. One *o'kheiluf* argument does succeed and it does so by refuting -P not with a biblical proof text but with a fact drawn from everyday life.[127] Since this fact, once recognized, is strong evidence in support of P, this *o'kheiluf* argument does not suffer from the logical shortcomings that the Stoic found in all of the R. Ishmael examples. Namely, in those others the author is not justified in

---

[127] Sifra, Mekhilta de-Miluim, see Chapter Two, #11. It was pointed out that in this *o'kheiluf* argument as well as the other four in the Sifra, there is no biblical support at all for the launching claim P of the first qal v'homer argument nor for the launching claim -Q of the *kheiluf* qal v'homer. This is a signature feature of the R. Akiva school and not found at all in the R. Ishmael arguments (*o'kheiluf,* as well as other arguments). (The R.Ishmael *o'kheiluf* arguments are all launched from claims for which there is strong biblical support, which yet does not meet the very high standard of the R. Ishmael school for sufficient support.Therefore *o'kheiluf* ensues.) This *o'kheiluf* argument of the Sifra fits very well with the other four and is therefore, like those, most likely also authored by the R. Akiva school. It is hard to imagine that this argument could have been composed by the R. Ishmael school as Menahem Kahana suggests in his 2006b paper published in *The Literature of the Jewish People in the Period of the Second Temple and the Talmud. Volume III: The Literature of the Sages* (New York: Brill, 2006): 83-87.

believing that the initial evidence in support of P is strengthened by the *o'kheiluf.*

In the successful *o'kheiluf* of the Sifra[128], setting up the *o'kheiluf* argument helped the author reach an answer to the motivating legal question even though there was no biblical evidence for Premise 2 or Premise 2'. With the *kheiluf* qal v'homer concluding with -P, the author was stimulated to seek a way to refute -P and he found one. (Perhaps without the *o'kheiluf* the author could not see that a good way to establish that Premise 2, P, is true is by showing that -P must be false.) The other four *o'kheiluf* arguments of the Sifra that were also launched from premises for which there was no biblical evidence might have been engaged in exploratively with the hope of bringing to mind some fact that would be useful, as did happen in the one successful case.

Chapter Four argued that the four failed *o'kheiluf* arguments served the rhetorical function of justifying what followed in each case: a less natural method was applied to resolve the question of law after the more common and natural method of qal v'homer via *o'kheiluf* was exhausted and failed. The Stoic could point out that this rhetorical strategy should not have been as compelling as the authors hoped, because the *o'kheiluf* is not really an engagement with two different qal v'homer ideas but really with only one (as the sharing of Premise 1 in both Arguments 1 & 2 makes clear).

In presenting the failed *o'kheiluf* argument to answer the question at issue and then resorting to a less natural method based on some hermeneutical cue, the author was seeking acceptance for his less-than-compelling derivation by impressing upon the audience or his readers that he had first tried every qal v'homer he could think of and only after such sensible attempts at derivation failed did he resort to a less-compelling derivation. That less-compelling derivation is made more compelling in the eyes of the reader when it is seen as the best

---

[128] Ibid.

in a dearth of other possibilities. But since the *o'kheiluf* argument is really only one qal v'homer idea, the authors in the Sifra did not really apply exhaustive efforts before applying a hermeneutical rule. What they really did first is try one single qal v'homer idea. (And even that attempt was from the start not promising because with no biblical evidence for P or for -Q, i.e. for Premise 2 or Premise 2', there was little chance of being able to show that Argument 1 or Argument 2 was true.) Thus with the *o'kheiluf* arguments of the Sifra the R. Akiva school presented less exhaustive attempts than even they thought they were presenting.

Of the Sifre Devarim

In the *o'kheiluf* arguments of the Sifre Devarim the authors have biblical evidence for P but not what meets their high standard for conclusive evidence. Their standard of proof and evidence is very much like that of the R. Ishmael school. When the *kheiluf* qal v'homer concludes with -P as the Stoic has explained earlier that it must, the authors do not continue with the format seen in the R. Ishmael argument of pointing out that -P contradicts the biblical evidence for P and therefore must be false. Like the R. Ishmael school, they too do not seem to know that the *kheiluf* qal v'homer must conclude with -P and so the conclusion reached prompts them to consider: is it necessarily true that the biblical evidence for P makes -P impossible?

They consider the possibility that their original interpretation of that verse was not justified. If they can reinterpret what was seen as the biblical evidence in support of P so that it does not contradict -P then the *kheiluf* qal v'homer would still be possibly true. In three of the *o'kheiluf* arguments of the Sifre Devarim the authors suggest cogent reinterpretations of a verse. In two of those, further examination of the verses further strengthens the reasonableness of their reinterpretation. With the evidence reinterpreted so that it does not contradict -P, the *kheiluf* qal v'homer is not refuted and remains a possibility. With two possible and contradictory qal v'homer arguments and no way to decide between them, the *o'kheiluf* fails to reach an answer to the legal question that prompted engagement with *o'kheiluf*. (This serves the author's purpose, as it justifies the need for the explicit biblical phrase that in thought was omitted from the relevant verse at the start of the argument. For further discussion see Chapter Two, # 12-14.)

The Stoic would not have much criticism for the authors of the *o'kheiluf* arguments of the Sifre Devarim. Even though the authors do not understand *a priori* that the *kheiluf* must conclude with -P, when they do reach that result (by thinking through the content rather than the form of the argument) they are stimulated to check whether their evidence for P is incontrovertible. In two cases the reinterpretations of the evidence are reasonable. In the third case, the reinterpretation is shown to not be justified by other verses considered and so no opportunity is seen to save the *kheiluf* qal v'homer. The argument continues on to a resolution.

This third case in Sifre Devarim, piska 244, is prompted by the question of whether or not the seducer in Exod. 22:15 faces penalties only if his victim is a young woman, a *naarah*. The first qal v'homer launched is from the claim P, based on Deut. 22:28, that the penalties that follow in 22:29 are only imposed on the rapist if his victim was a young woman. But the evidence is only suggestive, not explicit. The verse says, "[I]f a man finds a young girl, a virgin, who was not betrothed, and he seizes her and lies with her and they are found." The next verse, 29, describes the reparations he must make: "Then the man who lay with her shall pay the father of the virgin who was not betrothed 50 silver coins and she will be a wife to him and he may never send her away."

The *kheiluf* qal v'homer concludes as it must with -P. But like the other two *o'kheiluf* arguments in piska 244, the author does not — as do all 6 *o'kheiluf* arguments of the R. Ishmael school — rush to point out that -P is contradicted by the evidence for P on the basis of which the first qal v'homer was launched. But rather, faced with the fact that the *kheiluf* qal v'homer has concluded -P, the author considers whether it is possible to reinterpret Deut. 22:28 such that instead of serving as suggestive evidence for P it serves as reasonable evidence for -P. Following in the same vein as the other two arguments in piska 244, the author suggests that perhaps the reference of *naarah* is not to the conditions under which verse 29 follows for the rapist but rather its reference is to the father in verse 29. That is, if the victim is a young woman then the rapist gives the fifty silver coins to her father instead of to the victim herself. But the author realizes that this is not a reasonable reading of the word *naarah* in verse 28 because *naarah* is repeated with regard to the father, "he gives to the father of the *naarah* 50 silver coins." The word *naarah* in 29 in the phrase containing "father" serves that function most reasonably and so (also very reasonably) it is not the function of the word *naarah* in 28. The reinterpretation of Deut. 22:28 is seen as not plausible. Thus the first interpretation of Deut. 22:28, the only one that is still viable, P, gains more support. Since the conclusion -P contradicts that reading of Deut. 22:28, it is refuted.

The argument continues with the R. Ishmael format. Since the conclusion of the *kheiluf* qal v'homer is refuted, that entire qal v'homer is refuted. The first qal v'homer, which is the only one left standing, is declared (by default) correct.

As with this last *o'kheiluf* argument, all of the *o'kheiluf* arguments of the R. Ishmael school were likewise launched because the authors did not find (the less than explicit) evidence for P convincing. The result of all the R. Ishmael school's *o'kheiluf* arguments however is, as the Stoic has explained, unjustified increased confidence in the strength of that same biblical evidence for P and therefore unjustified increased confidence in the first qal v'homer that is launched from P. (Earlier in this chapter, in the Stoic's analysis of Example ii, it was shown why this increased confidence is unjustified. The Stoic explains that by logic, specifically *modus tollens*, the *kheiluf* must always conclude with -P regardless of the particular contents of P. And whatever evidence exists for P, whether very weak or very strong, will contradict the contents of -P.)

Not so with this *o'kheiluf* argument in the Sifre Devarim. The *o'kheiluf* results in another plausible way to read the biblical evidence for P, followed by a demonstration that this second reading is unjustified. With this second reading eliminated, the first reading (whose plausibility cannot be refuted) seems even more likely to be true. With justified increased confidence in P the author asserts that the first qal v'homer launched from P is correct.

I have been referring to an *o'kheiluf* argument as successful if it is able to declare one of the two qal v'homer arguments considered, the original or the *kheiluf*, correct. As it happens the arguments are ordered such that when the *o'kheiluf* succeeds it is the first qal v'homer that turns out to be the correct one. The successful *o'kheiluf* succeeds by strengthening the initial support for the launching premise P of the first qal v'homer. The evidence for P was originally not viewed as sufficiently strong and it is for this reason that complete confidence in the conclusion of that qal v'homer argument, Q, was lacking and *o'kheiluf* ensued. Thus the successful *o'kheiluf* argument succeeds by strengthening the evidence in support of P.

The Stoic has shown that although in the *o'kheiluf* arguments of the R. Ishmael school, the author thinks he justifies his increased confidence in the truth of P, he is mistaken. He is not justified in having any more confidence in the truth of the launching premise P than he had at the start. In this sense these arguments are not logically coherent. But this is not true for the *o'kheiluf* arguments of the R. Akiva school. In the two *o'kheiluf* arguments that succeed (i.e that are not determined to require the application of another method), one from the Sifra, the other from Sifre Devarim, piska 244, the authors are justified in believing that they have established more support for P than they had at the start and that they therefore have reason for increased confidence in the truth of the first qal v'homer argument. The only successful *o'kheiluf* arguments that are indeed coherent in this sense, that are not logically in error, are these two of the R. Akiva school. The other two *o'kheiluf* arguments in Sifre

233

Devarim, piska 244, also of the R. Akiva school are fully coherent in this sense as well. The remaining *o'kheiluf* arguments of the R. Akiva school, those that do not succeed without turning to another method, are not logically problematic.

5.4: Summary of Conclusions

As the Stoic has shown, the qal v'homer argument can be viewed as a combination of a syllogism along with a rhetorical argument for the truth of its first premise, the conditional premise, by *a fortiori* reasoning from two facts. If both premises of the syllogism are true statements then the conclusion is a true statement. Thus the truth of the qal v'homer argument, that is, that its conclusion is true, can be challenged by challenging the truth of either of its two premises.

As pointed out a number of times above, the *o'kheiluf* arises in the (unusual) situation where the tannaitic author of usually a qal v'homer argument did not have strong confidence in his evidence for the claim that lines up with Premise 2 of the syllogism part of the argument. He was therefore logically justified in lacking confidence in the truth of the conclusion of the argument, i.e. in the truth of the conclusion of the representing syllogism. The author was therefore further justified logically in entertaining the possibility of the contradiction of the truth of that conclusion, that is, he was justified in attacking the conclusion of the original qal v'homer argument. The Stoic's analysis shows that the *o'kheiluf* argument challenges the conclusion of (what is usually) a qal v'homer argument (but sometimes instead a just-as argument) by challenging the truth of Premise 2 while remaining committed to the truth of the conditional premise, Premise 1.

In the Stoic's analysis, the *o'kheiluf* arguments of the R. Ishmael and the R. Akiva schools betray blanket ignorance of basic Greek and Stoic logic. These arguments would not have been so constructed had the Tannaim known (or known enough to ask the Stoic philosophers about) in particular, the contents of *modus tollens* and that taking the contrapositive of a conditional statement does not

234

change the truth value of the conditional statement. The Tannaim of the two schools were not able to recognize that the *kheiluf* qal v'homer must conclude with the negation of Premise 2, regardless of the details of the case.

For the R. Ishmael school, this ignorance cost their *o'kheiluf* arguments logical coherence. Lacking confidence in the biblical evidence for Premise 2, **P**, they engaged in *o'kheiluf* launched from the negation of the conclusion of the first qal v'homer.[129] When that second qal v'homer concluded with **-P** (as unbeknownst to them it must) they asserted that it must be false because of the original biblical evidence, weak as it might be, on the basis of which the first qal v'homer was launched. The R. Ishmael school, in each *o'kheiluf* made the logical mistake of thinking that their evidence for **P** had been strengthened by using it to refute **-P**. These *o'kheiluf* arguments did not accomplish what they set out to do: they did not replace a tentative answer to the question sought with an answer in which they were indeed justified in having more confidence.

The *o'kheiluf* arguments of the R. Akiva school do not suffer from logical incoherence. When the *kheiluf* qal v'homer concluded (again as unbeknownst to the Tannaim it must) with **-P**, this served to prod the authors to check whether their original biblical evidence in favor of **P** was irrefutable. Sometimes they found that it was not. In the case where they found that reinterpretations of the biblical evidence could not be maintained, they then had no basis for supporting **-P**. Their subsequent increased confidence in their original (reading of the)

---

[129] For easy reference, here again is the symbolic formulation of the *o'kheiluf* argument, (4') from Chapter One:

Since **A, B** & **P** must-it-not-follows-that **Q** ?!

או חילוף

Since **A, B** & **-Q** must-it-not-follow-that **-P** ?!   (4')

where **A, B** represent propositions known to be true, **P** represents a proposition whose truth is not established by strong biblical evidence. **-Q** is the negation of **Q** and likewise for **P**. (Thus for example **-P** is the statement 'It is not true that **P**'.) Further, each of the two rhetorical questions sandwiching the phrase או חילוף represents a qal v'homer argument.

235

evidence in support of **P**, after having considered other ways to interpret that evidence, was then indeed justified. Thus the *o'kheiluf* argument of the R. Akiva school, when successful, did achieve what it was aimed to do: it answered the question at issue with more justifiable confidence then they could claim for their originally posited qal v'homer solution.

As described above, the *o'kheiluf* arguments of the R. Ishmael school are not logically sound while those of the R. Akiva school are logically justified. Comparison of the *o'kheiluf* arguments of the two schools, by the lights of the imagined Stoic philosopher, has exposed the R. Akiva school as by far the superior logicians. *O'kheiluf* argumentation involved some of the logically most challenging reasoning of the tannaitic era and while the *o'kheiluf* arguments number only fifteen, their dispersal across all tannaitic literature reveals that this type of argument was well-entrenched in the reasoning of that period.[130]

5.5: Addendum: Other Sorts of Tannaitic Attacks on Qal V'Homer

In tannaitic literature the *o'kheiluf* is not the only sort of attempt to challenge a qal v'homer argument. Unlike the *o'kheiluf* which is a challenge to Premise 2, most attempts at challenging a qal v'homer argument seek to refute Premise 1, the qal v'homer conditional. These other ways of attacking a qal v'homer argument are logically simpler and unlike the *o'kheiluf* are fully logically coherent. It is in fact not uncommon to see a qal v'homer argument which is offered as a derivation of a certain law, legitimately challenged, shown to be false, and then followed by a different derivation of the law at issue.

By applying the Stoic's analysis of the qal v'homer presented in the context of the *o'kheiluf* argument, to one common type of attack on a qal v'homer argument which begins with the word 'No!', it will be easy

---

[130] See Conclusions to Chapter Four for more on this point and how it relates to Heschel's view of the school of R. Akiva.

to demonstrate that this type of attack presents a legitimate challenge not to Premise 2, as in the *o'kheiluf*, but to the conditional premise, Premise 1.

The following is one typical example of this type of attack from Sifre Bamidbar, Parashat Naso, piska 26:

Speaking of the nazirite, the words לאביו ולאמו לא יטמא in Num. 6:7 are redundant if interpreted literally, "For his father and his mother he will not defile himself [with their burial]." This is because the previous verse states, "All the days of his abstinence (נזרו) for the Lord he shall not come into contact with the dead."

The Sifre explains how these words should be interpreted so as not to be expressing a restriction already mentioned in an earlier verse: *For his father and mother the nazirite must not defile himself but he must defile himself for a mait mitzvah.* The Sifre continues with justification for this derash by showing that the obvious qal v'homer argument that one would assume to be the way to derive the nazirite's obligation in *mait mitzvah* is in fact defective and therefore some other means of derivation is needed.

The author challenges the qal v'homer that draws from the case of the high priest to that of the nazirite to conclude that the nazirite should also be obligated in *mait mitzvah*. A *mait mitzvah, mait* meaning a dead person, and *mitzvah* meaning a religious obligation, refers to the obligation to immediately tend to the burial needs of a neglected corpse found along one's path.

The qal v'homer argument goes as follows:

And given that the High Priest whose holiness is an eternal holiness, behold he defiles himself for a mait mitzvah,
the nazirite whose holiness is just for a limited time,
must it not follow that he should become defiled for (the sake of) a mait mitzvah ?!

The qal v'homer is immediately challenged, the rhetorical question is answered not with the expected 'Yes, of course' but instead as follows:

No!
If you said regarding the High Priest [that he becomes defiled for the mait mitzvah], well he does not [have to] bring a sacrifice to purify himself after defilement, that is why he defiles himself for a mait mitzvah. Would you not say regarding the nazirite who must bring a sacrifice to purify himself after defilement, that he should not defile himself for a mait mitzvah?!

The Stoic would analyze the qal v'homer argument as follows:

Premise 1: If the High Priest defiles himself for a *mait mitzvah* then the nazirite defiles himself for a *mait mitzvah*. *****
Premise 2: The High Priest does defile himself for a *mait mitzvah*.

Conclusion: The nazirite defiles himself for a *mait mitzvah*.

***** by virtue of *a fortiori* reasoning from the following facts:

The High Priest's holiness is eternal.
The nazirite's holiness lasts only for the period of time during which he is a nazirite.

In terms of this analysis, the challenge to the qal v'homer is specifically a challenge to the truth of Premise 1. Premise 1 is believed to be true on the basis of *a fortiori* reasoning regarding the facts about the duration of the High Priest's holiness as compared to that of the *nazir*. (The implication being that since the High Priest's holiness is for a far longer period than that of the *nazir*, the former is holier than the latter.) Premise 1 is challenged by the contention that the durations of their respective holiness are not the relevant properties by which to relate the obligations of these two individuals. The relevant properties instead are the measures that each would

238

have to undergo to purify himself after the defilement: the *nazir* would have to bring a sacrifice while the High Priest would not require such an involved process. It would therefore seem that obligating the High Priest, who would not need to bring a sacrifice to purify himself after defilement from a corpse in *mait mitzvah,* does not imply that the *nazir* who would need to bring such a sacrifice should be similarly obligated in *mait mitzvah.* Thus the law obligating the *nazir* in *mait mitzvah* could not be derived by what would appear at first as the most compelling qal v'homer argument.

Therefore, it is argued, the teaching is derived from the otherwise redundant specification that the nazirite, "for his father and his mother he will not defile himself [with their burial]" (Num. 6:7). In other words, these superfluous-seeming words were included in the Torah as a source to derive the law about *mait mitzvah* because this law could not be reached through qal v'homer or other reasoning from the Torah minus the superfluous-seeming phrase interpreted as a source for this law.

CHAPTER SIX: *O'Kheiluf* in the Mishnah

6.1: The Same Symbolic Formulation

The phrase *o'kheiluf*, או חלוף, occurs exactly once in the Mishnah, in M. Pesahim 6:2. It is often translated[131] as 'or the reverse', which is a context-dependent phrase i.e. from the context one can determine what 'the reverse' must mean, but not without a context. Although it has never been recognized before this work, the phrase או חלוף actually does have a precise context-independent meaning which it shares with each of its other occurrences in tannaitic works (where the spelling is או חילוף).

Chapter Two contained a complete listing and labeling of all those other 15 occurrences, one of which was analyzed in depth in Chapter One and others were examined further in Chapter Four. Each occurrence of the phrase או חילוף in the Midrash Halakhah is preceded by a qal v'homer argument[132] and is followed by another qal

---

[131] See for example the ArtScroll Publications translation of Talmud Bavli, Tractate Pesahim 69a¹.

Herbert Danby's translation of the phrase *o'kheiluf* in his *The Mishnah* (Massachusetts: Hendrickson Publishers, 2012) is much more problematic than the vague 'the reverse'. He translates it on p.143 of the Second Division: Moed, as 'Nay, on the contrary!' 'The contrary' does not convey some sort of reversing of the different parts of the argument. Rather 'the contrary' would seem to apply to a single proposition, presumably the proposition that sprinkling overrides the Sabbath restrictions. Further, 'Nay' is simply wrong: R. Akiva is not saying 'No, you are in error, it is as follows.' He is saying 'or', that is, he is pointing out that there is another equally likely possibility.

[132] Except for one of the cases, Sifre Bamidbar, piska 155, (Chapter Two, #6) where it is a just-as argument that precedes and another just-as argument that follows the phrase או חילוף :

'A & B, just-as P so too Q'

או חילוף

v'homer argument.[133] I have been referring to the two qal v'homer arguments together with the phrase between them, as the first part of the o'kheiluf argument.

The central claim of this chapter is that the single occurrence of או חילוף in the Mishnah has exactly the same meaning as do all of those that appear in the Midrash Halakhah and that the (first part of the) argument in which the phrase appears can be symbolized precisely as was shown in Chapter Two for all those other 15 occurrences whether of the R. Ishmael school or the R. Akiva school:

Since A, B and P must-it-not-follow that Q ?!

או חילוף

Since B, A and -Q must-it-not-follow that -P ?!   (1)

where A and B represent biblical or well known facts and P represents a proposition for which the evidence is less than compelling. Each of the two expressions ending in '?!' is a rhetorically-questioning qal v'homer argument.[134] (The author has no evidence to support or refute Q.)

As shown in the earlier chapters, in the Midrash Halakhah the sources for facts A and B are biblical verses or common sense (which is also the case for the more usual qal v'homer arguments that are not part of o'kheiluf arguments). In the midrash of the R. Akiva school though, A or B may not quite express the content of a biblical verse but rather a reasonable conclusion from the content of a biblical

---

[133] 'B & A, just-as -Q so too -P'

[134] Except for the one o'kheiluf argument of the R. Ishmael school, Chapter Two, #6, where the two arguments are just-as arguments, or comparisons of equals, rather than qal v'homer arguments.

verse. In the *o'kheiluf* arguments in the Midrash Halakhah, whatever inconclusive evidence exists for the proposition P is biblical.[135]

In the Mishnah, the textual sources for facts A, B and P of a qal v'homer argument, in addition to the above may also be other lines of Mishnah. To the Tannaim of the Mishnah, in addition to biblical verses and common sense facts, well known legal facts that are reflected in mishnaic statements also have the status of facts. Therefore it is not surprising that in a mishnaic *o'kheiluf* argument, textual source for facts A and B might also be other mishnaic rulings.

In a tannaitic *o'kheiluf* argument, unlike in typical qal v'homer arguments, P is a proposition for which the evidence is inconclusive. When the *o'kheiluf* argument is mishnaic, the inconclusive evidence might be biblical as in the Midrash Halakhah but it could also be a line of Mishnah whose truth is not fixed but under consideration.

Putting the above definition into words, the *kheiluf* of one qal v'homer which argues 'P, therefore Q', is another qal v'homer, using the same facts A & B and arguing '-Q therefore -P'. As discussed in Chapter One, the Tannaim were aware that if one qal v'homer argues 'P, therefore Q', the *kheiluf* argument will start from -Q. But they were not aware that it will consistently end with the contents of -P.

The above claim that the single occurrence of the phrase או חלוף in the Mishnah has indeed precisely the meaning captured by (1), the same meaning as have all the other 15 tannaitic occurrences of the phrase, will next be verified following some remarks about the contexts in which (1) arises.

---

[135] For each of the *o'kheiluf* arguments of the R. Ishmael school and of Sifre Devarim of the R. Akiva school, there is some biblical evidence for P. For several of the former (Chapter Two, #3,4,5) and several of the latter (Chapter Two, #12,13,14) there is more than just mild evidence for P, but not what meets the high standards of these authors for conclusive evidence. For the 5 *o'kheiluf* arguments of the Sifra there is no biblical evidence at all for P (or -Q).

In all of the tannaitic cases including the mishnah in Pesahim, (1) describes the first half of what is referred to in this work as the *o'kheiluf* argument. Despite having the same setup as every *o'kheiluf* argument of the Midrash Halakhah, the single *o'kheiluf* argument in the Mishnah does not arise from the same circumstances as those in the Midrash Halakhah.

The Midrash Halakhah presents tannaitic legal discussion in the form of a running commentary to the Pentateuch, deriving teachings and laws from the biblical verses. In general, the qal v'homer argument in the Midrash Halakhah is an argument which, from something stated in a biblical verse, infers by *a fortiori* reasoning some new teaching.[136] As discussed at length in Chapter One, the *o'kheiluf* arises when the biblical evidence for the launching statement of the qal v'homer argument is not thought to be strong.[137] The Tanna is therefore not confident about the conclusion of the qal v'homer argument and is thus led to consider the *kheiluf* of that argument which is an argument that begins from the denial of that conclusion.

The Mishnah on the other hand does not claim to derive every, or even most, rulings from the Torah. Thus it need not in general present sources for its rulings. The qal v'homer argument in the Mishnah is not often used to derive laws[138] but rather is usually used to test different mishnaic rulings against each other for consistency, particularly related rulings that do not rest on rulings in other mishnayot. Thus the launching claim in a qal v'homer argument in the Mishnah, labeled here P, tends to be a line of Mishnah rather than an expression of a biblical verse. (For some examples, see M. Eduyot 6:2, M. Zevahim 12:3, M. Yevamot 8:3.) There are instances though

---

[136] For more on the role of the qal v'homer, see the section in 1.1 with heading 'Some brief preliminary background on the rabbinic *a fortiori*'.

[137] In the *o'kheiluf* arguments of the Sifra, there is no evidence for the launching premise P. In these examples P is a guess and it is assumed true in the qal v'homer launched from it.

[138] See M. Nazir 7:4. After R. Akiva derives a legal position from a qal v'homer argument, he relays that R. Eliezer's response was, "What is this Akiva, we don't rule from a qal v'homer [argument]."

where a mishnaic qal v'homer argument is refuted by a biblical verse or even by a derash on one or more biblical verses.[139]

The single o'kheiluf argument in the Mishnah occurs in a situation that arises often in the Mishnah, where two rulings in the same mishnah seem to be inconsistent. (See M.Yevamot 8:3 for an example of this.) Referring to one ruling as P and the other as -S, to test the consistency of the compound P & -S, a qal v'homer is argued starting from P and concluding S, where S is the negation of -S. To uphold the two rulings in the mishnah, P & -S, it must be successfully argued that this qal v'homer argument is defective. There are a number of ways this can be done, including attacking the relevance of the properties with regard to which the a fortiori comparison is made between the two topics, or by offering a biblical or other disproof of S (even though the mishnah did not offer a biblical proof text to justify -S).

As will be seen, in order to uphold the P & -S rulings of M. Pesahim 6:1, R. Akiva counters the challenge of R. Eliezer's qal v'homer argument that 'P therefore S', by presenting a counterexample to the claim S. R. Eliezer rejects the disproof of S via another qal v'homer argument and R. Akiva responds with an o'kheiluf to discredit the last qal v'homer.

The single o'kheiluf argument of the Mishnah located in M. Pesahim 6:2 and following on the contents of the preceding mishnah, M. Pesahim 6:1, is a very well-known argument, quoted and cited widely in academic literature as well.[140] The mishnayot concern whether the Passover sacrifice may be brought on the Sabbath. This is clearly an important topic, but both the Bavli and Yerushalmi on this mishnah go

---

[139] Examples of this: M. Sotah 6:3; M. Hullin 10:1; M. Behorot 9:1; M. Pesahim 6:2 discussed above.

[140] See for example, Reuven Hammer, Akiva: Life, Legend, Legacy by Reuven Hammer (Philadelphia: University of Nebraska Press, 2015); Barry W.Holtz, Rabbi Akiva: Sage of the Talmud (New Haven: Yale University Press, 2017): 95-96; Jeffrey L. Rubenstein, The Culture of the Babylonian Talmud (Baltimore: John Hopkins University Press, 2003):57.

further and attach paramount importance to this question: each Gemara cites a baraita that tells the story of how, on the sole basis of Hillel's ability to answer this question, the *bnei Beterah* stepping aside appointed him *nasi.*[141]

Given the popularity of these two mishnayot, the number of times they have been referenced in other rabbinic works as well as their treatment by many modern scholars, it is especially surprising that up until now, the precise meaning given above of the phrase חלוף או has remained unknown. It will be shown that this knowledge is key to correctly grasping R. Akiva's argument in the Mishnah, something that previous authors have not been able to do.[142]

Since, as established in this work, the phrase has a uniform meaning everywhere it is found in tannaitic writings, comparing the argument found in these two mishnayot to all other arguments where the phrase או חילוף is found, adds clarification to these two mishnayot which is absent in the Gemara's treatment. That is, the Gemara did not refer to the technical meaning of the phrase חלוף או or compare its presence in these mishnayot to its presence in other tannaitic passages. This analysis also appears to be absent from commentaries to the Gemara.

Here is the argument in M. Pesahim 6:1-2 and its context:

According to the Torah a Paschal offering is supposed to be made in the afternoon of the 14th of the first month, and eaten afterwards that night, the first night of Passover.[143] Activities like slaughtering are normally prohibited on the Sabbath so there is a question as to how to deal with the commandment to prepare the Paschal offering on the 14th of the first month when that day falls out on the Sabbath. This is the situation M. Pesahim 6:1 deals with. The Mishnah states that the slaughtering of the Paschal offering, the splashing of its blood [on the

---

[141] B. Pesahim 66a, Y. Pesahim 6:1, 39a.
[142] Including the authors cited in footnote 140.
[143] Exod. 12:6

altar], removal of the innards and the burning of its fats, do supersede the Sabbath restrictions and should be done on the Sabbath. Roasting and washing the innards of the offering do not supersede the Sabbath restrictions.

M. Pesahim 6:1 goes on to list other activities involved in preparing the Paschal sacrifice that should not be done on the Sabbath: carrying and bringing the animal from outside the *tekhum* to serve as the offering and cutting off the animal's warts do not override the Sabbath restrictions.[144] R. Eliezer disagrees: he says that these other activities needed for performing the sacrifice properly should also be done on that Sabbath.

Using the labeling introduced above, the two laws that R. Eliezer responds to are,

P = 'Slaughtering the Paschal offering overrides the Sabbath prohibitions.'

-S = 'Other activities needed for performing the sacrifice, specifically carrying and bringing the animal from outside the *tekhum* to serve as the Paschal offering and cutting off the animal's warts, do not override the Sabbath restrictions.'

R. Eliezer opposes the rulings -S. He is cited as asserting S, that the preparatory activities for overriding the Paschal sacrifice, also override the Sabbath restrictions.

In M. Pesahim 6:2, R. Eliezer argues this position:

"Is this not *din!* If slaughtering which is work[145], overrides the Sabbath, then must it not follow that these associated activities that

---

[144] *Tekhum* (Shabbat) is the distance a person may walk on Shabbat. See M. Eruvin 4:1, 3.
[145] Slaughtering is one of the 39 primary categories of work prohibited on the Sabbath listed in M. Shabbat 7:2.

are only rabbinically[146] prohibited, should certainly override the Sabbath?!"

In terms of the symbolic notation introduced above, R. Eliezer argues by qal v'homer that contrary to the legal statements of the sages, P certainly implies S.

R. Yehoshua attacks R. Eliezer's *a fortiori* reasoning from the laws concerning festivals where work (such as cooking) is permitted yet certain prohibitions that are only rabbinic are forbidden. R. Eliezer dismisses this example that runs counter to the reasoning in his qal v'homer by distinguishing the Paschal offering from eating on a festival on the basis that the former is a *mitzvah* and the second is a voluntary act.

Following up, R. Akiva presents his counterexample to R. Eliezer's qal v'homer conclusion:

"Let sprinkling [with the waters of purification] prove it. It is performed because it is a *mitzvah* and it is forbidden to be done on the Sabbath only rabbinically, yet it does not override the Sabbath. So too, do not be surprised by these, that although they are a *mitzvah* and doing them on the Sabbath is only forbidden rabbinically, they do not override the Sabbath."

Letting -Q = 'Sprinkling the waters of purification does not override the Sabbath,' -Q is R. Akiva's example of a rabbinic law that is a *mitzvah* that does not override the Sabbath. It is a counterexample to the conclusion of R. Eliezer's qal v'homer argument, S, and one that the latter cannot dismiss on the grounds that it is only a rabbinic enactment (for *shvut*) for it is not that but instead a *mitzvah*. Thus it

---

[146] He is referring to the rabbinic enactment that certain activities should be forbidden on the Sabbath in order to promote *shivut*, resting on the Sabbath, and not because these activities belong to one of the 39 categories of work forbidden on the Sabbath.

would appear that R. Akiva has successfully refuted R. Eliezer's qal v'homer argument.

But R. Eliezer responds, saying he disagrees with the ruling -Q. In fact he argues by the same qal v'homer reasoning he used earlier (i.e. that P implies S), that P certainly implies Q. Namely, that sprinkling does override the Sabbath restrictions.

Here is R. Eliezer's *a fortiori*, dissenting:

ועליה אני דן,

ומה אם שחיטה שהיא משום מלאכה דוחה את השבת, הזאה שהיא משום שבות,

אינו דין שדוחה את השבת !?

"But regarding that itself, I also argue! If slaughtering, which is work [forbidden generally on the Sabbath] overrides the Sabbath [in this situation], then sprinkling [a defiled person to complete his purification process] which is prohibited only rabbinically, must it not logically [also] override the Sabbath?!"

R. Eliezer has thus disagreed with both the last part of the ruling in 6:1, -S, and with R. Akiva's report on the sprinkling ruling, -Q. His disagreement with these rulings is based on *a fortiori* reasoning starting from the ruling in the first part of M. Pesahim 6:1, P, that slaughtering the Paschal offering does override Sabbath restrictions. Thus R. Eliezer's opposing views are based on his firm commitment to the first part of 6:1, while questioning the last part. He has treated that first half, in particular the ruling on slaughtering, as incontrovertible, but rejected both the rulings in the last part of 6:1 and R. Akiva's report on the ruling on sprinkling. The *a fortiori* property R. Eliezer argues distinguishes having a strong authoritative source from having only a weak authoritative source for the prohibition.

The rulings in the two parts of M. Pesahim 6:1 are presented in the anonymous voice and with no justification. In 6:2, R. Akiva's counter to R. Eliezer, quoted below, is meant to question the basis of R.

Eliezer's certainty with regard to only the first part of Mishnah 6:1. R. Akiva is pointing out that the rulings of the two parts of the mishnah and the ruling on sprinkling do not obviously differ in how reliable and incontrovertible they are, both are anonymous pronouncements given without justifications. R. Akiva argues that R. Eliezer's second qal v'homer, concluding from slaughtering to sprinkling, is no stronger a possibility than the qal v'homer that can be run instead from 'sprinkling doesn't override the Sabbath' to 'slaughtering does not override the Sabbath', i.e. the kheiluf qal v'homer:

אמר לו רבי עקיבא:

או חלוף,

מה אם הזאה שהיא משום שבות, אינה דוחה את השבת, שחיטה שהיא משום
מלאכה, אינו דין שלא תדחה את השבת ?!

Rabbi Akiva responded:

"Or the kheiluf:
If sprinkling, which is only [rabbinically] forbidden in order to impose rest, does not override the Sabbath [restrictions], then slaughtering which is forbidden biblically, must-it-not-follow [by din] that it [also] should not override the Sabbath?! "

Turning now to symbolize the last two arguments from M. Pesahim 6:2, as done in Chapters One and Two for the o'kheiluf arguments of the Midrash Halakhah, I will label the propositions that express known facts with the symbols A and B; P as above will represent the ruling in the mishnah that R. Eliezer accepts as the binding law, although its correctness might be questioned. The labeling will reveal that the argument presented by R. Akiva, introduced with the phrase או חילוף (o'kheiluf) does indeed have the form described above in (1). Again, this form is identical to the form of all the arguments in the Midrash Halakhah that likewise contain the phrase o'kheiluf.

R. Eliezer's qal v'homer argument:

250

A = ומה אם שחיטה שהיא משום מלאכה

P = [שחיטה] דוחה את השבת

B = הזאה שהיא משום שבות

אינו דין

Q = שדוחה [הזאה] את השבת ?!

A= 'Slaughtering is [a primary category of] work prohibited on the Sabbath'

P= 'Slaughtering [the Pesach offering] overrides the Sabbath [work prohibition]'

B= 'Sprinkling is [only] rabbinically prohibited on the Sabbath[147]

Q= 'Sprinkling overrides the Sabbath [work prohibition]'

A and B are mishnaic facts.[148] Referring to M. Pesahim 6:1 as Mishnah 1 and to M. Pesahim 6:2 as Mishnah 2, P represents a proposition whose only evidence is Mishnah 1, which states it anonymously. R. Eliezer finds the last part of Mishnah 1, -S, to be inconsistent with P.

Since R. Eliezer doubts the last part of Mishnah 1, -S, the rest of the Mishnah, in particular, P, is also cast into doubt according to R. Akiva. Q is the conclusion R. Eliezer arrives at by qal v'homer from A, P and B, namely, that sprinkling overrides the Sabbath prohibitions.

R. Akiva's counter with a qal v'homer argument:

או חלוף,

מה אם

---

[147] The Tannaim added certain further restrictions to activity on the Sabbath (not by deriving them from biblical prohibitions but rather) in order to promote resting, shvut, (שבות) on the Sabbath. Sabbath has the same root as שבות and the Torah refers to it as a day of rest.

[148] Slaughtering is listed as one of the 39 primary categories of work forbidden on the Sabbath, in M.Sabbath 7: 2.

הזאה שהיא משום שבות = B
אינה דוחה את השבת = Q-

שחיטה שהיא משום מלאכה =A
אינו דין
שלא תדחה את השבת ?! = P-

B= 'Sprinkling is [only] rabbinically prohibited on the Sabbath.'
-Q= 'Sprinkling does not override the Sabbath [work prohibition]'
A= 'Slaughtering is [a primary category of] work prohibited on the Sabbath.'
-P= 'Slaughtering [the Passover sacrifice] does not override the Sabbath [work prohibition].'

Indeed what is labeled -Q, namely, 'sprinkling does not override the Sabbath prohibitions,' is in fact the negation of what has been labeled Q. Likewise with -P.

Thus it is clear that R. Eliezer's qal v'homer argument can be symbolized by,

'Since A & P & B must-it-not-follow-that Q ?!'[149]

and R. Akiva's qal v'homer argument, introduced by the words או חילוף, can be symbolized by,

'Since B & -Q & A must-it-not-follow-that -P ?!',[150]

where A and B are facts while P is not known with certainty to be true. The last is because the latter half of the mishnah has been called into question and P is no more of a certainty than the rest of the mishnah.

---

[149] Refer to Appendix I and to Chapter One which refers to the former for explanation of why the symbolic formulation of a qal v'homer argument begins with the word 'since' rather than 'if' which is the literal translation of the Hebrew אם.
[150] Ibid.

It is thus clear that the exchange of qal v'homer arguments between R. Eliezer and R. Akiva separated by the phrase *o'kheiluf* can be symbolized together by (1). In Chapter One this was referred to as the first part of the *o'kheiluf* argument. The argument continues with the second part to decide which of the two qal v'homer arguments is the correct one, i.e. concludes with the correct legal ruling. It begins as follows:

R. Eliezer then objects to R. Akiva's qal v'homer, pointing out that its conclusion, -P, that slaughtering [the Paschal sacrifice] does not override the Sabbath restrictions, contradicts Scripture. He says,
'Akiva, you have uprooted what is written in the Torah, "in the afternoon", "in its appointed time", whether [it falls out] on a weekday or on the Sabbath!' R. Eliezer has presented a scriptural proof, a phrase from Num. 9:2, indicating that the Passover offering must be offered at its designated time, and as 9:3 goes on and describes, during the afternoon of the fourteenth of the first month with no qualifications mentioned regarding what day of the week the fourteenth falls out on.

With his qal v'homer, R. Akiva was arguing that a qal v'homer from -Q to -P is just as possible as a qal v'homer that argues from P to Q and therefore there are no grounds for assuming that in Mishnah 1, P is known more certainly than is -S. The latter is the basis for R. Eliezer's argument, 'P, therefore S'. But with the scriptural proof above, R. Eliezer is able to refute R. Akiva's claim. The first qal v'homer from P to Q, is superior to the other, going from -Q to -P, because it can be argued that there is scriptural evidence for P.

Given what has been learned from the *o'kheiluf* arguments in the Midrash Halakhah, it would be expected that unless R. Akiva is able to give a different interpretation[151] to the phrase "in its appointed time"

---

[151] The author of two *o'kheiluf* arguments of the R. Akiva school, found in Sifre Devarim, piska 244, succeed in doing this and thereby preventing a refutation of -P and thereby of the whole *kheiluf* qal v'homer argument. See Chapters Two and Four for more details.

thereby rejecting the scriptural refutation of -P, R. Eliezer or the Mishnah's anonymous voice would conclude as do all the R. Ishmael cases (and two cases from the school of R. Akiva) with the following declaration with the grammar adjusted to the situation:

דנתי, חלפת, בטל או חלוף וזכינו לדון כבתחיל

"I argued a qal v'homer, you switched it around, the *o'kheiluf* qal v'homer argument was found to be invalid and so we merited to deduce via qal v'homer as at first."

It would be expected that R. Eliezer would follow this declaration by repeating this time as an assertion, the first qal v'homer. R. Eliezer's qal v'homer argument would then by this default process be validated.

In other words, it would seem from all the other *o'kheiluf* arguments in the Midrash Halakhah where a scriptural disproof of the *kheiluf* argument is offered, that R. Akiva is boxed in. R. Eliezer first presented a qal v'homer, R. Akiva opposed it with a qal v'homer that assumed the contrary, Rabbi Akiva's qal v'homer was then successfully refuted by a scriptural phrase. R. Akiva would then seem to have no choice but to accept R. Eliezer's original qal v'homer unless (as in the *o'kheiluf* arguments of the Sifre Devarim, piska 244, of his school) R. Akiva could reinterpret the proof text to have a different meaning.

That is how all those other *o'kheiluf* arguments proceed (although the other examples are framed in one anonymous voice, and not as a debate between two individuals): Once the debate or the debaters implicitly assume(s) the proof technique, namely, that the two matters of law must be related to each other by qal v'homer the debate or the debaters cannot step outside this framework before exhausting it.

The argument up to this point can be symbolized as follows:

R. Eliezer: Since A & B and P must-it-not-follow that Q ?!

R. Akiva: או חילוף ,
Since B & A and -Q must-it-not-follow that -P ?!

R. Eliezer: -P contradicts the biblical verse "in its time" [so -P must be false and therefore the entire argument from -Q to -P is false]!

And this is where R. Akiva does something totally original in comparison to what was seen in all of the other tanniatic o'kheiluf arguments. He manages to sidestep the almost inevitable conclusion that since his qal v'homer argument was invalidated, the remaining viable qal v'homer argument, R. Eliezer's, must be correct. R. Akiva does this by rejecting the original framing of the debate over these laws, that the issues are related by a fortiori reasoning between activities that the Mishnah in Shabbat defines as work prohibited on the Sabbath, and activities only rabbinically prohibited on the Sabbath. R. Akiva in a brilliant move shows himself to be uniquely able to think outside the hermeneutical box.

R. Eliezer had used the biblical proof text "in its time" to disprove the conclusion of R. Akiva's qal v'homer argument i.e. he proved that slaughtering the Passover sacrifice does indeed override the prohibition of work on the Sabbath. R. Akiva uses that very same scriptural proof text "in its time" to supply a different (and superior) argument that upholds that sprinkling does not override the Sabbath restriction, i.e. -Q, while slaughtering the Paschal offering does override the Sabbath restrictions, i.e. P. In this way R. Akiva upholds P & -Q.

The Stoic from Chapter Five would explain R. Akiva's rejection of the framing of the debate, a bit more formally:

The Stoic would describe R. Akiva's qal v'homer argument as the following type 1 indemonstrable (modus ponens),

Premise 1: If sprinkling does not override the Sabbath
then slaughtering does not override the Sabbath   *****

Premise 2: Sprinkling does not override the Sabbath restrictions.

Conclusion: Slaughter does not override the Sabbath restrictions

***** argued to be true by *a fortiori* reasoning using the facts:

> Sprinkling is forbidden on the Sabbath only by rabbinic
> enactment.

> Slaughtering is a primary category of work forbidden on the
> Sabbath.

Since the Conclusion was shown to be false, as it contradicts the
biblical verse "in its appointed time," and since as a type 1
indemonstrable this argument is a valid argument, at least one of
Premises 1 & 2 must be false as well. R. Eliezer would say,
consistent with his qal v'homer argument, that Premise 2 is false. R.
Akiva does not acquiesce; he instead argues that it is Premise 1 that
is false. He rejects the qal v'homer premise as the way to relate the
two issues, slaughtering and sprinkling, and he uses the proof text
itself to provide a different way to relate the two issues.

R. Akiva replies to R. Eliezer, shooting down his qal v'homer:

"My Master, [the proof text you quote is "in the appointed time",] bring
me an appointed time for these like the appointed time for slaughter!"

Akiva is here arguing, rather than comparing slaughter with the
activities in the last part of Mishnah 1 and with sprinkling, along the
axis that the former (is a major category of) work prohibited on the
Sabbath (according to Mishnah Shabbat) and the latter are only
rabbinically prohibited on the Sabbath, there is a more relevant
distinction between the two. With regard to slaughtering the Passover

offering it says to do it "in its time", while on the other hand, no time is specified for other associated activities such as sprinkling. Thus P & -Q should be the law, the Passover sacrifice is slaughtered on the Sabbath when the 14th of Nissan falls out on the Sabbath but an individual who needs sprinkling in order to complete a purification process [the Gemara elaborates, in order to partake of the Paschal offering] may not undergo it even on that Sabbath.

R. Akiva concludes with an unforced and elegant explanation for why the law should be as stated in the mishnah, i.e. P&-S, that slaughter does override the Sabbath while certain rabbinically forbidden activities involved in preparing the offering do not. "Rabbi Akiva stated a general rule: [With regard to the Paschal offering] any (usually forbidden) labor that can be done before the Sabbath does not override the Sabbath [and should be done before the Sabbath]. Slaughter which cannot be done before the Sabbath (when the 14th of the first month is on Sabbath) overrides the Sabbath."

R. Akiva thus succeeds in his original objective, upholding the two rulings of Mishnah 1, denoted above as P & -S.

6.2: Comparing *O'Kheiluf* in the Mishnah and Midrash Halakhah

The first part of the *o'kheiluf* argument in the case in the Mishnah is just like all fifteen cases of the Midrash Halakhah: they may all be represented symbolically precisely as in (1) with a qal v'homer argument followed by the phrase *o'kheiluf* which then introduces the *kheiluf* qal v'homer argument.[152] One difference however is that unlike in our Mishnah, those other *o'kheiluf* arguments are presented in one anonymous voice. That is, while in the Midrash Halakhah the *o'kheiluf* is an argument between two positions, the mishnaic *o'kheiluf* argument is between two positions held by two different people. None

---

[152]See footnote 6.

of those other *o'kheiluf* arguments consists of a dispute between two parties.

As is the case in M. Pesahim 6:2, in each *o'kheiluf* argument in the Midrash Halakhah of the school of R. Ishmael, the second or *kheiluf* qal v'homer argument is disproved by scriptural evidence.[153] After the scriptural phrase which contradicts the conclusion of the second qal v'homer is presented, each of the *o'kheiluf* arguments of the school of R. Ishmael (and one argument of the school of R. Akiva[154]) follows with the following expression or something nearly identical:

(2)   דנתי, חלפתי, בטל או חילוף, וזכיתי לדון כבתחילה

"I inferred by qal v'homer, I then switched around [and executed the *kheiluf* qal v'homer]. The *o'kheiluf* [was then found to be] invalid, and [so] I merited to infer as at first."

These words (or a very slight variation) then conclude with a repetition of the first qal v'homer argument. Thus two qal v'homer arguments are presented where one is the *kheiluf* of the other. The *kheiluf* is then determined by scriptural proof to be false. The *kheiluf* qal v'homer is therefore discarded and with confidence the original qal v'homer argument is asserted to be correct. It is viewed as true by default: there were two possibilities and one was eliminated.

Hence if our mishnaic *o'kheiluf* argument was to continue in the style of the Midrash Halakhah, after R. Eliezer presented the scriptural refutation "in its appointed time" of the second qal v'homer argument,

---

[153] Since each of the two qal v'homers in the argument is the *kheiluf* of the other, it is not surprising that in the Midrash Halakhah the format could be maintained whereby the qal v'homer that is disproved is always the second qal v'homer, i.e. positioned after the words *o'kheiluf*.

[154] Plus another argument of the school of R. Akiva, from the Sifra, Mekhilta de-Miluim, quoted in Chapter Two, uses common sense rather than a scriptural verse to discredit the *kheiluf* qal v'homer argument. The *o'kheiluf* argument then continues with the expression quoted above, "I inferred by qal v'homer then I switched it around…"

he would conclude as described earlier with a grammatical adaptation
of (2), something like,

דנתי, חלפת, בטל או חילוף, וזכינו לדון כבתחילה

followed by a repetition of the first qal v'homer argument, his,
declaring it to be true. But this is not how part two of the mishnaic
o'kheiluf argument proceeds.

R. Eliezer did not argue by himself, it was R. Akiva who introduced
the *kheiluf*. Therefore in considering how R. Akiva finishes off the
o'kheiluf argument we should compare his treatment to the *o'kheiluf*
arguments of the Midrash Halakhah, specifically of the school of R.
Akiva.

As discussed in Chapter Four, in each of the five *o'kheiluf* arguments
of the Sifra, the claim represented by P is really a guess; there is no
biblical evidence at all for or against P. In any *o'kheiluf* argument of
the Midrash Halakhah, as is typical of qal v'homer arguments, there is
no biblical expression supporting Q or -Q. Thus with no evidence for
any of P, -P, Q or -Q, each of the *o'kheiluf* arguments of the Sifra
after presenting two qal v'homer alternatives, the first and the *kheiluf*,
usually has no way to eliminate either qal v'homer argument.[155] The
argument concludes from this that the law sought cannot be arrived at

---

[155] The only one of the 5 that succeeds in the Sifra is the *o'kheiluf* in the
Mekhilta de-Miluim. It succeeds by applying an everyday common sense fact
to eliminate -P. See Chapter Four for a full discussion of all the *o'kheiluf*
arguments of the school of R. Akiva including those found in the Sifre
Devarim.
In the *o'kheiluf* arguments found in the Sifre Devarim there is biblical
evidence for the launching premise P. But that evidence is not quite explicit
and so does not meet the high standards of the R. Akiva school, and
therefore *o'kheiluf* ensues. The R. Akiva school is (unlike the R. Ishmael
school) very skilled at finding ways to reinterpret that biblical evidence in
another reasonable way such that it does not refute -P. When the author is
able to do this, he is left with two contradictory qal v'homer arguments and
no way to refute one of them, and the *o'kheiluf* fails to provide an answer to
the question that motivated it.

by qal v'homer reasoning. Another method, based on identifying some hermeneutical cue, is then presented by which the law in question is determined. Chapter Four argued that the purpose in presenting the failed *o'kheiluf* argument, which is then followed by another method to arrive at the law in question, is to justify that other method, to show that qal v'homer could not yield the answer and therefore some other method needed to be applied.

In Mishnah 2, R. Akiva pursues an agenda similar to that identified in all of those other *o'kheiluf* arguments of his school in the Sifra described above and in Chapter Four. As discussed, Mishnah 1 contains two rulings which have been denoted above as P & -S. P denotes the ruling that slaughtering the Passover sacrifice overrides the Sabbath prohibitions and -S denotes the ruling that several preparatory activities for the Passover sacrifice that are only prohibited by rabbinic injunction do not override the Sabbath prohibitions. R. Eliezer finds the two rulings inconsistent. He believes that by qal v'homer reasoning P implies S and that therefore Mishnah 1 should rule P&S. R. Akiva clearly motivated by the desire to uphold the rulings in the Mishnah, P& -S, rather than the dissenting opinion of R. Eliezer, attempts to destroy R. Eliezer's qal v'homer argument with a counterexample to its logic.

R. Akiva presents sprinkling [for purification] as an example which like slaughtering the Passover offering is a *mitzvah*, a commandment to perform, but which despite being prohibited on the Sabbath only by rabbinic injunction does not override the Sabbath. Thus he argues, -S is the law just as -Q is the law. R. Eliezer does not accept the counterexample, he responds that he in fact rules differently on the sprinkling matter: in line with his ruling that P implies S, he rules that P implies Q, where Q denotes that sprinkling does override the Sabbath.

R. Akiva then attacks the conclusion from P to Q by questioning the basis for R. Eliezer's confidence that P is true. R. Eliezer believes P but questions -S. But the source for both P and -S is Mishnah 1. R.

Akiva argues that P is no more certain than is -S, after all the source for P is the very Mishnah that asserts -S which R. Eliezer rejects. Thus, why reject -S and agree with P, why not vice versa and reject P? If he succeeds in showing that the argument '-Q therefore -P' is just as likely as the argument 'P therefore Q' he will also have refuted the necessity of concluding that S follows because P is true. He would then be able to uphold the rabbinic rulings P & -S.

R. Akiva acknowledges that R. Eliezer's qal v'homer from P to Q is possible but he adds *o'kheiluf*, or just as possible is the *kheiluf* argument:

-Q implies -P.

To summarize what has been put forward,

R. Eliezer: A & B and P must-it-not-follow-that Q ?!
R. Akiva: *o'kheiluf*,
             A & B and -Q must-it-not-follow-that -P ?!

With no evidence (mentioned in this mishnah or in another mishnah) for or against either P or -Q, R. Akiva is in a situation seen in the *o'kheiluf* arguments in the Midrash Halakhah of his school in the Sifra, but never seen in the arguments of the R. Ishmael school. Following a style of applying the *o'kheiluf* which is characteristic of his school, R. Akiva was about to point out that there is no way to decide between R. Eliezer's qal v'homer argument and his own qal v'homer argument and therefore some other technique is needed to establish the truth of P.

The method that R. Akiva would offer would surely have resulted in also upholding –S. This is clear because from the start of his engagement with R. Eliezer's argument, R. Akiva had been trying to uphold the two statements of Mishnah 1 which R. Eliezer found contradictory, i.e. P & -S.

With the exception of one brilliant argument where *o'kheiluf* does yield a solution,[156] all of the *o'kheiluf* arguments in the Sifra of R. Akiva's school work in this way. The *o'kheiluf* arguments of the Sifra first present the *o'kheiluf* to show that qal v'homer cannot decide the issue of law in question and that therefore some other method is needed. But in those other examples the method that is introduced after the *o'kheiluf* fails is more contrived than the qal v'homer that preceded it. In fact the purpose of first introducing the *o'kheiluf* is to justify the later method involving some hermeneutical cue, as simply the best that could be found to answer the question, after the far more compelling qal v'homer method failed. The *o'kheiluf* in the works of R. Akiva's school thus often has the rhetorical function of making a less convincing proof appear more palatable.

Distinct from all of those in the Sifra, the *o'kheiluf* argument of R. Akiva in the mishnah under discussion, is the only *o'kheiluf* argument whose expected failure was then meant to be followed not by a more contrived method but by a clearly intelligent method that is shown to make more sense to use in this particular case than qal v'homer. Very likely the property that R. Akiva had in mind all along, by which to distinguish the list of actions that Mishnah 1 rules may be performed on the Sabbath in order to offer the Passover sacrifice, from the list of actions that it forbids, was with regard to which things can be done in advance and which things cannot.

In all of the *o'kheiluf* arguments in the Sifra that fail, the hermeneutical cue that is then introduced to answer the question of law, answers the question only with regard to P. It does not weigh in on the law regarding Q. Q in these cases was only introduced as an aid to examine the law with regard to P. Once qal v'homer is seen to have failed, the aid, the question of law with regard to Q is abandoned. Seeing the similarity between R. Akiva's *o'kheiluf* to those spawned of his school, suggests that the new method R. Akiva intended to introduce would determine the law with regard to P. Since R. Akiva's

---

[156] Sifra, Mekhilta de Milium on Parashat Shemini, Lev. 9:22-23.

goal was to support the rulings P & -S of the sages, that method was surely intended to also establish -S.

Comparing R. Akiva's *o'kheiluf* argument in the Mishnah to those other ones in the Midrash Halakhah of his school that are similar, i.e. to those in the Sifra, does suggest that in introducing the *o'kheiluf* qal v'homer, R. Akiva was not in earnest. That is, R. Akiva did not think that -P should be the law. This is clear as R. Akiva was at first trying to defend -S against R. Eliezer, who committed to P, refused -S. Rather, R. Akiva was making a rhetorical move. Similar to all the *o'kheiluf* arguments from the Sifra, R. Akiva in the argument of the Mishnah introduced the *o'kheiluf* qal v'homer for the purpose of showing that a qal v'homer focusing on the properties of forbidden work versus only rabbinically prohibited work, would not succeed because it would produce two viable possibilities, not one answer. Once that would be made clear, R. Akiva would introduce some other method that did succeed in deciding the law for the two different matters and likely that method was intended from the start, to be with regard to which things can be done in advance and which things cannot.

R. Akiva's plan was frustrated because although he had not thought of it, there was what could be interpreted as biblical support for one of the claims, for P. Instead of folding and allowing R. Eliezer to announce that the first qal v'homer was correct, R. Akiva quickly came up with a way to use the content of the proof text itself as the new method of comparison in place of qal v'homer to decide the two issues so as to maintain the rulings of the Mishnah.

As will be seen shortly the Gemara is very puzzled by this *o'kheiluf* argument.[157] It seems likely that if the Amoraim had a better understanding of *o'kheiluf* in the Midrash Halakhah as advanced in the present work, then by comparing this mishnaic story to the *o'kheiluf* arguments of R. Akiva's school in the Sifra and the Sifre

---

[157] Chapter Eight is focused on the *o'kheiluf* arguments in the Bavli and Chapter Nine on those in the Yerushalmi.

Devarim, they would have come to a simpler understanding of the mishnah, the understanding described above.

6.3: The Bavli and Yerushalmi on the Mishnaic *O'Kheiluf*

Both the Bavli and the Yerushalmi start out by highlighting the importance of the question in these mishnayot about whether the Passover offering may be slaughtered on the Sabbath. B. Pesahim 66a quotes a baraita (and the Yerushalmi, Pesahim 3:1, 20a quotes a similar one) that tells the story of how on the basis of his ability to answer this question, Hillel, who had come to Israel from Babylonia (and was therefore referred to as Hillel the Babylonian) was installed as the *nasi*.[158] In this baraita, Hillel uses the same biblical phrase that the Mishnah cites, "in its appointed time," to prove that the slaughter of the Paschal offering is not postponed when the 14th of the first month falls out on the Sabbath. But the proof he presents is different from the one in the Mishnah. To the Mishnah, the cited biblical phrase, which refers to the Passover offering, is clear proof. But the proof in the baraita does not rely only on the sense of the cited phrase. It draws an analogy to the daily *tamid* offering of which it is also stated that it needs to be offered "in its appointed time". Just as the offering of the *tamid* puts off the Shabbat restrictions so too the slaughter of the Paschal offering puts off the Sabbath restrictions. The Bavli refines the baraita's proof, citing a phrase in Num. 28:10 that makes clear that the *tamid* is offered also on the Sabbath.[159]

---

[158] See footnote 6.

[159] From Num. 28:10: עולת שבת בשבתו על עולת התמיד. The Bavli points out that it is from this explicit phrase that it is known that the *tamid* is brought on the Sabbath. The phrase "in its appointed time" that appears both in reference to the *tamid* and the Paschal offering is used to draw a *gezerah shavah* between the two: just as the tamid is offered on the Sabbath so too the Paschal offering of which it likewise says "in its appointed time" is also brought on the Sabbath (when the 14th of Nisan falls out on the Sabbath). It could be argued that the Bavli does no more than spell out a bit further the proof intended by the baraita, i.e. that the baraita was relying on the biblical verses that make clear that the *tamid* is offered on the Sabbath, and not just

The Bavli does not however register the brilliance of R. Akiva's move, how he managed to step outside the dialectical box in which he found himself constrained. The Gemara as well as the medieval commentaries do not cite the list of tannaitic arguments where the phrase o'kheiluf arises and compare the occurrence of the phrase in this mishnah to those others. The Bavli does not point out how although the argument set-up identifies it as clearly having the essential style of (what has been referred to in this book as) the o'kheiluf argument found in the Midrash Halakhah of the R. Akiva school, R. Akiva's response in the Mishnah stands apart from all those other cases in the following two ways. First, after a proof text is supplied refuting one qal v'homer argument, R. Akiva who is unable or unwilling to reinterpret the proof text to mean something different, succeeds at sidestepping the default conclusion that the other qal v'homer must therefore be correct. Second, unlike most of the o'kheiluf arguments of the school of R. Akiva found in the Sifra, the method R. Akiva introduces here in place of the o'kheiluf is not somewhat contrived but is actually a natural and elegant method clearly more compelling than the discarded qal v'homer.

In trying to make sense of R. Akiva's qal v'homer, the baraita and Gemara on B. Pesahim 69a are very focused on and puzzled by how R. Akiva could offer a qal v'homer that concludes with a falsity, i.e. the false ruling that the slaughter of the Paschal sacrifice does not override the Sabbath. After all, R. Akiva's motive in arguing with R. Eliezer appears to be his desire to maintain the words of the sages, labeled above P and −S where P represents the ruling that the slaughter of the Passover sacrifice does override the Sabbath. So it is not possible that R. Akiva believes that the conclusion of his qal v'homer, -P, could be true. Why then did he present it? The Gemara is perplexed.

---

on the phrase "in its appointed time" that appears both in reference to the tamid and the Paschal offering. This baraita is part of a passage found in T. Pesahim 4:11. (Like the baraita on B. Pesahim 66a, it also cites Hillel's proof by qal v'homer but it does not reference the bnei Beterah.)

The baraita and the Bavli clearly do not demonstrate a good understanding as put forward in this work, of the *o'kheiluf* arguments of the school of R. Akiva found in the Sifra, even though one of those arguments occurs as a baraita in B. Temurah.[160] They do not recognize the strategic way in which the R. Akiva school uses the *o'kheiluf* argument and that R. Akiva himself is employing that strategy in his *o'kheiluf* in Mishnah 2.

R. Akiva is trying to discredit R. Eliezer's qal v'homer by showing that there is no way to decide between R. Eliezer's and his qal v'homer, and that therefore another method is needed to distinguish between what can and cannot be done on the Sabbath to prepare for Passover offering. R. Akiva is not committed to the conclusion of his qal v'homer argument; the fact that his argument concludes with a ruling he believes to be false is not a mystery in the context of *o'kheiluf* argumentation. His qal v'homer shows what follows, via R. Eliezer's *a fortiori* comparison of things biblically forbidden versus rabbinically prohibited, from the supposition that sprinkling does not override the Sabbath. Although he believes his launching premise to be true, he views it as a supposition as he does not have strong evidence to directly refute R. Eliezer's contrary ruling, similarly no strong evidence (beyond that the sages hold that way) has been provided for R. Eliezer's launching premise. This is why R. Akiva is engaged in *o'kheiluf.* He is also not committed to the qal v'homer conditional shared by his and R. Eliezer's qal v'homer arguments. R. Akiva is trying to show via *o'kheiluf* that the two contradictory qal v'homer arguments are possible and in this way refute the validity of the qal v'homer conditional, i.e. the relevance of comparing the activities with regard to which are biblically versus only rabbinically prohibited. The Bavli does not recognize any of this. Instead, the Gemara needs a whole other tale in order to resolve how it is that R. Akiva proposes a false law.

---

[160] See Chapter Two, # 7.

R. Akiva in defending himself from his teacher R. Eliezer for daring to conclude that the Passover sacrifice does not override the Sabbath restrictions says, what amounts to, 'I launched a qal v'homer argument from what I knew to be true because you taught it to me, that sprinkling does not override the Sabbath. The qal v'homer comparison that you set up led to the conclusion that the Passover sacrifice does not override the Sabbath restrictions.' Here's the baraita:

R. Eliezer: "You answered me [flippantly] with slaughter — through slaughter shall be his death!"

R. Akiva entreats him: "My teacher, do not deny me in this moment of debate! This is the teaching I received from you: Sprinkling is only forbidden rabbinically and it does not override the Sabbath."

The Bavli understands this to be an admission that R. Akiva believes that his conclusion, that the Passover sacrifice does not override the Sabbath restrictions, is false. As mentioned above, R. Akiva's motive in M. Pesahim 6:2 was clearly to defend rulings P and –S of 6:1, where P is the label given above for the ruling that the slaughter of the Passover offering does override the Sabbath restrictions. But the Bavli cannot then give a very cogent explanation, along the lines of all the o'kheiluf arguments in the Sifra, for why R. Akiva offered that qal v'homer argument. The Bavli puts forward the idea that in concluding with something he knew was false R. Akiva was showing strong commitment to the premise, i.e. that sprinkling overrides the Sabbath restrictions. And that the purpose of showing that commitment was to remind his teacher that he had taught Akiva the law about sprinkling (to complete the purification from defilement by contact with a corpse in order to be permitted to partake of the Paschal offering) which he, R. Eliezer, had apparently forgotten.[161]

---

[161] The Bavli discusses this further a few pages later, on folio 69a.

The thinking offered here is along the lines that his teacher would wonder, 'Why is my student Akiva presenting an argument that ends with a conclusion that he must believe is false? Oh, it must be to draw my attention to the premise of that argument that he is showing himself to be so committed to, despite that it leads him to an outright falsity.' "Why not tell him right out?" the Bavli asks. In order not to embarrass his teacher, the Bavli answers.

The Bavli seeks to resolve the puzzle of how R. Akiva could present a qal v'homer argument whose conclusion is a false law with a story that also takes into account how it is that R. Akiva has a different teaching with regard to the law of sprinkling than does his teacher, R. Eliezer. From where would Akiva have gotten this teaching? He must have received it from his teacher, R. Eliezer. But R. Eliezer forgot it. In order not to remind him without embarrassing him, R. Akiva resorts to presenting a strange argument, a qal v'homer that ends with a falsity.

The Talmud Yerushalmi similarly does not understand what R. Akiva was up to. It exclaims in amazement on Y. Pesahim 6:3, 42b[162]: "Is there a person anywhere who says to his teacher o'kheiluf?" It answers by explaining how R. Eliezer was R. Akiva's teacher, and that R. Eliezer had taught him the law about sprinkling but now forgot it.

Thus both the Bavli and the Yerushalmi, bewildered by R. Akiva's argument and lacking expertise in tannatic o'kheiluf argumentation especially of the R. Akiva school, find no way to explain R. Akiva's argument other than by attributing to R. Eliezer a most astonishing thing, a memory slip. R. Eliezer's (ben Hyrcanus) ability to retain his learning was legendary. M. Pirkei Avot 2:8 cites R. Yohanan ben Zakai's praise for his students where he describes R. Eliezer as "a cemented cistern that loses not a drop." Since it was so shocking and would so undermine R. Eliezer's unique intellectual gift, R. Akiva had

---

[162] ואית בר נש אמר לרביה, או חילוף? לפי שהיה רבי ליעזר מלמדו הלכה ובא שאין חגיגה דוחה שבת וכפר בו בשעת הדין. לפום כך הוא אמר ליה, או חילוף.

to remind him by presenting a very puzzling argument, a qal v'homer that concludes with a legal ruling that R. Akiva knows is false.

Looking to the collection of o'kheiluf arguments in the Midrash Halakhah of the R. Akiva school (which were analyzed in Chapters Two and Four) to make sense of this argument in the Mishnah, leads to the recognition of a rhetorical rather than a substantive role for R. Akiva's qal v'homer argument.

R. Akiva is committed to the two statements in Mishnah 1 under consideration, the first one being the ruling that the Paschal offering overrides the Sabbath. R. Eliezer accepts the first statement but questions the other one. (R. Akiva's first argument attempts to defend that other ruling about preparatory activities that R. Eliezer has thrown into doubt.) R. Akiva's objective is to uphold the validity of both statements of the Mishnah. R. Akiva argues by way of qal v'homer, that R. Eliezer is entitled to doubt part of Mishnah 1 but if he does so he may not ascribe certainty to another part. This is because the evidence for each part of Mishnah 1, R. Akiva is arguing implicitly, is precisely the statements in that mishnah. There is no further textual evidence mishnaic or biblical, he believes, for any part of Mishnah 1.[163] Thus R. Eliezer in doubting the later statement in the mishnah is not entitled to ascribe certainty to the first part, in particular the ruling that the Passover sacrifice overrides the Sabbath restrictions. Once R. Eliezer has cast doubt on the later statement of the mishnah, the first statement is also thrown into doubt. Therefore, as shown in earlier chapters of this work for the whole collection of tannaitic o'kheiluf arguments studied in this work, it is precisely because the launching premise of R. Eliezer's qal v'homer argument is not a certainty that an o'kheiluf argument is possible, i.e. it is possible to entertain a qal v'homer argument that begins with the negation of the conclusion of the original qal v'homer argument. This is the source of

---

[163] Later he accepts correction on this, that במועדו, "in its appointed time" mentioned with regard to the Paschal offering is a biblical source implying that the offering must be brought at its appointed time, even when that day falls out on a Sabbath.

the logical legitimacy of R. Akiva's move to start a qal v'homer from the negation of R. Eliezer's conclusion. It is R. Eliezer who has created this logical and interpretive possibility.

R. Eliezer does present biblical evidence for what is his launching premise but he only does so after R. Akiva presents his qal v'homer. R. Eliezer presents the biblical proof text as a refutation of R. Akiva's conclusion.

The Gemara seems to miss all this about what R. Akiva was really up to and how cleverly he sidestepped handing R. Eliezer an expected victory. There is no elaboration in either the Bavli or in the Yerushalmi highlighting the brilliant basis by which R. Akiva is able to split the activities that do and do not override the Sabbath prohibitions in the preparation of the Passover sacrifice. The gemara on 69b on the last line of Mishna 2 expressing R. Akiva's *klal*, his general rule, does not analyze the expression further. R. Yehuda quotes Rav as stating that the law follows R. Akiva and the gemara goes on to relate this ruling to the law regarding circumcision.

The last line of Mishnah 2:
R. Akiva stated a general rule: [With regard to the Paschal offering] any (usually forbidden) labor that can be done before the Sabbath does not override the Sabbath [and should be done before the Sabbath]. Slaughter which cannot be done before the Sabbath (when the 14th of Nisan is on Sabbath) overrides the Sabbath.

6.4: Conclusions

The single *o'kheiluf* argument of the Mishnah found in M.Pesahim 6:1-2, although structured as debate between two people, has precisely the same form as all of those of the Midrash Halakhah identified earlier in this book. This *o'kheiluf* argument like all the others may be symbolized as,

Since A, B and P must-it-not-follow that Q ?!

או חילוף

Since B, A and -Q must-it-not-follow that -P ?!   (1)

where A and B represent facts and P represents a proposition for which the evidence is less than compelling. (The author of the argument has no evidence to support or refute Q.) Each of the two expressions ending in '?!' is a rhetorically-questioning qal v'homer argument.[164]

In the Midrash Halakhah facts A and B are biblical or common sense facts, while in the mishnaic o'kheiluf argument A and B are facts in the world of the Mishnah and so may have their sources in well-accepted mishnaic rulings.

The Bavli and the Yerushalmi as well as later commentators have no clue as to what R. Akiva is up to in arguing a qal v'homer argument that concludes that the Passover sacrifice does not put off the Sabbath restrictions. To explain it, the Bavli (building on a baraita) resorts to positing a most astonishing thing, that R. Eliezer forgot his own teaching regarding sprinkling which he had taught his student R. Akiva. R. Eliezer's memory was legendary (M. Pirkei Avot 2:9) and so to point out gently without embarrassing him that he had actually forgotten one of his own teachings, R. Akiva presented a strange argument, a qal v'homer launched from that teaching but concluding with a flat-out false law. This bizarre argument according to the Bavli was aimed at making R. Eliezer realize that he had forgotten his teaching.

---

[164] Except for the one o'kheiluf argument of the school of R. Ishmael, Chapter Two, #6, where the two arguments are just-as arguments, or comparisons of equals, rather than qal v'homer arguments.

The identification and study of the *o'kheiluf* arguments of the Midrash Halakhah advanced in this book leads to a simple understanding of R. Akiva's brilliant argument, which is recognized as fitting his school's style of *o'kheiluf* argumentation, particularly as seen in the Sifra.

CHAPTER SEVEN: Talmudic Consideration of *O'Kheiluf* Arguments of the Midrash Halakhah

In Chapter Six, the Bavli's analysis of the sole *o'kheiluf* argument of the Mishnah exposed a limited grasp of the functions served by the tannaitic *o'kheiluf*. With regard to the Midrash Halakhah, only one of its 15 *o'kheiluf* arguments is found to be discussed in the Bavli (and none are found in the Yerushalmi). The next chapter will examine the passage on B. Temurah 28b which contains that single *o'kheiluf* argument. But first, this chapter takes up the question of why it is that the Bavli, which incorporates so many baraitot, did not make use of the other 14 *o'kheiluf* arguments of the Midrash Halakhah? Is this because the Bavli found these arguments wanting and if so for what reasons?[165]

For easy reference, here again is the symbolic formulation of the set up of the *o'kheiluf* argument, developed in Chapter One and used throughout this work:

Since **A, B & P** must-it-not-follow-that **Q**?!

או חילוף

Since **A, B & -Q** must-it-not-follow-that **-P** ?!   (*)

---

[165] The stance being taken here is that on a folio of the Bavli, the statements of the different named Amoraim along with the later anonymous (*stam*) strata, all together reflect one editorial voice referred to as 'the Bavli' and of which one can ask what 'it thinks'. For justification of this position see Moulie Vidas, *Tradition and the Formation of the Talmud*, (Princeton: Princeton University Press, 2014) and scholarship cited there. See David Weiss Halivni, *The Formation of the Babylonian Talmud* (Oxford: Oxford University Press, 2013) for discussion of how the *stam* worked with earlier terse amoraic statements to create a *sugya*, a talmudic passage.

where **A** and **B** represent biblical or common sense facts and **P** represents a proposition for which the evidence is recognized as less than compelling. (The tannaitic author has no evidence that supports or refutes **Q**.) −**Q** is the negation of **Q** and likewise for **P**. The ending '?!' is used to indicate that the expression is a rhetorically questioning qal v'homer argument.

Many of the answers to questions of law that were arrived at through *o'kheiluf* arguments in the Midrash Halakhah occur as rulings announced in the Mishnah. By examining the Bavli's treatment of these mishnaic rulings, especially the answer it gives to the question it invariably raises 'from where does the Mishnah know this?,' it is possible to infer something of the Talmud's opinion about the parallel *o'kheiluf* argument. Other questions of law raised by *o'kheiluf* in the Midrash Halakhah but not directly by any mishnah are often also raised by the Bavli in dealing with a mishnaic ruling on a closely related issue.

Because the Bavli, on each of these questions, includes derashot that are found in the Midrash Halakhah on the same topic, some right before the *o'kheiluf* argument is presented and some occurring after, it is hard to argue that any of these *o'kheiluf* arguments is absent from the Bavli simply because it was overlooked by the Amoraim and the editors of the Bavli. The absence of each of these *o'kheiluf* arguments in the Bavli should therefore be assumed to indicate that they were rejected for inclusion, and often in favor of other tannaitic material.

7.1: Inferring Reasons for Omission

Through this approach it is possible to infer five different reasons for why the Bavli does not contain the other 14 *o'kheiluf* arguments of the Midrash Halakhah as baraitot. They are as follows:

1. Sometimes the Bavli does not incorporate an *o'kheiluf* argument of the Midrash Halakhah

because it does not find the substance of the two qal v'homer inferences to be compelling. In such cases, the Bavli finds that the properties the qal v'homer focuses on, what is labeled **A & B** in the formulation of the *o'kheiluf* argument, do not capture the relevant difference between the two subjects of the qal v'homer.[166] This is the case for the *o'kheiluf* argument found in Sifre Bamidbar piska 123 about the yoke (#3 in Chapter Two).

2. Other times, the reason the Bavli passes over an *o'kheiluf* argument of the R. Ishmael school is because it is able to find strong support for the launching premise of the starting qal v'homer of the *o'kheiluf* argument, i.e. for **P** in the formulation above, and therefore has no need for *o'kheiluf*. Also the Bavli sometimes passes over a tannaitic qal v'homer in favor of other tannaitic material that arrives at the law in question by expounding a biblical phrase, finding the latter sometimes (depending on the particular phrase) to be a more reliable method of proof. Both of these are the case with the *o'kheiluf* argument found in the Mekhilta,

---

[166] Recall, the imagined Stoic philosopher in Chapter Five showed that the *o'kheiluf* argument can be described as the following pair of arguments where in each, the first two lines are the two premises and the third, following the drawn line, is the conclusion:

P

If P then Q ←- argued to be true, on the basis of properties A & B

   Q

   O'kheiluf!

   -Q

If -Q then -P ←- argued to be true on the basis of properties A & B

   -P

the goring ox and the *eglah arufah* (#1 in Chapter Two).

3. With regard to other *o'kheiluf* arguments of the R. Ishmael school where the Gemara does approve of the comparison to properties **A** & **B** set up by the qal v'homer arguments of the *o'kheiluf*, one may infer that the Amoraim did not have quite as high a standard for what would constitute a proof text as the R. Ishmael school sometimes had. In these cases the Gemara found the evidence in favor of **P** to be compelling and therefore the first qal v'homer to be valid. Thus the Bavli found no grounds for *o'kheiluf*, i.e. for considering the *kheiluf* qal v'homer. In such cases the Bavli just cites the first qal v'homer of the *o'kheiluf* argument. This is the case for the *o'kheiluf* argument found in the Sifre Bamidbar piska 155 (#6 in Chapter Two) about the father and husband.

It is also the case for *o'kheiluf* argument found in the Sifre Bamidbar piska 123 (#3 in Chapter Two) about the yoke. With regard to the latter, the Yerushalmi, Y. Sotah 9:5, 42a, similarly to the Bavli, does not share the high standards of the Tannaim and views the evidence for **P** in piska 123 as sufficiently strong to accept as the basis from which to draw a *gezerah shavah*.

In another case also we see that the Bavli, on Ketubot 39a, does not have the same high standard as does the Sifre Devarim, piska 249, of the R. Akivah school, for demonstrating that the words "one who was not betrothed and not divorced" mean to make the exclusion they seem to make, i.e. to which of the victims of a rape receive compensation from the perpetrator. The Sifre's high standard is what motivated the entire *o'kheiluf* argument. See the Bavli's justification for R. Yossi HaGilili's position in the mishnah under discussion there (M. Ketubot 3:3).

4. In some of the *o'kheiluf* arguments of the R. Akiva school, *o'kheiluf* and its failure are introduced to motivate a less transparent derivation of the law in question. Sometimes in deriving that same law, the Bavli does not feel the need to motivate the derivation with the failed *o'kheiluf* argument. This is the case with the *asham, asham* argument in the Sifra, Dibbura de-Khova, parshata 12 (#8, 9, 10 in Chapter Two) and also for the Ammonite/*mamzer* argument in the Sifre Devarim piska 249 (#15 in Chapter Two).

5. For some of the *o'kheiluf* arguments of the Midrash Halakhah the questions of law that they raise and answer are paralleled in tractates of the Mishnah for which there is no Bavli (or Yerushalmi). For this reason, the Bavli does not discuss these questions. (Sometimes though in covering other tractates the Bavli does quote those lines of Mishnah.) This is the case for the *o'kheiluf* argument in Sifre Bamidbar piska 125 (#4 in Chapter Two) concerning the dying person and the *sheretz*; its parallel rulings occur in M. Oholot for which there is no Bavli or Yerushalmi.

Examination of the examples for each of 1-5 follows:

1. On B.Sotah 46a which deals with analyzing M.Sotah 9:5-6 about the *eglah arufah*, the Bavli asks for the source of a parallel law regarding the red heifer, "I know only that a yoke disqualifies a red

heifer, from where do I know that other types of labors likewise disqualify the red heifer?"

The Bavli cites a baraita which gives the first qal v'homer in the o'kheiluf argument in the Sifre as the answer to the question:

אמרת קל וחומר: ומה עגלה שאין מום פוסל בה שאר עבודות פוסלות בה, פרה שמום פוסל בה אינו דין ששאר עבודות פוסלות בה.

Say, [it is by] qal v'homer: since the calf of the *eglah arufah* rite which is not invalidated by a blemish is invalidated by (even) work that does not involve a yoke, the red heifer which is invalidated by a blemish must-it-not-follow-that that it is invalidated (even) by work that does not involve a yoke?!

The Bavli continues, citing the rest of the baraita:

ואם נפשך לומר, נאמר כאן עול ונאמר להלן עול מה להלן שאר עבודות פוסלות בה אף כאן שאר עבודות פוסלות

And if you want to say that this *a fortiori* inference is unsound, you can instead learn this law through a verbal analogy: It is stated here, with regard to the red heifer, "yoke" (Num. 19:2), and it is stated there, with regard to the heifer whose neck is broken, "yoke" (Deut. 21:3). Just as there, other types of labor disqualify it, so too here in the case of the red heifer other types of labor disqualify it.

The Bavli asks, "What is the baraita referring to, i.e. what could be wrong about the qal v'homer argument?" The Bavli explains that the comparison set up in the qal v'homer between the *eglah arufah* and the red heifer is not made with respect to the relevant difference between the two. What is unique about a heifer whose neck is broken is that it is disqualified by years, which is not the case for a red heifer. Another problem with the qal v'homer arguments is that it could be argued that the case of sacred offerings is a counterexample to the inference of the qal v'homer (i.e. to the qal v'homer conditional): a blemish disqualifies them, but labor does not disqualify them.

The Yerushalmi offers the same *gezerah shavah* on Y. Sotah 9:5, 42a, but not the qal v'homer argument above found in the Bavli which is also part of the *o'kheiluf* argument in the Sifre Bamidbar. It would seem that the Yerushalmi agrees with the Bavli's objection above to that qal v'homer and instead offered a proof by *gezerah shavah* it found compelling.

2. The question driving the *o'kheiluf* argument in the Mekhilta is whether or not the ox that gored is forbidden to be made use of. The *o'kheiluf* argument draws an association from the *eglah arufah* to the ox that gored. If the *eglah arufah* which atones for sins is forbidden to be benefitted from must-it-not-certainly-follow-that the ox that gored and thus added sin to the world is forbidden to be benefitted from?! But the biblical evidence that the *eglah arufah* may not be benefitted from is only suggestive and therefore can be doubted. *O'kheiluf* ensues, upholding the first qal v'homer and thus concluding that the goring ox may not be used for benefit. Accepting that qal v'homer also entails upholding the truth of its launching premise, i.e. that the *eglah arufah* is forbidden to be used for benefit.

On B. Avodah Zarah 29b, the mishnah under discussion, M. Avodah Zarah 2:3, lists items that belong to idol worshipers and are prohibited [to Jews] and from which it is prohibited to derive any benefit. One of the items in the list is wine belonging to an idol worshiper.

The Bavli in its analysis of this mishnah asks, "From where [in the Torah] is it known that wine belonging to an idol worshiper is prohibited?" That is, what is the biblical basis for these rulings by the Mishnah. The answers it gives can be schematized as follows: wine → sacrifice → corpse → *eglah arufah*.

The Bavli argues that the law about wine is learned from the law regarding offerings of idol worshipers which is derived from the law prohibiting deriving benefit from a corpse which in turn is derived from the law that prohibits benefitting from the *eglah arufah*.

279

"And how is the last law known, that no benefit may be obtained from the *eglah arufah*," the Bavli asks. The Bavli is able to supply a derivation: "The school of R. Yannai said, 'It is written *kapparah* by it just as by *kodshim* [sacrificial animals].'"[167]

The purpose of the *eglah arufah* is to atone for the people (Deut. 21:4) who live in the city in which a corpse of a slain person is found and the murderer cannot be identified, and it is said of sacrificial animals that they atone for the sins of the people. Just as the latter which also serve the function of atoning for people are prohibited to be used for benefit, so too the former may not be used for benefit.

The Bavli's proof focuses on the shared word *kapparah*, meaning atonement, which describes the function of the *eglah arufah* as well as that of the sacrificial animals, to argue that the law prohibiting deriving benefit from the latter must be true of the former as well. Because the Bavli is able to derive the law, it does not need to suppose the law true as the Mekhilta does (perhaps based on context). Furthermore, the confidence established in this law means that unlike the Mekhilta the Bavli would have no reason to engage in *o'kheiluf*.

---

[167] The Bavli also does not use the proof from the Sifre Devarim, piska 207, on Deut, 21:4, which goes as follows: With regard to the word *v'arpu* (וערפו),'and you will break its neck' the same verb is used by the firstborn, the *peter rekhem,* of the donkey (Exod.13:13). If a person does not want to redeem the firstborn of the donkey by giving the priest a sheep he must axe the neck of the donkey. He cannot benefit from the carcass of the donkey (as he killed it because he was not willing to give the priest a sheep instead). Since the same verb is used by the *eglah arufah*, by analogy it carries the same connotations as when used for the axed donkey, including that the carcass may not be used for benefit.

Interestingly, the Mekhilta in Mesekhta de-Piskha, in commenting on Exod.13:13, uses the same analogy based on the same verb, to argue in the other direction: Since the *eglah arufah* may not be used for benefit the same applies to the axed firstborn donkey. The Mekhilta believes the former to be true because *o'kheiluf* resulted in strong confidence in the contextual evidence that the carcass of the *eglah arufah* may not be used for benefit.

The Bavli does not use its finding that the *eglah arufah* is prohibited to be used for benefit, to drive a qal v'homer to the case of the goring ox. That is, the Bavli does not appropriate the first qal v'homer of the Mekhilta's *o'kheiluf* argument.

For the Talmud's position on whether the goring ox is prohibited to be benefitted from, B. Kiddushin 56b is examined. The Mishnah under discussion is M. Kiddushin 2:9 which gives a whole list of items including the goring ox and the *eglah arufah*, such that if one betrothed a wife with any of those, his nuptials are invalid:

מתני'. המקדש בערלה, בכלאי הכרם, בשור הנסקל, ובעגלה ערופה, בצפורי
מצורע, ובשער נזיר, ופטר חמור, ובשר בחלב, וחולין שנשחטו בעזרה - אינה
מקודשת. מכרן, וקידש בדמיהן – מקודשת

The Bavli asks for the biblical source for the Mishnah's ruling that the carcass of an ox that gored cannot be given to a woman to accomplish betrothal. The Bavli answers with a baraita, the first part covered in the first paragraph below is found in the Mekhilta right before the *o'kheiluf* argument between the *eglah arufah* and goring ox:

From the fact that it says (Exod. 21:28) "the ox will be stoned," do I not know that it is a *neveilah*, an animal that died without being properly slaughtered, and a *neveilah* is forbidden for eating? Why then was it necessary for the Torah to state in Exod. 21:28, לא יאכל את בשרו, i.e. its flesh may not be eaten? It informs that even if the ox's owner slaughtered it after its sentence was finalized but before it was stoned, the meat is nevertheless forbidden for eating.

From where do we know that it is forbidden for (other) benefit as well? *Talmud lomar*, the Torah states (at the end of Exod. 21:28), ובעל השור נקי, and the owner of the ox is clean. What does this mean? Shimon ben Zoma says: It is similar to when a man says to his fellow, 'so-

281

and-so has gone out clean of his possessions,' i.e he has no benefit at all from them.[168]

The Bavli then takes issue with the first part of the baraita, the interpretation of לא יאכל את בשרו, pointing out that no source is given for it and that perhaps it is wrong and the ox slaughtered properly before it is stoned is permitted to be eaten. What then is the function of the otherwise– as raised in the first part of the baraita — seemingly redundant phrase, "its flesh may not be eaten"? To teach that it is forbidden to benefit from the stoned ox. (The Yerushalmi, Y.Avodah Zarah 5:12, 36b in commenting on M. Avodah Zarah 5:9, gives the same teaching from the redundant phrase "its flesh may not be eaten" that the stoned ox is forbidden to be benefited from.)

The Bavli goes on and says that the interpretation it has just given is supported by what R. Abahu said in the name of R. Elazar: 'Wherever the Torah says "he may not eat", "you may not eat" or "you [plural] may not eat," it is to be understand as a prohibition against both eating and obtaining benefit unless the Torah specifies otherwise as it does in the case of a *neveilah*.'[169]

The Bavli turns around and casts doubt on the support from R. Abahu's teaching. The anonymous voice argues that R. Abahu's teaching that the words "it may not be eaten" also prohibit deriving benefit, only applies when those same words are the source for the prohibition on eating. In this case, the prohibition on eating is derived from the words "the ox will be stoned." Conceding this, if one wanted to claim that the function of the words "he may not eat" is solely to prohibit the deriving of benefit from the stoned ox, one is left with the question of why would the Torah not simply state that and instead state "he may not eat."

---

[168] Similar to the 20th century American expression "They took him to the cleaners!"

[169] Deut.14:21 states "You shall not eat any *neveilah*. To the stranger who is within your gates you may give it so that he may eat it or you may sell it to a gentile." A *neveilah* is an animal that died without proper slaughter.

Even if one does allow R. Abahu's principle to apply in this case, and "it may not be eaten" teaches that the stoned ox is prohibited to be used for benefit, why did the verse need to say "its flesh" in "its flesh may not be eaten"? The Bavli answers that it means to teach that even if the stoned ox was (first) properly slaughtered, it is not permitted to be eaten.

The Bavli then asks, 'Now that we have derived both the prohibition of eating and the prohibition of benefit from the words "it may not be eaten" what then is the function of the words "the owner of the ox is clean"?'[170] The Gemara answers that it comes to teach that the hide of the ox may not be used for benefit. Without that phrase one might otherwise have thought that since it is written "its flesh may not be eaten" that the flesh is prohibited for eating or to be benefited from but that the hide is permitted for benefit.[171]

Thus the Bavli learns out directly from the words "the owner of the ox is clean" or from the words "it may not be eaten" via R. Abahu's teaching (in R. Elazar's name) that the ox that gored is forbidden to be benefitted from. These proofs are direct; their sources are the immediate biblical words describing the law of the goring ox.

The Bavli apparently finds this proof more rigorous and compelling than using the law known about the eglah arufah, by analogy with sacrifices that are also described as atoning, to derive by the first qal v'homer of the o'kheiluf argument in the Mekhilta (now launched from a fact), that the stoned ox is also forbidden to be benefitted from.

The Yerushalmi also does not choose qal v'homer between eglah arufah and the stoned ox to derive these laws. Avodah Zarah 5:9 lists

---

[170] For further discussion see B. Kiddushin 56b and commentaries. Here we cite only what is directly relevant to our question of why the Gemara does not use the o'kheiluf argument on this subject from the Mekhilta.

[171] In the Mekhilta, after discussion, this law follows from the law prohibiting benefitting from the gored ox.

the stoned ox and the *eglah arufah* amongst items that are completely forbidden, even in the tiniest amounts. Exod. 21:28 states that the stoned ox may not be eaten. The Yerushalmi, Y. Avodah Zarah 5:12, asks, "From the fact that it [the verse] says 'the ox must be stoned' don't we know that it cannot be eaten? What then is the purpose of the phrase 'it may not be eaten'?" The Yerushalmi answers that the phrase teaches that it is forbidden *bi-hana-ah*, i.e. it is forbidden to benefit from it or enjoy it in any way. With regard to the *eglah arufah*, the Yerushalmi derives by a *gezerah shavah* on the word *sham*, meaning 'there', used in reference to both the *eglah arufah* and burying Miriam (Num. 20:1), that just as a corpse may not be used for any benefit the same is the law for the *eglah arufah*. (The Bavli, B. Avodah Zarah 29b, used this *gezerah shavah* in the other direction from knowing the law regarding the *eglah arufah* to derive the law for a corpse.)

3. The question motivating the *o'kheiluf* argument found in the Sifre Bamidbar, piska 123, is whether the statement in Num.19:2 that the red heifer may not have born a yoke, also implies that the animal chosen may not have done any other work as well. *O'kheiluf* by comparison with the case of the *eglah arufah* leads to an answer.

There is no mishnah that rules on this question. M.Sotah 9:5-6 which deals with the *eglah arufah* process details the requirements on the calf chosen, that it must not have pulled a yoke but that it need not be blemish-free. These details about the *eglah arufah* are the very same details that drive the *o'kheiluf* argument in the Sifre about the red heifer. The Bavli on B. Sotah 46a uses these details to answer the question it raises, the very same question of the *o'kheiluf* in the Sifre about whether other work invalidates the red heifer:

Rav Yehuda says that Rav says, "If one places a bundle of sacks on a red heifer, it is disqualified; and as for the calf [for the *eglah arufah* rite] it is not disqualified until it pulls a burden." The Gemara raises an objection to these rulings from a baraita:

"From the word עול [אשר לא עלה עליה] (Num.19:2), I know only that a yoke disqualifies a red heifer, from where do I know that other types of labors likewise disqualify the red heifer?"

אמרת קל וחומר: ומה עגלה שאין מום פוסל בה שאר עבודות פוסלות בה, פרה שמום פוסל בה אינו דין ששאר עבודות פוסלות בה !?

By qal v'homer: since the calf [for the *eglah arufah* rite] which is not disqualified by a blemish, is though disqualified by other types labor, the heifer [for the red heifer rite] which is disqualified by a blemish, must-it-not-follow that it is disqualified by other types of labor ?!

This is the same qal v'homer argument that forms the basis of the associated *o'kheiluf* argument in the Sifre.

As in the *o'kheiluf* in the Sifre, in the above baraita, Deut. 21:3 is understood as meaning that any work involving a yoke or work not involving a yoke disqualifies the calf. Unlike (this baraita cited by the) Gemara which expresses confidence in this understanding of the verse, the *o'kheiluf* in the Sifre is motivated by lack of full confidence in this reading of the verse.

The Bavli is comfortable with this understanding of the verse which is also the content of the launching premise P in the *o'kheiluf* argument in the Sifre. Since the Bavli is confident of its truth, it has no basis for suggesting *o'kheiluf* as in the Sifre. (Recall that *o'kheiluf* occurs when the truth of the conclusion of a qal v'homer may be doubted precisely because there is less than complete confidence in the truth of the launching premise, P, of that qal v'homer argument.)

The Yerusahlmi like the Bavli is comfortable with the evidence for P and has no basis to doubt it as does the Sifre. The Yerushalmi uses (only proof by) a *gezerah shavah* from P to show that the red heifer is also disqualified by any type of work, not just drawing a yoke.

The situation is the same regarding the *o'kheiluf* argument in the Sifre Numbers, piska 155 about the respective rights of the father and the husband to annul the vows made by a female. From verses Num. 30:14,17 the Sifre understands that the husband may annul any vow a woman makes that could cause her harm or regarding a matter that is between her and her husband. The Sifre however is not certain that these are the sum total of the vows a husband may annul.[172] Since it is not certain of this claim, the Sifre cannot be certain of the conclusion of the just-as argument launched from that claim. Therefore o'kheiluf ensues, concluding that, yes indeed, those are the sum total of vows the husband may annul and so too therefore is the case for the father.

M. Nedarim 11:1, on the other hand, using the same expression as the Sifre in piska 155, ענוי נפש, starts off by declaring that the oaths that he [the husband or the father] may annul are those that would cause the woman suffering. As is quite common in the Mishnah, no biblical verse is cited as a source for this ruling. The fruit examples in M. Nedarim 11:2 also appear in the Sifre.

נדרים פרק יא משנה א-ב:

ואלו דברים שהוא מפר דברים שיש בהם ענוי נפש, אם ארחץ ואם לא ארחץ , אם אתקשט ואם לא אתקשט. אמר רבי יוסי, אין אלו נדרי ענוי נפש.

---

[172] However there is another derash a bit further on in piska 155 that does see the biblical evidence for the claim that the husband only annuls the two classes of vows, as conclusive and launches a qal v'homer from that claim. Beginning from the claim that those two categories are the only oaths that the husband nullifies and drawing a qal v'homer concludes that the same is the case for the father of the girl. That qal v'homer is refuted on the grounds that the axis of comparison, the husband annuls when the wife is a mature woman while the father does not, is not the most relevant way to compare the two. That is, it is not true that the husband has rights in more circumstances than the father. It is because the rights of the father could not be derived by qal v'homer, the midrash argues, that the Torah included the following words from which a hekesh must be drawn: 'אלה החקים אשר צוה ה. את משה בין איש לאשתו ובין אב לביתו. One is forced to draw a hekesh from the husband to the father. That is, just as the husband annuls only those oaths that his wife might take that would cause her harm so too the father with regard to his daughter annuls only such vows.

286

ואלו הן נדרי עינוי נפש, אמרה קונם פרות העולם עלי, הרי זה יכול להפר. פרות מדינה עלי, יביא לה מהמדינה אחרת. פרות חנוני זה עלי, אינו יכול להפר. ואם לא היתה פרנסתה אלא ממנו, הרי זה יפר, דברי רבי יוסי.

Turning now to the treatment of M. Nedarim 11:1-2 on B. Nedarim 79a, the Bavli raises a question with regard to the ruling in 11:1, "Is it only vows that cause suffering (עינוי נפש) that the husband may nullify so that he may not nullify any vows that do not cause the woman to suffer?" A baraita is presented that answers this question: The biblical phrase "בין איש לאשתו בן אב לבתו" (Num.30:14) teaches that a husband can nullify any of his wife's vows that concern matters between the two of them even if the vow would not cause the wife to suffer:

נדרי עינוי נפש הוא דמפר שאין בהן עינוי נפש אינו מפר והא תניא "בין איש לאשתו בן אב לבתו" מלמד שהבעל מפר נדרים שבינו לבינה

This baraita could certainly have been taken directly from the Sifre Bamidbar because as we saw, piska 155 does contain this remark.

Thus the Bavli adding to the mishnaic ruling "these are the things [oaths] that he annuls, those that involve suffering, for example..," the content of the baraita that the husband may also annul vows concerning matters between him and his wife, now has a complete list of the vows the husband may annul.

As for the Mishnah's source for its ruling that the husband may annul any oath his wife makes that would cause her to suffer, Rava in the Bavli takes for granted that the source is the explicit statement in Num.30:17. This is the same source that Sifre Bamidbar cites. Thus Num.30:17 and the baraita that cites Num. 30:14 are the sources for the Bavli's position that these exhaust the oaths that the husband may annul, namely, oaths that may cause her pain and those that concern matters between the two of them.

The Sifre Bamidbar suggests that these are the sum total of the oaths the husband may annul. But unlike the Bavli, the Sifre is not certain of this. The Sifre demands stronger proof than the Bavli. It is because the Sifre is uncertain of this claim that it engages in o'kheiluf.

The Yerushalmi, similarly to the Bavli, not having as high a standard of proof as does the Sifre Bamidbar, is confident in the evidence for the premise that the husband may annul precisely the oaths his wife takes that may cause her harm or that concern matters between the two of them. The Yerushalmi therefore confidently drives a qal v'homer from this premise to reach a conclusion that it would have no grounds to doubt and therefore no basis to engage in o'kheiluf. This qal v'homer derives which oaths the father may annul. The Bavli, on the other hand, does not focus on the father.

Y. Nedarim 11:1, 35b-36a:

כתיב, [במדבר ל: יד] "כל נדר וכל שבועת אסר לענות נפש" אין לי אלא נדרים שיש בהן עינוי נפש. נדרים שבינו לבינה מניין? "בין איש לאשתו". עד כדון בבעל. באב מניין [בין אב לבתו] מה הבעל אינו מיפר אלא נדרים שיש בהן עינוי נפש ונדרים שבינו לבינה. אף האב אינו מיפר אלא נדרים שיש בהן עינוי נפש ונדרים שבינו לבינה

4. Three o'kheiluf arguments in the Sifra, Diburah DeKhova, chapter 12, arise to answer a question prompted by reading Lev. 5:17, namely, whether the asham offering, brought by a person who unknowingly commits a forbidden act, i.e. a lo taaseh, should be brought even when that sin is a minor sin. All three of these arguments of the R. Akiva school fail (because there is no evidence whatsoever for either P or -Q or -P or Q in each of the arguments). Failure of these qal v'homer arguments is seen as justifying the more opaque derivation that follows: The word asham is mentioned in Lev. 4:27 and in Lev. 5:17 to draw a gezerah shavah between the two, just as in the former the asham refers to a matter whose intentional violation is punishable by extirpation and whose unintentional violation requires a sin offering and whose doubtful violation requires

an asham offering so too is the meaning of the word *asham* in Lev. 5:17.

This conclusion in the Sifra is also a teaching in the last line of M. Keritot 6:3:

כריתות 6:3:

רבי אליעזר אומר, מתנדב אדם אשם תלוי בכל יום ובכל שעה שירצה, והיא נקראת אשם חסידים. אמרו עליו על בבא בן בוטי, שהיה מתנדב אשם תלוי בכל יום, חוץ מאחר יום הכפורים יום אחד. אמר, המעון הזה, אלו היו מניחים לי, הייתי מביא, אלא אומרים לי, המתן עד שתכנס לספק. <u>וחכמים אומרים, אין מביאים אשם תלוי אלא על דבר שזדונו כרת ושגגתו חטאת.</u>

-

The Bavli in its analysis of this mishnah on B. Keritot 25b quotes Rava as asking for the reason for the mishnaic ruling that the provisional *asham* offering is only brought when one is in doubt of having performed a sin whose unintentional performance requires a sin offering and whose intentional violation is punishable by extirpation. The answer given is the same *gezerah shavah* that the Sifra gives relating the same verses, Lev 4:27 and 5:17, but based on the presence in both of the word *mitzvot* rather than the word *asham*. The Bavli makes no mention of the failed *o'kheiluf* arguments in the Sifra that motivated the derivation there by *gezerah shavah*.

There is no Yerushalmi on Keritot as it is in the order of Kodshim.

The situation is similar for the *o'kheiluf* argument in Sifre Devarim, piska 249 which deals with the law concerning the *mamzer* and the law about the Moabite and Ammonite. The conclusions of the argument also appear as rulings in the first and last statements of M. Yevamot 8:3.

The Bavli in discussing this mishnah on B.Yevamot 76b cites a baraita that gives the same derivations that the Sifre Devarim gives of the references of the two laws, that *mamzer* refers to both male and female and that Maobite and Ammonite refer to only males. But the Bavli does not incorporate the failed *o'kheiluf* argument of the Sifre

Devarim that precedes and motivates its final derivations of the references of the two laws. (Yerushalmi Kiddushin 3:12, 40a, in the name of the Ammora R. Abahu, also explains *mamzer* as a contraction of *mum zar*, i.e. a strange blemish.)

5. The *o'kheiluf* argument in piska 125 of Sifre Bamidbar concerns whether a dying person and whether a *sheretz* convey impurity while in the throes of death or only after they have died. The *o'kheiluf* argument starts out as follows:

מת חמור

אינו מטמא עד שעה שימות

שרץ הקל

אינו דין שלא יטמא עד שימות !?

This is followed by *o'kheiluf* which is refuted on the evidence for מת אינו מטמא עד שעה שימות, which is the redundant language in Num. 19:13: בנפש האדם אשר <u>ימות</u> כל הנוגע <u>במת</u>. The first argument, the argument above, is thereby proven to express the correct law, that for both man and *sheretz*, they only convey ritual impurity once they are actually dead.

There is a parallel mishnah, M. Oholot 1:6, to this *o'kheiluf* argument that declares these same conclusions as the law, i.e. that for both man and animal they only convey impurity once they are actually dead and not while in the throes of death. However there is no Gemara on this Mishnah tractate.

<u>אהלות א:ו</u> :

אדם אינו מטמא עד שתצא נפשו. ואפלו מגיד ואפלו גוסס. זוקק ליבום ופוטר מן היבום, מאכיל בתרומה ופוסל בתרומה. וכן בהמה וחיה אינן מטמאין עד שתצא נפשם. התזו ראשיהם, אף על פי שמפרכסים, טמאים, כגון זנב של לטאה שהיא מפרכסת.

The חיה in the above mishnah appears to include things that are in the class of *sheretz*. The animal it gives as an example of one who moves after its head is cut off, is the לטאה, the lizard. Since such movement is that (of the tail) of an already dead animal, one who touches it in that state becomes ritually impure. The לטאה is in the list given in Lev.11:30 of type of שרץ (i.e. *sheretz*) that is *tameh*.

There is no Gemara on M.Oholot so it is not surprising that we do not find any reference in the Bavli to the corresponding *o'kheiluf* argument. The first part of the mishnah is cited in B.Yevamot 120b, and B. Nazir 43b for different purposes. The Gemara in both places understands the mishnah in a straightforward way and accepts its ruling that a dying person imparts impurity only once he is dead. The Gemara in these different places does not ask for the source of the mishnah's ruling.

7.2: Did the Bavli Find Tannaitic *O'Kheiluf* Arguments Unsound?

We have given five reasons to explain why 14 out of the 15 *o'kheiluf* arguments in the Midrash Halakhah did not find their way into the Bavli as a baraita. None of these reasons indicates that the Bavli found the *o'kheiluf* arguments to be logically incoherent and for that reason passed them over. As for the *o'kheiluf* arguments of the R. Akiva school, where the impossibility of eliminating either qal v'homer motivated a less transparent derivation of the law in question, the Bavli often only copied the final derivation skipping the preliminary *o'kheiluf* argument with its failed pair of qal v'homer arguments. In these cases the Bavli, unlike the Midrash Halakhah, found the final derivations compelling and clearly not in need of explicit motivation.

In Chapter Five the (imagined) Stoic philosopher's analysis showed that the *o'kheiluf* argument of the Tannaim betrayed blanket ignorance of Greek and Stoic logic. In particular they did not know about *modus tollens* and that taking the contrapositive of a conditional statement does not change the truth value of the conditional statement. The Tannaim of the two schools were not able to recognize that the *kheiluf* qal v'homer must conclude with the

291

negation of the launching premise of the original qal v'homer, regardless of the particulars of the case.

For the R. Ishmael school, this ignorance cost their *o'kheiluf* arguments logical coherence. They engaged in *o'kheiluf* because they lacked confidence in the biblical evidence for the launching premise P of their qal v'homer argument. When the *kheiluf* qal v'homer concluded with –P, they refuted this conclusion with the biblical evidence for P. The school of R. Ishmael in each *o'kheiluf* made the logical mistake of thinking that their evidence for P had been strengthened by using it to refute -P. The *o'kheiluf* arguments did not fulfill their intended purpose: they did not replace a tentative answer to the question at issue with an answer meriting more confidence.

The Stoic showed that although in the *o'kheiluf* arguments of the school of R. Ishmael, the author thinks he justifies his increased confidence in the truth of P, he is wrong. He is not justified in having any more confidence in the truth of the launching premise P than he had at the start. In this sense these arguments are not logically coherent.

But the Bavli did not see any of the problems with the tannaitic *o'kheiluf* arguments that the Stoic saw. The Bavli had a lower standard for what constitutes a biblical proof text for claim P, more in line with some of the midrash of the R. Akiva school.[173] As explained in reason three, what the R. Ishmael school saw as weak biblical evidence in support of P, the Bavli saw as sufficient evidence and therefore the Bavli had no basis for questioning the conclusion of the qal v'homer from P and suggesting *o'kheiluf*. Therefore wherever the Bavli found the substance of the parallel *o'kheiluf* argument cogent, i.e. the topics being compared and the properties with respect to which the comparison is made, the Bavli only incorporated the first

---

[173] Although some of the midrash of the school of R. Akiva witnesses the same very high evidence for proof of a claim, namely, the *o'kheiluf* arguments in the Sifre Devarim. See Chapter Two.

qal v'homer going from P to Q. The Bavli's likely attitude about the *kheiluf* qal v'homer and its refutation in the R. Ishmael passage leaving only the original qal v'homer, is that it was unnecessary as the Bavli found the evidence for P to be sufficiently strong.

7.3: Conclusions

Only one of the 15 *o'kheiluf* arguments of the Midrash Halakhah can be found included as a baraita in the Talmuds. Yet many of the conclusions of these *o'kheiluf* arguments occur as succinct rulings of the Mishnah. The Bavli (and the Yerushalmi) on these mishnayot does not answer the question it invariably raises, 'from where is this known', with the relevant *o'kheiluf* argument, but answers instead using some other tannaitic material. This may lead one to wonder whether the Talmuds found the reasoning in *o'kheiluf* arguments to be wanting. Did the Talmuds see the logical problems that the imagined Stoic philosopher pointed out in Chapter Five and is that the reason the Talmuds did not incorporate these *o'kheiluf* arguments?

This chapter examined the Bavli's as well as the Yerushalmi's sources for each of the laws that occur as conclusions of *o'kheiluf* arguments of the Midrash Halakhah, to try and determine why the Talmuds preferred some other tannaitic derivation over the corresponding *o'kheiluf* argument. Five different reasons were given to explain why the Talmuds eschewed proof by *o'kheiluf*.

Sometimes the Gemara objected to the choice of properties (i.e. A & B in formulation (*)) with respect to which the two topics in the *o'kheiluf* argument are compared. Other times the Gemara, unlike the Midrash Halakhah, found the biblical evidence for the launching premise of the *o'kheiluf* argument to be sufficiently strong and therefore *o'kheiluf* was not warranted. Other times, the Gemara, unlike the Midrash Halakhah, was able to provide biblical support for the launching premise of an *o'kheiluf* argument and therefore had no reason to engage in *o'kheiluf*. With respect to *o'kheiluf* arguments of the R. Akiva school that failed and were only presented in order to motivate the more opaque derivation of the law that followed, the Bavli would sometimes just copy the opaque derivation, not believing that the latter needed to be justified.

All of these reasons that the Bavli and Yerushalmi had for not choosing to incorporate an *o'kheiluf* argument from the Midrash Halakhah, were focused on the content of the particular *o'kheiluf* argument, and the biblical support its claims rely upon. None of the reasons were focused on the form or format of the *o'kheiluf* argument. The Bavli did not reject any of the *o'kheiluf* arguments because it found them logically problematic. The Bavli did not see the serious logical shortcomings inherent in the *o'kheiluf* argument that the imagined Stoic philosopher laid out in Chapter Five.

As the next chapter will further demonstrate, like the Tannaim of the two schools, the rabbis of the Talmud were not able to recognize that the *kheiluf* qal v'homer must conclude with the negation of the launching premise of the original qal v'homer, regardless of the particulars of the case. The Talmud could therefore not point out that the evidence for the launching premise of the first qal v'homer was in no way strengthened when the *kheiluf* qal v'homer concluded (as it must) with the negation of the launching premise. Further, that the contrapositive of a conditional statement has the same truth value as the conditional is not something that the rabbis knew or could even consider.

CHAPTER EIGHT: *O'Kheiluf* of the Bavli

8.1: Overview

This chapter examines the two *o'kheiluf* arguments that appear in the Bavli. One appears on B.Temurah 28b as a baraita and is a copy of an *o'kheiluf* argument from the Sifra. The other *o'kheiluf* argument on B.Avodah Zarah 46b is of amoraic origin and original to the Bavli.

In its discussion of the argument from the Sifra, the Bavli reads its own objectives into the passage in a way that reveals serious errors in grasping the structure and function of the second part of that *o'kheiluf* argument following its set-up. In considering how a reading of a different verse suggested by an Amora may impact conclusions from the *o'kheiluf* argument, the Bavli is stilted, showing itself to be unable to enter into the logical game of the second part of the *o'kheiluf* argument to yield an answer faithful to the tannaitic *o'kheiluf* argument. But unlike in the tannaitic passage from the Sifra, the Bavli is concerned to justify how biblical cues are matched to particular derivations.

As will be shown, the Amoraim applied the phrase *o'kheiluf* exactly as did the Tannaim: the phrase *o'kheiluf* followed one qal v'homer and announced another qal v'homer that began from (what is) the negation of the conclusion of the first. Symbolically, the first part of the amoraic *o'kheiluf* argument can be represented like all of the tannaitic *o'kheiluf* arguments by,

> Since **A**, **B** & **P** must-it-not-follows-that **Q** ?!
> *o'kheiluf*
> Since **A**, **B** & **-Q** must-it-not-follow-that **-P** ?!

where A and B are known to be true from biblical verses and the evidence for P (and –Q) is at most weak.

But the amoraic *o'kheiluf* argument in Avodah Zarah is different from all of the tannaitic *o'kheiluf* arguments in that weak evidence is given for the launching premises of both qal v'homer arguments, i.e. not just for P but also for –Q. The Bavli does not notice this difference and its significance, neither Rav Pappa nor the stam, the later anonymous voice of the Bavli. And this is why Rav Pappa tries to compare this argument to the *o'kheiluf* argument on M. Pesahim 6:2. The Bavli also does not recognize the reason Rava needs to introduce a way to resolve the argument that the Tannaim did not use in their *o'kheiluf* arguments.

Because each of the two qal v'homer arguments of the amoraic *o'kheiluf* argument is launched from a proposition supported by weak biblical evidence, it is impossible to resolve the argument either as the R. Ishmael school did by eliminating one of the two qal v'homers or as the R. Akiva school usually did, by arguing that since there is no information at all about the claims of either qal v'homer, the two should be dropped, and another method introduced to yield an answer to the question at issue. The principle that Rava introduces to resolve the *o'kheiluf* argument that he is engaged in with Rav Huna the son of Rav Yehoshua, abolishes this argument form. The principle dictates that one must not even suggest a qal v'homer that leads to a leniency if there is another one that leads to a stringent ruling.

The principle Rava introduces to resolve the argument would invalidate all of the tannaitic *o'kheiluf* arguments, if it was meant to apply to all *o'kheiluf* arguments irrespective of whether or not there is any biblical evidence for both launching premises. The medieval commentaries, the Tosafot, certainly did not recognize the importance of the distinction between this amoraic *o'kheiluf* argument and all of the tannaitic *o'kheiluf* arguments, the distinction between the presence or absence of evidence for each launching claim, and this is why they sought to reconcile Rava's principle with the tannaitic *o'kheiluf* argument from the Sifra on B.Temurah 28b. Their resolution is ad hoc and cannot justify many of the *o'kheiluf* arguments of the Midrash Halakhah while upholding Rava's principle.

Later generations of Amoraim and the Stammaim would not launch a qal v'homer from a claim for which the only supporting evidence is the absence of any biblical statement to the contrary. But they did not raise objections to tannaitic material (incorporated into the Bavli) that witnesses the Tannaim doing exactly that.[174] Explanation is offered, in what follows, for why the Gemara developed this standard that it does not share with the Tannaim in the Midrash Halakhah.

8.2: B.Temurah 28b: Faulty Understanding of the *O'Kheiluf* Baraita

The *o'kheiluf* argument from the Sifra, Dibbura de-Nedavah which was discussed in Chapters Two and Four, appears also as a baraita on B.Temurah 28b. It is the only *o'kheiluf* argument from the Midrash Halakhah that appears in the Talmud. Its treatment in the Bavli will be shown to expose a lack of real familiarity and facility with the second or concluding part of the *o'kheiluf* arguments of the Midrash Halakhah and with how they operate, especially those of the R. Akiva school. (The argument does not appear in the Talmud Yerushalmi as there is no Yerushalmi on M.Temurah (or on any of the other tractates in the

---

[174]See David Weiss Halivni, *Peshat and Derash, Plain and Applied Meaning in Rabbinic Exegesis* (Oxford: Oxford University Press, 1991): 26-27. Weiss Halivni there makes a similar observation about the practice of 'reading in' to the text (what might not appear to be in the text):
"Despite the discontinuation of reading in, the rabbis of the talmudic period did not seriously challenge the right of their predecessors to have used that method. They seem to have granted the right to their predecessors but not to themselves. Their conviction against reading in was not absolute or thorough enough to impel them to criticize their authoritative predecessors. Their aversion, derived from their interpretive state of mind, was sufficiently strong to prevent them from doing it themselves, but not strong enough to question the legitimacy of such an activity when done in earlier times, having become by now a part of the tradition. The past thus remained beyond criticism."

fifth order, Kodshim).) After analysis, the question of why this *o'kheiluf* argument was favored to be the single one incorporated in the Bavli as a baraita is taken up.

The Sifra, the Midrash Halakhah to Leviticus, follows the order of the verses. Leviticus begins with the topic of sacrifices offered voluntarily. Lev. 1:2 reads as follows:

דבר אל בני ישראל ואמרת אליהם, אדם כי יקריב מכם קרבן לה', מן הבהמה מן הבקר ומן הצאן תקריבו את קרבנכם.

Speak to the children of Israel and say to them, 'when a person amongst you brings a sacrifice to the Lord, from the domestic animals, from the cattle or from the sheep you shall offer your sacrifices.

The commentary interprets the phrase "from the domestic animals" as intending to exclude certain animals as unfit to be sacrifices, particularly those used for sodomy and bestiality, and then justifies that interpretation before moving on to interpret the phrase "from the cattle" as excluding animals that were worshiped. The *o'kheiluf* argument based on the law regarding the gift to a prostitute and the price of a dog, follows. Its function is to justify the interpretation of "from the cattle," by showing that the law excluding the worshiped animal could not be derived by qal v'homer reasoning and so some otherwise extraneous textual cue was needed as a source for the law.

The Sifra is attributed to the school of R. Akiva and the hermeneutical practice that draws biblically intended exclusions from the word *min*, meaning 'from', is typical of this school.

This same *o'kheiluf* argument which justifies the interpretation of the biblical phrase "from the cattle" as excluding a worshiped animal from those animals permitted to be sacrificed on the altar, occurs in the Talmud Bavli, Temurah 28b. But there, unlike in the Midrash Halakhah, it does not arise simply to interpret Lev.1:1, but rather for the further goal of providing a biblical source for the mishnaic law announced in the mishnah under discussion.

298

B. Temurah 28a begins with a copy of M.Temurah 6:1:

כל האסורין לגבי מזבח אוסרין בכל שהן הרובע והנרבע והמוקצה והנעבד והאתנן
ומחיר והכלאים והטרפה ויוצא דופן. איזהו מוקצה המוקצה לעבודת כוכבים הוא
אסור ומה שעליו מותר ואיזהו הנעבד כל שעובדין אותו הוא ומה שעליו אסור וזה
וזה מותר באכילה.

With regard to all animals whose sacrifice on the altar is prohibited, they
prohibit in any amount.[These are the animals whose sacrifice is prohibited:]
an animal that copulated with a person or that was sodomized, the animal
that was set aside, and one that was worshiped, an animal that was given to
a prostitute as payment, and the price [of a dog], or an animal crossbred
from a mixture of diverse kinds, a *treifah* (i.e. an animal ripped to death in the
wild) or an animal born by caesarean section. What is the set aside animal?
An animal set aside for worship to the stars. It is prohibited [as a sacrifice]
and what is on it is permitted. What is a worshiped animal? Any animal that
is worshiped. And what is upon it is prohibited. Both of those are permitted
for consumption.

In the course of analyzing the Mishnah phrase by phrase as is usual,
the Bavli seeks the biblical source for the Mishnah's exclusion first of
the *rova v'nirva* ,רובע והנרבע, and then for the worshiped animal (and
what is upon it). A baraita which is almost an exact copy of the Sifra
referred to above, addresses these two issues. The worshiped animal
is known to be excluded because of the phrase "from the cattle," and
the baraita continues with the *o'kheiluf* argument which supports this
interpretation by showing that no qal v'homer argument could derive
the teaching. Therefore the Torah needed to include the extra phrase
"from the cattle," to limit the cattle that may be brought as sacrifices,
i.e. to indicate that worshiped animals are to be excluded.

The baraita on B.Temurah 28a which is a copy from Sifra, Dibbura
de-Nedavah, parsha 2 (see #7 in Chapter Two of this book):

והלא דין הוא,
ומה אתנן ומחיר שציפויין מותרין הן אסורין, נעבד שציפוין אסור אינו דין שהוא
אסור !?

299

או חילוף

ומה אתנן ומחיר שהן אסורין ציפוייהן מותרין, נעבד שמותר יהא ציפויו מותר ?!

אם כן ביטלת "לא תחמוד כסף וזהב עליהם ולקחת לך".

אניי אקיימנו לא תחמד כסף וזהב בדבר שאין בו רוח חיים, אבל בדבר שיש בו רוח חיים הואיל והן מותר, יכול יהא ציפוי מותר. תלמוד לומר: "מן הבקר" להוציא את הנעבד.

The translated argument as labeled in Chapter Two:

While
A = 'The coverings of the gift given to a prostitute and the price paid for a dog are permitted [to be used]',
B = 'The gift given to a prostitute and the price paid for a dog are prohibited on the altar [as a sacrifice]'.
Therefore,
Since
P = 'The coverings of a worshiped animal are not permitted [to be used]'
must-it-not-follow-that
Q = 'A worshiped animal may not be put on the altar [as a sacrifice]'
?!

O'kheiluf

While
B = 'The gift given to a prostitute and the price paid for a dog are prohibited on the altar [as a sacrifice]',
A = 'The coverings of the gift given to a prostitute and the price paid for a dog are permitted [to be used]'.
Therefore,
Since
-Q = 'A worshiped animal may be offered as a sacrifice on the altar'
must-it-not-follow-that
-P = 'The coverings of a worshiped animal are permitted [to be used]'
?!

As laid out in detail in Chapter Two, the problem with this *o'kheiluf* argument is that there is no evidence for the claim that corresponds to **P** or the claim that corresponds to -**Q**.

The evidence for fact **B** is a biblical verse, Deut. 23:19, while the evidence for fact **A** is a derash on the last two words of that verse.

After presenting the *kheiluf* qal v'homer the Sifra offers, "[D]o not covet the silver and gold that is on them and take it for yourselves" from Deut. 7:25 as biblical disproof of the conclusion of the *kheiluf* qal v'homer argument, -**P**. The entire verse Deut. 7:25 reads as follows: "The carved images of their gods you shall burn in the fire, do not covet the silver and gold that is on them and take it for yourselves." The disproof is then rejected because the verse is clearly referring to inanimate idols and not to living animals that are worshiped as gods.

With no evidence whatsoever for **P**, **Q**, or -**P** or -**Q**, it is impossible to choose between the original qal v'homer argument and the *kheiluf* argument. Since the two qal v'homer arguments contradict each other they cannot both be right, and so the *o'kheiluf* argument fails to arrive at a conclusion as to whether a worshiped animal may or may not serve as a sacrifice. Two irrefutable contradictory *din* arguments remain with no way to decide between them. The Sifra therefore turns to a different way to decide the matter of law, deriving it from the biblical phrase "from the cattle."

The medieval commentator Rashi comments on this baraita on B. Temurah 28a. He elaborates on the words אז חילוף : "If the text had not written it [referring to the biblical phrase "from the cattle"] it would be possible לחלופי דינא [i.e. to turn the qal v'homer around; he is referring to arguing instead the qal v'homer that follows the phrase אז חילוף]." This confuses the structure of the *o'kheiluf* argument, putting the cart before the horse.[175] The *o'kheiluf* argument is prior, it

---

[175] Rabbeinu Hillel (Hillel ben Eliakim,12th century) in his commentary to (Torat Kohanim, i.e.) the Sifra, makes the same mistake. The Sifra contains

301

represents an implied exhaustive attempt to derive the law regarding whether or not the worshiped animal is allowed on the altar, by compelling reason, namely, qal v'homer reasoning. The *o'kheiluf* argument is meant to show that this fails, thus motivating a more opaque derivation of the law, in particular that the law may be derived as an exclusion from the phrase "from the cattle". It is because this law could not be deduced by reason from the statements of the Torah that the Torah had to include another phrase with the exclusionary cue "from" to serve as a source from which to derive this law.

In line with the Bavli's analysis which follows, Rashi has another comment that is not faithful to the second part of this tannaitic *o'kheiluf* argument from the Sifra. He comments on the concluding words of the *o'kheiluf* argument,

תלמוד לומר, "מן הבקר" ולא כל הבקר, להוציא את הנעבד,

that having established that worshiped animals are forbidden on the altar, it follows (from the baraita) that their coverings are forbidden even for ordinary use because of the biblical expression, "you shall not covet the gold silver upon them and take them for yourselves.." (Deut. 7:25).

---

5 arguments that this book identifies as *o'kheiluf* arguments. Despite his works focused on clarifying the Midrash Halakhah, Rabbeinu Hillel was apparently not able to apprehend the structure and function of the *o'kheiluf* argument.

The notes in the ArtScroll translation of Temurah 28b following Rashi display a confused or contrived understanding of the *o'kheiluf* argument. See especially the use of the word "restored" in "restored qal v'homer". These just get the whole set up and rhetorical function of the *o'kheiluf* argument wrong. It is very unusual to find conceptual misunderstandings in the ArtScroll translation of either Talmud. The scholars, translators and editors, have first rate command of not just the Talmud but of the vast literature of commentaries as well. It is thus clear from this book that in order to reach an understanding of the logical form and function of the *o'kheiluf*, it is helpful to examine the collection of tannaitic *o'kheiluf* arguments together. But of course to think of doing this, one must suspect that the phrase *o'kheiluf* serves a technical function and is not just the everyday word it appears to be.

But this last line about the coverings is not the intent of those last words of the baraita o'kheiluf argument. While the Mishnah includes a ruling about the coverings, the o'kheiluf argument of the Sifra has no conclusion about the coverings. As with all o'kheiluf arguments of the Midrash Halakhah, its focus is on the question that motivated the o'kheiluf argument. Once the situation of the coverings is not found to be useful to answer the question at issue about the worshiped animal, the midrash is no longer interested in it.[176] The second part of the o'kheiluf argument dispensed with verse Deut. 7:25 as a source prohibiting the coverings of a live animal. Returning to that verse to argue that once it is established that a live worshiped animal is forbidden on the altar, then what Deut. 7:25 teaches about an inanimate idol should be seen as intended for a living idol as well, is a totally separate derash that is not part of the o'kheiluf argument and apparently not part of any other known baraita either. The Bavli has the Amora Rav Hananya referring to this apparently amoraic argument.

The Bavli follows the baraita containing the o'kheiluf argument with an amoraic attack on it:

מתקיף לה רב חנניא: טעמא דמעטי' קרא הא לא מעטי' קרא ציפוי מותר והכתיב
(דברים יב, ג) ואבדתם את שמם כל העשוי לשמם

Rav Hananya attacks [the baraita as follows]:
"[According to the baraita] the only reason [that the coverings of the worshiped animal are prohibited for even ordinary use] is because of the restrictive phrase 'from the cattle' [which restricts any worshiped animal from being offered as a sacrifice]. Had the Torah not included the restrictive phrase 'from the cattle,' those coverings would have been permissible. But this conclusion cannot be correct because Deut. 12:3 commands that 'and you shall annihilate their names,' i.e. all that is made for their names."

---

[176] See in Chapters Two and Four the o'kheiluf arguments in the Sifra, excluding the one in Mekhilta de-Miluim.

According to Rav Hananya, the baraita implies that the coverings of a worshiped animal are forbidden to be used, and that this is learned out from "from the cattle".

Let us consider now what can be made of this claim. The *o'kheiluf* concludes that "from the cattle," teaches that a worshiped animal is not permitted on the altar. The *o'kheiluf* argument in getting to that conclusion also asserts that "you shall not covet the silver and gold upon them [i.e. the graven images] and take them for yourselves," does not refer also to live animals that are worshiped. This makes the second qal v'homer just as much a possibility as the first qal v'homer, but the two are contradictory. Thus the law is learned out, not by qal v'homer but from the exclusionary phrase "from the cattle." The baraita does not rule either way on the coverings of the worshiped animal.

Rav Hananya's objection is based on his tacit assertion that the baraita's conclusion excluding worshiped animals from the altar, further implies that the coverings of the worshiped animal are also prohibited even from ordinary use. How can this be claimed? Rashi addresses this, invoking Deut. 7:25 referred to already in the baraita, as follows: 'Now that it is known from the phrase "from the cattle" that worshiped animals are forbidden on the altar, the contents of Deut. 7:25 can be extended to live worshiped animals. The verse says, "The carved images of their gods you shall burn in the fire, do not covet the silver and gold that is on them and take it for yourselves." This law may be applied not just to a statue that is worshiped but also to a live animal that is worshiped since the law for that animal (it is now known) parallels the law of the carved statue. The latter may not be used, it must be burned and the former may not be offered on the altar.'

That the former may be consumed while the latter cannot be made any use of and must be burned is not seen by Rashi as breaking the analogy. Perhaps because eating a holy idol is itself an act of desecrating the god, and further, in keeping with the Torah value of not being wasteful of food, it is therefore preferable for individuals to feed one's family from the worshiped animal rather than to burn it to ashes.

Thus Rav Hananya understands the baraita as making the following assertions: the phrase "from the cattle" is needed to teach that the worshiped animal is forbidden from the altar and further, from this conclusion it is known that coverings of worshiped animals are forbidden even for ordinary use, and that there is no other way to derive that law. But Rav Hananya, even as understood by Rashi, is mistaken in attributing the last claim to the baraita. The baraita is completely uninterested in settling the matter of whether or not coverings of worshiped animals are forbidden for ordinary use.

As is typical of o'kheiluf arguments, the issue of coverings was only raised to aid in answering the question of whether or not a worshiped animal is forbidden on the altar. Once qal v'homer with the use of this aid failed, the aid was of no interest to the baraita and it did not return to focus on it.[177] This question of the status of the coverings is, on the other hand, important to the Bavli because the mishnah under analysis, M. Temurah 6:1, states further on that the coverings of the worshiped animals are forbidden to be used. The Bavli, as is typical, would seek the biblical source of this law.

The baraita found in the Sifra, the running commentary of the Midrash Halakhah on Leviticus, is interested in what can be understood from the biblical verse under consideration. In all of the o'kheiluf arguments where one qal v'homer wins out over the other and is declared true, both the premise and the conclusion of that qal v'homer argument are thereby established as operative laws.[178] But in those o'kheiluf

---

[177] See the other o'kheiluf arguments from the Sifra in Chapter Two. They all share the feature that a question of law raised by an approach that is abandoned once it is seen that qal v'homer cannot yield the answer to the issue that prompted the inquiry, is also abandoned.

[178] See in Chapter Two each of the o'kheiluf arguments of the R. Ishmael school, the Mekhilta and the Sifre Bamidbar. See there also the o'kheiluf

arguments where some other method answers the question of law (because neither of the qal v'homer arguments of the *o'kheiluf* may be ruled out as false) that other method answers only the question of law at issue. It does not weigh in on the truth or falsity of the premise of the corresponding qal v'homer argument (which is the conclusion of the alternate qal v'homer argument).[179] If Rav Hananya or the Amoraim preserving his teaching had understood the structure of *o'kheiluf* arguments they would not have attributed the claim described above to the baraita.

Rav Hananya argues that the law that coverings of the worshiped animal are not permitted even for ordinary use is known from Deut. 12:3. It is therefore not necessary, he argues, to prove that worshiped animals are prohibited from the altar to arrive at the law for coverings. The law for coverings is known directly from Deut. 12:3 which says, "You shall tear down their altars, smash their monuments, burn their *asherim* with fire, cut down the graven images of their gods, and destroy their name from that place." Rav Hananya argues that eradicating their name would include not appropriating their coverings for everyday use. The Bavli then attacks his interpretation of Deut. 12:3.

But as it stands, Rav Hananya's point is reasonable not as an attack on the baraita but as arguing that there is a biblical prohibition on coverings and the law prohibiting worshiped animals derived only from the words "from the cattle" need not be called on to derive the law prohibiting the use of the coverings. This is not an attack on the baraita.

But the implications of Rav Hananya's point are indeed an attack on the baraita. They are not recorded; they do not appear to have been recognized by Rav Hananya nor are they recognized by the

---

arguments in the Sifra in Mekhilta de-Miluim, in Sifre Devarim, piska 249, the middle argument on the word '*naarah*'.

[179] See all of the *o'kheiluf* arguments in Chapter Two not included in Note 3, all are of the R. Akiva school.

anonymous (*stam*) strata of the Bavli. They are as follows: once it is known from a biblical verse, Deut. 12:3, that the coverings of a worshiped animal are prohibited for even ordinary use, that is, once there is biblical evidence that **P** is true, then by the first qal v'homer of the *o'kheiluf* argument it follows that worshiped animals are forbidden on the altar. The first qal v'homer is thus launched from a premise for which there is some evidence, namely Deut. 12:3. The *kheiluf* argument launched from what is only a guess would be ruled out because its conclusion would be deemed false as it contradicts the evidence that exists, i.e. Deut. 12:3, for its negation. Thus only the first qal v'homer would remain standing and would therefore be declared correct. By (the first) qal v'homer, it would be known that worshiped animals are forbidden on the altar. (This is precisely how all of the *o'kheiluf* arguments of the R. Ishmael school proceed to a resolution, as well as those of the R. Akiva school where there is some evidence for the launching premises of one of the two qal v'homer arguments.[180]) There would thus be no need to use the exclusionary "from" in "from the cattle" to derive the law excluding worshiped animals from the altar.

All this suggests that the Amoraim lacked a deep familiarity with the *o'kheiluf* argumentation of the Midrash Halakhah. The whole *o'kheiluf* argument is lifted as a unit from the Sifra in the Midrash Halakhah and quoted in the Bavli. The Bavli certainly understands the first part of the *o'kheiluf* argument, that two proposed qal v'homer arguments to answer the matter of law are presented and that the *kheiluf* qal v'homer starts from what is (in the language of this work) the negation of the conclusion of the first qal v'homer argument. But as for the second and concluding part of the *o'kheiluf* argument, the Bavli claims for this baraita a purpose its authors did not intend, thus opening the interpretive possibility that this distortion is not artful but presented truly out of ignorance. And not just ignorance of the existence of a collection of tannaitic *o'kheiluf* arguments all sharing

---

[180] See in Chapters Two and Four all of the *o'kheiluf* arguments of the R.Ishmael school, as well as the one on the word '*naarah*' in Sifre Devarim, piska 249.

features in common (such as not weighing in on the law involved in an approach abandoned as the argument advances), for the Bavli also clearly displays here ignorance of what can be learned from a single o'kheiluf argument. The Bavli shows that it does not know how to apply new information it considers, i.e. evidence from Deut. 12:3, to the o'kheiluf argument. The Bavli does not have the reasoning facility that the Tannaim had with the o'kheiluf argument. The Bavli does not understand well (by tannaitic standards) the mechanism of the o'kheiluf argument, the different gears from which it is composed.

The stam refutes Rav Hananya's claim that the prohibition on the coverings comes directly from Deut 12:3. The Bavli says "destroy their name" refers literally to the names of the gods and it commands the people to corrupt the names of the gods. That is, one should not refer to a particular god by the name its followers use but rather by a derogatory derivative name.

With this different understanding of Deut. 12:3, the Talmud refutes the claim that there is a biblical source prohibiting use of the coverings. Thus the Talmud believes it has refuted Rav Hananya's claim and eliminated the argument that the phrase "from the cattle" is needed not just as the source prohibiting worshiped animals from the altar but also for the teaching that the latter further implies, that the coverings are forbidden to be used.

But this is not quite what the Talmud has achieved, again because the baraita issues no conclusion about the status of the coverings of the worshiped animal.

What the Talmud can be said to have done is refuted Rav Hananya's claim that Deut. 12:3 prohibits the coverings. And further, because by the unrecognized implications of Rav Hananya's claim, the first qal v'homer is conclusive and there should be no need for the phrase "from the cattle" to prohibit worshiped animals from the altar, what the Talmud has unwittingly done is reaffirmed the need for the phrase "from the cattle," to teach the law prohibiting worshiped animals on the altar.

Thus Rav Hananya's objection is most coherent if reduced to simply offering another proof text countering the conclusion to the second or *kheiluf* qal v'homer in the *o'kheiluf* argument. In that tannaitic argument, Deut. 7:25 was offered as a countering proof text to the conclusion of the second or *kheiluf* qal v'homer. If correct it would have invalidated the *kheiluf* qal v'homer and left only the first one as viable. But this proof text was immediately shot down: it was pointed out that the biblical verse is referring to an inanimate idol not a living idol. (Thus the *o'kheiluf* argument concluded that neither qal v'homer can be eliminated and therefore another source of proof is needed. The derash then offered the phrase "from the cattle," as the source for the law.)

Deut. 12:3 should be seen (as functioning similarly to Deut. 7:25) as a refutation to the conclusion of the *kheiluf* qal v'homer. This biblical source is interpreted by Rav Hananya as saying that the coverings are indeed prohibited. If this interpretation was deemed correct, as the midrash attempted with Deut. 7:25, it would invalidate the *kheiluf* qal v'homer argument. The first qal v'homer could then be declared correct in the fashion of all successful *o'kheiluf* arguments. The Bavli does not view the interpretation of Deut. 12:3 as correct and so can be seen as unwittingly blocking this refutation of the *kheiluf* argument and the success of the first qal v'homer in the *o'kheiluf* argument and thus upholding the baraita's conclusion that the phrase "from the cattle," is needed to serve as the biblical cue for excluding a worshiped animal from the altar.

Unable to recognize these possibilities for Deut. 12:3 in impacting the *o'kheiluf* argument, Rav Hananya and the authors of the anonymous layer of the Bavli, the *stam*, are exposed as lacking real familiarity with the *o'kheiluf* arguments of the Midrash Halakhah individually and as a collection representing a type of argument. Consequently they lack facility and fluency with *o'kheiluf* argumentation.

The Bavli Shows Concern to Correctly Match Biblical Cues to Derived Teachings: איפוך אנא

Once it affirms that the baraita is correct, that qal v'homer will not work and a limiting phrase is needed to derive the law forbidding a worshiped animal from the altar, the Bavli asks, "Why specifically does 'from the cattle' exclude the worshiped animal, and from the earlier analysis, why does 'from the domestic animals' exclude animals that copulated with a person or sodomized a person?" Perhaps, the Bavli asks, the two assignments should be reversed. The Bavli uses the phrase, איפוך אנא, transliterated *eepukh ana,* meaning 'perhaps we should switch them'. The type of switch the Bavli is suggesting is exactly the sort of tannaitic operation shown in Chapter Three to be referred to with the phrase חילוף הדברים. By using the Aramaic איפוך אנא rather than חילוף הדברים the Bavli keeps track of what is of tannaitic origin as opposed to amoraic origin, even though the operation called for in the two phrases is the same.

The reason for the choice of pairing of the specific phrases with the references, i.e. "from the cattle," to exclude specifically the worshiped animals and the other phrase "from the domestic animals," to indicate that animals that copulated with people must be excluded, is not a question posed by the Sifra which concludes each of the two arguments by making the two assignments. This difference between the treatment in the Midrash Halakhah and the Gemara can perhaps be viewed as evidence of a later amoraic demand for more rigor as the Bavli seeks to make explicit what it is about cue x that would indicate that the thing it means to exclude is y. The Bavli succeeds in giving an answer that does sensibly connect the cues to the sin excluded: the law regarding the sin of sodomy is expressed in terms of a domestic animal (Lev. 20:15-16) while the prohibition of idolatry is described in terms of an animal of the herd (Psalms 106:19-20).

The Bavli is still not very comfortable with derivations of these laws from the phrases "from the domestic animals, from the cattle". A different source for these laws follows and other laws are described that could be derived instead from the phrases "from the domestic animals, from the cattle".[181]

---

[181] After discussing the animal that gored, the Bavli cites another baraita that relates the *rova v'nirva* animal to a blemished animal. The Bavli emends the baraita, saying it is incomplete, which leads to a teaching by the school of R. Ishmael that everywhere in the Torah where corruption is stated it refers only to sexual immorality and idol worship. Since the term corruption is also used with regard to blemished animals, the following may be derived: In any case in which a blemish disqualifies an animal from the altar, a matter of sexual immorality, such as an animal that copulated with a person or an animal that was the object of bestiality, or the use of the animal as an object of idol worship, also disqualifies the animal. Thus the laws that the *rova v'nirva* and the worshiped animal are not permitted on the altar may be derived from the law regarding a blemished animal instead of from the limiting phrases "from the domestic animals, from the cattle".

But this different source characteristically leads the Bavli to the following questions and assignments, (and very interestingly ends by explaining that the reason the Tanna of the R. Ishmael school did not align himself with the previous derash, is because he understood the biblical words being explicated in that derash, in keeping with the R. Ishmael school's principle, that the Torah's language is in keeping with the conventions of how people speak, דברה תורה בלשון בני אדם, discussed earlier in the book):

The Bavli then asks: "According to the Tanna of R. Yishmael school, who says that the disqualifications of an animal that copulated with a person and an animal that was the object of bestiality, the set-aside, and the worshiped animal, are derived from the case of blemished animals, what does he derive from the phrase, "from the cattle, from the herd or from the flock" which is the source of these disqualifications according to the earlier baraita?" The Bavli answers that he needs these three terms to exclude sick, old, and filthy animals, which may not be sacrificed.

The Bavli asks, "From where does the first Tanna, who derives from these verses the law of an animal that copulated with a person and an animal that was the object of bestiality, derive the ruling that animals that are sick, or old, or filthy are disqualified from being sacrificed on the altar?" The Bavli answers that he derives it from the verse (Lev.1:10), "[A]nd if his offering be of the flock, whether of the sheep or of the goats". The Bavli comments that according to the Tanna of the school of R. Yishmael these laws would not be derived from that verse, because it is simply the manner of the Torah to speak like this (i.e. to state the general category of flock before specifying sheep and goats).

Why does this *o'kheiluf* argument appear in its entirety as a baraita in the Bavli? Why did the Bavli not just incorporate the part of the *o'kheiluf* argument it found useful, its conclusion, as it did with other *o'kheiluf* arguments from the Midrash Halakhah?

It was pointed out at the start of this chapter that this is the only *o'kheiluf* argument of the Midrash Halakhah that appears in its entirety as a baraita in the Bavli. What is so special about this argument that it was singled out for inclusion? Perhaps the *o'kheiluf* argument to compare it to is another *o'kheiluf* argument of the R. Akiva school also found in the Sifra about the provisional *asham* offering. The Bavli cites the conclusion that draws a *gezerah shavah* between two biblical verses to yield that the *lo taaseh*, the negative prohibition, whose doubtful violation requires the *asham taluy* (אשם תלוי) is one whose intentional violation is punishable by extirpation and whose unintentional violation requires a sin offering. (See discussion of '4.' in Chapter Seven.)

On B.Temurah 28b the Bavli similarly cites the Sifra's derivation that "from the cattle" is the source for the law stated in the Mishnah under analysis, excluding the worshiped animal from serving on the altar. But unlike the *gezerah shavah* from two verses that do appear to speak to one another, "from the cattle" is not as compelling a proof that the "from" is meant to exclude worshiped animals. By copying as well the whole passage in the Sifra that motivates this more opaque derivation after more reasonable attempts are exhausted, via *a fortiori*, the Bavli renders this proof more believable. Thus perhaps the Bavli included this prelude and, taken together, the entire *o'kheiluf* argument in the Sifra because in the case of (only) this particular argument of the Sifra, the Bavli was in agreement with the Sifra, that the opaque derivation at the end needed to be motivated by showing first that more reasonable methods were tried but failed.

8.3: Tosafists on the O'Kheiluf

The Tosafists in commenting on B.Temurah 28b, raise the question of why the baraita is not able to reconcile between the two conflicting qal v'homer arguments (that this book recognizes as contained in an o'kheiluf argument), by appealing to the principle cited on B.Avodah Zarah 46b, that when there is both a possibility of a qal v'homer argument that leads to a stringency and one that leads to a leniency (regarding the same question), the qal v'homer leading to a stringency is chosen. This topic is taken up later when the discussion turns to the amoraic o'kheiluf argument on B. Avodah Zarah 46b. Here I only point out that such a principle is at odds with the conclusions of the other o'kheiluf arguments of the Sifra as well as the conclusions of at least half of the o'kheiluf arguments of the R. Ishmael school (some of which occur in mishnaic rulings as well) where the o'kheiluf argument concludes by upholding the position of the more lenient qal v'homer as the correct one of the two possibilities.[182]

The answer Tosafot gives to the question it raises, seeks to characterize this pair of qal v'homer arguments as an exception to which the principle does not apply. Tosafot says that with regard to animals the rabbinic position is to try to avoid rendering them prohibited and therefore a qal v'homer argument that leads to a lenient conclusion may also be entertained. But many of the o'kheiluf arguments of both schools of Midrash Halakhah, which by the very nature of o'kheiluf consist of two qal v'homer arguments whose respective conclusions are of opposite valency — one being a leniency with respect to the other's stringency — do not concern rendering an animal prohibited and their conclusions parallel succinct mishnaic rulings. Thus the exceptional case described by Tosafot, where the issue concerns rendering an animal prohibited, could not

---

[182] See Chapter Two (#2,) #4, #5, #6; #8-10 i.e.Sifre Bamidbar (piska 118,) piska 125, piska 126, piska 155; Sifra Dibbura de-Khova parshata 12; Chapter Two #13, i.e. Sifre Devarim, piska 244.

account for the many o'kheiluf arguments in the Midrash Halakhah whose existence defies the above principle stated in the Bavli.[183]

It is clear that the Tannaim held no such general principle. When B. Avodah Zarah 46b is taken up, an original version of the above principle is presented, one that was not realized by R. Pappa and the stam or even much later by the Tosafists but that is consistent with the arguments of the Midrash Halakhah.

8.4: The Amoraic O'Kheiluf Argument on B. Avodah Zarah 46b

On B. Avodah Zarah 46b we find the single o'kheiluf argument of amoraic origin in the Bavli. The argument arises as a debate between Amoraim.

M. Avodah Zarah 3:5 is found on B. Avodah Zarah 45a. The beginning of the mishnah is as follows:

If non-Jews worship mountains and hills, they [the mountains and the hills] are permitted for benefit, but what is upon them is prohibited. As it is stated, "You shall not covet the silver and gold that is upon them" (Deut. 7:25).

Rabbi Yossi HaGillili says, "[The Torah says] 'their gods on the mountain' but not the mountains themselves. [The verse continues] 'their gods on the hills', but the hills themselves are not their gods."

---

[183] Namely, Chapter Two #2, #4, #5, #6, #8-10, #13.
For discussion of other areas of the different Tosafists' intellectual engagement outside of Talmud proper, particularly their interest in the Midrash Halakhah and their own biblical exegesis see Ephraim Kanarfogel, *The Intellectual History and Rabbinic Culture of Medieval Ashkenaz*, (Wayne State University Press, 2012).

After dealing with the law of a mountain which does not become prohibited from use after having been worshiped, the Bavli discusses the law for stones that were dislodged from a mountain but it is unable to reach a conclusion.[184] In the course of the discussion, the Bavli points out that an animal that was worshiped, which clearly is not attached to the ground, is permitted for ordinary use and consumption.

The Bavli records a series of inquiries about the use of worshiped objects for sacred purposes, e.g. as offerings in the Temple. As discussed earlier, it is known from B.Temurah 28b-29a that although an animal that was worshiped is permitted for ordinary benefit, it may not be used for sacred purposes. In its first inquiry, the Bavli quotes Rami bar Khama asking whether the stones of a worshiped mountain may be used to build an altar:

בעי רמי בר חמא: המשתחוה להר אבניו מהו למזבח?

Rami bar Khama next shows that his question can be broken down into 2 parts:

1) יש נעבד במחובר אצל גבוה או אין נעבד במחובר אצל גבוה ?
Does the prohibition of a worshiped object disqualify that which is attached to the ground as an offering on the altar, or not?

2) אם תמצי לומר יש נעבד במחובר אצל גבוה, מכשירי קרבן כקרבן דמו או לא?
If the answer to 1) is 'yes', that they are prohibited from being offered on the altar, may these objects be used as accessories when offering sacrifices on the altar?

Rava answers both parts of the question.

אמר רבא: קל וחומר,

_____

[184] Maimonides in Hilkhot Avodat Kokhavim 8:2 rules that they are permitted for use.

315

ומה אתנן שמותר בתלוש להדיוט   A =

אסור במחובר לגבוה, דכתיב: "לא תביא אתנן זונה ומחיר כלב" - לא שנא תלוש

ולא שנא במחובר,   = P

נעבד שאסור בתלוש להדיוט   = B

אינו דין שאסור במחובר לגבוה   = Q

?!

Rava said, "[By] qal v'homer,

Since

A = *A gift given to a prostitute, which if detached from the ground is permitted for ordinary usage*

P = *when it is attached to the ground, it is forbidden for the service of the Most High.*

(For it says, "Do not bring the gift to a prostitute or the sale price of a dog" without distinguishing whether these are attached to the ground or not.)

With regard to,

B = *Any worshiped object, which if detached, is forbidden for ordinary use.*

Must-it-not-follow-that

Q = *if attached to the ground, it is forbidden for the service of the Most High*

?! "

We have labeled the parts of Rava's qal v'homer argument in the same way we labeled each qal v'homer in each tannaitic *o'kheiluf* argument.[185] The facts, known from some biblical verses are labeled **A** and **B**. Using **A** and **B** the qal v'homer concludes **Q** from **P**.

The qal v'homer argument represented symbolically:

A, P & B, must-it-not-follow-that **Q** ?!

In an ordinary qal v'homer argument in the Midrash Halakhah there is biblical evidence for the proposition in position P, in the Mishnah

---

[185] See Chapter Two.

sometimes the evidence for P is not biblical but is rather another line of Mishnah. In both cases though, it is on the strength of the evidence for P, biblical or mishnaic, that the qal v'homer, using facts A and B, derives Q as a compelling conclusion.

When the biblical evidence for P is strong, and when properties A and B are viewed as relevant aspects with regard to which to compare the two topics of P and Q, the qal v'homer conclusion cannot be refuted. It is the result of facts A, B and P, and the recognized relevance of the comparison set up between the two topics. On the other hand, in every *o'kheiluf* argument, the truth of the conclusion of the first qal v'homer is called into question and an alternative qal v'homer argument is launched from the negation of that conclusion. The truth of the conclusion of the first qal v'homer argument is subject to doubt in such arguments because the evidence for P is either weak, as in all of the R. Ishmael *o'kheiluf* arguments, or non-existent, as in some of those of the R. Akiva school found in the Sifra. In the latter case, P is just a guess.

In the above qal v'homer argument that Rava presents, the evidence for P is weak as it is in all of the *o'kheiluf* arguments of the Midrash Halakhah of the R. Ishmael school. As with all of those arguments, this is the reason that the conclusion of this qal v'homer also can be called into question. Rav Huna, the son of Rav Yehoshua, does just that, launching a new qal v'homer from the negation of the conclusion and using the same qal v'homer conditional, i.e. the same comparison between the same objects.

Rava was a fourth generation Babylonian Amora. Rav Huna b. R. Yehoshua was a fifth generation Babylonian Amora, a student of both Rava and Abaye.[186] He was Rav Pappa's partner in study and in business and thus assisted Rav Pappa in leading the new academy in Naresh.

---

[186] See Strack and Stermberger, *Introduction to the Talmud and Midrash* (Fortress Press, 1996).

The evidence for A and B in Rava's qal v'homer argument is strong and so these are viewed as facts.

A = *The gift given to a prostitute, an object detached from the ground, is permitted for secular use.* The evidence for **A** is simply that the Torah recognizes the gift given to a prostitute and does not command that such an object cannot be used for ordinary purposes. The Torah states that these gifts may not however be used in the Temple.

B = *Any detached object that is worshiped is forbidden for ordinary use.* **B** is known to be true from a number of verses including the first part of Deut. 7:25 which states, "[T]he carved images of their gods you shall burn in the fire."

The weak evidence for **P** = *[T]he gift given to a prostitute even when it is attached to the ground is forbidden for the service of the Most High,* is Deut 23:19:

לא תביא אתנן זונה ומחיר כלב בית ה' אלקיך לכל נדר כי תועבת ה' אלקיך גם שניהם.

"You shall not bring the gift of the prostitute or the price of a dog to the House of the Lord your God, to fulfill any oath, because those two are an abomination to the Lord, your God."

But the verse does not seem to refer to **P** as it does not specify that it applies even if the item was attached to the ground. Rava argues however that the verse should be applied to items that are attached to the ground. He says that because the verse does not specify attached or detached, the verse does not distinguish between the two, and therefore it should be read as forbidding any item whether or not it was attached to the ground. This is clearly not a strong proof text for prohibiting items that are attached to the ground and given to a prostitute.

Because of the weak evidence for **P**, Rav Huna is not committed to the conclusion of Rava's qal v'homer argument. Rav Huna counters it with a qal v'homer that begins by asserting **-Q**, the contrary of the

318

conclusion of that first qal v'homer argument. He correctly refers to his qal v'homer argument as או חילוף, that is, Rav Huna's qal v'homer argument is indeed the *kheiluf* of Rava's, consistent with the precise meaning of *o'kheiluf* uncovered in this book. The first qal v'homer starting from **P**, concludes with **Q**, and the *kheiluf* qal v'homer starts from **-Q** and concludes **-P**. In symbols,

אמר ליה רב הונא בריה דרב יהושע לרבא:

או חילוף,

ומה נעבד שאסור בתלוש אצל הדיוט = **B**

מותר במחובר לגבוה, שנאמר: "אלהיהם על ההרים", ולא ההרים אלהיהם, לא שנא להדיוט ולא שנא לגבוה = **Q-**

אתנן שמותר בתלוש להדיוט = **A**

אינו דין שמותר במחובר לגבוה !? = **P-**

Rav Huna the son of Rav Yehoshua said to Rava,

O'kheiluf:

Since

B = *Any worshiped object, which if detached from the ground is forbidden for ordinary use,*

-Q = *is permitted to be used in the service of the Most High if it is attached to the ground*

(*For it says: "Their gods are on the mountains", and not the mountains are their gods, without distinguishing whether these are attached to the ground or not.*)

With regard to,

A = *Any gift given to a prostitute, which if detached from the ground is permitted for ordinary usage*

must-it-not-follow-that

-P = *when it is attached to the ground, it is permitted for the service of the Most High*

?!

Thus Rava and Rav Huna engage in an *o'kheiluf* argument that shares the exact same form found in this work to hold for all of the tannaitic *o'kheiluf* arguments:

A, B & P must-it-not-follow-that Q ?!

או חילוף

A, B & -Q must-it-not-follow-that -P ?!   (*)

where A and B are known to be true from biblical verses and the evidence for P and -Q is at most weak.

But there is an important difference between this *o'kheiluf* argument and all of the *o'kheiluf* arguments of tannaitic origin (which have all been examined in this work): in this argument biblical support is presented for -Q. In all of the *o'kheiluf* arguments of the R. Ishmael school and in some of the R. Akiva school, the first qal v'homer is launched, as is Rava's above, from a proposition P for which there is some weak biblical evidence. Further, because of this weak evidence the conclusion Q may not be true and a qal v'homer beginning from -Q is considered. In these arguments there is no scriptural evidence for -Q. -Q is possibly true only because Q is not known with certainty to be true and this is because Q was derived from P for which there is only weak biblical evidence. Unlike all of those *o'kheiluf* arguments, in this one in the Bavli, in the *kheiluf* qal v'homer presented by Rav Huna beginning from -Q, Rav Huna offers biblical support for -Q. This support is the same sort of weak evidence Rava presented for P.

-Q = *Any worshiped object that is attached to the ground is permitted to be used for the Most High.*

The proof Rav Huna offers immediately in support of his assertion of -Q is that the verse Deut. 12:2 says,

אבד תאבדון את כל המקומות אשר עבדו שם הגוים אשר אתם ירשים אותם את
אלהיהם על ההרים הרמים ועל הגבעות ותחת כל עץ רענן .

320

You must destroy all the sites at which the nations you are to dispossess worshiped their gods whether on lofty mountains or under any leafy trees.

The verse that Rav Huna references (Deut. 12:2) is the very same verse that R. Yose HaGlili quotes in the Mishnah in support of the preceding line, that if the mountains and hills are worshiped they themselves remain permitted for use. R. Yose HaGlili says," 'Their gods on the mountains' is what it says and not 'the mountains, their gods'." Thus according to R. Yose the verse implies that the gods on the mountains must be destroyed and so may not be used, but if the mountain itself is worshiped it need not be destroyed and therefore can be used. Rav Huna adds to this that a worshiped mountain may be used for sacred purposes as well, arguing that because the verse does not distinguish between secular or sacrificial use it applies to both.

The evidence that Rav Huna presents for the claim -**Q** is weak in very much the same way as is the evidence Rava presented for **P**. With regard to **P**, Deut. 23:19,"[Y]ou shall not bring the fee of a prostitute or the price of a dog to the house of the Lord, your God to fulfill any vow..," does not specify whether the gift to the prostitute is something that is or is not attached to the ground. Rava argues that the verse should therefore be interpreted as including both, i.e. whether or not the gift to the prostitute is something attached to the ground or not, it may not be offered to or used for the Most High. Similarly, Rav Huna argues that Deut. 12:2 orders the destruction of only the detached gods on the mountain and therefore allows the gods that are attached to the ground to be used. But the verse says nothing about secular versus sacred use. Thus the conclusion that gods that are attached to the ground are permitted to be used, should be understood according to Rav Huna as including both secular and sacred use.

Rav Huna's evidence for his launching premise is similar to that for Rava's launching premise, they are both based on the absence of distinction in a proof text and this is why the respective evidence for the two premises are similarly weak. This is an important aspect of Rav Huna's challenge to Rava's qal v'homer argument. Rav Huna challenges Rava's qal v'homer argument with a qal v'homer that is launched from premise -Q. Rav Huna presents evidence for -Q which he is able to argue is no weaker than the evidence that Rava presents for his launching premise P from which Q followed by qal v'homer. Since the launching premises of the two contradictory qal v'homer arguments are equally weak, Rava cannot claim that his qal v'homer argument is based on stronger evidence.

Rav Huna anticipates that Rava will improve upon his evidence for his launching premise P, namely, that he will draw attention to the perhaps otherwise superfluous use of the word "house" in Deut. 23:19, as alluding to items that are attached to the ground. Rav Huna preemptively argues that this superfluous word is needed for a different teaching in the following baraita:'"The house of the Lord, your God," to exclude the red heifer which does not enter the House of G-d. These are the words of R. Eliezer, but the sages say "[those words serve a different purpose,] to include the beaten plates of gold [that decorated the walls of the Holy of Holies]".'

In this o'kheiluf argument between Rava and Rav Huna, P and -Q are supported by only weak biblical evidence. This is unlike all of the tannaitic examples of the R. Ishmael case, where there is weak evidence for P and no evidence for -Q.[187] In all but one of the examples from the Sifra, which is Midrash Halakhah of the R. Akiva school, we saw (in Chapters Two and Four) that there was no evidence at all for P or for -Q. As is true for all the tannaitic o'kheiluf arguments, if the evidence for P was strong, Rav Huna would not have been able to question the conclusion of the first qal v'homer argument, i.e. Rava's, and consider the kheiluf qal v'homer argument.

As with all other o'kheiluf arguments, this amoraic one consists of two contradictory alternative qal v'homer arguments. But in this one, the two qal v'homer arguments are launched from premises that are

---

[187] See Chapter Two and Six.

supported by equally weak evidence and therefore it is not possible to eliminate one in favor of the other. In the *o'kheiluf* arguments in the Sifra it was likewise not possible to eliminate one qal v'homer argument for the other, but there it was because the same degree of evidence shared by the launching premises respectively was zero evidence.[188] In the *o'kheiluf* arguments of the Sifra, including the one also found in B.Temurah 28b as a baraita, there is no evidence for P or for -Q, so each is possibly true and there is no way to eliminate the qal v'homer launched from P in favor of the qal v'homer launched from -Q or vice versa.

In the Sifra, including the baraita on B.Temurah 28b, the inability to eliminate one of the two qal v'homer arguments justifies the need for a different hermeneutical technique to yield the answer to the question at issue. But here in this amoraic *o'kheiluf* argument where there is indeed equally weak evidence for P and -Q, leaving the two qal v'homer arguments of the *o'kheiluf* alone and invoking some other hermeneutical method to answer the question of whether a worshiped object attached to the ground may be used for sacred purposes, would still require dealing with the weak evidence for whichever of P or -Q contradicts the answer found.

Thus to resolve this *o'kheiluf* argument, more evidence needs to be located for either **P** or **-Q**. If the evidence for **P** can thus be strengthened the first qal v'homer argument would be conclusive. If instead the evidence for **-Q** could be strengthened, the second qal v'homer argument would be compelling and efforts would then be made to neutralize the weak evidence for **P**. But the Bavli is apparently not able to find such evidence.

---

[188] In the *o'kheiluf* arguments in the Sifra, all of which are from the R. Akiva school, as we saw there is no biblical evidence at all for either of P, or -Q (or Q or -P). Therefore P may be entertained as true, and a qal v'homer drawn from P to Q, and likewise -Q may be entertained as true, and a qal v'homer launched from it concluding with -P.

Another possible way to resolve the o'kheiluf is to discredit the qal v'homer conditional, i.e. to argue that the comparison being made between being permissible or forbidden for ordinary use as a movable object and being prohibited for sacred use as an attached object, is not the most relevant way to compare the gift to the prostitute and the worshiped animal. That is, the o'kheiluf could be resolved by arguing that the qal v'homer conditional is not compelling and therefore it is not necessarily true.[189] Perhaps because the Bavli had the same difficulty as the Tannaim at recognizing that the two qal v'homer arguments share only one qal v'homer idea, i.e. that they are committed to the same qal v'homer conditional, the Bavli did not pursue this standard avenue.[190] If the Bavli had done this, it could discredit each of the two qal v'homer arguments of the o'kheiluf argument and it could instead uphold both claims **P** and **-Q** on the basis of the weak evidence that exists for each. This is not a possibility that is explored by the Bavli.[191]

---

[189] See Chapter Four for the careful discussion of the qal v'homer conditional in the Stoic analysis.

[190] Refuting what we have described in Chapter Five as the qal v'homer conditional is often how a qal v'homer argument in the Talmud is refuted. See for example B.Sotah 46a discussed in Chapter Seven. The refutation there, as in many other instances in the Bavli, is introduced with the phrase איכא למיפרך. See also B. Berakhot 21a. In the Midrash Halakhah refutation focused on the qal v'homer conditional is introduced with לא!, i.e. 'no!' as an answer to the rhetorical question must-it-not-follow-that. There are many such examples in the Mekhilta. See also the example in the Addendum to Chapter Five (although there after the refutation the same conclusion is reached by a different means). An especially compelling such refutation is found in M. Yadayim 4:7:

אומרים צדוקין, קובלין אנו עליכם, פרושים, שאתם אומרים, שורי וחמורי שהזיקו, חיבין. ועבדי ואמתי שהזיקו, פטורין. מה אם שורי וחמורי, שאיני חיב בהם מצות, הרי אני חיב בנזקן. עבדי ואמתי, שאני חיב בהן מצות, אינו דין שאהא חיב בנזקן. אמרו להם, לא. אם אמרתם בשורי וחמורי, שאין בהם דעת, תאמרו בעבדי ובאמתי, שיש בהם דעת. שאם אקניטם, ילך וידליק גדישו של אחר ואהא חיב לשלם.

[191] The rationale for doing this would be in line with the thinking of the R. Ishmael school, that each inference in a chain starting from a premise in

324

Instead, Rava seeks to resolve the *o'kheiluf* argument by eliminating Rav Huna's qal v'homer argument on the following grounds:

אנא קאמינא לחומרא ואת אמרת לקולא. קולא וחומרא, לחומרא פרכינן.[192]

Rava says, "My qal v'homer concludes with a stringency and your qal v'homer concludes with a leniency. *Kula v'khumra, l'khumra farkheenon*: If there are two possibilities, one leading to a leniency and the other leading to a stringency we apply the qal v'homer that leads to a stringency."

8.5: Rava's Principle and the Bavli's Understanding of the Tannaitic *O'Kheiluf* Arguments

Rava's Principle: *kula v'khumra, l'khumra farkheenon*

---

which there is a certain amount of confidence, introduces further possible error. This is the basis for their limiting practice of *lamed min ha-lamed*, למד מן הלמד. The Bavli is not interested in applying this principle of the R. Ishmael school probably because this principle encourages restraint in making more and more derivations. The Bavli would therefore not be interested in a conclusion that is pessimistic of its entire dialectic enterprise, i.e taking P and -Q to be true on the weak evidence for them because there is even less confidence possible in conclusions drawn from either of them.
Indeed the Bavli limited the restriction of למד מן הלמד, to issues of *Kodshin*, i.e. sacrificial animals. See the passage on B.Temurah 21b:

אמר ר' יוחנן: כל התורה כולה למדין למד מן הלמד, חוץ מן הקדשים שאין למדין למד מן הלמד

[192] See B.Yevamot 8a for the same expression for the parallel principle regarding conclusions by *hekesh*: לקולא וחומרא, לחומרא מקשינן.

When the Two Options Exist, Choose the Qal V'homer that Leads to a Stringency over the one that Leads to a Leniency.

The nature of qal v'homer which argues *a fortiori* from P to Q, given facts A and B, is that P and Q usually come down in the same direction. That is, Q is a stringency because P is a stringency: if P is stringent must it not certainly be the case, that because of A and B, Q is also a stringency?! Similarly, a case where the conclusion of a qal v'homer is a leniency obtains, as in Rav Huna's, because the launching premise is a leniency: -P is a leniency because -Q is a leniency.[193]

If Rava's qal v'homer is accepted as correct, it is not just the conclusion that is accepted as a true statement but also the launching premise, and the relevance of the comparison set up by the qal v'homer i.e. the qal v'homer conditional. As discussed in Chapter Five, the qal v'homer can be broken down into the following claims, that is, the truth of the qal v'homer entails the truth of each of these. The conclusion, Q, is true by virtue of the truth of the two premises that precede it below:

P

If P then it must certainly follow that Q ← argued to be true on the basis of facts A &B

———————

Q

Thus it is not only relevant, as Rava's language implies, that the conclusion of his qal v'homer is a stringent ruling. Acceptance of his

---

[193] Among the qal v'homer arguments that make up the *o'kheiluf* arguments in the Midrash Halakhah there is one exception to this: the qal v'homer arguments of the *o'kheiluf* argument in the Sifra, Mekhilta de-Miluim concerning washing and blessing. See Chapter Two.

qal v'homer includes affirming the truth of **P** as well, in this case that the gift of a prostitute, (even) if it is an object attached to the ground, may not be donated to serve sacred purposes. It is clear from Rava's language that he does not recognize that in asserting his qal v'homer to be true, he is not just asserting the truth of **Q** but also the truth of **P**. In a typical qal v'homer this is not something that needs to be recognized because a typical qal v'homer is launched from a known fact P. But a qal v'homer argument that is part of an *o'kheiluf* argument is launched from a claim for which there is only weak and not conclusive evidence and therefore asserting one qal v'homer argument to be true entails asserting the truth of the launching claim.

Rava's resolution of the *o'kheiluf* argument is to dismiss Rav Huna's *kheiluf* qal v'homer on the basis of the principle that when faced with two possibilities, a qal v'homer that concludes with a stringent ruling and one that concludes with a lenient ruling, one is to choose to argue the former. In this way Rava upholds his own qal v'homer argument and chastises Rav Huna for even daring to present his *kheiluf* qal v'homer argument.

Rav Pappa attempts to invalidate Rava's refutation of Rav Huna's argument. Rava invoked the principle that when faced with the choice of a qal v'homer that concludes with a stringency and one that concludes with a leniency, the practice is to apply the former. Rav Pappa calls into question whether this is indeed the practice, by pointing as a counterexample to R. Akiva's dispute with R. Eliezer in, what is, the single *o'kheiluf* argument recorded in the Mishnah. (This *o'kheiluf* argument was carefully studied in Chapter Six.) He asks, "Is it true that whenever there is a choice between a qal v'homer that leads to a leniency and one that leads to a stringency, we do not apply the qal v'homer that leads to a leniency?"

Rav Pappa describes the argument over whether sprinkling, to enable a contaminated person to bring the Passover offering, overrides the Sabbath. This is referring to a situation where the seventh day of an individual's purification process falls out on what is both the Sabbath and the 14th day of the first month. A seven day purification ritual from corpse impurity is completed after the individual is sprinkled a second time with a mix of spring water and ashes from a red heifer. Rabbinically, the sprinkling may not be done on a Sabbath and should be put off to the next day. But in the case that the seventh day is also the 14th of the first month, the month of Nisan, if the individual may not complete his purification on that day then he will not be permitted to prepare or partake of the Passover offering. The question is debated in M. Pesahim 6:1, whether the rabbinic prohibition against sprinkling on the Sabbath is set aside.

R. Eliezer and R. Akiva dispute the matter, R. Eliezer rules that the rabbinic prohibition is set aside and the individual should undergo sprinkling so that he may participate in the Paschal offering. R. Akiva asserts that the rabbinic prohibition is not set aside and concludes by qal v'homer from this that the Paschal offering may not be slaughtered on the Sabbath. Rav Huna characterizes R. Eliezer's position as stringency, likely in the sense that R. Eliezer is taking a stringent position on the requirement to bring the Passover offering. He characterizes R. Akiva's position, that the individual may not undergo sprinkling and therefore may not participate in the Passover offering, as a leniency presumably in terms of the person's obligation to partake in the Passover offering. Thus according to Rav Pappa, R. Eliezer presented a qal v'homer argument that concluded with a stringent position and then R. Akiva countered with a qal v'homer that concluded with a lenient position. Rav Pappa's point is that R. Akiva would not have countered with a leniency if indeed there is a principle that when there is a choice between a qal v'homer that leads to a stringency and one that leads to a leniency, the former is chosen over the latter.

Rav Pappa's characterization of the debate as one pitting a stringent position against a lenient position is a forced stretch if not a distortion of what it means to take a stringent as opposed to a lenient position in rabbinic law. R. Akiva's position cannot be described as a lenient position at all, as it does not simply free the individual who needs sprinkling from the obligation to participate in the Passover offering. What it does do is, in fact, prohibit that individual's participation in the Paschal offering. According to R. Akiva, the individual would remain contaminated, as he is not permitted to undergo the sprinkling, and therefore he would not be permitted to partake of the Passover offering.

Rav Pappa also does not realize the important distinction between the example he invoked and Rava's dispute with Rav Huna. The two qal v'homer arguments in the o'kheiluf from the Mishnah are not launched from any evidence, for at first R. Akiva is under the impression that there is no biblical evidence for R. Eliezer's qal v'homer argument. Typical of many tannaitic o'kheiluf arguments, especially of the R. Akiva school, the two qal v'homer arguments are launched from suppositions. However the qal v'homer arguments in the o'kheiluf between Rava and Rav Huna are each launched from a claim supported by weak biblical evidence.[194]

The anonymous Bavli does not recognize this distinction either and does not point out that the debate between R. Akiva and R. Eliezer does not fit the stringency-versus-leniency model well. The Bavli accepts Rav Pappa's characterization and seeks to refute the counterexample it implies, that since R. Akiva offered a qal v'homer that concludes with a leniency, as a counter to R. Eliezer's qal v'homer that concluded with a stringent ruling, it cannot be the case that a qal v'homer leading to the stringency is in principle favored over one leading to a lenient ruling. The Bavli's refutation is that R. Akiva did not mean for his qal v'homer to be taken seriously as a counter to R. Eliezer's qal v'homer. Rather, he presented it only to remind R. Eliezer, who had forgotten his own teaching about sprinkling and had just contradicted it.

---

[194] In the R. Ishmael examples in the Midrash Halakhah, the first qal v'homer in the o'kheiluf argument is launched from what is seen as weak evidence. See Chapters One and Two.

The Bavli's point that R. Akiva did not intend to be taken seriously and only meant to remind his teacher R. Eliezer of this halakhah that he had taught him, is elaborated upon more fully in B. Pesahim 69a.[195] The discussion there is motivated by the need to explain how R. Akiva could have presented a qal v'homer whose conclusion is refuted by the Torah. Chapter Six pointed out that the lengths the Talmud goes to, elaborating on a story to explain R. Akiva's qal v'homer, shows clearly that the Bavli finds R. Akiva's argument to be odd. All this shows that the Bavli did not have a deep understanding of the o'kheiluf argument and its function. The Bavli's refutation of Rav Pappa's counterexample similarly exposes a lack of understanding of tannaitic o'kheiluf argumentation.

Thus the Bavli upholds that there is indeed a principle that when one has two competing qal v'homer arguments where one concludes with a stringency and the other with a leniency, the one that concludes with a stringency should be chosen. This principle most certainly was not in force during tannaitic times. For if it had been, it would have scratched out all of the o'kheiluf argument of the Midrash Halakhah.

Three of the six o'kheiluf arguments of the R. Ishmael school can be understood as a contest between a qal v'homer leading to stringent results and another leading to lenient results, where the qal v'homer

---

[195] On Y.Pesahim 6:3, 42b, the Yerushalmi asks in amazement, 'Is there any student who would dare say 'o'kheiluf!' in response to his teacher's argument. ‏ואית בר נש אמר לרביה או חילוף?!‏ .

To which, the Yerushalmi replied that R. Akiva argued o'kheiluf because it was R. Eliezer who had previously taught him that sprinkling does not override the Sabbath and was now in debate with him asserting the contrary. (The Bavli says R. Akiva sought to remind his teacher of what he had taught him without embarrassing him and this is why he argued by o'kheiluf a qal v'homer whose conclusion is false according to the Torah.)
The Bavli does not have this explicit comment about how dare a student argue o'kheiluf that contradicts his teacher's argument. Interestingly the amoraic o'kheiluf argument on B. Avodah Zarah 46b discussed in Chapter Eight is also a debate between a teacher and his student, Rava and Rav Huna ben Yehoshua, respectively. The Yerushalmi apparently would have a problem with this but the Bavli raises no such objection.

with the lenient rulings is shown to be the correct one. At least one of the *o'kheiluf* arguments of the R. Akiva school likewise decides in favor of the qal v'homer with the lenient rulings.[196] Further, whether a qal v'homer led to a stringency or a leniency was not something that entered into the logic of deciding between the two qal v'homer arguments in a tannaitic *o'kheiluf* argument. If this had been a consideration in the *o'kheiluf* argument, the argument would have been reduced to comparing the conclusions of the two qal v'homer arguments to determine which is more stringent.

8.6: Correcting Tosafot: A New Understanding of Rava's Principle

One could instead understand this principle as introduced to be applied to the uniquely amoraic adaptation of the *o'kheiluf* argument of which the single *o'kheiluf* argument in Avodah Zarah is the only example recorded in the Bavli. This *o'kheiluf* argument is different from all those of tannaitic origin, including the baraita in Temurah (lifted from the Sifra) in the way described in the last section: In each of the two qal v'homer arguments that make up the statement of the *o'kheiluf* argument, the launching premise of each is presented along with supporting biblical evidence. This is not something that the Tosafists recognized.

On B.Temurah 28b discussed above, Tosafot tries to justify a baraita, which we identified as an *o'kheiluf* argument from the Sifra. Of the two qal v'homer arguments that make up the set-up of the *o'kheiluf* argument, one leads to the conclusion that a worshiped animal may not be offered as a sacrifice on the altar, while the other leads to the conclusion that the covers of the worshiped animal are permitted for use. Tosafot asks, "How can there be a contest between the two qal v'homer arguments, that is, why is the second qal v'homer even considered, given the principle cited on B. Avodah Zarah 46b in the name of Rava that when two qal v'homer arguments are possible we

---

[196] See footnote Chapter Two, #13.

choose to argue the one that leads to a stringent ruling over the one that leads to a lenient ruling?"

The ad hoc answer that Tosafot gives to justify the presentation of the second argument was discussed earlier in this chapter. The point being made here is that the Tosafot are reading the incorrect *stammaic* understanding of Rava's principle into the activity of the Tannaim. Had this idea been applied in the indiscriminate way that the Tosafot suggests with regard to the baraita in Temurah from the Sifra, i.e. without realizing the way in which the tannaitic arguments were unlike the argument between Rava and Rav Huna in terms of supporting evidence for launching claims, it would have scratched out many of the *o'kheiluf* arguments in the Midrash Halakhah.

The unique amoraic *o'kheiluf* argument in the Bavli is distinguished from all of the tannaitic *o'kheiluf* arguments by the fact that each of the two qal v'homer arguments is launched from a proposition for which there is some biblical evidence. Because that biblical evidence is not explicit and needs to be justified as supporting evidence, each of Rava and Rav Huna, after stating his launching claim presents the biblical evidence with the expression, "for it says," followed by the biblical quote and then justification for how those words can be seen to include what the debater claims they include. It would be expected that other, perhaps not recorded, amoraic *o'kheiluf* arguments would tend to share this property of always arguing from evidence, be it biblical, mishnaic or amoraic. The Amoraim were reluctant to launch a qal v'homer argument from a claim whose entire support was the absence of any evidence to the contrary, and they would have avoided doing so even in a qal v'homer that counters another qal v'homer argument (as the *kheiluf* does in the *o'kheiluf* argument).

With such reluctance, it would have been unlikely to see any amoraic *o'kheiluf* arguments like any of the tannaitic ones. In each of the latter at least one of the pair of qal v'homer arguments, the *kheiluf*, is launched from a claim supported only by the absence of a biblical phrase asserting the contrary. In any amoraic *o'kheiluf* argument it

332

would be expected that each of the two qal v'homer arguments would be launched from some evidence.[197] It would therefore be difficult or impossible to decide between the two qal v'homer arguments, just as in the debate between Rava and Rav Huna. And so there would be a need to do away with having such arguments, such as by declaring as Rava did, that when a stringent qal v'homer can be presented one should not even consider the qal v'homer leading to a lenient ruling on the associated matters.

Why were the Amoraim reluctant to launch a qal v'homer from a claim whose entire support was the absence of biblical evidence to the contrary, while the Tannaim were not as reluctant? As seen earlier, the *kheiluf* qal v'homer of each of the R. Ishmael *o'kheiluf* arguments of the Midrash Halakhah, were all launched from evidence from absence.

To the R. Ishmael school, who restricted possible launching premises of qal v'homer arguments to not include propositions that were conclusions reached from other arguments, i.e. למד מן הלמד, *lamed min ha-lamed*, biblical statements and everyday facts were the only possible sources for any launching claim of a qal v'homer argument.[198] Thus if a Tanna could point out that no biblical verse could be used to claim the contrary of his claim, that was reasonable evidence for that claim. But for the Amoraim who considered conclusions of arguments based on the Torah or Mishnah or amoraic discussion to be valid evidence from which to launch a qal v'homer, it would have been much harder to be certain that no such evidence

---

[197] B. Berakhot 21a may seem like an exception to this generalization. On such a reading, the pair of qal v'homer arguments are together inconsistent as they include inconsistent claims, yet both are taken by R. Yohanan to be true. (The pair thus does not form an *o'kheiluf* argument.) But if we read the first qal v'homer as launched instead from the claim 'no verse demands that a blessing be made before eating' then the two arguments do not contradict each other nor do they violate the generalization as there is positive evidence for the above claim and for the claim that there is no verse that demands a blessing after learning Torah.

[198] See footnote 191.

exists for the contrary of a launching claim of a qal v'homer. The possibilities to consider to be confident of complete absence of any possible conclusion contrary to the considered claim, would simply be a far larger pool, by orders of magnitude.

But even for the Midrash Halakhah of the R. Akiva school that did not adhere to a general principle of avoiding למד מן הלמד, *lamed min ha-lamed*, when claiming that there is no evidence for the contrary to a particular proposition, they did not have to consider the manifold of possibilities for such evidence outside the Torah that the Bavli would have had to consider, including mishnaic statements and amoraic conclusions. The R. Akiva school could therefore with more confidence assert the absence of any evidence contrary to the considered proposition.

8.7: Did the Amoraim Recognize the Logical Shortcomings of the Tannaitic *O'Kheiluf* Arguments?

Did such recognition lead them to avoid constructing *o'kheiluf* arguments that were similar to those?

There are no amoraic *o'kheiluf* arguments like those of the R. Ishmael school where the first qal v'homer is launched from weak biblical evidence but the evidence for the launching claim of the second or *kheiluf* qal v'homer is the absence of any biblical statement to the contrary. The Amoraim would avoid constructing such arguments because they would want to launch a qal v'homer only from positive evidence.

The Amoraim and the later editors of the Bavli did not avoid constructing *o'kheiluf* arguments like those of the R. Ishmael school because of any recognition of the logical shortcomings of these arguments, as explained by the Stoic in Chapter Five. Namely, the Bavli did not come to realize that the *kheiluf* argument must always conclude with the negation of the launching premise of the first qal v'homer, i.e. with -P, regardless of the content of the argument. Further, there is no indication that the Bavli came to realize that the fact that -P contradicts whatever evidence exists for P, in no way strengthens the original evidence for P. The Bavli did not realize that when a R. Ishmael argument concludes with the first qal v'homer, the author is mistaken in concluding that as a result of o'kheiluf he is justified in having more confidence in his original qal v'homer.

As pointed out above in section 8.5, Rava's response to Rav Huna makes clear that he does not understand the logically prior point that in asserting his qal v'homer from P to Q to be true, he is not only asserting the truth of Q but also of P. Rava thinks he is only asserting Q. (He does not recognize that his qal v'homer is made up of three assertions: P, the qal v'homer conditional, and Q.)

Surprisingly, though reluctant to entertain evidence from absence as does the Midrash Halakhah, the Bavli sometimes has a lower standard for what counts as a sufficiently strong proof text than does much of the Midrash Halakhah. As described in Chapter Seven, the Bavli's view of those R. Ishmael o'kheiluf arguments whose content it approved of, is simply that the kheiluf qal v'homer was overkill. This is because, by the Bavli's lower standards for what counts as a proof text, the evidence for the launching premise of the original qal v'homer was sufficiently strong for the Bavli and therefore there was no reason to doubt the conclusion of that qal v'homer argument and to engage in o'kheiluf.

In maintaining a lower standard for what counts as a proof text than the R. Ishmael midrash (or the R. Akiva midrash in Sifre Devarim), the Bavli was motivated by practicality. The Bavli avoided having an impossibly high standard of what would count as biblical proof because it was engaged in the project of finding sources for as many oral and mishnaic laws as possible. With so many laws to derive the Bavli could not afford to be as demanding of certitude from biblical texts.

335

There are also no Babylonian amoraic o'kheiluf arguments like the baraita on B.Temurah 28b of the R. Akiva school, with no evidence for the launching claims of either the original or the kheiluf qal v'homer. In the Sifra, the school of R. Akiva used such arguments to motivate more opaque methods to derive the law in question, seeking to convey that they had exhausted all transparent avenues before resorting to the more opaque method.

The Bavli did not steer clear from engaging in such arguments out of any recognition that, as the Stoic explains in Chapter Five, the R. Akiva school had not actually attempted all that much. That is, since both qal v'homer arguments are committed to the same qal v'homer conditional, it is only one qal v'homer idea that is attempted before the R. Akiva school gives up and seeks a hermeneutical cue to obtain the answer to the question at issue. The Bavli does not seem to recognize this shortcoming at all; it is certainly not a difficulty the Bavli brings up with regard to the baraita on B.Temurah 28b. Rather, o'kheiluf arguments like those of the Sifra do not appear in the Bavli simply because the Bavli would not be inclined to launch a qal v'homer argument from a guess.

The Bavli would be reluctant to launch a qal v'homer from a claim that was a guess or whose biblical support was only the absence of any biblical statement to the contrary. It is for this reason that we do not find amoraic o'kheiluf arguments that are like the tannaitic o'kheiluf arguments all of which contain such qal v'homer arguments. But the logical shortcomings of the tannaitic o'kheiluf arguments did not register with the Bavli. The Amoraim were oblivious to any logical problems with the tannaitic o'kheiluf arguments and these problems did not lead the Amoraim to avoid constructing similar o'kheiluf arguments.

8.8: Why Did the *O'Kheiluf* Argument Peter Out?

Why did the *o'kheiluf* argument die out in the Bavli which only records one amoraic *o'kheiluf* argument between fourth or fifth generation Amoraim?

Since the Amoraim in the Bavli were not inclined to view evidence from absence to the contrary as sufficiently strong evidence, each of the two qal v'homer arguments in an amoriac *o'kheiluf* argument would be expected to be launched from a claim for which there was some positive evidence. But of course that evidence would have to be weak because otherwise the conclusion of the original qal v'homer could not be doubted (while maintaining commitment to the truth of the qal v'homer conditional shared by both qal v'homer arguments, as explained in Chapter Five). This is exactly what was seen in the *o'kheiluf* argument consisting of the debate between Rava and Rav Huna. But how is it possible to choose between two qal v'homer arguments (that share the same qal v'homer conditional and) that are each launched from equally weak biblical evidence?

Neither can be eliminated because of the weak biblical evidence that exists for the launching premise of each. The amoraic *o'kheiluf* argument is thus not resolvable. Rava suggested a principle by which to decide between the two qal v'homer arguments: Do not even suggest the qal v'homer argument that leads to a lenient ruling when the conflicting qal v'homer argument leads to a stringent ruling. That is, do not set up an *o'kheiluf* argument just argue the possible qal v'homer argument that leads to the stringent conclusion. The Bavli's acceptance of this principle certainly discouraged future *o'kheiluf* arguments.

The Amoraim could not see how to adjust their reasoning about qal v'homer arguments launched from facts, to a qal v'homer argument launched from weak evidence. In particular, Rava and then the *stam* did not realize that declaring a qal v'homer true when it is launched from weak evidence, implies commitment to that launching premise as well and not just to the conclusion of the qal v'homer argument.

The two characteristics of the Bavli discussed above worked together to bring the *o'kheiluf* argument to an end: the practice of providing positive supporting evidence for any claim made, and a lower standard than the R. Ishmael midrash for what constitutes a biblical proof text. Because of the first, any amoraic *o'kheiluf* argument would have to be like the debate between Rava and Rav Huna where the launching claim of each qal v'homer argument is supported by some positive evidence and not just absence of evidence for the contrary claim. With weak biblical evidence for both launching claims, there was no easy procedure to decide between the two qal v'homer arguments. As for the second characteristic, situations that would lead to *o'kheiluf* were greatly reduced because the Amoraim and the later rabbis did not have as high a standard for conclusive biblical evidence as did the R. Ishmael school of the Midrash Halakhah. Consequently, the evidence in support of the launching claim of a qal v'homer argument was less likely to be found insufficient by the Bavli and therefore the conditions that warrant *o'kheiluf,* in particular, grounds for doubting the conclusion of the qal v'homer argument, were less frequently met.

The Bavli did not discover the logical shortcomings of the tannaitic *o'kheiluf* argument; the Bavli was oblivious to them. The Bavli did not understand about any of the *o'kheiluf* arguments that there were logical problems (as mentioned above and discussed at length in Chapter Five) with the structure of the argument.

8.9: Conclusions

This chapter examined the two *o'kheiluf* arguments that appear in the Bavli. One appears on B.Temurah 28b as a baraita and is a faithful copy of an *o'kheiluf* argument from the Midrash Halakhah. (There is no Talmud Yerusahlmi on Temurah.) In the Sifra, Dibbura de-

Nedavah, parsha 2, this *o'kheiluf* argument (#7 in Chapter Two) arises as commentary to Lev. 1.1, while on B. Temurah 28b the Bavli introduces it as the source for the ruling in the mishnah under discussion, M. Temurah 6:1, that a worshiped animal may not be offered as a sacrifice, which is the conclusion of the *o'kheiluf* argument.

This is the only *o'kheiluf* argument of the Midrash Halakhah that occurs in its entirety in the Bavli: the entire failed argument followed by the derivation of the law from the hermeneutical cue 'from' in the phrase "from the cattle." The Bavli did not only copy the successful derivation at the end, as it did in the case of other *o'kheiluf* arguments of the R. Akiva school, but it also included the failed *o'kheiluf* argument that was only presented in order to motivate the more contrived derivation that followed. Apparently in this case, the Bavli agreed with the Sifra that the derivation was only made compelling by the failure first of more natural qal v'homer efforts.

According to the Bavli, the baraita intended the further teaching that the coverings of the worshiped animal are prohibited even for ordinary use. Chapters Two and Four on the *o'kheiluf* arguments of the Midrash Halakhah, specifically of the R. Akiva school, make clear that the authors of this *o'kheiluf* argument that makes up the baraita, intended no such further teaching. As with all of the other *o'kheiluf* arguments of the Midrash Halakhah, the focus is on the question that motivated the *o'kheiluf* argument. The issue of coverings was only raised to aid in answering the question of whether or not a worshiped animal may be sacrificed. Once the qal v'homer with the use of this aid failed, the aid was no longer of interest to the *o'kheiluf* argument and it did not return to focus on it.

The Bavli, on the other hand, is interested in finding a source for the law regarding the coverings because the same mishnah, M. Temurah 6:1, includes a statement that they are forbidden. Thus the Bavli reads into the baraita its own concern which is not a concern of the baraita, doing violence to the second part of the *o'kheiluf* argument, the part that follows the set-up of the argument. **The Bavli's misinterpretation of the baraita does not appear to be intentional. Rather it seems to suggest that the Bavli's knowledge and use of *o'kheiluf* is not based on a careful study (as carried out in this book) of the collection of tannaitic *o'kheiluf* arguments, but rather on an evolved common practice of *o'kheiluf* argumentation.**

The Bavli also displays a lack of real facility with the individual *o'kheiluf* argument from the Midrash Halakhah. What the Bavli describes as R. Hananya's attack on the baraita is not that at all, but the implications of his point are an attack on the baraita in a way that to date has not been recognized: The verse he points to, Deut. 12:3, as a source prohibiting use of the coverings, would render the first qal v'homer of the *o'kheiluf* argument conclusive. There would therefore be no need for the biblical phrase "from the cattle," as the *o'kheiluf* baraita argues, to derive that a worshiped animal may not be offered on the altar.

The Bavli exposes weak skills in the tannaitic practice of *o'kheiluf* argumentation. The Bavli refutes R. Hananya's interpretation of Deut. 12:3, but then does not understand correctly how this refutation really does serve the *o'kheiluf* argument.

The other *o'kheiluf* argument in the Bavli, B. Avodah Zarah 46b, is of amoraic origin and original to the Bavli. Examining it, reveals that the Amoraim used the phrase *o'kheiluf* exactly as the Tannaim did: the phrase o'kheiluf follows one qal v'homer and announces another qal v'homer that begins from (what is) the negation of the conclusion of the first. Symbolically the first part of the amoraic *o'kheiluf* argument can be represented like all of the tannaitic *o'kheiluf* arguments by,

A, B & P must-it-not-follow-that Q ?!

או חילוף

340

A, B & -Q must-it-not-follow-that -P ?!

where A and B are known to be true from biblical verses and the evidence for P (and −Q) is at most weak.

The argument is a debate between two Amoraim (just as the *o'kheiluf* argument in Mishnah Pesahim is an argument between two Tannaim). But this amoraic *o'kheiluf* argument is different from all of the tannaitic *o'kheiluf* arguments in that evidence is given for the launching premises of both qal v'homer arguments, P and −Q. With two qal v'homer arguments, each launched from weak evidence, there is no way to eliminate one of them as false, leaving only one viable qal v'homer argument (and there is no way to dismiss the two qal v'homer arguments in favor of some other method of derivation and just forget about the weak evidence for the two respective propositions).

Rava, who presented the first qal v'homer of the *o'kheiluf* argument, seeks to resolve the *o'kheiluf* argument by eliminating his opponent's qal v'homer argument through the following principal he introduces:
Kula v'khumra, l'khumra farkheenon. When faced with two possible contradictory qal v'homer arguments, one leading to a leniency and the other leading to a stringency, the qal v'homer that leads to a stringency should be chosen.

It is clear from Rava's language that he does not recognize that in asserting his qal v'homer, he is not just asserting the truth of Q but also the truth of P. In a typical qal v'homer this is not something that needs to be recognized because a typical qal v'homer is launched from a known fact P. But a qal v'homer that is part of an *o'kheiluf* argument, is launched from a claim for which there is only (at most) weak and not conclusive evidence and therefore asserting a qal v'homer argument to be true entails asserting the truth of the launching claim.

Rav Pappa in defending R. Huna's qal v'homer against Rava, turns to the *o'kheiluf* argument in Mishnah Pesahim discussed in Chapter Six, not recognizing the important distinction between the two. In the *o'kheiluf* argument in the Mishnah neither qal v'homer is launched from a proposition for which there is biblical evidence (for at first R. Akiva is under the impression that there is no biblical evidence for R. Eliezer's qal v'homer argument). Typical of many tannaitic *o'kheiluf* arguments, especially of the R. Akiva school, the two qal v'homer arguments are launched from suppositions. However the qal v'homer arguments in the *o'kheiluf* between Rava and Rav Huna, which unlike usual qal v'homer arguments are not launched from facts, are each launched from a claim supported by weak biblical evidence.

The debate between R. Akiva and R. Eliezer does not fit the stringency-versus-leniency model Rav Pappa imposes upon it. The Bavli (incorrectly) accepts Rav Pappa's characterization of the argument in M. Pesahim 6:1-2 and seeks to refute the counterexample it implies.

The Bavli's refutation of Rav Pappa's counterexample from the *o'kheiluf* argument in the Mishnah exposes a lack of deep understanding of tannaitic *o'kheiluf* argumentation. With Rav Pappa refuted, the Bavli upholds that there is indeed a principle that when one has two competing qal v'homer arguments and one concludes with a stringency and the other with a leniency, the one that concludes with a stringency should be chosen as reflecting the law. This principle most certainly was not in force during tannaitic times. For if it had been, it would have invalidated all of the *o'kheiluf* arguments of the Midrash Halakhah.

I offer instead a charitable reading of the principle Rava introduced, one that is compatible with the body of *o'kheiluf* arguments of the Midrash Halakhah. I claim that the principle was intended to be applied specifically in a situation where each of two competing qal v'homers are launched from propositions supported by weak biblical evidence of the same strength. Such is the situation in the amoraic

342

adaptation of the *o'kheiluf* argument of which the single *o'kheiluf* argument in Avodah Zarah is the only example recorded in the Bavli. This *o'kheiluf* argument is different from all those of tannaitic origin, including the baraita in Temurah (lifted from the Sifra) in the way described above. The distinction between this argument and the tannaitic *o'kheiluf* arguments is not something that the Bavli or, much later, the Tosafists recognized.

The Tosafot on B.Temurah 28b points out with regard to the passage on B. Avodah Zarah 46b, identified in this chapter as the other *o'kheiluf* argument in the Bavli, that the latter argument seems to deny Rava's principle that the qal v'homer that leads to a stringent position should be chosen over the one that leads to a leniency. Tosafot's point is that if such a principle was followed in the passage on B.Temurah 28b, there would be no reason for debate between the two qal v'homer arguments. That is, there would be no *o'kheiluf* argument. Tosafot offers a solution to the problem this presents for Rava's principle, by appealing to the subject matter of the argument. Tosafot claims that the argument in B.Temurah is an exception to Rava's principle made because it involves animals and the Torah tries not to render the use of any animals prohibited. The problem with Tosafot's solution is that it cannot be used to save more than half of the *o'kheiluf* arguments of the Midrash Halakhah from the chopping block of Rava's principle. This is because many of the *o'kheiluf* arguments of the Midrash Halakhah do not concern prohibiting an animal from consumption yet conclude choosing the lenient ruling.

Tosafot is ignorant of the distinction between the amoraic *o'kheiluf* argument and any of the body of tannaitic *o'kheiluf* arguments because it does not recognize the significant difference between typical qal v'homer arguments and those of which an *o'kheiluf* argument is composed. A qal v'homer of the latter is launched either from a guess or from weak evidence while a typical qal v'homer is launched from a proposition in which there is strong confidence. In the single amoraic *o'kheiluf* of the Bavli, both qal v'homer arguments are launched from weak evidence while in the

343

tannaitic *o'kheiluf* arguments at most one is launched from weak evidence, with the other being launched from a guess. The reasons why the Tannaim were willing to consider a qal v'homer launched from a guess while the Amoraim required positive evidence, likely concern the far greater volume of material the Amoraim would have to (mentally) check in order to be confident of the truth of a guess.

The two characteristics of the Bavli discussed above worked together to bring the *o'kheiluf* argument to an end: the practice of providing positive supporting evidence for any claim, and sometimes (as seen in Chapter Seven) a lower standard than the R. Ishmael midrash and the Sifre Devarim of the R. Akiva school for what constitutes a biblical proof text. The Bavli avoided having an impossibly high standard of what would count as biblical proof because it was engaged in the project of finding sources for as many oral and mishnaic laws as possible. With so many laws to derive, the Bavli could not afford to be as demanding of certitude from biblical texts.

Because of the first characteristic, any amoraic *o'kheiluf* argument would have to be like the debate between Rava and Rav Huna where the launching claim of each qal v'homer argument is supported by some positive evidence and not just absence of evidence for the contrary claim. With weak biblical evidence for both launching claims, there was no easy procedure to decide between the two qal v'homer arguments. As for the second, situations that would lead to *o'kheiluf* were greatly reduced because the Amoraim and the later rabbis did not always have as high a standard for conclusive biblical evidence as did the R. Ishmael school of the Midrash Halakhah. Consequently, the evidence in support of the launching claim of a qal v'homer argument was less likely to be found insufficient by the Bavli, and therefore the conditions that warrant engaging in *o'kheiluf* were less frequently met.

The logical shortcomings of the *o'kheiluf* argument as discussed in Chapter Five, however, played no role in the demise of this argument form in the Bavli. The Bavli did not discover any of the logical shortcomings of the tanniatic *o'kheiluf* arguments; the Bavli was oblivious to them. The Bavli did not recognize that there were logical problems with the structure of the *o'kheiluf* argument.

CHAPTER NINE: *O'Kheiluf* in the Yerushalmi

This chapter examines the two amoraic *o'kheiluf* arguments that are unique to the Yerushalmi. They are found to display the same expertise at forming the negation of a complex claim seen in the tannaitic *o'kheiluf* arguments and they use the phrase *o'kheiluf* exactly as do the Tannaim in the Midrash Halakhah and the Mishnah (and as continued by the Bavli). They are very much like the tannaitic *o'kheiluf* arguments in that the second or *kheiluf* qal v'homer is never launched from any biblical evidence. But unlike all those other *o'kheiluf* arguments, after setting up the two possibilities, the original and the *kheiluf*, the Yerushalmi does not pursue determining which of the two is correct. Each of the two Yerushalmi *o'kheiluf* arguments is examined in turn to discover why this is the case.

The understanding of the *o'kheiluf* argument developed in this book will be shown to illuminate a popular and widely quoted but somewhat misunderstood statement that appears on Y. Sanhedrin 4:1, 21a and is paralleled on B. Sanhedrin 17a. The statement in the Yerushalmi precedes one of the two amoraic *o'kheiluf* arguments of the Yerushalmi. Examining that *o'kheiluf* argument will shed light on the Talmuds' interpretation of the popular statement.

The noun *kheiluf*, חילוף, in the Yerushalmi

The noun חילוף shows up in the Yerushalmi (and always spelled there with the letter *yud*) in only two sorts of phrases: 'או חילוף' and 'חילוף הדברים' (considered together with חילוף היו הדברים). The two phrases maintain the respective meanings they were shown in

Chapters One and Three to have in tannaitic works.[199] In the Yerushalmi, in 2 out of the 12 occurrences of the word חילוף, which is 2 out of 5 occurrences of the word in an amoraic expression, we do not witness the strict care seen in the tannaitic sources and carried on in the Bavli, to distinguish the *o'kheiluf* operation from the *kheiluf ha-devarim* (i.e. חילוף הדברים) operation by matching the respective terminology to the correct operation. That is, in the Yerushalmi, twice when a statement undergoes what according to the Tannaim would be described as חילוף הדברים, the Yerushalmi refers to it as או חילוף. (See Y. Hagigah 1:1, 3b and Y. Avodah Zarah 5:12, 3b.)

In the Mishnah the word חלוף appears in nine places and always without the letter *yud*. Chapter six examined one occurrence of the word in M. Pesahim 6:2 in the phrase או חלוף, where the phrase signifies a bona fide *o'kheiluf* argument. The other eight occurrences of the word are found in the phrase 'חלוף הדברים'. Chapter Three discussed the uniformly precise logico-linguistic meaning characterizing every occurrence of the phrase 'חלוף הדברים' (or חילוף הדברים) whether in the Mishnah or the Midrash Halakhah, which is completely distinct from the meaning of או חלוף (or או חילוף) whether in the Mishnah or the Midrash Halakhah.

---

[199]Other nouns from the same root do appear in the Yerushalmi such as בחליפיו, meaning, in referring to physical objects, for its exchange, in Y. Kiddushin 3:6.
In the Mishnah no *yud* occurs in the phrase *o'kheiluf* or in *kheiluf* in any of the occurrences of *kheiluf ha-devarim*. In the Midrash Halakhah the phrase *o'kheiluf* occurs with and without the letter *yud*. In the *o'kheiluf* argument from the Mekhilta, the phrase occurs with a *yud*, but the phrase *ha-kheiluf* in the conclusion of the argument, has no *yud*. In three of the arguments of the Sifre Bamidbar the phrase occurs without a *yud*, and in two others it occurs with a *yud*; but in the conclusion of 4 out of the 5, *o'kheiluf* or *ha-kheiluf* occurs with a yud. In all three arguments of the Sifra, the phrase occurs with a *yud*. In of the arguments of the Sifre Devarim the phrase occurs with a *yud*. The two instances of *kheiluf ha-devarim* in the Sifra which also occur in the Mishnah occur in the former however with a *yud*. The one occurrence of *kheiluf hem ha-devarim* in the Sifre Devarim which is not found in the Mishnah contains a *yud* in the word *kheiluf*.

The 8 occurrences in the Mishnah of the phrase חלוף הדברים are as follows: Bava Batra 5:10, Gittin 5:4, Yevamot 10:3 (2), Shevi'it 4:2, Kailim 26:8, Mikvaot 6:9, Eduyot 7:8. Tractates Kelim and Mikvaot are in Seder Tohorot of which Talmud Yerushalmi only contains Nidah. Thus those two mishnayot do not appear in Talmud Yerushalmi. There is no tractate Eduyot in either Talmud Bavli or Talmud Yerushalmi and so M. Eduyot does not occur in the Yerushalmi. The other four mishnayot are copied into the Yerushalmi and analyzed there.

In addition to those four occurrences, the phrase חלוף הדברים shows up in the Yerushalmi, Shabbat 3:1, 22a and Terumot 2:1,12a, in a tannaitic passage that also occurs in the Tosefta Shabbat 3:6. In this passage from the Tosefta the phrase bears the same meaning it has everywhere in the Mishnah and the Midrash Halakhah. In the Yerushalmi, as in the Bavli, there is no phrase of amoraic origin containing the phrase חילוף הדברים.

All other instances of the word חילוף in the Yerushalmi show up as part of the phrase או חילוף. The phrase חילוף או occurs in the Yerushalmi in four different amoraic passages besides in the copy of M. Pesahim 6:2 and in the analysis that follows it. In two of the passages, as in both the mishnah and the gemara on Y. Pesahim 6:3, 42a, the phrase signifies an o'kheiluf argument. These two arguments on Y. Bava Batra 8:1, 22a and Y. Sanhedrin 4:1, 21a, respectively, forms the subject of this chapter. In the other two occurrences of amoraic origin pointed out above, the phrase functions as what the Mishnah and Midrash Halakhah would refer to as חלוף הדברים. (In the Bavli, as in the Yerushalmi, the spelling is with a *yud*, חילוף).

In the two amoraic *o'kheiluf* arguments of the Yerushalmi, the phrase או חילוף (i.e. *o'kheiluf*) shares the same precise logico-linguistic meaning it was shown to have in all 15 of the passages of Midrash Halakhah in which it is found. This shared meaning is conveyed by the faithful symbolic representation of the argument:

Since A, B & P must-it-not-follow-that Q ?!

או חילוף

Since A, B & -Q must-it-not-follow-that -P ?!

where A and B are known to be true from biblical verses or common sense, the evidence for P is at most weak, and there is no evidence for or against –Q.

All of this will be confirmed first for the *o'kheiluf* argument on Y. Bava Batra 8:1, 22a. The context of this argument makes clear why the Yerushalmi does not include a conclusion to this *o'kheiluf* argument. This is unlike what we find with all of the *o'kheiluf* arguments of the Midrash Halakhah, Mishnah and Talmud Bavli which all reach a resolution.

9.1:   *O'Kheiluf* on Y. Bava Batra 8:1, 22a

Y. Bava Batra 8:1,22a parallels B. Bava Batra 108a. The mishnah on the parallel folios, M. Bava Batra 8:1, discusses who inherits who and who bequeaths to whom. One of the clauses in this mishnah, is that the sons inherit the father, והבנים את האב. This is understood to mean that the sons inherit the entire estate and the daughters do not inherit a share along with them.

Both Talmuds inquire as to how the Mishnah knows this law, that is, what is the biblical basis for this law that only the sons inherit from the father and not the man's daughters (provided he has sons). They both give the same biblical source, Num. 27:8: "If a man dies and he has no sons then you will pass the father's property to his daughter."
Since the verse makes clear that this is to happen if the man has no sons, it is understood that the daughters do not inherit if the man does have sons.

350

The implication drawn from Num. 27:8 about what the law is if a man has both a son and a daughter is not seen as convincing. The Yerushalmi cites the wise men of the gentiles (i.e. ע"כום) and the Bavli cites Rav Pappa speaking to Abaye, as interpreting the verse to mean that if a man has both a son and a daughter the inheritance is divided equally between the two of them. Should a man only have a son then he inherits everything and likewise if the man only has a daughter then the whole inheritance goes to her.

The Bavli tries to dismiss Rav Pappa's interpretation, citing different sages that offer different biblical proofs. But these are in turn refuted. The Bavli ends the discussion by upholding Num. 27:8 as the best support for the mishnaic clause. (It also offers Lev. 25:46 which speaks of bequeathing *livinaikhem* (i.e. לבניכם), to your children, but literally the word means 'to your sons'.)

The next issue discussed in the Yerushalmi, and on folio 111 in the Bavli, is the biblical source for the mishnaic clause stating that a man inherits from his mother but does not bequeath to her. Both Talmuds quote Num.36:8 which states, "[A]nd every daughter who inherits a portion from the tribes of the children of Israel." It is pointed out (in the Bavli it is from a baraita) that the daughter can only inherit from plural tribes if her parents were from two different tribes and she inherits from both her father and her mother.

The Talmuds want to know the biblical source by which it is known that the son also inherits from his mother. They answer (in the Bavli the baraita continues with), "It is known by qal v'homer from the case of the daughter."

"Since a daughter, who is weak when it comes to inheriting her father's property (i.e. she only inherits if there is no son) yet she does inherit from her mother; a son, who is strong in inheriting from his father must-it-not-follow-that he inherits from his mother?!"

351

But now the question remains, if a woman is survived by her son and her daughter, does the son precede the daughter? That is, is the situation the same as inheriting from the father so that if there is a son (or children of the son) he gets the estate and the daughter only inherits from her mother if there is no son?

The baraita in Bavli continues with, "From the inference drawn, just as there, with regard to a father's property, a son precedes a daughter, so too here, with regard to a mother's property, a son precedes a daughter."

The baraita in the Bavli as well as the Yerushalmi then cite Tannaim that hold differently (in the name of R. Zechariah ben HaKatzav): "The son and daughter are equal in inheriting from their mother."

The Yerushalmi goes on to cite Amoraim that assert that the citations presented are incorrect and that the law does not follow R. Zechariah. The Bavli recounts how different Amoraim wanted to rule in accordance with R. Zechariah but R. Nachman strong-armed and intimidated them from doing so.

Next, in both Talmuds, R. Yehuda Nesi'ah enters the picture. In the Yerushalmi passage he is referred to by the name R. Yudan Nesi'ah. ('Nesi'ah' is Aramaic for 'the prince' which in Hebrew is 'HaNasi'.) He is the grandson of Rabbi Yehuda HaNasi and seems unwilling to just accept the rulings of other prominent rabbis. The Bavli describes how he approached the elderly R. Yannai who seemed to dislike him from the past. (R. Yannai makes a negative remark to his attendant about Yehuda Nesi'ah's cloak.)

In the Bavli, Yehuda Nesi'ah asks R. Yannai, "From where is it derived that a son precedes a daughter with regard to inheriting the mother's property?" R. Yannai answers that the verse Num. 27:8 uses the word 'tribes' thereby making an association, i.e. a hekesh, between the father's tribe and the mother's tribe: Just as with regard to the father's tribe, the son precedes the daughter, so too, with regard to the mother's tribe, the son precedes the daughter.

R. Yehuda Nesi'ah responds, "If indeed that is right and there is a *hekesh* between the mother's tribe and the father's tribe established by the word in the verse 'tribes', then the following should also be derived from the *hekesh*: Just as with regard to the father's tribe, the *bekhor*, the eldest son, receives double the inheritance of the other sons, so too with regard to the mother's tribe, her *bekhor* should receive a double inheritance."

R. Yannai then turns to his attendant and says, "Take me away from here this man does not want to learn."

Apparently what R. Yehuda Nesi'ah was aiming for was a sort of *reductio ad absurdum*, showing R. Yannai what further trouble his method of derivation leads to and therefore why his position (in keeping with the above baraita) is faulty. R. Yannai apparently did not have a better derivation to offer for the ruling that the son also precedes the daughter in inheriting from the mother, one that R. Yehuda Nesi'ah would not be able to critique. Therefore all he could do was criticize R. Yehuda Nesi'ah, describing him as one who does not ask honest questions and therefore a person he should not waste his time on.

The Bavli continues citing different Amoraim to refute R. Yehuda's conclusion, finding objections to their refutations and concluding with Rava's derivation from Deut. 21:17 that the double inheritance is only when inheriting from the father.

In the Yerushalmi, R. Yudan Nesi'ah takes a different, bolder route to try and make R. Yannai change his position (which matches the baraita above). He throws into question R. Yannai's premise, whose source is the mishnah (M. Bava Batra 8:1).[200] The Yerushalmi recounts as follows:

R. Yannai and R. Yohanan were sitting together. R. Yudan Nesi'ah came and asked them, "What do we learn from the verse, Num. 36:8, '[A]nd any daughter who inherits from tribes'?" They answered, "The verse juxtaposes (i.e. makes a *hekesh* between) the father's tribe and the mother's tribe. This teaches that just as for the father's tribe, the son precedes the daughter, so for the mother's tribe, the son precedes the daughter."

מה מטה האב אין לבת במקום הבן אף מטה האם אין לבת במקום בן.

To which R. Yudan Nesi'ah replied:

או חילוף,

מה מטה האם יש לבת במקום בן אף מטה האב יש לבת במקום בן.

R. Yannai & R. Yohanan were in effect saying,

"Just as, with regard to inheritance from the father's tribe, the daughter does not get any when there is a son, so too, with regard to inheritance from the mother's tribe, the daughter doesn't get any when there is a son."

R. Yudan Nesi'ah responds:

---

[200] In the Bavli's account, R. Yehuda Nesi'ah, attacks the conditional in the argument (see Stoic Analysis in Chapter Five for more details), i.e. the first premise in the following description of the argument:

If P so-too Q ←--- by virtue of the word 'tribes' relating the father's tribe with the mother's tribe

P

Q

O'kheiluf, i.e or perhaps the *kheiluf!* :

"Just as with regard to inheritance from the mother's tribe, the daughter does receive a share when there is a son, so too, with regard to inheritance from the father's tribe, the daughter does receive a share when there is a son."

In the Bavli, as discussed above, R. Yehuda Nesi'ah says about the just-as conditional, that it would further imply that the *bekhor* of the mother gets a double inheritance just like the *bekhor* of the father. In the Yerushalmi's account unlike in the Bavli, R. Yehuda Nesi'ah (referred to as R. Yudan Nesi'ah) is committed to the truth of the so-too conditional and instead attacks the truth of the second premise, P.

He argues the *kheiluf* which keeps the conditional:

If **P** so-too **Q**
-Q

_____

-P

where **P** and **Q** represent the following propositions:

P = *When there is a son, the daughter does not receive a share in inheritance from her father.*
Q = *When there is a son, the daughter does not receive a share in inheritance from her mother.*

The negations of **P** and of **Q**, respectively, are then the following propositions:

-P = *When there is a son, the daughter does receive a share in inheritance from her father.*
-Q = *When there is a son, the daughter does receive a share in inheritance from her mother.*

The debate between R. Yannai and R. Yohanan with R. Yudan Nesi'ah can therefore be symbolized as follows:

Since **P**, so too **Q**.

או חילוף

Since -**Q**, so too -**P**.

This o'kheiluf argument is similar to the o'kheiluf argument in Sifre Bamidbar, piska 155, as it does not involve qal v'homer arguments but rather just-as arguments.[201] These two o'kheiluf arguments therefore have stronger association to the contrapositive than do all the others. (See Chapter One for discussion comparing the o'kheiluf argument to the contrapositive of a conditional statement.)

R. Yohanan does not respond with, 'Oh, take a look, the conclusion of your argument is patently false because it contradicts the mishnah which is based on Num 27:8. Therefore your whole argument is wrong.' He does not continue with, as the argument in Sifre Bamidbar, piska 155, 'We've disproven your argument therefore by default only the first remains, i.e. our argument, which therefore must be correct.' That is, R. Yohanan does not bring the debate to a conclusion by responding in line with the Sifre Bamidbar, piska 155, with,

כתיב, "איש כי ימות [ובן אין לו והעברתם את נחלתו לבתו]" ..... .
דנתי, חלפת, בטל החילוף וזכינו לדון כבתחילה:
מה מטה האב אין לבת במקום הבן אף מטה האם אין לבת במקום בן.

Instead what R. Yohanan says is, similar to the story in the Bavli,

"We can see here that this person does not want to learn Torah."

The question remains, why did R. Yohanan not bring the o'kheiluf argument to a conclusion by disproving his opponent's argument as

---

[201] See Chapters Two and Five.

sketched above? Why did he simply insult his opponent and give up the argument? The o'kheiluf arguments uncovered and discussed in this book provide an answer.

Each o'kheiluf argument in the Midrash Halakhah arose because of the unusual situation that a first argument, usually a qal v'homer argument, was launched from a premise for which there did not exist strong evidence. Usually a qal v'homer argument or any other argument that argues for a certain conclusion is, unsurprisingly, launched from a premise that is believed to be true, a premise for which there is strong evidence. O'kheiluf occurs in the unusual situation where this is not the case. Because there is absent strong evidence in support of the launching premise, it is possible to doubt the conclusion of such an argument and to consider the possibility that the contrary of the conclusion is true and then o'kheiluf ensues.

Thus in suggesting o'kheiluf, i.e or perhaps the kheiluf, R. Yudan Nesi'ah was indicating that he was not convinced of the conclusion of R. Yohanan and R. Yannai's qal v'homer argument precisely because he was not convinced of the truth of the launching premise of their argument, the ruling understood from the mishnah, M. Bava Batra 8:1, that if there is a son, he alone inherits the father.[202] As discussed above, the Talmuds found that the verse Num. 38:7 was the biblical basis of this mishnaic law. But this verse was not seen to be compelling evidence supporting the content of the mishnaic law. (For example, Rav Pappa in the Bavli saw the verse as evidence for the contrary position, which is R. Yehuda Nesi'ah's position.) For this reason the Talmud presented attempts to find stronger biblical evidence but it was forced to conclude that no stronger evidence exists.

---

[202] See Chapter Five, the Stoics analysis, for discussion about how in an o'kheiluf argument both qal v'homer arguments are committed to the truth of the shared qal v'homer conditional. Thus if the conclusion of one of the qal v'homer arguments is deemed false this must imply that Premise 2 is false as Premise1, the qal v'homer conditional shared by the two qal v'homer arguments, is assumed true for the sake of engaging in the o'kheiluf argument.

R. Yohanan and R. Yannai realized that R. Yudan Nesi'ah disapproved of the mishnaic position and that he found Num. 38:7 to not be convincing evidence in support of the mishnah's position. (As pointed out above, the anonymous voice of the Talmud does not find this evidence very convincing either.) Therefore saying to R. Yudan Nesi'ah, 'Oh, you are contradicting the mishnah which bases its ruling on Num 38:7,' would just have given R. Yudan Nesi'ah an opportunity to point out explicitly that their ruling limiting when a daughter might inherit from the mother is based on a very questionable premise, i.e. a mishnaic statement based on questionable or very weak biblical support. Since R. Yohanan knew this and since he did not have stronger evidence to offer in support of the mishnaic ruling, he was reduced to having no counter other than to insult R. Yudan Nesi'ah. Since R. Yudan Nesi'ah did not accept the mishnah's statement and the questionable biblical support for it, R. Yohanan described him as "a man who does not want to learn Torah."

R.Yohanan was a first generation Amora. To the Bavli he often had the status of a Tanna and there are places in the Bavli where he is seen behaving that way, ruling contrary to anonymous statements in the Mishnah.[203] Thus R. Yehuda Nesi'ah's attempt to get R. Yohanan to rule contrary to a baraita and maybe also (on a related point) in opposition to the Mishnah, was likely in earnest as R. Yohanan sometimes would do this.

This o'kheiluf argument, just like the single mishnaic o'kheiluf discussed in Chapter Six and the amoraic o'kheiluf in the Bavli discussed in Chapter Eight, was framed as a debate between two parties or individuals. It is now clear why this amoraic o'kheiluf argument of the Yerushalmi, unlike those others, does not reach a conclusion, and this does not reflect any deficiency in the argument. The passage demonstrates real facility at o'kheiluf argumentation and the stalemate the parties reached is reflective of that facility. Next we

---

[203] See for example B.Yevamot 42b–43a.

turn to examine the other one of the two *o'kheiluf* arguments of amoraic origin found in the Yerushalmi.

9.2: Y. Sanhedrin 4:1, 21a: On Rendering the Reptile Pure

The amoraic *o'kheiluf* argument found on Y. Sanhedrin 4:1, 21a follows a popular and widely quoted directive, a similar version of which appears on B. Sanhedrin 17a and B. Eruvin 13b. Our analysis of that *o'kheiluf* argument, following the understanding of the *o'kheiluf* argument developed in this book, supports a new reading of the activity proposed by the popular directive. We start off by examining the parallel passage on B. Sanhedrin 17a.

B. Sanhedrin 17a

In chapter one, 17a, where the Bavli is still analyzing the mishnayot (in chapter 1 of M. Sanhedrin) introduced on B. Sanhedrin 2a, Rav Kahana is quoted as saying, "In a Sanhedrin where all the judges saw fit to convict the defendant in a case of capital law, they must acquit him." The Bavli asks for the rationale behind this judicial practice. It is learned that suspension of the trial overnight is necessary in order to make acquittal possible. The law is that the judges may not issue the guilty verdict on the same day that the evidence was heard. This is to allow for the possibility that overnight one of the judges will think of a reason to acquit the defendant. If the judges all saw fit to convict the defendant they will not see any further possibility to acquit him, because there will not be anyone arguing for such a verdict. Therefore they must acquit him.

This is followed by R. Yohanan's requirements of someone chosen to be a judge. Rabbi Yoḥanan says, "They place on the Great Sanhedrin only tall men of wisdom who have a pleasant appearance, and are of suitable age so that they will be respected. Also, they must be masters of sorcery, so that they can judge sorcerers, and they must know all seventy languages in order that the Sanhedrin will not need to hear testimony from the mouth of a translator in a case where a witness speaks a different language."

This is followed by,

אמר רב יהודה, אמר רב: אין מושיבין בסנהדרין אלא מי שיודע לטהר את השרץ מהתורה

Rav Yehuda says that Rav said, "They place on the Sanhedrin only one who knows how to render [the carcass of] a *sheretz* pure by Torah law."

A *sheretz* is any of a collection of insects and reptiles that may defile a person. A person who touches one of their dead bodies is rendered impure until the evening. This is all stated explicitly in Leviticus, chapter 11.

Rav Yehuda's declaration in the name of Rav is in the spirit of the earlier statement in the Bavli that if all of the judges see fit to convict the defendant, if no judge sees any evidence in favor of the defendant, the judges are deemed biased against the defendant and the court is ordered to acquit him. R. Yehuda's statement suggests that he has little tolerance for the position that sometimes it is impossible to find any evidence in favor of the defendant. To assure that judges will exhaust every possibility to find in favor of the defendant and avoid convicting to death an innocent man, R. Yehuda declares that only those who can find a way to render pure by Torah law the *sheretz*, which is known very clearly from Lev. 11:29-30 to be impure, may serve as judges. If a sage can find a way to exonerate the *sheretz*, who is so clearly guilty of being impure, and find it to be pure, such a sage may be able to look past obvious and blatant evidence of guilt to consider each of the other details of the case that could possibly lead in a different direction.

Saul Lieberman reads this directive as reflecting rabbinic appropriations of Roman rhetorical methods. He wrote, "The judge must thus be a rhetor who can *disputare in utramque partem* and prove at one and the same time the two opposite points of view."[204] As Hidary explains, "In quoting this one Latin phrase, Lieberman associates the rabbinic court system with the basic foundation of the rhetorical enterprise – arguing both sides of any issue." The rabbis were certainly familiar with the Roman court system, and disapproved of some of its features. Here with his directive, Rav insists that the rabbinic court take a page from the other's book, and apply Roman rhetorical methods to the best of their ability to prevent convicting an innocent man to death.[205]

But weighed against the vast body of debate found in the Talmud, a demand to render pure what the Torah explicitly declares impure, seems like an altogether different matter, an impossible one. The quality that Rav is seeking in a court judge is very clear, but how tight is his analogy to the particular trait in Torah study he is describing? Is this test, to be able to render pure by Torah law the clearly impure *sheretz*, meant in earnest or is it an exaggeration to convey Rav's emphasis on the thoroughness and open-mindedness he demands of those who would be judges of the high court? While Rav's actual words may sound like a demand, as Lieberman writes, to be able to argue 'both sides' of the issue of the purity/impurity of a *sheretz*, is that what Rav demonstrates he can do?

---

[204] See Saul Lieberman, *Hellenism in Jewish Palestine* (New York: Jewish Theological Seminary, 1962):62:
"Rab maintained that no one is to be appointed a member of the high court (Sanhedrin) unless he is able to prove from Biblical texts the ritual cleanliness of a reptile (although reptiles are definitely declared unclean in Lev. 11:29). The reason for this requirement can be inferred from the statement of a younger contemporary of our Rabbi. R. Johanan asserted that a man who is not qualified to offer hundred arguments for declaring a reptile ritually clean or unclean will not know how to open [the trial of capital cases] with reasons for acquittal. The judge must thus be a rhetor who can *disputare in utramque partem* and prove at one and the same time the two opposite points of view."
[205] For more discussion see Richard Hidary, "Chapter 6: The Role of Lawyers in Roman and Rabbinic Courts," in *Rabbis and Classical Rhetoric* (Cambridge: Cambridge University Press, 2017).

The Bavli quotes Rav as saying that he can indeed do this, that in fact he will succeed in rendering the *sheretz* pure. He uses the word אדון, which can be translated as "I will judge" or also from the root to judge, "I will derive by a qal v'homer".[206] Thus Rav means that his directive, that judges have the skill to render the *sheretz* pure, be taken literally.

But this first generation Amora is considered one of the three greatest Amoraim of the greatest generation of Amoraim so if he cannot prove the *sheretz* pure then it is unlikely that such a proof is feasible. If the Bavli can show that Rav's demonstration fails, then it would follow that Rav's insistence that only judges who can do this are eligible to serve, should be viewed only as hyperbole to get the idea across that the judges must be individuals who will leave no detail unexamined in their search for reasons to acquit an innocent man.

The Bavli follows with Rav's demonstration:

ומה נחש שממית ומרבה טומאה טהור שרץ שאינו ממית ומרבה טומאה אינו דין שיהא טהור ?!

"Since a snake, which kills other creatures whose carcasses are impure and thereby increases impurity in the world, is yet itself pure, then concerning a creeping animal that does not kill and does not increase impurity, must-it-not-follow that it should be pure?!"

The Stoic analysis described in Chapter Five, would put this qal v'homer argument into the following form:

Premise 1: If a snake is pure then the *sheretz* is pure. *****

Premise 2: The snake is pure.

Conclusion: The *sheretz* is pure.

****** by virtue of *a fortiori* reasoning using the following facts:

> The snake kills and thereby increases impurity [in the world by increasing carcasses that convey impurity to people that touch them].

> The *sheretz* does not kill and therefore does not increase impurity [in the world].

The *stam*, the anonymous voice of the Bavli, refutes Rav's qal v'homer, by refuting Premise 1:

ולא היא מידי דהוה אקוץ בעלמא

"But it is not so, for it is [like] an ordinary thorn."

Premise 1 is believed to be true on the basis of *a fortiori* reasoning regarding the facts that a snake kills [other animals and people] and a *sheretz* does not, and that killing and thereby increasing the amount of impurity in the world makes something more likely to be impure itself. That is, Premise 1 is believed to be true because it is conceivable to think that an animal that kills and thereby produces impurity is more likely to be ruled impure than one that does not and thus if an animal that kills is ruled to be pure then most certainly an animal that does not kill must be determined to be pure. The Bavli refutes Premise 1 by refuting that being a killer (and thereby increasing *tumah* in the world) is related to being impure. It refutes the assumption about the nature of purity and impurity, that being a killer and being impure are related, and it does this by presenting a counter example: an ordinary thorn kills [people and animals] and yet it is pure.

The nature of purity and impurity, the essence of what makes something impure is not something that is discussed in the Torah. The Torah lists particular things that are impure and situations that make a person impure but it does not describe any intrinsic property by virtue of which impure things are impure. Rav's qal v'homer argument attempts at least a partial theory of what makes an animal impure such that contact with it defiles a person and the refutation of the qal v'homer shoots down this theory. (It is not surprising that no such theory would be left standing, since laws regarding purity and impurity are described as being in the category of khok (חוק, pl. חוקים), laws for which no rationale can be given, as opposed to the mishpatim (משפטים).)

The Bavli refutes the qal v'homer with a counterexample to the implication in Premise 1, that whether or not something kills is associated with its being pure. The counterexample, a thorn, shows that comparing the snake to the sheretz with respect to killer status is irrelevant for concluding whether or not the sheretz is pure. The thorn is a particularly strong counterexample showing that impurity cannot possibly be determined by killing capacity because if it was otherwise then the common ubiquitous thorn would have to be impure. There would then be no end to the number of impure objects in the world that would entail a purification process and thus such a definition of impurity would be entirely impractical.

Notice that the Bavli does not begin its refutation in the usual way seen throughout the Midrash Halakhah, the Mishnah and elsewhere in the Bavli, in the case where a qal v'homer concludes with a contradiction of a biblical verse. Namely, the Bavli does not point out that this qal v'homer argument must be wrong because its conclusion contradicts the biblical verses Lev.11:29-31, and the Bavli does not follow up on this by showing, with the counterexample, that this false conclusion was reached because (what is labeled above) Premise 1 is false. The reason that the Bavli does not do this is because it has accepted the terms of Rav's game.

From Lev.11:29-31 it is known that the eight classes of sheretz presented, defile a person who touches the carcass of one of those animals. The language also implies that this list is complete, no other animal is impure i.e. defiles a person in this way. The snake is not on the list of eight and therefore it follows that it is not impure. Rav claims to know the second, that in particular the snake is pure, but he imagines that Lev. 11:29-31 is absent from the Torah. Rav's conclusion from the claim that the snake is pure, does not contradict (Torah)' where (Torah)' denotes all of the Torah except Lev. 11:29-31. Since Rav is arguing from (Torah)', the Bavli does not point out that Rav has contradicted a verse in the Torah (that is not in (Torah)').

The Bavli could also have criticized Rav's argument by pointing out that his grounds for Premise 2 that the snake is pure, must be precisely verses Lev.11:29-30. Thus the first generation Amora is launching a qal v'homer from an accepted belief for which he does not have strong source evidence, as he is imagining the verses that imply that the snake is pure, to be absent from the Torah. But the reason the Bavli does not do this is because it is able to refute the stronger argument that it sees Rav as making in its defense of the *sheretz*. Namely, that the complete listing of the impure animals, by the lights of the Torah, does not make sense. How can it be that both the mouse is impure and the snake is pure? The snake kills and yet is pure, should not then the mouse be pure as well? The Bavli shows that this conclusive listing is not self-contradicting as the Torah's concept of impurity is not tied to the status of being a killer. Proof: A thorn kills and yet it is not impure.

Rav in defending the *sheretz*, exploited what he tried to argue is a conceptual inconsistency in the law that specifies the eight impure animals, based on assumptions he made about the nature of purity and impurity. The Bavli shows that he failed.

Thus the anonymous voice of the Bavli finds that even Rav, one of the three greatest Amoraim, cannot give a demonstration that the *sheretz* is pure. Surely then, Rav was aiming too high when he declared that this ability should be required of judges. The Bavli is trying to walk back his directive that trial judges need to have precisely that skill in Torah study.

But the Bavli's refutation of Rav's argument to render the *sheretz* pure also reveals its understanding of his argument. As discussed

365

above, the Bavli understands Rav to be arguing not from the Torah but from the Torah minus verses Lev. 11:29-31. The Bavli therefore recognizes that it would be no criticism of Rav's argument at all to point out that its conclusion contradicts Lev. 11:29-31.

But where did Rav get the idea for this intellectual exercise of proving from some subset of the Torah the contrary of what is stated explicitly elsewhere in the Torah?

This question will be taken up after we examine the related passage in the Yerushalmi which through an *o'kheiluf* argument makes more explicit than does the Bavli, the understanding the former shares with the latter, of what both Rav and R. Yohanan meant by "rendering the *sheretz* pure from the Torah."

Y. Sanhedrin 4:1, 21a

Chapter four of Y. Sanhedrin begins on folio 20b with the mishnah describing the difference between judging monetary cases and capital offenses. The end of the mishnah states that in monetary cases, the judges may begin with a reason to favor the defendant or with a reason to find him liable. Capital cases on the other hand, must be opened only with reasons to acquit the defendant, and not with reasons to convict him.

The Yerushalmi takes up the issue of how the judges should go about trying to acquit a defendant of murder. In the context of this discussion the early Amora, R. Yohanan is quoted:

אמר ר' יוחנן כל שאינו יודע לדון את השרץ לטהרו ולטמאו מאה פעמים אין יכול לפתוח בזכות.

"Anyone who does not know how to judge a *sheretz*, to find one hundred reasons why it should be ruled pure and why it should be ruled impure, cannot open a case in such a way as to find for the defendant [and therefore may not be chosen as a judge]."

R. Yohanan's directive is very similar to that attributed to Rav in B. Sanhedrin 17a examined above. There are some small differences between the two. Although the directive in the Bavli is attributed to Rav rather than R. Yohanan, the two Amoraim share the characteristic of being considered two of the three greatest Amoraim of the early generations of Amoraim.[207] Also, in the Bavli the directive follows another ruling by R. Yohanan listing other qualities that judges must have such as being tall, and of suitable age. Another difference between the directives in the Bavli and the Yerushalmi is that the latter is more extravagant and demanding: A prospective judge must be able to find one hundred ways to demonstrate that the *sheretz* is pure and to demonstrate that it is impure. While for the Bavli, being able to give one demonstration from the Torah that the *sheretz* is pure is all that is required.

Like Rav in the Bavli, R. Yohanan in the Yerushalmi can be understood as referring to the *sheretz* to draw the following analogy. Since the *sheretz* is perfectly well known to be impure from Lev. 11:29-31, it would be hard to set this knowledge aside and come up with arguments from perhaps other verses in the Torah that would seem to point to the *sheretz* being pure (or to other arguments for why it must be impure). A judge must be someone who when faced with a defendant who seems as guilty of a crime as the *sheretz* appears guilty of being impure, can study the case in so unbiased a manner, looking at every detail, such that he can come up with an abundance of reasons that would favor the defendant.

The Yerushalmi is not content to see R. Yohanan's words as hyperbole aimed at making the point that the judge must be someone who can remain unbiased and able to search and find reasons to acquit the defendant. The Yerushalmi asks pointedly and perhaps skeptically,

---

[207] Shmuel is the missing third from the list. See Strack and Stemberger,1996.

How indeed do we judge the *sheretz* so as to acquit it of being impure, i.e. how can one argue that it is pure [when Lev. 11:29-30 clearly says that it is impure]? As mentioned above with regard to the Bavli, the word דנין means to judge but it also has the related meaning of drawing a qal v'homer inference. With this sense of the word, the question can be understood as, how by qal v'homer could one arrive at the conclusion that the *sheretz* is pure, if the statement in Lev. 11:29-30 to the contrary is ignored?

This seems like a surprising thing to suggest doing, to try by some other route to prove that the *sheretz* — which the Torah explicitly decrees impure — is pure. It is not just surprising because the products of this activity would contradict what is stated in the Torah, but also because the activity seems foreign to the whole function of qal v'homer reasoning in tannaitic works.

Conclusions to qal v'homer arguments that are at odds with the Torah do not sit undisturbed side by side with other qal v'homer arguments in rabbinic works nor are they shunned as impious and therefore to be avoided. The qal v'homer is often used as a tool to probe the text, be it the Pentateuch in the case of Midrash Halakhah or other lines of Mishnah in the case of the Mishnah.

In the Midrash Halakhah, qal v'homer uses (what are viewed as) biblical or common sense facts to derive conclusions about points not made explicit in the Torah. Sometimes a qal v'homer does conclude with a contradiction to some statement in the Torah, but then the qal v'homer is examined to discover the spot where the reasoning is faulty. Thus any qal v'homer whose conclusion contradicts some verse in the Torah is immediately attacked and cogently refuted in whatever work it appears.

This is also how the Bavli treats the qal v'homer presented by Rav on B. Sanhedrin 17a which concludes that the *sheretz* is pure, contrary to Lev 11:29-31. Rav's qal v'homer drew a relation between being a killer and being impure. The Bavli refuted the qal v'homer with a counterexample from the Torah, showing that the Torah's concept of purity and impurity cannot be understood as involving a direct relationship between being an animal that kills and being an animal that is impure. (That is, the Bavli refuted the qal v'homer argument by refuting what was described in Chapter Five as the qal v'homer conditional in the Stoic's logical analysis of qal v'homer.)

Thus the intellectual activity that R. Yohanan is promoting seems at first blush to be at odds with what we know of rabbinic hermeneutics and debate. Analysis of the rest of the Yerushalmi passage, in particular the *o'kheiluf* argument advanced, will yield more clues about this activity.

R. Yannai, a first generation Amora who had studied under Rabbi Yehuda HaNasi, takes up the challenge to derive that a *sheretz* is pure. His qal v'homer argument is identical to Rav's in the Bavli except that instead of deriving about the general *sheretz* that it is pure, he derives for the particular *sheretz*, the mouse, that it is pure:

Since a snake, which kills, is pure, a mouse which does not kill must-it-not-follow-that it should be pure?!

The anonymous voice of the Yerushalmi presents a counter to R. Yannai's argument:

O'kheiluf!

The mouse which does not kill is impure, [therefore] the snake, which does kill, must-it-not-follow-that it is impure?!

R. Yannai's original qal v'homer argument together with the Yerushalmi's counter qal v'homer argument introduced with the phrase *o'kheiluf* constitute a bona fide *o'kheiluf* argument identical in form to all the other tannaitic and amoraic *o'kheiluf* arguments studied in this work:

A = 'נחש ממית'	מה אם הנחש שממית
P = 'נחש טהור'	טהור
B = 'עכבר אינו ממית'	עכבר שאין ממית
Q = 'העכבר טהור'	אינו דין להיות טהור ?!
	או חילוף
B = 'עכבר אינו ממית'	עכבר שאין ממית
-Q = 'העכבר טמא'	טמא,
A = 'נחש ממית'	נחש שממית
-P = 'הנחש טמא'	אינו דין להיות טמא ?!

A & B are facts well known from everyday experience. The two arguments together clearly have the form described throughout this book:

Since A, B & P must-it-not-follow-that Q ?!

או חילוף

Since A, B & -Q must-it-not-follow-that -P ?!

In the first qal v'homer, R. Yannai is committed to the claim that the snake is pure but he is clearly not committed to the content in Lev. 11:29-31 that states that the mouse is impure. R. Yannai is trying to prove the *sheretz* to be pure from all of the Torah minus the statement that the mouse and the other seven creatures are impure. We will again (as we did in discussing the parallel argument in the Bavli) refer to this resulting set of propositions by (Torah)'. R. Yannai is imagining those statements to be absent from the Torah. The language of Lev. 11:29-31 indicates that the eight creeping creatures listed make up the complete list of impure creeping creatures and therefore the snake is pure. Thus the snake is pure. R. Yannai (maybe by implication from Lev. 11:42) does not consider the proposition, that any creeping creature that is not one of the eight listed is pure, to be absent from (Torah)'. Or perhaps he does not have in mind the biblical source of this law about the snake but just that it is commonly held knowledge. Thus it is from (Torah)', that R. Yannai assuming that the snake is pure, argues that therefore so is the mouse.

R. Yannai, similar to Rav in the Bavli, can be understood as arguing that the mouse being impure and the snake being pure are not consistent rules. By qal v'homer he argues that the snake being pure implies that the mouse is pure. In this way R. Yannai believes he has defended the mouse against the charge of being impure.

Like the Bavli, the Yerushalmi does not refute R. Yannai's qal v'homer by pointing out that its conclusion contradicts Lev. 11:29-31. This is because like the Bavli, the Yerushalmi accepts the terms of the challenge, that these verses be imagined for the sake of the argument, omitted from the Torah. But this means to the Yerushalmi that the launching premise of R. Yannai's qal v'homer, that the snake is pure, can be doubted. Since the launching premise can be doubted, as is the case in every o'kheiluf argument, so can the conclusion of the qal v'homer. And as in every o'kheiluf argument, this is why o'kheiluf may ensue.

The Yerushalmi, accepting the comparison drawn between the different creeping creatures with regards to who is a killer, i.e. committed to the truth of the qal v'homer conditional, concedes that it could be argued that the two rules, about the mouse and the snake, are inconsistent. But the Yerushalmi does not see that reason therefore implies that the mouse should be ruled pure as R. Yannai argued on the mouse's behalf.

The Yerushalmi sees Lev. 11:29-31 as divisible into two propositions:
1. The 8 creeping animals listed are impure i.e. they defile a person who comes into contact with one of their carcasses, until the evening.
2. Any creeping creature not on that list of 8 is pure; thus, for example, the snake is a pure animal.

The Yerushalmi argues that the possibility that the verses express two inconsistent propositions does not imply that the second, in particular that the snake is pure, is the more reasonable of the two. One can instead, o'kheiluf, starting from the biblical rule that the mouse is impure, call into question the reasonableness of the second proposition. Hence the Yerushalmi argues the same qal v'homer idea from (Torah)", i.e. from the entire Torah minus the two propositions in Lev. 11:29-31. The Yerushalmi argues that the belief that the mouse is impure would imply that the snake is impure.

This is the same line of reasoning as in the argument (discussed in Chapter Six) in M. Pesahim 6:1-2 between R. Eliezer and R. Akiva, that leads to o'kheiluf. R. Eliezer believes that two laws are inconsistent and from the first derives the contradiction of the second. R. Akiva responds by pointing out that while R. Eliezer may describe grounds with respect to which the two laws are inconsistent, he has no basis for favoring the first over the second. R. Akiva points out that starting from the second, R. Eliezer's qal v'homer comparison implies the negation of the first. R. Akiva is committed to both rulings in the mishnah and the point he raised was meant to undermine R. Eliezer's rejection of the second ruling. The Yerushalmi appreciates that Lev. 11:29-31 includes propositions 1 and 2 and refutes R. Yannai's disproof of proposition 1 contained in Lev. 11:29-31 using the same strategy as seen in M. Pesahim 6:2.

Similar to R. Akiva in the mishnah, the Yerushalmi counters R. Yannai's proof that the mouse is pure by pointing out that the position he takes that the two propositions 1 and 2 about the mouse and the snake, respectively, are inconsistent, does not give priority to the proposition about the snake. That is, a claim that the two statements

372

are inconsistent does not imply that the one about the snake is the one that makes sense. If instead priority is given to the statement about the mouse, that it is impure, then it can be concluded that the statement that the snake is pure does not make sense. Thus in the eyes of the Yerushalmi, R. Yannai was not able to prove that the mouse is pure. Believing the two statements to be inconsistent, because the snake is a killer and the mouse is not, would lead to two contradictory possibilities: either both the snake and the mouse are pure or they are both impure.

The o'kheiluf argument was possible, because the Yerushalmi considered the evidence for Premise 2, that the snake is pure, to be weak evidence. The Yerushalmi participated in R. Yannai's game of pretending Lev. 11:29-31 is absent from the Torah and examining what can be concluded from a Torah that has those verses removed and with these verses removed from consideration, there was no strong evidence for the purity of the snake. Unlike the Bavli, the Yerushalmi does not reason that since the snake is pure but the conclusion that the mouse is pure is false, there must be something wrong with, what is in this book referred to as the qal v'homer conditional or Premise 1.[208] The Yerushalmi does not proceed to prove that Premise 1 is false.

The Yerushalmi instead engages in o'kheiluf which entails commitment to Premise 1. The Yerushalmi casts into doubt Premise 2, that the snake is pure. It can only do this because it understands R.Yannai's argument as based on pretending that Lev. 11:29-31, which is also the biblical basis for the claim that the snake is pure, is absent from the Torah. By accepting R. Yannai's conditions that Lev. 11:29-31 is to be imagined absent from the Torah, the Yerushalmi can doubt Premise 2 and therefore the conclusion reached from it in R. Yannai's qal v'homer. It is only because it can doubt Premise 2 that the Yerushalmi can engage in o'kheiluf. This is how all the

---

[208] See Chapter Five.

o'kheiluf arguments presented in this book have been shown to operate.

Because Lev. 11:29-31 is imagined absent, the Yerushalmi's *kheiluf* qal v'homer starting from the contradiction of R. Yannai conclusion also lacks biblical support. Thus neither qal v'homer in the *o'kheiluf* argument is conclusive and yet neither can be eliminated.

After the *o'kheiluf* is presented, the fourth generation Amora, R. Pinkhus, tries to invalidate the *kheiluf* qal v'homer.[209] [210] He does not try to refute the *kheiluf* in the way that it is done in the Midrash Halakhah, by presenting biblical evidence that the conclusion, that the snake is impure, is wrong. R. Pinkhus cannot do this, again because in the thought experiment, the biblical evidence that would refute the conclusion, the wording of Lev.11:29-31, is imagined absent from the Torah. That is, the *kheiluf* qal v'homer is an argument in (Torah)". Instead, he seeks to refute the qal v'homer conditional in the *kheiluf* argument that relates purity to killing behavior: If an animal that does not kill is impure then certainly an animal that kills must be impure. R. Pinkhus tries to refute the qal v'homer conditional by presenting a

---

[209] Most likely R. Pinkhus bar Hama, a fourth generation Amora who spent most of his life in the Land of Israel. See Strack and Stemberger, *Introduction to the Talmud*.

[210] Hidary's discussion of this argument on p.198 of his *Rabbis and Classical Rhetoric*, suffers from errors due to unfamiliarity with how (what I have identified in this work as) the *o'kheiluf* argument functions. As a case of *o'kheiluf,* this passage does not reflect, as Hidary writes, rabbinic "deep ambivalence and skepticism about the application of qal v'homer reasoning" nor is it "casting doubt on its [qal v'homer's] very reliability". (The rabbis had a much more sophisticated and well-defined program for applying qal v'homer and for applying an *o'kheiluf* qal v'homer than Hidary suggests. See Chapter One, Two, and Five of this work.) Contrary to Hidary, the Talmud does not uphold R. Yannai's qal v'homer. What the Talmud does by refuting R. Pinkhus (Hidary's spelling is 'Pinehas') is uphold the *o'kheiluf*, i.e. the two contradictory qal v'homer arguments with no way to decide between them. The Yerushalmi like the Bavli refutes the claim that the greatest Amora can prove the *sheretz* pure. R. Pinkhus does not recognize that the original qal v'homer and the *kheiluf* share the same qal v'homer conditional (as the contrapositive of a conditional is equivalent to that conditional); see Chapter Five.

counterexample to the claim it makes, that the scorpion kills and yet it is pure. If successful, it would refute the whole o'kheiluf argument including R. Yannai's qal v'homer.

The Yerushalmi demolishes the counterexample with the following: "We found that there is a Tanna who says that the case of the snake and that of the scorpion are the same." Meaning, the kheiluf qal v'homer beginning from the claim that the mouse is impure can conclude with the case of the scorpion just as well as with the case of the snake. What this is implying is that the scorpion is only known to be pure from exactly the same source from which it is known that the snake is pure: Neither is contained in the list of sheratzim (the plural of sheretz) in Lev. 11:29-30. The kheiluf qal v'homer takes place in (Torah)" where there is no evidence that creeping creatures other than the 8 are pure, i.e. that the scorpion just as the snake is pure. Where this proposition is imagined absent from the Torah, i.e. where it is imagined that the Torah is (Torah)", it is not possible to refute the kheiluf qal v'homer with the scorpion as a counterexample to the conclusion (and to the qal v'homer conditional that purity status and being a killer should be related).

Hence there is no way to choose between the two contradictory qal v'homer arguments. When this happens in the o'kheiluf arguments of the Sifra (including the one that occurs as a baraita on B. Temurah 28b) the authors use this situation to advance a different, less compelling method to answer the question at issue. Pointing out that since qal v'homer was shown to fail, some other hermeneutical cue needed to be found (and was purposefully placed in the Torah) to answer the question.

But here, as in the cases of o'kheiluf in the Sifre Devarim, o'kheiluf arises because certain verses or (in the Sifre Devarim) words are imagined absent from the Pentateuch. In the Sifre Devarim, the inability to eliminate either of the two contradictory qal v'homer arguments in the o'kheiluf argument, proves that the words imagined absent from the Torah are indeed needed and not superfluous.[211] But the Yerushalmi is not looking (just) to conclude that Lev. 11:29-31 is needed in the Torah and that otherwise we would not know that the mouse is impure. Rather it is seeking to test whether had those three verses been left out of the Torah, one would be led to the opposite conclusion, that the mouse is pure.

The o'kheiluf argument has failed. The Yerushalmi has shown that both R. Yannai's qal v'homer and its kheiluf are possibilities that cannot be eliminated. The o'kheiluf has shown that qal v'homer drawn between the case of the mouse and that of the snake cannot yield an answer as to whether or not the mouse is pure (i.e. does not confer impurity).

Thus R. Yannai's argument has led to two possibilities, either the mouse is pure or it is impure. In the eyes of the Yerushalmi he has clearly failed to prove that the mouse is pure. In particular, he has failed to make a sound inference (from the Torah excluding Lev. 11:29-30) that for the particular sheretz, the mouse, it can be concluded to be pure. This parallels the Bavli's refutation of Rav's attempt to render the sheretz pure. Hence the Yerushalmi, just like the Bavli, does not know of any Amora who can satisfy R. Yohanan's criterion to qualify to serve as a trial judge. R. Yohanan and Rav's shared standards do appear too high.

Thus the Yerushalmi, clearly skeptical that any Amora is able to come up with compelling demonstrations that the sheretz is pure, is perhaps suggesting perhaps that R. Yohanan not be taken quite so literally. Instead, as described above with reference to Rav in the Bavli, R. Yohanan should simply be understood as stressing that those chosen as judges should be individuals capable of the highest degree of intellectual detachment and unbiased thinking; that they be individuals who will try every avenue to exonerate a defendant who

---

[211] See in Chapter Two, the Sifre Devarim o'kheiluf arguments #12, #14. These are further discussed in Chapter Four.

appears as guilty of the capital offense he is standing trial for as a *sheretz* is guilty of being impure.

The Yerushalmi's next remark points out that there is a tradition that in the past, there were Tannaim who were able to come up with valid qal v'homer arguments from the Torah minus Lev. 11:29-31, to render the *sheretz* pure. The Yerushalmi cites the illustrious Tanna, Rabbi Yehuda HaNasi, who references the finding of ways to render the *sheretz* pure as a tannaitic activity in Torah study, but one that had its critics:

Rabbi [Yehudah HaNasi] said, "Rabbi Meir had an elder student, and he would be finding the *sheretz* pure and impure via one hundred different ways. They said that this student did not know how to rule (i.e. he never rose to the status of teacher or rabbi, hence he was referred to as an elder student)."[212]

(This is immediately followed by, 'Rabbi Yaakov bar Dosai said, "This student was cut off from the Torah of Sinai".' R. Yaakov bar Dosai was a fifth generation Amora living in Palestine.)

These words in the Yerushalmi witness that trying to render the *sheretz* pure was a tannaitic activity that took place in the realm of Torah study where it was not unanimously appreciated. Apparently R.Yohanan did not himself come up with the idea of doing this.[213] R.

---

[212] According to Jastrow, ותיק means enduring; trusty; strong; distinguished; and תלמיד ותיק is a faithful student, or a distinguished scholar. It has these many senses since the root is related to the biblical Hebrew עתיק meaning, very old.

[213] B.Eruvin 13b also indicates that the concept of finding arguments to render the *sheretz* pure was of tannaitic origin; it quotes a baraita. Like in the Bavli and Yerushalmi versions of the above passage in Sanhedrin, B. Erusin 13b presents an actual attempt at such an argument only by an Amora, Ravina. Ravina's argument is essentially the same as Rav's in the Bavli and R. Yannai's in the Yerushalmi above. The Bavli's refutation of Ravina's is the same as its refutation of Rav's in Sanhedrin:

תנא : תלמיד ותיק היה ביבנה שהיה מטהר את השרץ במאה וחמשים טעמים

Yohanan's contribution rather, was to draw a connection between this intellectual activity that existed in the realm of tannaitic hermeneutics and the issue of fitness requirements of trial judges, when he declared that someone who could not succeed at rendering the *sheretz* pure would not be fit to serve as a trial judge.

This leaves the question of what kind of tannaitic intellectual activity this was that R. Yohanan was referencing. How did it arise and how did it fit into what we know from the Midrash Halakhah and the Misnah constituted the Torah study and research of the Tannaim? And why was Rabbi Meir's student criticized?

9.3: What Type of Tannaitic Intellectual Activity was R. Yohanan Referencing?

As demonstrated repeatedly in the early chapters of this book, *o'kheiluf* is engaged only when the launching premise of the original qal v'homer argument is not backed by strong evidence, i.e. the evidence for P is at most weak in,

Since A, B & P must-it-not-follow-that Q ?!

או חילוף

Since A, B & -Q must-it-not-follow-that –P ?!,

where A and B are facts.

Thus, as discussed above, the *o'kheiluf* argument that follows R. Yohanan's directive is clear evidence that according to the Yerushalmi the launching premise of R. Yannai's qal v'homer argument is not based on strong evidence and therefore cannot be

---

אמר רבינא : אני אדון ואטהרנו: ומה נחש שממית ומרבה טומאה טהור, שרץ שאין ממית ומרבה טומאה, לא כל שכן ?! ולא היא: מעשה קוץ בעלמא קעביד.

based on the verses Lev. 11:29-31. That is, R. Yannai's qal v'homer imagines Lev. 11:29-31 to be absent from the Torah. Hence, the attempt to prove from the Torah that the *sheretz* is pure when in fact Lev. 11:29-31 says clearly that it is not, should be understood as an attempt to prove this contrary-to-Torah proposition from (Torah)" where (Torah)" refers to all of Torah minus Lev. 11:29-31 and its implications. And this is the sort of activity that is seen repeatedly in the Midrash Halakhah.

The Midrash Halakhah, both of the R. Ishmael and the R. Akiva schools, subscribes to a principle of biblical parsimony. That is, a belief that the Torah does not contain superfluous words. The school of R. Ishmael has the less extreme version of such a belief, sometimes explaining away words that appear superfluous with "the Torah speaks in the language of people." i.e. the Torah used extra words to describe something because in the particular case that is how people talk.[214]

When some words in the Torah that detail a law appear redundant, the midrash of either school often engages in a thought experiment whereby the words are imagined absent and it is shown that in such an imagined situation either it is possible to prove the opposite of that law or it is not possible to derive the law or its negation at all. This demonstration confirms that indeed the words that were imagined absent from the Torah are most certainly not redundant, but serve an informational role in the Torah.[215]

Often the Midrash Halakhah asks the question: Did we really need to be given this law explicitly? Could we not have derived it from... other statements in the Torah? Is the statement of the law in question, superfluous? The midrash then imagines the statement absent and shows that the law at issue could not have been derived even if the midrash uses everything else in the Torah. Sometimes though the law

---

[214] See Sifre Numbers, piska 112 : דברה תורה כלשון בני אדם
[215] See Chapter Two, each of the *o'kheiluf* arguments from the Sifre Devarim, #12-15.

could be derived from other statements in the Torah and therefore its expression does appear redundant. The midrash then defends the apparent redundancy by trying to show that it in fact does add content and is required. Sometimes, for example, stating that otherwise it would not be possible for a person to incur punishment for the violation of a law expressed in the statement, because punishment is not meted out for violating a law that was derived by qal v'homer, i.e. אין עונשין מן הדין (transliterated, *ayn onshin min ha-din*).[216] That is, punishment is incurred only for violating a law stated explicitly in the Torah.

The attempt to render the *sheretz* pure can be understood as attempting to show that indeed the law expressed in Lev.11:29-31 that the *sheretz* is impure and that touching its carcass defiles a person until the evening, needed to be stated explicitly and could not be derived from the rest of the Torah. That a particular biblical phrase is not redundant is something commonly demonstrated in the Midrash Halakhah regarding the expression of many different laws.

But to try to render the *sheretz* pure is actually to try to do more than this. It is clearly more challenging to show not just that without the explicit statement of this law in the Torah we would not know the contents of the law in question, but that in fact without the statement of this law one could be led by the rest of the Torah to conclude the contrary of this law, that in fact the *sheretz* is a pure animal. There are many such more challenging examples in the Midrash Halakhah.[217]

---

[216] See Mekhilta, Masekhta de-Nezeikin, each of parsha 7, 11, 12; Sifre Bamidbar Parshat Naso, piska 1 and piska 23; Sifra Kedoshim, parsha 4, perek 11.

[217] There are many such examples in the Midrash Halakhah. See for example Sifre Bamidbar, piska 24 which considers the question of whether the nazirite is permitted products of the grapevine in the case of *akheelat tzar*. Some other examples in Sifre Bamidbar are in each of piska 7, 12, 22, 23, 34, 62, 107, 110. Such examples, contrary to Neusner's claims (in his translations to the Sifre Bamidbar and the Sifra), do not show that logic is secondary to Scripture and that Scripture at times takes a stand against logic

or "unfettered reasoning." For a full discussion see my paper "How are Scripture and Reason Related in the Midrash Halakhah? Refutation of Neusner's Influential View and its Serious Consequences," submitted for publication. What follows here are some of the salient points from the paper.

What the examples above from the Midrash Halakhah do show is that in a typical qal v'homer, Scripture is involved from the start, as the axioms from which the argument is launched are statements from the Torah. Contrary to Neusner, Scripture does not only show up at the end of an argument when a proof text is presented that contradicts the conclusion reached. The reasoning from the axioms and the axioms together make up the argument. In discussing the work of Midrash Halakhah it makes no sense to separate the two, Scripture and reasoning, or axioms and reasoning, as reasoning is constrained by the axioms with which it has to reason. Contrary to Neusner there is no "unfettered reasoning" in the Midrash Halakhah. (For similar objection to the last, see Janowitz and Lazarus,"Rabbinic Methods of Inference and the Rationality Debate," 497.)

When a qal v'homer reaches a conclusion from biblical axioms that contradicts another verse in the Torah, that is, another biblical axiom, this does not make the whole collection of axioms an inconsistent set of statements. This is because qal v'homer reasoning is inductive, not deductive. The possibility of inductively inferring from the original set of axioms the contradiction of the last axiom considered, demonstrates the need for including that last axiom in one's set of axioms, i.e. in the Torah.

An everyday example can be used to demonstrate this last point. A list of rules is often adjusted by adding in another rule to block certain unwanted possible inductive inferences from the original list. When we do this we are not guilty of 'favoring our rules over logic.' For example, suppose a middle school is setting up a dress code. The code may be set up as a set of rules or axioms. The following are three conceivable axioms in such a code:

1. The girls must wear dresses.
2. The dresses must be black.
3. The sleeves of each dress must reach the elbows.

Mothers shopping for appropriate clothing for their child might draw the following inductive inference from these three rules which seem to be setting modesty standards:

Conclusion A: Since for a middle school girl a short dress is immodest, dress lengths must be well below the knee.

A different possible inference is that since the dress code says nothing about the length, it should be understood that the code places no restrictions on dress length:

Conclusion B: The dress code places no restrictions on dress length.

Since these sorts of demonstrations occur throughout the Midrash Halakhah and they show that no words in the Torah are superfluous, why is R. Meir's student criticized for engaging in this kind of search? Perhaps it is because he looked for one hundred ways to show that the words of Lev.11:29-31 were needed. To show that these verses are not superfluous all he needed to do was to show that if they were absent from the Torah, certain other verses in the Torah could be used in a particular way to conclude the contrary of Lev.11:29-31, that the *sheretz* is pure. He did not need one hundred such demonstrations each from a different subset of verses in the Torah. One such demonstration shows that the three verses in Leviticus are not superfluous as they serve a unique function in the Torah. Once this is shown ninety nine more such demonstrations are not needed.

Looking for those other ninety nine is diverting time from real Torah questions. A student who wastes his time on such frivolous pursuits at the expense of more pressing Torah questions never completes his

---

The school then adds a fourth rule to the first three to add further specifications:

4. Dresses may be of any typical length, up to five inches above the knee.

The fourth rule or axiom contradicts each of the two possible conclusions mentioned above, Conclusion A and Conclusion B, drawn from the first three axioms and thereby renders those two conclusions false. Does this make the new set of axioms, all of 1, 2, 3, and 4, seem arbitrary and not sensible or even obtuse, unreasonable or even illogical? After all, the first three taken together suggested that these rules were all about modesty while the fourth seems to correct that induction from the first three. The answer is no.

It may not even be necessary to abandon the inductive interpretation that the rules are about implementing modesty. These rules or axioms could have been part of a dress code in the US in the 1960's motivated in part by considerations of modesty. But in the 1960s when skirts were at their all time shortest, mothers would have had a hard time finding dresses to purchase that were longer than 5 inches above the knee. But beside this practical point, when the fashion had skirts so very short, 5 inches above the knee would have appeared as a very respectable length for a dress and very much longer would have the girls appearing very odd and for both of these reasons such a length would have appeared to serve the purposes of modesty.

degree and becomes a rabbi he only ages into an old student. Since
he is diverting his attention off of the usual questions that preoccupy
the rabbis it is said of him that he is cut off from, presumably the
revelation of the oral law at, Sinai. And because the parallel passage
in the Bavli only asks of the prospective judge that he be able to
render the *sheretz* pure in one way, there is no baraita or amoraic
comment that this is not a good thing for a Torah student to be doing.
As described above, doing this once is in keeping with what is seen in
many passages in the Midrash Halakhah.

B. Eruvin 13b

There are other passages, one in Piskei de-Rav Kahana, a work of
aggadic midrash composed sometime between 500 CE and 700CE
most likely in Palestine, and another on B.Eruvin 13b, which praise
activities that might seem like those of R. Meir's student. But as will
be argued below, they are different from the latter in logically
important ways.[218]

---

[218]From Piskei de-Rav Kahana 4.2, on *Para Adumah*:

ר' יוסי ממליחייא ר' יהושע דסכנין בשם ר' לוי תינוקות בימי דוד עד שלא יטעמו
טעם חט היו יודעין לדרוש את התורה ארבעים ותשע פנים טמא וארבעים ותשע פנים טהור

From B.Eruvin 13b, the same sort of activity as in the passage from Piskei
de-Rav Kahana, although a rabbinic ruling had already been reached. The
reception is not entirely positive, as his conclusions were at odds with the
consensus:

אמר רבי אחא בר חנינא: גלוי וידוע לפני מי שאמר והיה העולם שאין בדורו של רבי מאיר
כמותו, ומפני מה לא קבעו הלכה כמותו? שלא יכלו חביריו לעמוד על סוף דעתו שהוא אומר
על טמא טהור ומראה לו פנים, על טהור טמא ומראה לו פנים.

Also from B. Eruvin 13b, a corrective remark a few lines further down:

אמר רבי אבהו אמר רבי יוחנן: תלמיד היה לו לרבי מאיר וסומכוס שמו, שהיה אומר על כל
דבר ודבר של טומאה ארבעים ושמונה טעמי טומאה, ועל כל דבר ודבר של טהרה
ארבעים ושמונה טעמי טהרה.

Unlike the baraita in the Bavli regarding the activity of R. Meir's student, a passage in the midrash Piskei de-Rav Kahana and a tradition reported on B. Eruvin 13b, respectively, find these other similar-seeming activities to be productive. The issues under consideration there concern matters not explicitly decided by the Torah, and the arguments referenced in the passage from Piskei de-Rav Kahana argue inductively for two opposing positions starting from the same premises. Such activities contribute to fleshing out different possibly relevant points and displaying all possibilities (perhaps before a best proof can be chosen from the collection). The rabbis therefore approved of these activities. The passage on B. Eruvin 13b, refers to rulings that have already become authoritative. With regard to these, finding a plethora of ways to demonstrate those rulings as deriving from the Torah is also viewed positively for the different possible connections it raises between the authoritative texts and the ruling under consideration.

The most important difference between proving the *sheretz* pure and the activities praised in the Piskei de-Rav Kahana and on B. Eruvin 13b is that in the latter all proofs are engaged in from a body of shared premises. Arguing first for and then against the same position from a body of shared premises was also a standard exercise given to students of Roman rhetoric. This is not the case with the debate between the Torah and Rav or between the Torah and R. Yannai. The earlier discussion in this chapter made clear that neither of these two rabbis is engaged in, or even thinks he is engaged in, proving a proposition contrary to the Torah from the same set of premises shared by the Torah. That the *sheretz* is impure is one of the axioms that make up the Torah, while as shown above, both Rav and R. Yannai's demonstrations rendering the *sheretz* pure are made from the set of premises that is a tweaked version of the Torah that does not contain the verses Lev. 11:29-31.

This chapter has shown that the origin of the concept of trying to prove the *sheretz* pure, at least as expressed by the Amoraim Rav and R. Yannai and understood by the Talmuds, lies within types of arguments often encountered in the Midrash Halakhah, some of them *o'kheiluf* arguments, to show that a certain biblical verse is not redundant. In taking on the intellectual challenge to render the *sheretz* pure, neither Amora can be understood as rejecting the truth that the Torah dictates that the *sheretz* is impure and that this ruling should be followed. Rather, they can be understood as testing their inferences about the nature of purity and impurity, which is not spelled out in the Torah alongside pronouncements of what sorts of things and situations cause impurity.

While the Talmud has limited enthusiasm for the proliferation of arguments to render the *sheretz* pure, the Talmud records much enthusiasm for the proliferation of, what are, inductive arguments reaching opposing conclusions starting from the collection of statements of the Torah as shared premises. And as explained earlier, being able to reach two opposing conclusions by arguing *inductively* from one set of axioms or premises does not make that set of axioms a contradictory set of statements.[219] (What it does is make the set incomplete, that is, if the contradictory statements are 'X is true' and 'X is false', then the set of axioms do not determine whether or not X is true; that information though perhaps relevant to the topic of the axioms cannot be obtained from the axioms.)

Explaining R. Yohanan's Spin

If, as I have argued, R. Yohanan was referring to standard activity of the Midrash Halakhah which R. Yannai then tried to engage in with the law of the *sheretz*, why did R. Yohanan phrase it in such a way that it is possible to read him as asking of prospective judges that they be able to prove contradictions to Torah laws from the Torah?

In the Bavli, R. Yohanan is describing how to pick judges. He instructs that those chosen to be judges should be tall, men of wisdom, pleasant looking, they must know the nature of sorcery,

---

[219] See footnote 217.

speak all seventy languages. Several of these criteria suggest that they must be people who can be found in a beit midrash. R. Yehuda in the name of Rav, adds a particular restriction on which individual Torah scholars may qualify: only those who can render the *sheretz* pure from the Torah.

Halakhah 1 (Mishnah 4:1) in the Yerushalmi, states that in capital cases the judges should open with arguments to exonerate the defendant. R. Yohanan says anyone who cannot find a way to render the *sheretz* pure and impure in one hundred ways will not be able to open with arguments to vindicate. R. Yohanan is providing a test by which to disqualify prospective candidates to the court who are coming from the beit midrash.

Why would R. Yohanan have the scholars of the beit midrash tested in this way for fitness to serve on the court? The kind of judging that a Torah scholar in the beit midrash would have had experience with is deciding private matters of ritual law. Queen Helena, for example, is featured prominently as someone who sought out the sages for rulings on different private matters that came up.[220] The closest previous experience anyone in a beit midrash could have to presenting arguments to exonerate someone who seems clearly guilty, may very well be inferring from a subset of the statements in the Torah the contrary of what is well known from a different verse.[221] The analogy with trial is made stronger by choosing that inference to be regarding the innocence of the *sheretz*, where a verse not in the subset under consideration establishes its guilt. Any scholar in the beit midrash who does not demonstrate such skill in Torah study, if put on a court, would not have the chops to find ways to try to exonerate a defendant who reeks of guilt.

---

[220] See M. Nazir 3:6, B. Sukkah 2b.

[221] Consistent with our reading that R. Yohanan is looking for relatable intellectual activities that someone sitting in a beit midrash could possibly have, is the fact that R. Ishmael's baraita of the list of 13 hermeneutical activities is recorded in the Tosefta in Sanhedrin, chapter 7, that deals with judging capital cases.

9.4: Conclusions

The two amoraic *o'kheiluf* arguments unique to the Yerushalmi were analyzed. Each displayed the same facility with the mechanics of the *o'kheiluf* argument, the same expertise at forming the negation of a complex claim that was seen in the tannaitic *o'kheiluf* arguments. The amoraic authors use the phrase *o'kheiluf* exactly as do the Tannaim in the Midrash Halakhah and the Mishnah and as continued by the Bavli. Both arguments are structured as debates between two people (or voices), just as in the *o'kheiluf* argument of the Mishnah, Pesahim 6:1-2. But unlike each of the tannaitic *o'kheiluf* arguments, after setting up the two possibilities, the original and the *kheiluf*, the Yerushalmi does not pursue determining which of the two is correct.

The first one considered, Y. Bava Batra 8:1, 22a, is an *o'kheiluf* argument between two just-as arguments (rather than two qal v'homer arguments).[222] The *o'kheiluf* argument is not pursued all the way to a conclusion because R. Yannai and R. Yohanan, who presented the initial qal v'homer of the *o'kheiluf* argument, know that R. Yehuda Nesi'ah, who presented the *kheiluf* qal v'homer, does not find the biblical evidence relied upon for the launching proposition of their qal v'homer argument to be sufficiently strong. R. Yohanan has no stronger biblical evidence to offer and he knows that if he responds to R. Yehuda Nesi'ah's *kheiluf* qal v'homer with, 'Look you have concluded with -P which contradicts the evidence for P !', R. Yehuda Nesi'ah will respond with, 'Precisely, I think your evidence for P does not hold up and I think P is wrong.' R. Yohanan, unable to refute R. Yehuda Nesi'ah's *kheiluf* argument, resorts to insulting him, referring to him as someone who does not want to learn Torah. (The parallel passage on B. Bava Batra 111a, does not involve an *o'kheiluf* argument. Instead, R. Yehuda Nesi'ah counters with a short *reductio ad absurdum* argument which earns him similar insults.[223])

---

[222] There is one such tannaitic *o'kheiluf* argument as well. See Chapter Two, #6, from Sifre Bamidbar, piska 155. It is also discussed in Chapter Five.

[223] In the Bavli, Bava Batra 11a-b, Yehuda Nesi'ah asks R. Yannai, "From where is it derived that a son precedes a daughter with regard to inheriting the mother's property?" R. Yannai answers that the verse, Num. 27:8, uses

The other amoraic *o'kheiluf* argument of the Yerushalmi, on Y. Sanhedrin 4:1, 21a which parallels B. Sanhedrin 17a, concerns R. Yohanan's famous pronouncement that a person who is not able to render the *sheretz* pure by Torah law, must not be appointed judge to the high court. The idea being that one who would be a judge should be clever and open-minded enough to examine every detail of the case in order to exonerate a defendant who seems as guilty of the crime he is on trial for, as a *sheretz* is guilty of being impure.

In the Bavli, Rav offers a demonstration from the Torah that a reptile (i.e. the *sheretz*) is pure and in the Yerushalmi, a very similar demonstration (regarding the particular *sheretz*, the mouse) is attributed to R. Yannai. Although the Yerushalmi's understanding of such demonstration matches the Bavli's, the Yerushalmi's understanding is made particularly transparent through its use of *o'kheiluf* argumentation. The actual arguments to render the *sheretz* pure are revealed as far less provocative than the directive. In fact they are typical of many arguments found much earlier in the Midrash Halakhah.

As seen throughout this book, a *qal v'homer* argument is countered with *o'kheiluf* only when its launching premise is either a guess or supported only by (what is viewed as) weak biblical evidence. Through its use of *o'kheiluf*, the *stam* makes clear that it understands R. Yohanan as pretending that the biblical verses listing the impure creeping creatures, Lev. 11:29-31, are absent from the Torah. It is

---

the word 'tribes' thereby making an association, i.e. a *hekesh*, between the father's tribe to the mother's tribe: just as with regard to the father's tribe, the son precedes the daughter, so too, with regard to the mother's tribe, the son precedes the daughter.

R. Yehuda Nesi'ah responds, "If indeed that is right and there is a *hekesh* between the mother's tribe and the father's tribe established by the word in the verse 'tribes', then the following should also be derived from the *hekesh*: just as with regard to the father's tribe, the *bekhor*, i.e. the eldest son, receives double the inheritance of the other sons, so too with regard to the mother's tribe, her *bekhor* should receive a double inheritance."

from such an imagined Torah as his set of premises, that R. Yannai gives his demonstration rendering the mouse pure. The *kheiluf* qal v'homer, that starts from the contrary conclusion, in order to respond to R. Yannai, must also argue from a Torah in which those verses are imagined absent.

In refuting R. Yannai's demonstration by showing that it does not rule out the *kheiluf* possibility, and so the *o'kheiluf* argument cannot proceed to a resolution, the Yerushalmi shows that it is not possible – at least for any Amora or later rabbi – to prove (even) from a Torah in which Lev.11:29-31 is omitted, that the mouse is pure.

The Yerushalmi next cites the illustrious Tanna, Rabbi Yehuda HaNasi, as witnessing that trying to render the *sheretz* pure was a tannaitic activity that took place in the realm of Torah study where it was not unanimously appreciated.[224] Apparently the Amora, R. Yohanan, in this passage of the Yerushalmi was not expressing an original idea. R. Yohanan's contribution rather, was to draw a connection between this intellectual activity that existed in the realm of tannaitic hermeneutics to the issue of fitness requirements of trial judges, declaring that someone who could not succeed at rendering the mouse pure would not be fit to serve as a trial judge.

Chapters Two and Four described *o'kheiluf* arguments from Sifre Devarim of the school of R. Akiva that proceed from the same sort of thought experiment as trying to prove the *sheretz* pure. The Midrash Halakhah, both of the R. Ishmael and the R. Akiva schools, subscribes to a principle of biblical parsimony, that is, a belief that the Torah does not contain superfluous words. To test whether some words in the Torah that detail a law appear redundant, the midrash often engages in a thought experiment whereby the words are imagined absent and it is shown that in such an imagined situation

---

[224] There are other passages, one in the midrashic work Piskei de-Rav Kahana and another on B. Eruvin 13b which praise activities that might seem like those of R. Meir's student but are different in logically important ways explained in the chapter.

either it is possible to prove the opposite of that law or it is not possible to derive the law or its negation at all. This demonstration confirms that indeed the words that were imagined absent from the Torah are most certainly not redundant, but serve an informational role in the Torah.[225]

If trying to prove the *sheretz* pure from the Torah minus Lev. 11:29-31 is the same sort of activity commonly seen in the Midrash Halakhah why, as the Yerushalmi suggests, did the former have fierce critics? Perhaps the criticism was aimed at the seeking of one hundred ways to do this when one way would have sufficed to show that the biblical words were not redundant. Looking for one hundred ways to do this served no function.

This leaves one question remaining. If R. Yohanan was really referring to argumentation that is actually standard in the Midrash Halakhah, why did he phrase his directive in such a way that it is possible to read him as asking of prospective judges that they be able to prove contradictions to Torah laws from the Torah? Why would R. Yohanan have the scholars of the beit midrash tested in this way for fitness to serve on the court? The kind of judging that a Torah scholar in the beit midrash would have had experience with is deciding private matters of ritual law. The closest previous experience anyone in a beit midrash could have to presenting arguments to exonerate someone who seems clearly guilty, would be inferring from a subset of the statements in the Torah the contrary of what is well known from a different verse.[226] The analogy with trial is made stronger by choosing that inference to be regarding the innocence of the *sheretz*, where a verse not in the subset under consideration establishes its guilt. Any scholar in the beit midrash who does not demonstrate such

---

[225] See Chapter Two, each of the *o'kheiluf* arguments from the Sifre Devarim, #12-15.

[226] Consistent with our reading that R. Yohanan is looking for relatable intellectual activities that someone sitting in a beit midrash could possibly have, is the fact that R. Ishmael's baraita of the list of 13 hermeneutical methods is recorded in the Tosefta in Sanhedrin, chapter 7, that deals with judging capital cases.

skill in Torah study, if put on a court, would not have the smarts to find ways to exonerate a defendant who reeks of guilt.

CHAPTER TEN: Summary of Conclusions, Further Results

In this book I have uncovered a type of tannaitic argument that was lost: neither traditional commentators nor academic scholars seem to have known of its existence. I located it scattered across the range of tannaitic literature – including in some well-trodden passages – which suggests that it was a widely practiced way of arguing. Everywhere it appears in tannaitic literature, this type of argument is signaled by the same phrase, *o'kheiluf*. The argument also appears in passages of amoraic origin in the Bavli and Yerushalmi Talmuds, also signaled by the same phrase.

This type of argument appears to have no precedent in Greek or Roman literature. It is uniquely tannaitic. The phrase by which it is identified, *o'kheiluf*, would seem to be an everyday expression, 'o' meaning 'or', and *kheiluf*, is a noun from the ordinary root, ח,ל,פ, meaning to switch or to exchange. It was therefore never recognized as signaling any precise operation. Yet this everyday-seeming expression was appropriated by the Tannaim to serve as technical terminology indicating the special type of argument. It is used in tannaitic literature exclusively for this purpose and, as shown in Chapters Two and Six, in every argument in which it appears it means precisely the same thing.[227]

The similar tannaitic phrase *kheiluf ha-devarim* has a precise meaning as well, one that is distinct from *o'kheiluf*. The Tannaim were very careful with the two phrases, applying them exactly where they belonged, never labeling an *o'kheiluf* argument as a case of *kheiluf ha-devarim* or vice versa. And these two terms truly functioned as technical terminology. That is, each occurs often as a stand-in for the entire argument (or proposition) that it represents, in this way keeping the overarching structure of the overall argument clear.

---

[227] Section 2.6 of this book argued that the single occurrence of the phrase *o'kheiluf* in Sifre Deuteronomy piska 260 is a later corruption of the text.

Because this argument has no Greek analogue, it was not possible to describe it with an English word or expression. I had to describe it in great detail and the clearest most efficient way to do this was to describe it symbolically. The *o'kheiluf* argument is a meta-argument that aims to determine which of two arguments related to one another in a highly specific way is correct. Everywhere the phrase occurs it refers to a precise set of logical changes to any member of a particular class of complex propositions. By the end of Chapter Five the logical connection between the phrase and the contrapositive is drawn out. But there is no Greek term for the collection of changes the phrase represents.

Thus, the phrase *o'kheiluf* is uniquely tannaitic logico-linguistic terminology. As described in Chapters One, Four and Five, executing the *o'kheiluf* argument involves yet further logical terminology also unique to the Tannaim.

In examining the *o'kheiluf* arguments in the Midrash Halakhah, stark differences were found between those of the R. Ishmael and R. Akiva schools. Most surprising, the authors of the school of R. Akiva emerged as, by far, the better logicians. This is at odds with the picture Heschel popularized, painting the school of R. Akiva as not focused on being logical.

The midrash of the R. Akiva school often resorts to treating biblical verses as codes to be deciphered, in ways that at times appear forced. In such midrashim the R. Akiva school may strike the reader as not reflecting our own reading practices. But the logically superior *o'kheiluf* arguments of the R. Akiva school supports the charitable view of such other midrash as presenting simply the best derivation possible rather than representing derivations that the R. Akiva school found most compelling. The school of R. Akiva sought to derive as many oral traditions as possible from the Torah and this goal at times led to a best possible derivation of a law, rather than a necessarily compelling derivation, even by their own lights. Not sufficiently appreciating the premises under which the R. Akiva midrash operated, Heschel was led to characterize the R. Akiva school as not focused on being logical. A study of the *o'kheiluf* arguments finds against Heschel's general picture.

I used the differences I found in the *o'kheiluf* arguments that I identified as characteristic of the two schools as markers for attributing school affiliation to particular passages where authorship is contested. I was able to thus identify certain passages in the Sifra as clearly in the *o'kheiluf* style of the R. Akiva school, refuting Menahem Kahana's attribution of these passages to the R. Ishmael school.

The *o'kheiluf* argument, with its uniquely tannaitic logical terminology, betrays blanket ignorance of Aristotelian and Stoic logic. The tannaitic logical terminology signals operations that a contemporaneous Stoic philosopher would see as cumbersome and largely unsuccessful attempts to make do without Western logic, particularly knowledge about the contrapositive and *modus tollens*. The Stoic would see the *o'kheiluf* argument as, in some sense, intended to compensate for ignorance about the truth value of the contrapositive and about all that goes into the Stoic syllogism we call *modus tollens*.

Our imagined Stoic philosopher in Chapter Five shows how Stoic logic could have demonstrated to the R. Ishmael school that their *o'kheiluf* arguments did not accomplish what they were intended for. The Tannaim of the two schools were not able to recognize that the *kheiluf* or second argument that the *o'kheiluf* presents, must conclude with the negation of the launching premise of the original argument, regardless of the particulars of the case. The evidence for the launching premise of the first argument is in no way strengthened when the *kheiluf* argument concludes, as it must, with the negation of the launching premise. Further, that the contrapositive of a conditional statement has the same truth value as the conditional is not something that the rabbis knew or could even consider.

Logic, especially Stoic logic, was of vital importance to the Stoic philosophers that were everywhere to be found in Roman times. Stoic logic was at the heart of Stoic philosophy (and intermixed throughout its different branches[228]). Logic was central to Stoic ethics.[229][230] Had the Tannaim been cognizant of Western logic and if they had real contact with Stoic philosophers they might have brought these arguments to a Stoic philosopher for analysis. But they clearly did not. The discoveries detailed in this book need to be taken into account by any theory of tannaitic participation in Hellenestic culture that wants to claim for the rabbis any real or deep knowledge and understanding of Stoic philosophy.

---

[228] See in A. A. Long, "The Dialectician as Stoic Sage," in *Stoic Studies* (Berkeley: University of California Press, 1996).

[229] Stoic logic was completely worked out by Chrysippus by the 3rd century BC. To the Stoics there were three areas of philosophy: logic, ethics and physics. Logic was divided into two 'sciences', dialectic and rhetoric. Dialectics was concerned with what we moderns would consider to be logic, including all of the Stoic syllogisms, and grammar. Dialectics was crucial for ethics because it is the tool for correctly assessing our impressions and our choices and their consequences.

The biographer Diogenes Laertius (180-240 AD) wrote:

Such then is the logic of the Stoics, which chiefly establishes their point that the wise man is the only dialectician. For all things are brought to light through the study in rational utterances, both the subject-matter of physics and again of ethics (as for logic that goes without saying), and (?without logic the wise man?) would not be able to speak about correctness of names, how the laws have made arrangements for actions. Of the two forms of inquiry which fall under the virtue (of dialectic), one considers what each thing that exists is, and the other what it is called. (VII.83)

Dialectics continued to form an important part of the Stoic curriculum during the imperial period.

The Greek philosopher Epictetus (died 135 AD) who was most interested in the practical purposes of philosophy, used methods and terminology that show great familiarity with the logical textbooks by Chrysippus and other Stoics. He stressed the wise man's need for dialectical competence, not as an end in itself but as a "measuring instrument" of our rational faculty. He speaks of the "necessity of logic" (Discourses II.25). For references and a fuller discussion, see Long, "The Dialectician as Stoic Sage".

[230] After the Romans conquered Greece they became very interested in Greek philosophy and the philosophy that became the most popular in the Roman Empire was Stoicism.(The Roman Emperor and Stoic philosopher, Marcus Aurelius lived 121 - 180 AD.)

To say that they were not familiar with Aristotelian and Stoic logic is not to say that the Tannaim did not employ the sort of reasoning with which the ancient logicians concerned themselves. Appendix II describes one robust example from the Tosefta of *reductio ad absurdum* which is the sort of ordinary reasoning whose underlying form the Stoics exposed by means of *modus tollens*. The Stoic logical investigations were aimed at uncovering the rules of correct reasoning that people had been using, such as *reductio ad absurdum*, without thinking about the underlying form of their reasoning. Applying these uncovered rules or forms, such as *modus tollens*, then enabled more reliable distinction between cases of correct reasoning from logical fallacies.

It is interesting that without having such rules the Tannaim were yet so highly skilled at correctly negating complex propositions, as seen in the *o'kheiluf* arguments in Chapter Two. From those arguments as well as from other attacks on a qal v'homer discussed at the end of Chapter Five, it is clear that the Tannaim also recognized that, as we would put it, the conclusion of an argument could be no more reliable than the degree to which the premises of the argument are reliable.

Later, the Amoraim studied some of the tannaitic passages that contain *o'kheiluf* arguments, most prominently the often-cited M. Pesahim 6:1-2. The Talmuds did not understand what R. Akiva was up to with his *o'kheiluf* that concludes with a false law, i.e. that the Passover sacrifice does not put off the Sabbath restrictions. To explain it, the Bavli, building on a baraita, resorts to the astonishing claim that R. Eliezer whose memory faculties were legendary had forgotten his own teaching regarding sprinkling which he had taught his student Akiva. To remind R. Eliezer of that teaching without embarrassing him, the Bavli reasons, R. Akiva presented the *kheiluf* that started from that teaching even though it concludes with a false law about the Passover sacrifice. According to the Bavli this bizarre argument was aimed at provoking R. Eliezer into realizing that he had forgotten his own teaching.

The Talmuds could not make sense of R. Akiva's argument. Their analysis was clearly not informed by a careful study of the collection of *o'kheiluf* arguments in the Midrash Halakhah of the R. Akiva school. The talmudic commentators fared no better. The identification and study of the *o'kheiluf* arguments of the Midrash Halakhah advanced in this book leads to a simple understanding of R. Akiva's brilliant argument. Chapter Six lays out how R. Akiva was arguing in the manner of *o'kheiluf* arguments (detailed in Chapter Four) typical of his school with the same objectives.

Only one of the *o'kheiluf* arguments of the Midrash Halakhah, from the Sifra (#7 of Chapter Two), appears in its entirety as a baraita in the Talmud, on B. Temurah 28b. The Bavli introduces it as the source for the ruling in the mishnah under discussion, M. Temurah 6:1, that a worshiped animal may not be offered as a sacrifice. The *o'kheiluf* argument concludes that the source for the ruling is the hermeneutical cue 'from' in the phrase "from the cattle". The Bavli did not only copy the successful derivation at the end (as it did with other *o'kheiluf* arguments of the R. Akiva school) but also included the failed attempts of the *o'kheiluf* that motivated the more contrived derivation that followed. Apparently in this case, the Bavli was in agreement with the Sifra that the derivation was only made compelling by the failure first of more natural methods.

According to the Bavli, the baraita intended the further teaching that the coverings of the worshiped animal are prohibited even for ordinary use. But the analysis in Chapters Two and Four of this book makes clear that the midrashist of this *o'kheiluf* argument from the Midrash Halakhah, intended no such further teaching. As with all of the other *o'kheiluf* arguments of the Midrash Halakhah, the focus is on the question that motivated the *o'kheiluf* argument. The issue of coverings was only raised to aid in answering the question of whether or not a worshiped animal may be sacrificed. Once the qal v'homer with the use of this aid failed, the aid was no longer of interest to the *o'kheiluf* argument and it did not return to focus on it.

The Bavli's interest in the status of the coverings arises because the mishnah, M. Temurah 6:1, rules that they are forbidden. The Bavli reads into the baraita its own concern (to find a biblical source for the ruling) which is not a concern of the baraita, doing violence to the second part of the o'kheiluf argument following the set-up. The Bavli's misinterpretation of the baraita does not appear to be intentional. Rather it seems to indicate that the Bavli's knowledge and use of o'kheiluf is not based on a careful study (as carried out in this book) of the collection of tannaitc o'kheiluf arguments, but instead on an evolved common practice of o'kheiluf argumentation.

The Bavli also shows a lack of facility in working with this o'kheiluf argument even to serve its own interests.[231] What the Bavli describes as R. Hananya's attack on the baraita is not that at all, but the implications of his point are an attack on the baraita in a way that to date has not been recognized. The verse he points to, Deut. 12:3, as a source prohibiting use of the coverings, would render the first qal v'homer of the o'kheiluf argument conclusive. There would therefore be no need for the biblical phrase "from the cattle," as the o'kheiluf baraita argues, to derive that a worshiped animal may not be offered on the altar. The Bavli displays weak skills in the tannaitic practice of o'kheiluf argumentation. The Bavli refutes R. Haninya's interpretation of Deut. 12:3, but then does not understand correctly how this refutation really does serve the o'kheiluf argument.

With regard to all of the other o'kheiluf arguments of the Midrash Halakhah that were not incorporated into the Bavli (or Yerushalmi), Chapter Seven examined what material the Talmuds chose to incorporate in their stead. Compelling reasons were offered for why the Gemaras omitted those o'kheiluf arguments. Concern over the logic of the o'kheiluf arguments was not found to be one of the reasons.

---

[231] Tosafot on B.Temorah 28b demonstrates that it too does not understand the tannaitic o'kheiluf argument. See Chapter Eight.

The *o'kheiluf* argument on B. Avodah Zarah 46b is of amoraic origin. The phrase *o'kheiluf* there satisfies the same symbolic form that was shown to characterize the tannaitic occurrences of the phrase. But as discussed in detail in Chapter Eight, Rava's principle to resolve that *o'kheiluf* argument, *kula v'khumra l'khumra farkheenon,* essentially ended *o'kheiluf* argumentation.

The chapter offered two related reasons to explain why the *o'kheiluf* argument form died out in the Bavli: amoraic insistence on positive supporting evidence for any claim, coupled with a lower standard (than the R. Ishmael midrash and the Sifre Devarim of the R. Akiva school) for what constitutes a biblical proof text. With regard to the second, the later generations of Amoraim and the anonymous authors of the Bavli avoided having an impossibly high standard of what would count as biblical proof because they were engaged in the project of finding sources for as many oral and mishnaic laws as possible. (Chapter Seven included evidence that this was also true of the Yerushalmi.) With so many laws to derive, the Bavli (as well as the Yerushalmi) could not afford to be as demanding of certitude from biblical proof texts. As for the first, the reason the Babylonian Amoraim, unlike the Tannaim before them, were unwilling to entertain an argument launched from a guess, likely concerned the far greater volume of material the Amoraim would have to check in order to be confident of the truth of a guess. If a Tanna could point out that no biblical verse could be used to claim the contrary of his guess that was mild evidence in favor of it. But for the Amoraim who recognized much more extensive source material including the Mishnah, an extensive body of baraitot and amoraic rulings, it would have been much harder for them to be certain that no evidence exists that would contradict a claim they were making without evidence. The possibilities the Amoraim would have had to consider to be confident of absence of evidence to the contrary of a conjectured claim for which there was no positive evidence, were simply too many.

Because of the first characteristic, any amoraic *o'kheiluf* argument in the Bavli would have to be like the debate between Rava and Rav

Huna where the launching claim of each qal v'homer argument is supported by some weak positive evidence and not just absence of evidence for the contrary claim. With weak biblical evidence for both launching claims, there was no easy procedure to decide between the two qal v'homer arguments. This naturally led to Rava's principle which would essentially do away with o'kheiluf arguments. As for the second, situations that would lead to o'kheiluf were greatly reduced because the Amoraim and the later rabbis did not always have as high a standard for conclusive biblical evidence as did the R. Ishmael school in the Midrash Halakhah. Consequently, the evidence in support of the launching claim of a qal v'homer argument was less likely to be found insufficient by the Bavli (or the Yerushalmi) and therefore the conditions that warrant engaging in o'kheiluf were less frequently met.

But the logical shortcomings of the o'kheiluf argument as discussed in Chapter Five appear to have played no role in the demise of this argument form in the Bavli. That the demise of the o'kheiluf argument came about for reasons uncritical of what was in fact problematic about this form of argument is very different from the situation regarding other types of tannaitic argument.[232]

---

[232] See for example, Yaakov Elman, "It is no Empty Thing: Nahmanides and the Search for Omnisignificance," The Torah U-Madda Journal,(1993): 1-83. On p.5 Elman points out that the tannaitic practice of deriving laws from an extraneous vav at the beginning of a biblical word, died out early in the amoraic period. He cites B. Yevamot 72b, to show R. Yochanan's disapproval of such derivations.
See B. Sanhedrin 50b, a baraita there describes an exchange between R. Ishmael and R. Akiva to suggest that even in tannaitic sources, the claim that a law had its source in an extra vav sometimes seemed hard to believe.

See also Michael Chernick's work on the gezerah shavah. (His spelling is shawah.) "Internal Constraints on Gezerah Shawah's Applications," in The Jewish Quarterly Review, LXXX, Nos.3-4 (January-April, 1990):253-282. Chernick finds that the Tannaim were well aware of the potential problems with this type of word analogy and therefore imposed reasonable constraints that would justify applying such analogy.

Chernick identified the different major forms of *gezerah shavah* and showed that in tannaitic works, the words involved in drawing a *gezerah shavah* had to satisfy one of several possible conditions and constraints. In this way there were internal controls on the application of *gezerah shavah*. An example of a condition: In the "simple" *gezerah shavah* the two occurrences of the same word or phrase being compared are the only appearances of that word or phrase in the Torah. An example of a constraint: *mufneh*, meaning, freed up for its use in conveying a meaning because other words right next to it already convey that meaning.

Chernick identified a type of word comparison where the phrase *gezerah shavah* is not invoked, but instead there is the phrase נאמר כאן. This type of interpretation is found without the above conditions and constraints being met. He points out that these types of interpretations, unlike those designated as *gezerah shavah*, are often challenged.

In the amoraic period derivations by נאמר כאן also began to be called *gezerah shavah*. He argues that this led to the impression that there were no internal restrictions on the application of *gezerah shavah* and therefore the worry that this rule of reference could be used to generate all sorts of incorrect halakhot. The Amoraim therefore imposed the following constraint on its application: "No one may create a gezerah shavah on his own":

אין אדם דן גזירה שוה מעצמו

Chernick writes, "...external controls were not necessary in the tannaitic period. The strict formal demands of the generative verses for "simple" *gezerah shawah* and requirement of a "free" pentateuchal element for mufnah acted as internal limitations on the application of *gezerah shawah*."

Y. Pesahim 44b cites the baraita of how Hillel resolved the problem of the *bnei biterah* of whether to slaughter the Pesach offering if the 14th of Nisan falls out on the Sabbath. When Hillel answered them with a *gezerah shavah* connecting the two instances of the word במועדו, "in its time" mentioned with regard to the Pesach offering and to the *tamid* offering, the *bnei Beterah* objected. They considered his proof to be invalid, because a person may not put together his own *gezerah shavah* argument. Only if it is a received tradition is it acceptable. As they explained: שאין אדם דן גזירה שוה מעצמו.

The Yerushalmi then justifies this bit of the baraita, showing by example that the *gezerah shavah*, drawing an association between two topics that share a word, is a rule that could lead to incorrect results and therefore is not a robust rule. The example the Gemara gives associates the biblical words for 'garment' and 'leather' that occur both with regard to a corpse and with regard to a *sheretz*. This association could be used to argue that the law of the *sheretz*, that a lentil-size bit confers defilement, applies as well to a human corpse and that the law of a corpse, that it defiles the tent in which it

402

That the rabbis were not familiar with Aristotelian logic or Stoic logic, might not be surprising especially since the Tannaim before them (who had lived amongst Stoic philosophers) were not either. But it has been suggested that Greek learning penetrated the Persian Empire, remaining on long after ancient Hellenistic rule, and reaching the Persian Empire through travel by Christians, Jews and others from the Greek East. In the Persian Empire, Greek works of philosophy were translated into Syriac and became part of the curriculum in Christian schools.[233] But the Bavli's handling of the widespread tannatic *o'kheiluf* argument, its obliviousness to its inherent logical shortcomings, makes it very hard to believe that Jews were studying any Western logic or even knew what it was.

Although the Amoraim were unfamiliar with Stoic logic and did not have knowledge of *modus tollens* or of the contrapositive there is much evidence (stronger than what exists for the Tannaim) that they did engage in the kind of reasoning that Stoic logic sought to clarify. *Modus tollens* exposes and formalizes the essential logical form of the rhetorical *reductio ad absurdum* argument and there are indeed many robust amoraic examples in the Bavli of (what is described in Appendix II as the simple type) of *reductio ad absurdum*. Further, in

---

lies applies likewise to the *sheretz*. However, these conclusions would be contrary to halakhah.

The Bavli on the same topic of Hillel's response to the *bnei biteirah* invokes the same principle, on B. Pesahim 66a, דאין אדם דן גזירה שוה מעצמו. It occurs there in the context of the Bavli's question: given that Hillel had a proof by *gezerah shavah,* why did he also offer the *bnei beterah* a solution by qal v'homer.

[233] It has been suggested that the Bavli's use of the phrase 'Greek Wisdom' (i.e. חכמת יונית) refers specifically to Aristotelian logic, suggesting that in amoraic times Jews were studying such topics. See Molie Vidas, "Greek Wisdom in Babylonia," in *Envisioning Judaism, Studies in Honor of Peter Schafer on the Occasion of his Seventieth Birthday* (Tübingen: Mohr Siebeck, 2013), and references therein.

Appendix II, I identify a strong example of actual *modus tollens* reasoning on B. Bava Kamma 29a.

But employing *reductio ad absurdum* without reflecting on its underlying form as the Stoics did, rendered the Amoraim less than reliably accurate in the use of such reasoning. As shown in Chapters Seven and Eight, the Bavli was oblivious to the logical shortcomings of the tannaitic *o'kheiluf* argument that were laid out in Chapter Five, including ignorance of the logically necessary way (that what is) a *modus tollens* argument must conclude irrespective of its semantic content. In Chapter Eight, the reader saw that Rava did not recognize how his qal v'homer argument divided up into premises and a conclusion and that in committing to the conclusion he was also committing to the premises. As pointed out earlier it is the nature of logical discoveries that they uncover the rules of the correct reasoning that people have been using and distinguish it from logical fallacies. Logic formalizes the valid reasoning that people have been using without thinking about the underlying form of their reasoning. Once established this logic is then useful for determining the validity of a new argument whose validity is in question.

That the rabbis did not study Western logic should not be taken to imply that they did not engage in arguments that can be described as logically interesting. As Michael Abraham, Dov Gabbay, Uri Schild and associates have shown, the rabbis of the Talmud developed novel inductive types of arguments whose logic these researchers are introducing to the Artificial Intelligence community.[234]

Chapter Nine examines the two amoraic *o'kheiluf* arguments found in the Yerushalmi. They are not like the amoraic argument in the Bavli between Rava and Rav Huna that led to Rava's principle. In that *o'kheiluf* argument, unlike in the tannaitic ones, both opponents have weak evidence to support their respective launching premises. The

---

[234] There have been fifteen volumes published to date in the series *Studies in Talmudic Logic*, put out by College Publications, King's College, London, edited by Michael Abraham, Dov Gabbay and Uri Schild.

o'kheiluf arguments in the Yerushalmi do not follow this doomed route. But unlike the tannaitic *o'kheiluf* arguments and the one in the Bavli, the two in the Yerushalmi are not aimed at finding the correct law but rather at showing that neither of the two contradictory possibilities presented in the *o'kheiluf* argument can be eliminated. Unlike the one in the Bavli, the resolutions of the two in the Yerushalmi do not contain logical errors. My impression is that the reason for the distinctive feature (not seen in any other *o'kheiluf* arguments) that neither argument in the Yerushalmi reaches a conclusion is because the involved parties (including the *stam*) are so practiced that they do not need conclusions spelled out for them. These two arguments suggest that the Yerushalmi had an evolved common practice of *o'kheiluf* argumentation that was more sophisticated and careful than that of the Bavli.

The chapter first discusses the *o'kheiluf* argument on Y. Bava Batra 8:1, 22a between R. Yohanan and R. Yehuda Nesi'ah. The other *o'kheiluf* argument on Y. Sanhedrin 4:1, 21a which parallels B. Sanhedrin 17a, concerns R. Yohanan's famous pronouncement: "One who does not know how to render the *sheretz* pure and to render it impure, in one hundred different ways by Torah law, would not be able to open [a defense] with arguments to acquit [a defendant, and so must not be appointed judge to the high court]." The idea being that one who would be judge should be clever and open-minded enough to examine every detail of the case in order to exonerate a defendant who seems as guilty of the crime he is on trial for, as a *sheretz* is guilty of being impure according to the Torah.

In the Bavli, Rav offers a demonstration from the Torah that a reptile (i.e. the *sheretz*) is pure and in the Yerushalmi, a very similar demonstration (regarding the particular *sheretz*, the mouse) is attributed to R. Yannai. The Bavli's understanding of such demonstration matches the Yerushalmi's which is made particularly transparent through the Yerushalmi's use of the *o'kheiluf* argument.

As seen thoughout this book, a qal v'homer argument is countered with *o'kheiluf* only when its launching premise is either a guess or supported only by (what is viewed as) weak biblical evidence. Through its use of *o'kheiluf*, the *stam* makes clear that it understands R. Yohanan to be pretending that the biblical verses listing the impure creatures, Lev. 11:29-31, are absent from the Torah. It is from such an imagined Torah as his set of premises, that R. Yannai gives his demonstration rendering the mouse pure. The *kheiluf* qal v'homer that starts from the contrary conclusion is only possible because from a Torah in which those verses are imagined absent, R. Yannai's launching premise that the snake is pure is based on (at most) weak evidence.

Chapters Two and Four described *o'kheiluf* arguments from Sifre Devarim of the school of R. Akiva that proceed from the same sort of thought experiment as trying to prove the *sheretz* pure. The Midrash Halakhah, both of the R. Ishmael and R. Akiva schools, subscribes to a principal of biblical parsimony, that is, a belief that the Torah does not contain superfluous words. To test whether some words in the Torah that detail a law appear redundant, the midrash engages in a thought experiment whereby the words are imagined absent and it is shown that in such an imagined situation either it is possible to prove the opposite of that law or it is not possible to derive the law or its negation. This demonstration confirms that indeed the words that were imagined absent from the Torah are most certainly not redundant, but serve an informational role in the Torah.[235]

The actual arguments to render the *sheretz* pure are thus far less provocative than the wording of the directive. The *o'kheiluf* argument makes clear that the Talmuds do not view, as some modern scholars have argued, the attempt to render the reptile pure as reflecting the rabbis' rejection of the existence of objective truth.[236] The Sophistic

---

[235] See Chapter Two, each of the *o'kheiluf* arguments from the Sifre Devarim, #12-15.

[236] For these types of claims see Hidary, *Rabbis and Classical Rhetoric*, 234, 235, 239 and the Conclusions.

idea invoked is that in giving – from a shared set of premises — both a proof that something is true and another proof that the same thing is false, the Sophists would show that there is no fact about the truth of the matter. But this is not what is going on in the debate between the Torah and R. Yannai (or between the Torah and Rav). Neither of these two Amoraim is engaged in (or even thinks he is engaged in) proving a proposition contrary to the Torah from the same set of premises shared by the Torah. That the *sheretz* is impure is one of the axioms that make up the Torah, while what the *o'kheiluf* argument makes particularly clear is that R. Yannai's proof rendering the *sheretz* pure is from the set of premises that is a tweaked version of the Torah that does not contain the verses Lev. 11:29-31.

The *o'kheiluf* argument that the Yerushalmi presents, when understood in light of the explication of *o'kheiluf* argumentation undertaken in this book, makes clear that the Talmud did not see R. Yannai's argument as anything novel. (As shown in Chapter Nine, this *o'kheiluf* argument is very similar to the *o'kheiluf* in Mishnah Pesahim.) Rather, the Talmuds see R. Yannai (and Rav's) demonstration as the application of an old and well-entrenched technique seen often in the Midrash Halakhah, including in the *o'kheiluf* arguments of the Sifre Devarim, to prove that particular words in the Torah are not superfluous but rather serve a function.

In refuting R. Yannai's demonstration by showing that it does not rule out the kheiluf possibility, and so the *o'kheiluf* argument cannot proceed to a resolution, the Yerushalmi shows that it is not possible – at least for any Amora or later rabbi – to prove even from a Torah in which Lev. 11:29-31 is omitted, that the mouse is pure.

The Yerushalmi next cites the illustrious Tanna, Rabbi Yehuda HaNasi, as witnessing that trying to render the *sheretz* pure was a tannaitic activity that took place in the realm of Torah study where it

---

See David Kraemer, *The Mind of the Talmud* (Oxford, Oxford University Press, 1990):140-144, for a similar idea, separating practice from truth in rabbinic thinking.

was not unanimously appreciated.[237] Section 9.3 takes up the questions that follow naturally from the above assertions: If trying to prove the *sheretz* pure from the Torah minus Lev. 11:29-31 is the same sort of activity commonly seen in the Midrash Halakhah then why, as the Yerushalmi suggests, did the former have fierce critics? If R. Yohanan was really referring to argumentation that is actually standard in the Midrash Halakhah, why did he phrase his directive in such a way that it is possible to read him as asking of prospective judges that they be able to prove contradictions to Torah laws from the Torah?

Reflections on the Methodology Introduced in This Work

The tool used throughout this work, to define the *o'kheiluf*; to verify that indeed every occurrence of the phrase in the Midrash Halakhah shares precisely that same meaning; to then note differences in how the R. Akiva and R. Ishmael schools implement the *o'kheiluf* argument; to demonstrate that the mishnaic *o'kheiluf* argument has the same form; and then to clarify R. Akiva's objective which the Talmuds are mystified about; and further on to clarify an argument in the Yerushalmi that has been misunderstood, is a tool well known in philosophy: symbolization of statements.

The use of symbols like alphabet letters to represent terms or to represent each proposition in a statement is a technique that has been used in philosophy since Aristotle, who used them as term-variables in his *Prior Analytics*.[238] Martha and William Kneale in their

---

[237] There are other passages which praise activities that might seem like those of R. Meir's student but are different in logically important ways explained in section 9.3. The most important difference between proving the *sheretz* pure and the similar sounding but praised activities of Piskei de-Rav Kahana and B. Eruvin 13b is that in the latter all of the (inductive) proofs are engaged in from a body of shared premises.

[238] See Kneale, *Development of Logic*, p61 and footnote:

Development of Logic are not exaggerating when they describe this as an "epoch-making device in logical technique."[239] The Stoics used ordinal numbers to represent propositions.[240] The technique continued to be applied later in medieval philosophy. In the early 1900's Bertrand Russell furthered this technique for his theory of definite descriptions in the philosophy of language and it is in this context that beginning philosophy students everywhere are introduced to this technique. Its value lies in exposing the structure of a statement by hiding the content that tends to distract the reader from apprehending the structure. (It is also the basis of how computers work.)

This basic approach to the structure of statements has been used throughout this work in part to uncover what the Tannaim saw themselves as doing and later, in particular in regard to passages in the Yerushalmi, it was used to clarify the reasoning of Amoraim. With the clarification achieved through symbols, it was then possible to apply formal logic to the rabbinic arguments. I have taken great pains to make my methodology transparent to readers who are not very accustomed to logic, in the hopes that my results will encourage others to apply my methodology to other literary and historical investigations of rabbinic texts. If my discoveries point to anything, it is that a bit of formal logic can help clarify rabbinic texts and correct previous scholarly misinterpretations. The moral is that today's

---

An. Pr. i. 2 (25ª 14). On p96, "It is one of the few passages in Aristotle's work involving the use of propositional variables, and it can be rendered as follows: If given that-P it is necessary that-Q, then given that-not-Q it is necessary that-not-P." footnote: An. Pr. ii. 2 (53ᵇ12).

[239] Ibid.

[240] See Mates, Stoic Logic, p70-71 for the inference-schema:

If the first, then the second.
Not the second.
Therefore, not the first.

If the first, then the second.
The first is.
Therefore, the second is.

student or professional scholar of Talmud, traditional or academic, would benefit from being equipped with the basic discoveries in logic.

A New Finding for the History of Logic

This work has shown that while the Tannaim were ignorant of Greek logic (Aristotelian and Stoic) they did coin and employ uniquely tannaitic logical terminology. This work uncovered the existence of a precise type of argument along with its associated uniquely tannaitic logico-linguistic terminology, which was lost to the history of rabbinic hermeneutics. As evidence for the existence of logical terminology independent of Greek logic, the o'kheiluf argument is a new finding for the history of logic. But the o'kheiluf may be important to the history of logic for yet a different reason.

Logic developed in Athens as a response to the introduction of democracy. Every citizen's right to vote meant that someone trying to get a measure passed in the Athenian Assembly needed to care about how ordinary individuals would vote. Such a person would often hire Sophists to sway potential voters to vote his way. It is in such an environment that philosophers developed logic, to protect people from falling for fallacious arguments presented by the commissioned Sophists. Stoic logic also was aimed at enabling an individual to recognize invalid arguments, often ones presented with the intent to deceive.

History has preserved examples of fallacious arguments such as those of the Sophists, and has bequeathed to us the works of Aristotelian and Stoic logic which set out the forms of valid arguments. Training in the latter would enable individuals to identify fallacious arguments as such. There are thus historical witnesses to both before and after the logical discoveries. History also witnesses times and places before rhetoric and logic were separated. The qal v'homer and the Indian a fortiori[241] are non-Western examples of

---

[241] See S.C. Vidyabhusana, *A History of Indian Logic* (Calcutta University: The Baptist Mission Press, 1921), 60, for an example:

these. As discussed in Chapter Five, if someone had pointed out to a Tanna — and perhaps the same could be said for an Indian rhetor — how to break up his argument into a logical argument and a rhetorical argument, he likely would not have been interested. These arguments were so organized to deliver a rhetorical punch that convinces, and separating out the logical structure would have destroyed the rhetorical force.

The o'kheiluf is a witness to none of these historical stages, i.e. it is not witness to a time before the need for Greek logic was felt, nor to attempts to fool people with defective arguments nor to formal logic later developed to identify such invalid arguments. Rather, it is an historical witness to an intellectual stage where, while possibly even unaware of the existence of Greek logic, individuals yet recognized in some sense, the need for logic in order to analyze the very rhetorical arguments they were composing themselves. It is a witness to people trying to analyze their own arguments but unable to separate out the logical elements from the rhetorical elements, and therefore engaging in cumbersome analysis.

An o'kheiluf argument arises in a situation where it is recognized that the conclusion of a particular argument, usually an a fortiori argument, might be incorrect. But the authors are unable to take the argument apart, to divide it up into a logical argument, and a separate logically prior rhetorical argument. Therefore in their analysis of what might be wrong with the a fortiori argument, they cannot consider the separate propositions and check each against its negation to determine which could be true. Instead they must carry around the entire argument at each step of their analysis.

This hill is fiery.
Because it is smoky.
Whatever is smoky is fiery, as a kitchen.
"So" is this hill (smoky).
Therefore, this hill is fiery.

The *o'kheiluf* argument represents a situation where the Tannaim saw themselves as needing what we refer to as Greek and Stoic logic. Unaware even of the existence of this knowledge, they made cumbersome moves to compensate for its absence. The *o'kheiluf* bears witness to an intermediate historical stage between not sensing any need for formal logic, and the development of formal logic to enable people to identify spurious arguments presented to them. This intermediate stage is the sensing of the need for formal logic — while not having it or knowing anything about it — to apply to one's own arguments to determine which are correct, and the struggle to analyze one's arguments without it. As far as I know, the *o'kheiluf* is the only identified witness to this historical intellectual stage. It would be interesting to know whether artifacts to this prior intermediate stage could be identified in other ancient literatures that have survived.

Appendix I: Correction to Louis Jacobs' Formulation of the Tannaitic Qal V'Homer

The Qal V'Homer cannot be Casted as a Conditional Statement

Introduction:

In his influential 1953 paper[242] *The Aristotelean Syllogism and the Qal Wa-Homer*, Louis Jacobs focused on refuting Adolf Schwarz's work[243] that claimed identity between the qal v'homer and the categorical syllogism.[244] Jacobs sought to prove the contrary, that the qal v'homer bears absolutely no similarity or relationship to Aristotle's categorical syllogism.

---

[242] L. Jacobs,"The Aristotelean Syllogism and the Qal Wa-Homer,"*The Journal of Jewish Studies*, 14:4 (1953):154-157.

[243] *Der Hermeneutische Syllogismus in der Talmudischen Litteratur, Eln Beitrag Zur Geschichte Der Logik Morgenlande* (Karlsruhe 1901) as cited in Jacobs, 154.

[244] To date, the only successful attempt to capture the logic of the qal v'homer is the work of Michael Abraham, Dov Gabbay, and Uri Schild. See chapter two of their *Studies in Talmudic Logic, Volume 10* (London: College Publications, 2013). They put forward a new form of induction, matrix abduction, which they are able to demonstrate successfully models the qal v'homer argument, even the especially complex one found on B. Kiddushin 5a-5b. See also their companion paper in Hebrew which offers more analysis of the qal v'homer and, in particular, of the argument on Kiddushin 5a-5b:

מידות הדרש ההגיוניות כאבני הבסיס להיסקים לא דדוקטיביים: מודל לוגי לקל וחומר בניין אב והצד השווה, בתוך: בד"ד 23 (תשע)

For some further refinements, see also Dov Gabbay and Karl Schelchta, *A New Perspective on Nonmonotonic Logics* (Switzerland: Springer International Publishing, 2016): chapter 12.

Jacobs distinguished between what he calls the simple and complex qal v'homer and then identified each of these as a particular sort of 'If, then' statement. He then presented a paradigmatic example of a rabbinic qal v'homer for comparison with the famous categorical syllogism: 'All men are mortal'; 'Socrates is a man'; 'therefore Socrates is mortal'. Jacobs' comparative analysis was directed at showing how very different the qal v'homer is from the categorical syllogism.

Citing (and explicating) Arnold Kunst, Jacobs' pointed out that the biggest difference between the categorical syllogism and the qal v'homer is that the former inference concerns the relationship between genus and species while the latter deals with sentences.[245] Jacobs uses as an example, the qal v'homer he cited earlier, to explain what Kunst meant by 'deals with sentences'. A more general and useful way to describe the difference would have been to note that the categorical syllogism is a deduction while the qal v'homer is an inductive type of inference.[246] Much confusion in understanding the role of qal v'homer, or *din* as it is also often referred to in rabbinic works, has resulted to a great extent from scholars not recognizing that a qal v'homer inference is not a deduction.[247] But the focus here is on something else.

---

[245] Arnold Kunst, "An Overlooked Type of Inference," *Bulletin of the School of Oriental and African Studies*, Vol. X, Part 4 (1942): 976-991.

[246] Although many publications repeat Louis Jacobs' refutation of Schwarz's claim, as far as I know, the first (and only) publications to point out that the qal v'homer is not a deduction but rather an inductive inference are the first two cited in footnote 244. The second paper of Abraham, Gabbay, and Schild in Hebrew, credits these points to the 1969 work of David Cohen, also known as HaRav HaNazir: קול הנבואה, הרב דוד כהן, מוסד הרב קוק, ירושלים, תשל.

See also my paper where I take pains to substantiate these points,
"How are Scripture and Reason Related in the Midrash Halakhah? Refutation of Neusner's Influential View and its Serious Consequences," submitted for publication.

[247] See Amelia Spivak, "How are Scripture and Reason Related in the Midrash Halakhah? Refutation of Neusner's Influential View and its Serious Consequences," submitted for publication.

This appendix focuses on the symbolic representation of the qal v'homer that Jacobs provided early in his paper and which figured importantly in his argument against relating the qal v'homer to the categorical syllogism. This appendix demonstrates, contrary to Louis Jacobs, that it is incorrect to symbolically represent the qal v'homer as an 'If,then' statement. No scholar is known to have ever addressed this aspect of Jacobs' work to correct it.[248]

Scholars since have tended unreflectively to describe the qal v'homer argument and translate particular qal v'homer arguments as 'If, then' statements. The question of whether the qal v'homer has the form of an 'if, then' argument or a 'since, therefore' argument or whether the form depends on context, sometimes having one form and sometimes the other is one of real significance. One of the reasons why the *o'kheiluf* argument, which is often built out of qal v'homer arguments and is the subject of this book, has never before been recognized nor have specific instances been understood correctly is because scholars have not had a well-formed consistent understanding of the form the qal v'homer takes.

The following is a quick overview of the contents of this appendix.

Jacobs' symbolic representation of the qal v'homer is presented. It clearly must have been intended to capture the qal v'homer argument that could be expressed as a statement. His argument against relating the qal v'homer to the categorical syllogism was therefore also limited to the statement-styled qal v'homer. It is shown how once established for the latter, Jacobs' conclusion could be extended to apply as well to the more ubiquitous rhetorically-questioning qal v'homer.

---

[248] For example, Alexander Samely, whose work on the logic of the qal v'homer in his *Rabbinic Interpretation of Scripture in the Mishnah* has many merits, like Jacobs though presents his own formulation of the qal v'homer on p.178, as a conditional or 'If,then' statement.

Jacobs' symbolic representation is then analyzed as composed of three propositions whose truth it is committed to and one that it is not committed to.

This is followed with an examination of Jacobs' example of a typical qal v'homer, which he sets up for comparison with the categorical syllogism. It is shown that it cannot be represented by Jacobs' own symbolic representations for qal v'homer arguments. Specifically it is shown that while the symbolic representation is committed to only three of four propositions contained in the qal v'homer argument, the example is committed to all four propositions being true. It is pointed out that these features of Jacobs' example are indeed typical of statement-styled qal v'homer arguments.

Another example of a statement-styled qal v'homer is presented, this one from the Mekhilta of R. Ishmael. This sort of qal v'homer argument is far more common than is Jacobs' own example in that it contains no quoted verses as proof texts and it therefore would seem a much better candidate for Jacobs' 'If,then' representation. That is, it does not contain within it, the evidence for any of the propositions it implicitly asserts.

Typical of most tannaitic qal v'homer arguments, the evidence for all three assertions it assumes, logically precede the qal v'homer. The source of at least one of the three is usually the biblical verse that prompts the comment containing the qal v'homer while the source of another is in an earlier nearby verse and the source of the remaining assertion is elsewhere in the Pentateuch. Analysis however shows that this typical qal v'homer argument from the Mekhilta likewise cannot be represented as an 'if, then' statement.

The change of tense that occurs in Jacobs' example is also highlighted ás further and independent evidence that the example cannot be represented by Jacobs' symbolic representation of the qal v'homer. The change in tense is typical of the vast majority of qal v'homer arguments and therefore they as well cannot be represented by Jacobs' formulation as an 'if, then' statement. A different formulation of the rabbinic qal v'homer that begins with the word 'Since' is offered.

Jacobs' symbolic representation of the qal v'homer as an 'If,then' sentence is incorrect. However the statement-styled qal v'homer, such as the one Jacobs presents for analysis, often does begin with the word אם or ואם which literally mean 'if' or 'and if', respectively. Other times it begins with "question words," such as the phrase ומה אם, 'and what if', or just ומה, 'and what'. The function and meaning of these words at the start of the statement-styled qal v'homer are determined by first analyzing their function in the more common rhetorical-questioning tannaitic qal v'homer.

Returning to the main thread, a third and final line of evidence that qal v'homer arguments cannot be described as 'If, then' statements is presented. This evidence is not related to Jacobs' example but instead has its source in the many tannaitic qal v'homer arguments presented and then refuted by the phrase *talmud lomar* followed by a quote from the Pentateuch. This is explained by way of a detailed example.

The question of whether the qal v'homer has the form of an 'if, then' argument or a 'since, therefore' argument is one of real significance. One of the reasons why the *o'kheiluf* argument, which is built out of qal v'homer arguments and is the subject of this book, has never before been recognized is, in part, because scholars have tended to thoughtlessly translate the qal v'homer as an 'if, then' statement or argument.

Further, modern scholars[249] following Daube[250] believe that when Cicero discusses (what was only much later, in the Middle Ages,

---

[249] For example, see Hidary, *Rabbis and Classical Rhetoric*, 174-212.
[250] D. Daube, "Rabbinic Methods of Interpretation and Hellenistic Rhetoric," *Hebrew Union College Annual* 22 (1949): 239-264.

termed) the *a fortiori*, he means very much the same thing as what Hillel the Elder or, later on, Rabbi Ishmael is understood to be referring to when they are represented as speaking of the qal v'homer. Although it is recognized that rabbinic uses for qal v'homer were often different from Roman uses for the *a fortiori*, the arguments themselves, the *a fortiori* and the qal v'homer are treated as identical. Without having a clear awareness of the form of the qal v'homer, any comparison of Cicero's *a fortiori* with the tannaitic qal v'homer is compromised.

There is one more reason why ascertaining that the qal v'homer cannot be expressed as a conditional statement is important: it relates to Louis Jacobs' paper which was focused on refuting work by the mathematician Adolf Schwarz who argued that the qal v'homer is identical to Aristotle's categorical syllogism (and that the rabbis developed this logic independently of the Greeks). Later authors[251] pointed out that scholarly discussion of possible Greek influence on the tannaitic qal v'homer, should not focus on Aristotelian logic but rather on the logic of philosophers dominant in the times of the Tannaim, the Stoics.

Stoic philosophers were very popular in Helenistic times and logic was at the center of their philosophy. If Jacobs' formulation of the qal v'homer as a conditional statement was correct, it could be argued that many tannaitic passages in which the qal v'homer argument is

---

In this often-cited article Daube argued that the rabbinic methods of interpretation derive from Hellenistic rhetoric. He writes that Hillel's famous seven norms of hermeneutics in accordance with which Scripture was to be interpreted (T. Sanhedrin vii) all betray the influence of the rhetorical teaching of that Hellenistic age. The first of these norms is *a fortiori,* or *a minori ad maius,* in Hebrew the qal v'homer. Cicero discusses this norm in his Topics (see 4.23): 'What applies to the *maius* must apply also to the *minus* and vice versa.' (See also footnote 122 in this book for how Cicero's phrase 'vice versa' relates to the *o'kheiluf* conditional.)

[251] See R. Berchman, "Rabbinic Syllogism: The Case of Mishnah-Tosefta Tohorot," in *Approaches to Ancient Judaism V: Studies in Judaism and its Greco-Roman Context*, ed. W.S. Green (Missoula: Scholars Press 1985): 81-98.

presented are composed of three distinct parts corresponding to an assertion followed by one conditional proposition representing the qal v'homer argument, and then a third part, an implied conclusion. These three together could be seen as forming a Stoic syllogism, specifically what is known to us as *modus ponens*. From this it could be concluded that the Tannaim were consciously engaged in formal reasoning along lines furthered and perfected by the Stoics, perhaps suggesting influence of the latter on the former. In refuting the 'if,then' formulation of the qal v'homer, this appendix eliminates the basis for arguing along such lines.

Section 1: Jacobs' symbolic representation of the qal v'homer is a sentence made up of four statements. The commitments to the truth of these statements are investigated.

Jacobs distinguishes two types of qal v'homer, what he calls the simple and the complex. He locates the source of the simple type in the Torah and states that the complex type is of later halakhic origin.[252] The complex type (also referred to as the rabbinic qal v'homer) is the more common type found in tannaitic literature.

Jacobs gives a symbolic representation for each of the two types of qal v'homer arguments. As symbolic representations these are meant to capture the general features and structure of the vast majority of qal v'homer arguments in biblical and tannaitic literature, respectively.

Simple:

If A has Y then B certainly has Y. (0)

---

[252] Tzvi Novick, "Rhetorical Markers in A Fortiori Argumentation in Biblical and Post-biblical Hebrew," in *The Reconfiguration of Hebrew in the Hellenistic Period*, ed. J. Joosten et al. (Leiden: Brill, 2012). Novick uses the term "Inequality Assertion" to make essentially the same distinction between the biblical and the tannaitic qal v'homer that Jacobs makes via the symbolic expressions (0) and (1).

Complex (or rabbinic):

If A, which lacks X, has Y then B, which has X, certainly has Y. (1) [253]

In the simple qal v'homer, lacking X is something that is either part of the definition of what A is or so obviously true of A that it need not be pointed out that 'A lacks X'. Likewise for, 'B has X'.

Any simple qal v'homer can be described as a complex one by spelling out what is only implied in the text: the X that A lacks but B has. But this complex representation would not represent what is actually written out in the text. It would rather represent the reasoning or logic of the argument of the text. (Thus the converse is not true, that every complex qal v'homer can be described as a simple one.)

Jacobs' representations (0) and (1) are meant to describe the vast number of qal v'homer arguments. However in tannaitic literature, qal v'homer arguments are more often expressed as rhetorical questions rather than as declarative statements.[254] Thus to be precise, (0) and (1) could only have been meant to represent those qal v'homer arguments that have the form of a statement. Correspondingly the particular qal v'homer that Jacobs set up for analysis and comparison

---

[253] See Jacobs, "The Aristotelean Syllogism," 155. Setting aside in an indented paragraph of its own, he writes with the italicies as shown and with extra spacing indicated between the words and symbols so as to give the impression of a formula unlike the sentences that precede and follow in the other paragraphs:
Symbolically the two types of *qal wa-homer* may be represented as follows:
  Simple: If *A* has *X* then *B* certainly has *X*.
  Complex: If *A*, which lacks *Y*, has *X* then *B*, which has *Y*, certainly has *X*.
[254] A search using the Responsa Project search engine, of key phrases אינו הוא דין, דין, and קל וחומר, in the Mishnah and Midrash Halakhah suggests that the two types of expression of qal v'homer arguments occur there in the ratio of roughly 171: 239 which is approximately 7:10.

420

with the categorical syllogism is also a qal v'homer that is expressed as a statement.

Why did Jacobs, in his choice of symbolic representation and then with a qal v'homer that matched this representation, decide to focus on the statement-styled qal v'homer rather than the more common questioning-styled qal v'homer? Recall that his goal was a comparison of the qal v'homer argument with the categorical syllogism for the purposes of showing that there is no connection between the two. The categorical syllogism consists of three statements, Jacobs may have reasoned that the qal v'homer of the statement form would have a better chance of resembling the categorical syllogism than one expressed as a rhetorical question. Once Jacobs would have succeeded in refuting the claim of any connection between the categorical syllogism and the statement-styled qal v'homer, the same conclusion would follow for the questioning-styled qal v'homer as well.[255]

The more ubiquitous questioning-styled qal v'homer arguments can be made to fit into symbolic representation (1), if one replaces the questioning aspect with a declarative aspect. (To do so, there are phrases in the formulation of the qal v'homer that would have to be replaced. For example in a typical qal v'homer like the one below, אינו דין, which by itself means 'it is not logical', borrows the מה אם, the 'what if', at the very beginning of the qal v'homer expression, to be correctly translated in context as 'is it not logical?' or 'must it not follow, by reasoning?' When replacing the questioning aspect with a declarative tone, 'אינו דין' i.e. 'is it not logical?', would have to be

---

[255] Note this meta-argument implied by Louis Jacobs is itself, an *a fortiori* argument! This is not very surprising as we use *a fortiori* and even the complex qal v'homer all the time to draw conclusions that are usually correct. See N. Janowitz and A. Lazarus' defense of the qal v'homer as cogent reasoning, most certainly not irrational reasoning in N. Janowitz and A. Lazarus, "Rabbinic Methods of Inference and the Rationality Debate,"*The Journal of Religion*, 72:4 (1992): 491-511.

replaced with 'it certainly follows' as for example via the phrase דין הוא.[256])

The contents of Jacobs' symbolic representations of statement-style qal v'homer arguments, (0) and (1), may be unpacked as follows:

(0) expresses a conditional statement, i.e. an 'If,then' statement. It does not claim that 'A has Y'. What it does claim is that if it is true that 'A has Y' then it will follow that 'B has Y' is also true.

Indeed (1) is more complex. It expresses a conditional statement, i.e. an 'if,then' statement, committed to two additional claims besides the conditional claim: A, must be something that lacks X and B, must be something that has X. If these two things are true, i.e. if whatever particular things A, X, Y, and B represent, it is true that A lacks X and that B has X, then according to formulation (1) it is true that 'If A has Y, then B has Y'. The formulation as written is not committed to 'A has Y' being true. This latter point is because that is how we (and the Torah, and the Tannaim) understand 'if' at the beginning of a statement.

Therefore, (1) is a compact sentence that expresses the following:

---

[256] Novick, "Rhetorical Markers," while not distinguishing between the statement-styled and the rhetorically-questioning qal v'homer varieties, demonstrates with many examples that for biblical qal v'homer arguments the rhetorical markers of the qal v'homer that precede the conclusion or the apodosis are אף כי and ואיך. I would add that the first is the marker for the statement-styled biblical qal v'homer and therefore corresponds to 'certainly' in (0) or (0') while the second is a marker for the rhetorically-questioning biblical qal v'homer and therefore corresponds to 'must-it-not-certainly-follow' in my expression (i) on the last page of this paper. In the tannaitic qal v'homer, דין הוא and קל וחומר and על אחת כמה וכמה are usual rhetorical markers of the statement-styled qal v'homer that precede what Novick calls the apodosis and therefore correspond to 'certainly' in (1) or (3'), while אינו דין is the usual marker of the rhetorically-questioning type and corresponds to 'must-it-not-therefore-follow' in my expression (5) which is relabeled (ii). Novick finds no evidence of qal v'homer arguments beginning with ואם prior to tannaitic literature.

A lacks X; B has X: If 'A has Y' then 'B has Y'.

Importantly, it does not claim that 'A has Y' is true.

Section 2: Checking whether Jacobs' example of a qal v'homer fits Jacobs' general symbolic representation of qal v'homer arguments

Consider the statement-styled qal v'homer that Jacobs sets up for comparison with a well-known categorical syllogism.[257] Jacobs argued that only the simple qal v'homer could possibly be entertained as bearing any similarity to the categorical syllogism. Of this class, only those whose origin is later than the Pentateuch could be claimed to have been influenced by Aristotelian logic. Therefore Jacobs sought an example from the small class of simple rabbinic qal v'homer. But the example he chose is more naturally viewed as complex than simple. Examining how well the example fits first into symbolic representation (1) and then into (0), makes this clear.

The example is from the Mishnah, M. Hullin 12:5:

חולין יב:ה :

ומה אם מצוה קלה קלה שהיא כאסר, אמרה תורה 'למען ייטב לך וארכת ימים' קל וחומר על מצות חמורות שבתורה.

Jacobs' translation:

If then, in regard to such a light precept (i.e. the law of sending away the dam-Deut. xxii, 6, 7) which concerns a matter that is worth but an *issar,* the Law has said *that it may be well with thee and that thou mayest prolong thy days,* how much more so in regard to the weightier precepts of the Law!

Jacobs' symbolic representation of the complex qal v'homer (1) is recopied here for convenience:

---

[257] All men are mortal. Socrates is a man. Therefore Socrates is mortal.

If A which lacks X has Y then B which has X certainly has Y. (1)

To determine the extent to which Jacobs' example of the qal v'homer from Hullin, fits into his symbolic characterization of qal v'homer arguments (1), A, X, Y, B will represent the values indicated below:

A= 'the law of sending away the dam'
X = 'weightiness'
(Evidence that A lacks X is that 'it is worth but an *issar*'.)
Y = 'it is said of it *it may be well with thee and that thou mayest prolong thy days* [if you do it]'
B= 'the weightier precepts of the Law'

Working from the Mishnah itself or from Jacobs' faithful translation, and substituting the symbols for their equivalent expressions, the contents of the Mishnah may be unpacked as follows:

A lacks X.
The proof that A lacks X is that 'it is worth but an *issar'*.
A has Y.
B has X.
How much more so, must it be the case that B has Y.

Notice, that as opposed to expression (1), which we pointed out, is not committed to the truth of 'A has Y', the Mishnah example states that 'A has Y' is true and it can be confirmed by checking the verse in Deuteronomy that indeed 'A has Y' true.

Putting all of this into a one-line argument:

A which lacks X has Y, how much more so must it be the case that B which has X has Y.

Or if we use the 'certainly' from Jacobs' formulation (1), we would express the argument as follows:

A which lacks X has Y, certainly then B which has X, has Y. (2)

Or if we put the 'certainly' where Jacobs' puts it:[258]

A which lacks X has Y, B which has X certainly has Y. (3)

What then is the role of the ומה אם at the beginning of the Mishnah, which corresponds to 'If then' in Jacobs' translation (although, as mentioned above, its literal translation is 'and what if')?

The 'if then' at the beginning of the Mishnah has the sole function of connecting the first part of the statement, everything before the "קל וחומר" (or in the translation the 'how much more so') to the second half, and to drive home the point that it is by virtue of the whole first half that the second half follows a fortiori. By inserting 'If then' at the start of (3) and seeing where that leads, it becomes clear that the words 'if then' in the Mishnah should not be taken literally.

When 'If then,' is inserted in front of (3) in an effort to keep our symbolic representation faithful to Jacobs' translation, (3) becomes:

If then, A which lacks X has Y, B which has X certainly has Y. (4)
Rearranging the words in (4) by just moving the 'then' in (4) and putting it right before 'B' yields (1):

If A which lacks X has Y, then B which has X certainly has Y. (1)

But (4), if it is to represent Jacobs' example of the qal v'homer from Mishnah Hullin cannot be put into the form of (1).

As shown above, (1) does not claim that 'A has Y'. What it does claim are the following three things:
I. A lacks X

---

[258] (2) is more accurate than (3), but for our purposes we need not fuss over a distinction between (2) and (3).

425

ii. B has X

iii. If A has Y then B has Y.

It does not however claim that A has Y.

On the other hand, if (4) represents the Mishnah in Hullin, then it must be making the claim that A has Y.

Statement (3), as opposed to Jacobs' symbolic formulation (1), does claim all of the following and in that respect fits the Mishnah example:

1. A lacks X
2. A has Y
3. B has X
4. By virtue of i,ii, and iii, B has Y.

In Jacobs' example, what corresponds to 'A has Y' is a fact, i.e something that the Tannaim would have viewed as true either because the Torah or another line of Mishnah makes that assertion or because the assertion expresses what is well known from everyday experience to be true. 'A has Y' = It is said [in the Torah] of the law of sending away the dam, 'it may be well with thee and that though mayest prolong thy days'; indeed Deut. 22:7 expresses the content of 'A has Y'. The Mishnah is reminding the audience of this fact and therefore expression (1) is incorrect as a symbolic representation of this qal v'homer. The statement represented by 'A has Y' in a qal v'homer argument is generally, as it is in this example, a fact to the tannaitic audience.

A similar analysis may be applied to determine how well Jacobs' example, which he viewed as a simple qal v'homer, fits his symbolic formulation of the simple qal v'homer, 'If A has Y then B certainly has Y' (0). In the example 'A' would represent 'a particular light mitzvah which we know for a fact to be light, because it concerns a matter worth only an *issar*' and as above 'Y' represents 'the property that the Law has said *that it may be well with thee and that thou mayest prolong thy days*' and 'B' represents 'a weightier precept'. As

426

discussed above, the Mishnah is indeed committed to the truth of 'A has Y' while (0) is not.

Section 3: A more typical statement-styled qal v'homer argument is checked for fit with Jacobs' symbolic representation

In Jacobs' example (viewed as a complex qal v'homer) it was clear that the particular proposition corresponding to 'A has Y' was a fact to the Tannaim. Thus showing that his example could not be described as a conditional statement was particularly straightforward. Most statement-styled qal v'homer arguments (especially from the Midrash Halakhah) on the other hand do not contain proof texts. For these, the evidence for the truth of 'A has Y' does not lie within the qal v'homer argument. It takes some attention to locate the evidence for 'A has Y' to show that the proposition corresponding to 'A has Y' is a fact to the Tannaim and that the qal v'homer argument expresses that it is a known fact.

In the Midrash Halakhah the evidence that 'A has Y' is usually contained in the biblical verse that prompts the tannaitic comment that presents the qal v'homer argument. Other times it is in another biblical verse often nearby. (The evidence for 'A lacks X' usually occurs in a nearby biblical verse that precedes the biblical verse that prompts the comment.) In the Mishnah, the evidence for 'A has Y' usually occurs in an earlier line of the Mishnah that contains the qal v'homer argument or in the preceding Mishnah. Thus in both the Midrash Halakhah and in the Mishnah the evidence for 'A has Y' is usually not interior to the qal v'homer argument itself.

Here is a typical example from the Mekhilta of R. Ishmael, Meshekhta de-Piskha, parsha 6, demonstrating this, it occurs as a comment to the following verse, Exod.12:9:

אל תאכלו ממנו נא ובשל מבושל במים, כי אם צלי אש ראשו על כרעיו ועל קרבו :

427

"[Speaking of the Passover sacrifice] Do not eat of it cooked in water, but rather [only] roasted with its head over its knees and its innards."

The Mekhilta comments on the words, ובשל מבושל במים, meaning, cooked in water: *From these words I know only that it is forbidden to cook it in water. From where do I know that cooking the Passover sacrifice in other fluids is also forbidden?*

R. Ishmael says, "*You say it is [known] by qal v'homer*":

ומה אם מים שאינן מפינין את טעמן הרי הן אסורין בבישול, שאר המשקין שהן מפינין את טעמן דין הוא שיהיו אסורין בבישול.

"*Water which does not impart its flavor [unto what it cooks] behold it is forbidden in cooking [the Passover sacrifice], other liquids that do impart their flavor [unto what they are cooking], it must follow (by din) that they should be forbidden for cooking [the Passover sacrifice].*"

Assigning the following symbols to phrases of the comment:

A= *water*
B= *other liquids*
X= *the property of imparting flavor onto what it cooks*
Y= *the property that it is forbidden to cook the Passover sacrifice in it*

With these symbols,
'A lacks X' = *Water does not impart flavor onto what it cooks.*
'A has Y' = *It is forbidden to cook the Passover sacrifice in water.*
'B has X' = *Other liquids do impart flavor onto what they cook.*
'B has Y'= *It is forbidden to cook the Passover sacrifice in other liquids.*

With these symbols the qal v'homer argument becomes,

'And what if', A which lacks X has Y, B which has X must certainly have Y. (5)

428

The propositions that corresponds to the labels 'A lacks X' and 'B have X' are well-known facts from everyday experience.

Again, as earlier, the expression (5) could equivalently be written as the following conditional statement only if the qal v'homer is not committed to the truth of 'A has Y':

If A which lacks X has Y, B which has X must certainly have Y.

However, 'A has Y' represents *'It is forbidden to cook the Passover sacrifice in water'* which is indeed a fact: the verse Exod. 12:9 which prompts the comment in the Mekhilta expresses this prohibition very clearly and the comment that introduces the qal v'homer repeats it. In the qal v'homer the word הרי, translated 'behold' or 'indeed', turns the phrase הרי הן אסורין into 'Behold! They <u>are</u> forbidden', i.e. 'we know this to be true that it is forbidden to cook the Passover sacrifice in water'. Thus because 'A has Y' is not a supposition but a fact and because its status as a fact is asserted within the qal v'homer, it is not possible to express (5) as a conditional statement.

Suppose the situation had been different and the qal v'homer used the fact 'A has Y' only as a supposition to draw out its implication so that no reference to its truth was contained within the qal v'homer argument itself. Then it would be possible to describe the derash in which the qal v'homer is embedded as consisting of the following propositions[259]:

A lacks X; B has X; A has Y.
If A which lacks X has Y then B which has X certainly has Y.

---

[259] Note how such hypothetical reasoning would be close to the formalized reasoning of the Stoics in what we refer to as *modus ponens*: If p then q; p; therefore q. The symbols p and q refer to propositions or statements.

But this is not the case. To the contrary, the qal v'homer example from the Mekhilta includes within it the implication that 'A has Y' is known to the audience to be a fact.

Taking into account the commitment within the qal v'homer argument to the truths of 'A lacks X', 'A has Y', and 'B has X', the ומה אם translated as 'And what if' should be rendered 'Since' in the symbolic representation, yielding,

Since A which lacks X has Y, B which has X certainly should have Y.

Section 4: Another line of evidence that for Jacobs' example and in general, the qal v'homer is not an 'if,then' statement, comes from changes of tense

What follows is a second line of evidence that what corresponds to 'A has Y' in the qal v'homer is a true fact. We turn to the Mishnah in Hullin again to pick up extra cues that were first overlooked. These cues are not captured in Jacobs' formulation yet they are very typical of the structure of a qal v'homer and their function is to emphasize to the audience that indeed what correspond to 'A lacks X', 'A has Y' and 'B has X' are facts known to the audience and on the basis of these facts the qal v'homer is arguing that 'B has Y' should be the case. These cues are changes in tense as the argument moves from the known facts to the advocated conclusion. The presence of these cues independently demonstrates that what corresponds to 'A has Y' is a fact to the audience of the qal v'homer and that therefore Jacobs' formulation (1) is incorrect.

Jacobs' example is typical of qal v'homer arguments in having a change in tense from past to present or from present to future, distinguishing the tense of the conclusion from what precedes it. The first phrase in the Mishnah which we symbolized by 'A lacks X' is 'A light precept which [concerns a matter] that is [worth] like an *issar* '.

430

The Mishnah is claiming that it is the case that 'A lacks X' is true.[260] The Mishnah goes on, in regard to this, 'The Law <u>has said</u> *that it may be well with thee and that thou mayest prolong thy days*. This is written in the past tense, אמרה meaning 'has said'. Thus it is indeed being claimed by the Mishnah that with regard to this light precept it is known *that it may be well with thee and that thou mayest prolong thy days,* because the Law has said it. This was symbolized above with the phrase 'A has Y'. So it is indeed being claimed by the Mishnah that 'A has Y' is the case, it is not a supposition but something to whose truth the argument is committed. The Mishnah goes on to discuss 'the weightier precepts'. Well, the weightier precepts are by definition weightier, i.e. the weightier precepts have weight. This was symbolized above by 'B has X'. This is certainly true by definition and it is being claimed by the Mishnah. The Mishnah concludes with 'how much more so [*that it may be well with thee and that <u>thou mayest prolong thy days</u>*]' in regard to the weightier precepts of the Law. This was symbolized above by 'B has Y'. The 'how much more so' follows i,ii,iii and implies that 'B has Y' is true and follows from i,ii and iii.

The changes in tense further serve to distinguish the first part of the argument, i.e. everything relevant that the listener already knows/ knew to be true, from the second part of the argument, namely, what is being argued should follow from the above. In many[261] qal v'homer arguments the part corresponding to 'B has Y' is more correctly

---

[260] Sometimes, as in the example from the Mekhilta in section 3, to emphasize that it is the case that 'A has Y', not only is the present tense used, but also extra emphasis is added that 'yes, it is the case that..' by using words like הרי, meaning 'behold' before the phrase so that it reads '*[B]ehold, it is the case that A has X*. See also the example in the footnote that follows.

[261] Here's an example from a rhetorically-questioning qal v'homer in M.Sotah.6:3 :

קל וחומר לעדות הראשונה מעתה: ומה אם עדות אחרונה שאוסרתה אסור עולם הרי היא מתקיימת בעד אחד. עדות הראשונה שאינה אוסרתה אסור עולם אינו דין שתתקים בעד אחד

The last verb is underlined, it is in the future tense while all the earlier verbs that correspond to lacking/having X are in the past tense and the verb that corresponds to A having Y is in the present tense.

captured by the future tense, 'B will have Y'. This role of the change in tenses is very similar to the role suggested above for the 'if then' or מה אם at the beginning of the argument and serves to further reinforce that effect.

It has thus been established that for the very example that Jacobs offers of the *a fortiori* argument, his symbolic formulations (0) or (1) as an 'if,then' conditional statement, is wrong. Since Jacobs' example is indeed a typical qal v'homer, it follows as well for the vast majority of qal v'homer arguments that they likewise are not correctly represented by (0) or (1).

Section 5: Correcting Jacobs' symbolic representation of the statement-style qal v'homer

Although many qal v'homer arguments begin as does Jacobs' example from Mishnah Hullin, with the phrase ומה אם which literally translates to 'and what if' in English (or others with just ומה, 'and what' or with only ואם, 'and if') these words should not be understood as 'what if' is normally understood, i.e. as hypothetical. In the statement-styled qal v'homer as in Jacobs' example, the phrase should rather be translated with an emphatic 'Since'. Thus the statement-styled complex qal v'homer is correctly characterized by putting 'Since' in front of (3) as follows:[262]

---

[262] There are those qal v'homer arguments that are better symbolized by:
Since A which has Z has Y, B which lacks Z certainly has Y (*).
The statement (*), like (3'), is also committed to the truth of three propositions from which it concludes a fourth. The three propositions are A has Z; A has Y; B lacks Z. From these three it is concluded that B has Y.
In claiming considerable generality for (3') our idea is that a qal v'homer argument of form (*) can, although somewhat cumbersomely, also be put into the form (3') by having Z represent 'a lacking of X'. So that 'A has Z' = 'A has a lacking of X' = 'A lacks X'.
As Samely, in chapter 7 of his *Rabbinic Interpretation of Scripture in the Mishnah,* makes the point, Jacobs' symbolic representation (1) is not sufficiently general to capture the logical structure of all qal v'homer arguments because sometimes rather than 'A lacks X' and 'B has X' the

432

**Since A which lacks X has Y, B which has X certainly has Y.
(3')**

And likewise, the statement-styled simple qal v'homer is correctly characterized by replacing 'If' with 'Since' in (0):

Since A has Y, B certainly has Y.   **(0')**

---

structure is more correctly described by A and B having X to varying degrees. For example see M.Yevamot 8:3.
The following symbolic formulation would more closely capture the structure of such qal v'homer arguments than does (3'):

Since A which has a bit of X has Y, then B which has more X [than does A] certainly has X. (**)

(**) is very much like (*) and (3'), in that it too is committed to the truth of three (in form, very similar) propositions from which a fourth proposition is concluded.
The three assertions are: A has a bit of X; A has Y; B has more X [than does A]. From these 'B has Y' follows.

In a similar manner to how it was done with (*) it is possible to force (**) into form (3').
Samely sought to get one, necessarily very elaborate, symbolic representation that naturally characterizes all three sorts of qal v'homer arguments that we described via (3'), (*) and (**). He does this in order to expose the underlying logic of the must-certainly or how-much-more-it-must-be-so property characteristic of the qal v'homer. By contrast, in this book I take for granted that the qal v'homer is a natural and cogent form of argument and I do not seek to analyze wherein lies its logical validity. Instead, in this work I am interested in articulating the overall structure of the qal v'homer. That is, I seek to expose with my symbolic representation the number and nature of the propositions that the qal v'homer argument holds as true and from which it seeks to draw a further conclusion. The simple formulation (3') suits these purposes. Further, as noted in footnote 3, Samely in laying out his formulation of the logic follows in Jacobs' footsteps and makes the error of describing the overall structure of the qal v'homer as an 'If,then' argument.

Section 6: A turn to the rhetorically-questioning qal v'homer to explain the true function and meaning of the "question words" with which the statement-style qal v'homer usually begins

It has been shown for Jacobs' example that the phrase 'and what if' or 'and if' functions to connect the two parts of the qal v'homer argument: what the audience knows to be true and what the argument urges should follow from that knowledge. The full role of the 'what if' at the beginning of the qal v'homer can only be appreciated by considering the rhetorical-questioning qal v'homer. Such examples lead to the suggestion that the phrase מה אם, literally 'if then', at the beginning of a statement-styled qal v'homer argument as in the example Jacobs cites, historically was adopted from its natural setting in the rhetorically-questioning qal v'homer.

Jacobs' example of a qal v'homer argument is of the declarative rather than the more common rhetorically-questioning sort. As seen above, even for his paradigmatic example, (0) and (1) are incorrect. Instead, (0') and (3') may serve as correct formulations replacing (0) and (1), respectively. The qal v'homer argument presented from the Mekhilta is certainly typical of the vast majority of declarative complex qal v'homer arguments and as was shown, it too could not be represented correctly by Jacobs' representations (1). Instead (3') fills that role. Thus the whole class of complex qal v'homers could also be represented by (3') and the whole class of simple ones by (0').

It will be shown that it is also true of the rhetorically-questioning qal v'homer arguments of the Tannaim that they too should not be construed as beginning with a conditional clause.

Since Jacobs chose his example from the Mishnah, an example of the rhetorically-questioning qal v'homer will be taken from the Mishnah as well. The role of the "question words" at the beginning of the rhetorically-questioning qal v'homer argument is very much the same whether the argument's source is the Mishnah or any of the works of Midrash Halakhah or other tannaitic works. Therefore the morals drawn from this example in Mishnah about the role of those words in this type of argument will apply to the occurrences of the rhetorically-questioning qal v'homer in the Midrash Halakhah as well.

In the following example of a rhetorically-questioning qal v'homer in M. Zevahim, the words אינו דין, which are typical of the rhetorically-questioning qal v'homer, literally mean 'it is not *din*'. In English the meaning is conveyed with the translation, 'it is not logically compelling' or 'reason does not dictate'. As discussed earlier, the 'if' or the questioning phrase at the beginning of a declarative qal v'homer argument function to connect on the one hand the facts the listener would know with what he is being urged to believe follows from those facts. The idea of this function for the beginning questioning words is most compelling for the rhetorically-questioning qal v'homer such as the example from Zevahim. But in this type of qal v'homer argument the question words at the beginning serve another function as well. They charge the phrase אינו דין, 'it is not *din*,' with a questioning aspect turning it into 'it is not *din*?' or as English speakers would arrange the phrasing 'is it not *din*?'

Just as in the earlier examples of the declarative qal v'homer argument, the phrase ומה אם, literally 'and what if', can be translated 'since' because what follows are true facts and that they are known to be true (to the audience of the argument) is part of what is being asserted and they are not being presented as a string of suppositions. Namely, the priests are indeed entitled to the meat of the *olah*[263] offering but not to its skins and they are not entitled to the meat of the most holy offerings. But the presence of the phrase ומה אם at the beginning of the argument turns אינו דין into a question which should be understood essentially as 'must-it-not-therefore-follow'.

זבחים, פרק י׳ב, משנה ג׳:

---

[263] A type of animal sacrifice that is burnt entirely on the altar; no part of it is eaten by any person, lay or priest. It is named *olah* meaning, [it] goes up, to reflect this. Biblical source: Leviticus, chapter 1.

....קל וחומר: מה אם עולה שלא זכו בבשרה זכו בעורה, קדשי קדשים שזכו
בבשרה אינו דין שיזכו בעורה ?!

<u>M. Zevahim 12:3:</u>

.... [with regard to the] olah offering whose meat the priests haven't been entitled to, they have [though] been entitled to its skins, [with regard to] the most holy offerings whose meat the priests have been entitled to, must-it-not-therefore follow that they would also be entitled to their skins?!

Recall (3'), our symbolic representation of the statement-styled complex qal v'homer (corrected from Jacobs' version (1)):

Since A which lacks X has Y, B which has X certainly has Y. (3')

Adapting (3') to represent a rhetorically-questioning qal v'homer rather than the statement-styled qal v'homer, leads to:

Since A which lacks X has Y, B which has X, must-it-not-therefore-follow that it will certainly have Y ?!   (3")

where '?!' denotes a rhetorical question.

It will be shown that with the following substitutions the example from Zev 12:3 can indeed be put into the form (3") :

A = *the olah offering*
X = *the property that kohanim have been entitled to its meat.*
Y = *the property that kohanim are entitled to the skins*
B = *the most holy offerings*

Thus,

'A lacks X' = *'The olah offering lacks the property that the priests have been entitled to its meat.'* = *'The priests have not been entitled to the meat of the olah offering.'*
'A has Y' = *The olah offering has the property that the priests are entitled to its skins.*

436

'B has X' = *The most holy offerings have the property that the priests have been entitled to their meats.*
'B should have Y' = *The most holy offerings should have the property that the priests are entitled to the skins.*

Like the example from the Mekhilta but unlike Jacobs' example, the qal v'homer cited above from Zevahim is typical of most qal v'homer arguments in that the evidence for the truth of the statements corresponding to 'A lacks X', 'A has Y', and 'B has X' are not contained within the qal v'homer itself. Instead, the evidence precedes the qal v'homer in the text (in which it occurs).

If the qal v'homer argument is contained in a Mishnah as in the example from Zevahim, the evidence for the statement corresponding to 'A has Y' (and also for 'A lacks X' and 'B has X' if these require evidence) is contained in lines from a Mishnah, usually the immediately preceding Mishnah. While if the qal v'homer is found in the Midrash Halakhah, the evidence for those statements is to be found in the Pentateuch, usually the verse that prompts the comment containing the qal v'homer, the verses that precede that verse in the same passage and a verse elsewhere in the Pentateuch that deals with the topic B.

In this example from Zevahim, the statements that correspond to 'A lacks X', 'A has Y' and 'B has X' are all known to be true. The evidence for the truth of the first two is that they are asserted in the immediately preceding mishnah, M. Zevahim 12:2, while the last is well-known from many mishnaic and biblical sources. (Also, the statement corresponding to 'A lacks X' is well-known from Leviticus.) The changes of tense within the example indicate acknowledgement that the three facts are indeed known to be true. Thus this qal v'homer could not be viewed as beginning with a conditional phrase.

Hence M.Zevahim 12:3 is essentially saying 'A lacks X', 'A has Y' and 'B has X' and 'should it therefore not also be the case that 'B should have Y' ?!.

With the substitutions made above, M.Zevahim 12:3 can indeed be symbolized as follows:

Since A which *lacks* X has Y, B which *has* X must-it-not-therefore-follow-that it will certainly have Y ?!   (3'')

It is clear that this symbolization most accurately represents the Mishnah. However for reasons of readability in English it is worth reordering (3'') as follows, thereby obtaining (6):

Since A which *lacks* X has Y must-it-not-therefore-follow that B which *has* X will certainly have Y ?!   (6)

The 'if' or 'what if' found at the beginning of the rhetorically-questioning qal v'homer, and supported with an example from the Mishnah, is not unique to the rabbinic qal v'homer argument. The 'if' in the latter has roughly the same function as an 'if' at the beginning of a typical rhetorically-questioning, *a fortiori* in the English language. There too the 'if' with which the argument begins is not the conditional 'if'. Here's an example of a rhetorically-questioning *a fortiori* argument in everyday English:

"If you've never been able to get this done in a week, you really think you can do this in one night?!"

It is clear in the example that the 'if' functions primarily to draw a connection between the two parts of the argument, to make the person see the connection between his past inability to get 'this' done in a week and his new idea to accomplish the very same thing in only one night. The second function of the questioning word 'if' is to charge the second part of the argument, 'you really think you can do this in one night' with a questioning quality, i.e. to turn it into a question asking him to really consider the reasoning of this argument. The argument is meant to convince the person that he cannot get the project done in one night, that he should face up to that and rather

438

than spend his time trying to accomplish the impossible he should make alternate plans.

The questioning words at the beginning of the rhetorically-questioning qal v'homer such as the example from Zevahim function very similarly to our example of a rhetorically-questioning *a fortiori* in English. They very clearly serve to connect the part of the argument that presents what the audience would agree to or (as is usual with the rabbinic arguments) knows to be true with the conclusion which it is being urged follows from the former. Secondly, the questioning words have a second related function of charging the phrase 'it must follow' in the qal v'homer with a questioning aspect so that it becomes the rhetorical question phrase 'must it not follow?!' We theorize that the presence of the questioning words at the start of the statement-styled qal v'homer derive from their presence at the start of the rhetorically-questioning qal v'homer i.e. that the questioning words have historically been adopted from the latter to the former.

It has been shown that the very example Jacobs offers of a qal v'homer is clearly not an 'if,then' statement and the same was shown for an example from the Mekhilta that is most typical of the vast majority of statement-styled qal v'homer arguments. Another line of evidence that a qal v'homer argument cannot be correctly described as a conditional statement was then presented: the tense is not uniform throughout a qal v'homer statement, when it moves to the conclusion the tense changes from past to present or from present to future. With expression (1) as well as (0) refuted, a corrected symbolic representation of the qal v'homer which does not begin with the word 'if' was presented. There remains the question of why the statement-styled qal v'homer typically begins with 'if' or with a questioning phrase such as 'and what' or 'and what if'. Turning to an example of a rhetorically-questioning qal v'homer made things clear. One of the two functions of the question words at the start of such arguments (and in such arguments 'if' at the start gives the statement a questioning quality) is to relate the early clauses of the qal v'homer to the conclusion in order to press the point that it is precisely by virtue of the three facts given that the conclusion of the qal v'homer follows. The symbolic representation of the rhetorically-questioning qal v'homer preserves the main features of the symbolic representation (3') of the statement-styled complex qal v'homer.

Section 6: A third and final source of evidence that the qal v'homer is not an 'If,then' argument

A third line of evidence showing that qal v'homer arguments were not viewed as 'if, then' arguments, does not come from Jacobs' example from Hullin. Instead it comes from the many tannaitic qal v'homer arguments, usually rhetorically-questioning, presented and then refuted by the phrase *talmud lomar* followed by a quote from the Torah or if the argument is found in the Mishnah, from an earlier statement in the Mishnah.

Any 'if,then' sentence may be represented by "If P then Q" where P and Q symbolize propositions. The statement "If P then Q" cannot be refuted by simply presenting proof that Q is false. That is, nothing about the truth or falsity of Q alone has any bearing on the truth of the claim 'If P then Q'. This would make no sense because of the conditional meaning of the word 'if'. For example, take the statement "If a woman has milk in her breasts then she has conceived". There the Q part is, 'she has conceived' and the contradiction of Q, that is, evidence that a woman exists who has not conceived, cannot disprove the conditional statement 'If she has milk in her breasts then she has conceived'.

The same can be said of the more complex 'if,then' statement with which Jacobs' defines the qal v'homer:

'If A which lacks X has Y then B which has X certainly has Y' (1). This statement could not be shown to be false by simply providing proof that 'B has Y' is false. As explained above, this refutation would not make sense to the modern reader or to the Tannaim.

440

Yet the Midrash Halakhah and the Mishnah include many cases where a — usually rhetorically-questioning — qal v'homer is offered and is then refuted with proof that the part 'B has Y' is false. If a qal v'homer did indeed have the 'if, then' form Jacobs suggests this would make no sense. However with the above description of the qal v'homer, the argumentation of the Tannaim does make sense: the statement,

'Since A which lacks X has Y, B which has X certainly has Y', is refuted if there is proof that B does not have Y.
And likewise,
'Since A which lacks X has Y, B which has X must-it-not-therefore-follow that it certainly has Y ?!', is refuted by proof that B does not have Y.

Here is a typical example chosen from the Mishnah of a qal v'homer refuted with the words *talmud lomar* introducing a biblical quote:

M.Sotah 6:3:

קל וחומר לעדות הראשונה מעתה:
ומה אם עדות אחרונה שאוסרתה אסור עולם, הרי היא מתקימת בעד אחד, עדות הראשונה שאין אוסרתה אסור עולם,
אינו דין שתתקים בעד אחד?!

תלמוד לומר: "כי מצא בה ערות דבר" ולהלן הוא אומר, "על פי שני עדים יקום דבר",מה להלן על פי שנים עדים, אף כאן על פי שנים עדים.

The conclusion of the qal v'homer, that "the first" testimony against the wife of a jealous man [that his wife might be involved with another man], can be established by [even only] one witness, is refuted by two biblical verses that together indicate that two witnesses are required in such a matter. But the refutation of the conclusion could not refute the qal v'homer argument if it were understood to be expressing an 'if,then' statement:

If "the last" witnessing which would forbid her for life [from being permitted to her husband], is upheld with only one witness, then "the first" witnessing which wouldn't forbid her for life [from being permitted to her husband] certainly is upheld by [the testimony of] one witness. Thus the ומה אם, literally 'and what if', at the start of the qal v'homer must be understood to mean 'Since'.

Section 7: Conclusion

Several different kinds of evidence were marshaled to demonstrate that Jacobs was mistaken in symbolizing the tannaitic qal v'homer as an 'if,then' statement. Having a corrected description of the qal v'homer is the necessary starting point for the work of this book. It is also important for several other reasons given in the introduction to this appendix, such as for making comparisons between Cicero's *a fortiori* and the qal v'homer and for assessing the scholarship relating the qal v'homer to *a fortiori* arguments that appear in the New Testament.[264]

Jacobs' symbolic representation of the simple qal v'homer,
'If A has Y then certainly B has Y' does not claim that indeed A has Y.

What it does claim is that *if* it is the case that A has Y then it is also true that B has Y. On the other hand, actual simple qal v'homers do claim that what corresponds to 'A has Y' is true.

It is therefore more correct to represent the simple qal v'homer by,
'Since A has Y then certainly B has Y.'

---

[264] Paul is said to have argued in the manner of the Pharisees, using the qal v'homer, for example in Romans 11:24. Maccoby argues that those are not bona fide qal v'homer arguments but more like Hellensitic *a fortiori* arguments. Maccoby points out that Paul's arguments do not adhere to the *dayo* principle. See Hyam Maccoby, *The Mythmaker: Paul and the Invention of Christianity* (New York: Barnes & Noble, 1998): 65.

For the same reason, Jacobs' description of the complex qal v'homer is also mistaken. We replace Jacobs' symbolic representation,

'If A which lacks X has Y then B which has X certainly has Y'

with the improved expression,

'Since A which lacks X has Y then B which has X must certainly have Y.'

While the qal v'homer does claim that 'A has Y' is true, the evidence for that claim is usually not inside the qal v'homer argument but rather in the biblical verse that prompts the qal v'homer argument in the Midrash Halakhah or in a previous line of Mishnah for the qal v'homer occurring in the Mishnah.

It was theorized that the "question words" at the start of the statement-styled qal v'homer have been adopted from the more ubiquitous rhetorically-questioning qal v'homer where their real non-conditional function is more transparent. Examples show that these words serve to tie the facts known to the audience to the conclusion being urged so as to impress upon the audience that it is precisely because of these facts which they know, that the conclusion being urged forces itself upon them with logical force. The "question words" at the start also function to charge the phrase 'it-must-follow' with a rhetorically-questioning meaning.

The rhetorically-questioning qal v'homer arguments — which Jacobs does not distinguish at all — are likewise more correctly symbolized as follows:

Simple qal v'homer:
'Since A has Y must-it-not-certainly-follow that B has Y ?!'

Complex qal v'homer:
'Since A which lacks X has Y, B which has X must-it-not-therefore-follow that it will certainly have Y ?!

For these as well, the evidence for the truth of 'A has Y' is usually not contained within the qal v'homer argument itself but rather is contained in the verse that prompts the qal v'homer comment or in the case of Mishnah, in an earlier line of the Mishnah containing the qal v'homer or in the preceding Mishnah.

Appendix II: *Reductio ad Absurdum* in Rabbinic Literature

In Plato's dialogues (380 BC), Socrates starts off by asking some fellow Athenian whether he believes a certain thing. When the Athenian says he does, Socrates shows that this belief logically leads finally to something false or absurd.[265] From this, Socrates infers that the original belief must also be false. The rhetorical technique of refuting a belief by showing that it leads to a falsehood is known to us by the Latin name *reductio ad absurdum*. The connective underlying the argument is "if-then". The ancient Greeks had a long tradition of arguing in this way.[266]

The Stoics reflected upon this technique which they used extensively and came to analyze its logical form. Because their arguments, especially about ethics, concerned consequences, they were led to explore forms that depended on the connectives "either/or", "if-then", or "not both". These investigations led to a collection of valid argument forms to which any argument must be reducible if it too is to be a valid argument. The first two of the list are the first and second demonstrables or as we have come to know them by the Latin name they were given in the Middle Ages, *modus ponens* and *modus tollens*. Specifically, one can see how *modus tollens* exposes and formalizes the essential logical form of the rhetorical *reductio ad absurdum* argument.[267]

Modus Ponens:	Modus Tollens:
Premise 1: If P then Q	Premise 1: If P then Q
Premise 2: P	Premise 2 : Not Q

---

[265] *Dialogues of Plato*, ed. C.B. Johnson (New York: Simon & Schuster Paperbacks, 2010).
[266] See Michael Shenefelt and Heidi White, *If A, then B: How Logic Shaped the World* New York: Columbia University Press, 2013), and references cited therein.
[267] Ibid.

Conclusion: Q   Conclusion: Not P

Where in both arguments P and Q are symbols representing propositions (or sentences).

The two main schools of philosophy during Hellenistic times were the Stoics and the Epicureans and the latter did not concern themselves with logic. In Chapter Five of this book, an imagined Stoic philosopher approached by a Tanna uses Stoic logic to reveal serious shortcomings with the tannaitic rhetorical technique of *o'kheiluf*. As the discussion there makes clear, these flaws would not have existed had the Tannaim been able to separate the rhetorical argument from the logical argument, and been able to express the latter in terms of its constituent propositions or in terms of syllogism, and certainly not if they had known of *modus tollens* or the truth value of the contrapositive.

It is the nature of logical discoveries that they uncover the rules of the correct reasoning that people have been using and distinguish it from logical fallacies. Logic formalizes valid reasoning that people have been using without thinking about the underlying form of their reasoning. One might therefore wonder, granted the Tannaim had none of the logical machinery mentioned above, but did the Tannaim have the sort of ordinary reasoning that the Stoics were investigating and which the latter succeeded in clarifying and formalizing by means of the discovery of *modus tollens*? That is, did the Tannaim argue in a manner resembling the *reductio ad absurdum*?

In his book *Studies in Talmudic Logic and Methodology*, Louis Jacobs has a chapter titled "The *Reductio ad Absurdum* argument in the Talmudic Literature" that begins with the claim that the *reductio ad absurdum* occupies an important place in the reasoning of both the tannaitic and amoraic periods and then goes on to offer many examples first in the Mishnah and then in Talmud Bavli. Jacobs distinguishes the expression that characterizes the argument in the

Mishnah from the expression used in the amoraic examples but he claims, incorrectly as will be argued, that the argument is essentially the same in both periods.

In Jacobs' examples from the Mishnah, most of the arguments which he characterizes as being cases of *reductio ad absurdum* have the following explicit or implicit structure. A possible legal position is considered and then rejected. To explain this rejection, consequences of imposing the original law are then described. Since the consequences presented are clearly undesirable it follows that rejecting the original possible legal position is justified. The reasoning involves rejecting the original premise/law because a conclusion/law it leads to is unacceptable. Also, the consequences of the entertained legal position are all closely related to that legal position, with a resulting situation that brings to mind the phrase 'infinite regress'.[268]

Here is one of Jacobs' examples with his analysis:

M. Pesahim 1:2:

'One need not fear that a weasel may have dragged (*hametz*, leaven, i.e. after the house has been searched for leaven on the night before Passover) from house to house, or from place to place; for if so from courtyard to courtyard, or from town to town: there is no end to the matter.'

Jacobs' analysis:

"The Mishnah suggests that there is no need for a number of persons to search for leaven simultaneously in order to avoid the possibility of a weasel dragging the leaven into the room after one person has searched for it, for if this were necessary then it would be necessary logically to search all the courtyards of the town simultaneously and

---

[268] For a similar observation, see Samely, *Rabbinic Interpretation of Scripture in the Mishnah,*192n58.

indeed all towns and this is obviously impossible. Here we have a clear *reductio ad absurdum* argument."

Although in Jacobs' examples the *absurdum* is not something that is logically impossible but rather something that is impractical to legislate or otherwise legally undesirable, still it can be argued that the reasoning is of the sort characteristic of the method of *reductio ad absurdum*. Namely, a proposition is considered, in the case of the Mishnah having the form 'the law should be X'. It is inferred that consequences that would naturally and inevitably then follow are considered. Since those consequences are obviously undesirable, it is recognized that to avoid those consequences it is necessary to not have the law be X.

The reasoning in Jacobs' examples from the Mishnah resembles simple cases of the Greek *reductio ad absurdum* but not the more complex uses seen in Socrates' elenchus technique. Socrates' famous examples occur as debates or arguments with very explicit steps while in the Mishnah examples some of the reasoning must be inferred. Second, as mentioned above, in the Mishnah examples the consequences of the proposed law are usually very closely related to the original proposition. There is consequently hardly any need to argue that they would follow from the proposition. These arguments are therefore simpler. Also, Socrates' elenchus involves a number of steps; they have the form: A implies B, and B implies C, and C implies D, but D is impossible, thus A must be false. In the examples from the Mishnah the format is shorter, typically: A implies B, but B would clearly be bad, therefore we cannot have A as the law.

In the examples Jacobs brings from the Mishnah we do not see arguments of the Socratic elenchus form: starting off believing A to be true, it is then shown that A implies B, and then that B implies C which implies D, but D is impossible so A must be false. The logical significance for us of these more complex arguments that are not seen in the Mishnah is that one simple thought does not connect A and D, yet the one who presents it, realizes that D being false implies that A is false. The reasoning in these complex arguments is closer than is the reasoning of the simple *reductio ad absurdum*, to approaching the reasoning involved in *modus tollens* which irrespective of the meaningful content of the statements, expresses that if A implies B and B is not true, then A cannot be true.

Socrates, mimicking the manner of the Sophists, set out to show the Athenians that they did not have knowledge that they thought they had. The Tannaim (who lived about 500 years later) constructed arguments for completely different reasons. They were busy extending the Torah, that is, deriving laws from the Torah about particular points of law not explicitly stated in the Torah. With such a project to uphold the Torah and extend its laws, and perhaps because of an associated conservative principle, the Tannaim did not have experience with the more complex form of *reductio ad absurdum*. Because of their conservative rule of refraining from למד מן הלמד, *lamed min ha-lamed*, no legal derivation was to be obtained from a previous derivation. If B is derived from A, one could not obtain C as a law via the reasoning A implies B which in turn implies C. In this way they limited the extent of possible error involved in deriving a law.[269]

Unlike those that Jacobs cites from the Mishnah and Tosefta, there are examples of tannaitic *reductio ad absurdum*, where A and B are not so obviously conceptually or practically related. In this sense, such arguments more closely approach a simple Greek *reductio ad absurdum* argument. One such example can be found in T. Pesahim, chap.4, halakha 6.[270]

With regard to the issue of other animals slaughtered to serve as paschal offerings, R. Eliezer rules these sacrifices invalid while R. Yehoshua declares them valid.

---

[269] For more discussion of this principle, see footnotes 94, 100.

[270] See Lieberman's edition. This example was referenced in Chapter Three because it also occurs as a baraita on B. Zevahim 11a containing the phrase או חילוף דברים.

R. Yehoshua presents a qal v'homer defense of his position. R. Eliezer follows, claiming that R. Yehoshua's argument suggests a similar qal v'homer argument that leads to the conclusion that the paschal offering offered at the right time, on the 14th of Nissan, may serve instead as some other sacrifice. Thus the absurd conclusion is reached that a paschal offering offered at the right time but not for its own sake is valid. He says incredulously, "And is this what you are saying?!"

R. Eliezer can therefore be said to have presented a *reductio ad absurdum* argument disproving R. Yehoshua's position. R. Yehoshua goes on to dispute R. Eliezer's claim that he has presented an argument that is just like his.[271]

Turning to Jacobs' examples of *reductio ad absurdum* arguments from the amoraic period we find that unlike the tannaitic examples he presented, there are many arguments where there is a conceptual leap between the initial claim A and the consequence B with B recognized as clearly impossible. These arguments are therefore more robust examples of intentional *reductio ad absurdum* reasoning.

Consider one of Jacobs' examples, this one from B. Bava Metzia 9a:

'Why does a rider (of a lost animal) fail to acquire it if he rides in the town? R. Kahana said: Because it is unusual for men to ride in the town (i.e. they dismount from their beasts in the town hence the act of riding does not constitute a valid act of acquisition in a town). R. Ashi said to R. Kahana: If so (*'ela me' attah*) if one lifts up a money-bag (that is abandoned and belongs to the one who acquires it) on the Sabbath (when it is forbidden to handle money), since it is unusual to lift a money-bag on the Sabbath, does this mean that he does not acquire it? But you must say that come what may he acquires it, here too, come what may he acquires it.'

---

[271] In the baraita version, R. Yehoshua attacks the qal v'homer conditional in R. Eliezer's qal v'homer argument, as not making sense.

R. Ashi uses *reductio ad absurdum* to disprove the claim that a rider of a lost animal does not acquire the animal by riding it in the town.

R. Kahana starts by supporting the claim that the rider does not acquire the animal by riding it in the town. He says it is so, because it is unusual for an owner to ride his animal in the town, riding the animal in the town does not constitute a valid act of acquisition. R. Ashi then argues that if an unusual act cannot be a valid act of acquisition, then picking up an abandoned bag of money on the Sabbath should not be a valid way to acquire the money. But it is known that it is! Thus it must be false that a rider does not acquire an animal by riding it in the town.

Another example, one not cited by Jacobs, is a passage on B. Bava Batra 11a-b discussed in Chapter Eight whose parallel in the Yerushalmi is an *o'kheiluf* argument.

R. Yehuda Nesi'ah asks R. Yannai, "From where is it derived that a son precedes a daughter with regard to inheriting the mother's property?" R. Yannai answers that the verse, Num. 27:8, uses the word 'tribes' thereby making an association, i.e. a *hekesh*, between the father's tribe to the mother's tribe: just as with regard to the father's tribe, the son precedes the daughter, so too, with regard to the mother's tribe, the son precedes the daughter.

R. Yehuda Nesi'ah responds, "If indeed that is right and there is a *hekesh* between the mother's tribe and the father's tribe established by the word in the verse 'tribes', then the following should also be derived from the *hekesh*: just as with regard to the father's tribe, the *bekhor*, i.e. the eldest son, receives double the inheritance of the other sons, so too with regard to the mother's tribe, her *bekhor* should receive a double inheritance."

R. Yannai turned to his attendant and said, "Take me away from here, this man does not want to learn."

451

R. Yehuda Nesi'ah was clearly aiming for a sort of *reductio ad absurdum*, showing R. Yannai that he errs in his position that the son precedes the daughter in inheriting from the mother. R. Yannai apparently did not have a better derivation for his ruling that the son precedes the daughter in inheriting from the mother just as he does from the father, one that R. Yehuda Nesi'ah would not be able to critique. Therefore all he could do is criticize R. Yehuda Nesi'ah, describing him as one who does not ask honest questions and therefore a person he should not waste his time on.

A Robust Example of *Modus Tollens* Reasoning in the Bavli

In the Bavli there are also arguments whose structure reflects *modus tollens* reasoning.[272]

---

[272] The passage in B. Bava Kamma 29a seems not to have ever been recognized as reflecting *modus tollens* reasoning. Luzzatto does not cite this passage as an example. The few examples he does give in either his *Derekh Tevunot* or *Sefer HaHigayon* (1742) of reasoning that fit *modus tollens* are too simple and contrived to be good examples representative of this type of argument.

Luzzatto does not describe what we know as *modus tollens* in a direct manner. He has no name for it, and he describes it in the context of refuting the conclusion of what we know as *modus ponens* which he calls, הקש התלוי. He does not use Greek or Latin terminology at all (or any symbols) rather he introduces his own Hebrew terminology. (Interestingly he does not deal with the contrapositive of a conditional and therefore has no term for it.) One of his two cited passages is not only very simple but is also a somewhat artificial example of *modus tollens*. Artificial, because the conditional premise is not really a conditional but rather an equality: if Rabbi Akiva and Rabbi Yossi agree in their rulings then they have the same exact set of rulings. See *Derekh Tevunut*, chapter seven, the passage from B. Pesahim 19a. The passage in Chapter 8 of *Derekh Tevunot*, citing B. Bava Kamma 84a, contains a trivially simple example, perhaps presented to convince his readers of the truth of *modus tollens* rather than as an argument whose validity is appreciated by apprehending that it has the logical form of *modus tollens*:

אם כל 'נתינה' שבתורה היא ממון, גם "כאשר יתן מום באדם" הוא ממון

"כאשר יתן מום" ודאי אינו ממון

אם כן, לא כל "נתינה" שבתורה ממון

452

The following second part of M. Bava Kamma 3:1 appears at the bottom of B.Bava Kamma 28a:

If his jug broke in the public domain and someone slipped in the water [that poured out of the jug] or was injured by the shards of the jug, he is liable [for the damages incurred]. R. Yehuda says, in a case where the owner acted with intent he is liable, while in a case where he acted without intent he is not liable.

After analyzing the anonymous statement of the mishnah which it later attributes to R. Meir, the Gemara takes up R. Yehuda's statement to consider what he means by 'acting with intent'. The Gemara cites Rabba who understands it to mean the following: Even if the owner intended no more than to lower the jug from his shoulder

---

Luzzatto uses his own Hebrew terminology to refer also to different ways of changing or exchanging parts of a categorical statement, making heavy use of the common roots ה,פ,כ, to turning over, and ח,ל,פ, to exchange. He uses ההפכיים to refer to opposites and הנגדים to refer to negatives. Luzzatto uses the word חלוף to refer to a number of different types of exchanges of parts of a statement. It is for this reason that I do not believe that he knew what has been spelled out in this book, that או חלוף, an expression he does not mention, does not mean different things in different passages but instead has a perfectly precise meaning throughout rabbinic literature. And further that this meaning is perfectly distinct from the precise tannaitic phrase, חלוף דברים, which he also does not mention.(I suspect that the reason he did not discover that או חלוף is perfectly precise logical terminology is perhaps because he was not adept at using symbols.There is no symbolization in his two books.) Luzzatto uses חלוף המאמר הפשוט and חלוף כולל to refer to the converse of a categorical statement, and חלוף קצתי or חלוף מקרי to refer to what might be called a limited converse. He also uses חלוף הפכי כולל to refer to the contrapositive of a categorical statement. He makes no mentions of the contrapositive of a conditional statement. Luzzatto does not locate examples of the limited converse or the contrapositive in the Talmud. Rather he cites a categorical statement from the Talmud and shows how to obtain its limited converse and its contrapositive which are not present in the talmudic passage. His stated aim with his books was to show the Talmud student what logical inferences could be made from different statements in the Talmud.

and in so doing accidentally breaks it, he is liable for the damages he caused.

It is clear that in the mishnah, R. Yehuda's statement is meant to limit the scope of R. Meir's blanket anonymous statement finding the owner liable. This is what Abaye is referring to when he points out to Rabba, that if R. Yehuda is to be understood as holding the owner liable if he so much as tried to lower the jug from his shoulder when it broke and caused damage then it must follow that R. Meir holds an individual liable for the damages even if the jug broke on its own unprecipitated by any intent even just to move the jug.

In the language of the Gemara, Abaye's response to Rabba's explanation of what R. Yehuda means by 'he intends' is, the following with מכלל meaning 'from this claim it would follow that':

מכלל, דמחייב רבי מאיר אפילו נפשרה ?!

Rabba responds that he is aware of this implication that follows from his claim on R. Yehuda's position. He says that indeed, even if the owner is holding the jug by its handle when the jug collapses, R. Meir would rule him liable for the damages his broken jug causes.

The Gemara goes on to consider whether indeed R. Meir would rule in this way. It quotes a baraita that describes his rulings (as compared to those of the Sages) on different cases ranging in the degree to which the perpetrator could be considered to have acted negligently. The last case concerns a person who put his pitchers on the roof to dry them out and then an atypically strong, completely unexpected type of wind blew them off and they caused damage. R. Meir agrees with the Sages in ruling the person not liable for the damages caused by these jugs. Evidently then R. Meir acknowledges that a person is not liable for damage caused by his property if it was not reasonable for him to anticipate these consequences, that is, where the circumstances were completely beyond his control.

This case from the baraita refutes the implication of Rabba's understanding of R. Yehuda's position, that even when there is no act of negligence attributable to the owner, he is liable for whatever damage his jug caused. But if the implication of Rabba's statement is false, the Gemara understands that his statement must also be false, and Rabba is not correctly interpreting R. Yehuda's disagreement with R. Meir. Abaye then moves on to suggest a different understanding of the substance of the disagreement between R. Meir and R. Yehuda.

In summary,

Rabba claims that by 'if he intended' R. Yehuda means, if the owner so much as intended to lower the jug off his shoulder and this led to the jug accidentally breaking, then the owner is liable for damages it causes.

Abaye then points out:
[If R. Yehuda holds that an owner is liable for damages his jug causes as unintended results of the owner trying to lower the jug off his shoulder] then it follows that R. Meir holds that even if the jug's breaking is not precipitated by any act at all by the owner, he is liable for the damages it causes.

The Gemara then examines what direct evidence it has for this conclusion and finds that it has evidence that refutes it.

The Gemara attributes this realization to Abaye, on the basis of which it is understood that Rabba is wrong and R. Yehuda does not mean that 'if he intends' refers to lowering the jug from his shoulder, that the owner would be liable for any damages caused by the jug from any resulting accident.

The Gemara follows with "Rather, Abaye says, what R. Meir and R. Yehuda are disagreeing about is instead...."

With the following symbols,

P = 'R. Yehuda holds that an owner is liable for the damage his jug causes as unintended results of the owner trying to lower the jug off his shoulder'

Q = 'R. Meir holds that even if the jug's breaking is not precipitated by any act at all by the owner he is liable for the damages it causes',

the argument can be represented as follows:[273]

Abaye: If **P** then **Q**

Gemara. **Q** is false

Abaye: Therefore, **P** is false

---

[273] This passage from the Bavli is a robust example of *modus tollens* reasoning in that the two premises and the conclusion are expressed explicitly in the Bavli's development of the argument, none of these needs to be inferred in order to make the case that the argument is an example of *modus tollens* reasoning. This is not the situation with the biblical arguments that Adina Moshavi discusses in "Two Types of Argumentation Involving Rhetorical Questions in Biblical Hebrew Dialogues," Biblical Studies on the Web, Vol 90 (2009) p. 32-46. Following on the work of Van Selms and Douglas Walton, Moshavi applies pragmatic argument theory to *reconstruct* (her expression) certain biblical rhetorical questions as *modus tollens* arguments in order to argue that they can be represented as sound arguments. (She reconstructs other biblical rhetorical questions as denying the antecedent in a conditional statement to yield the negation of the consequent, and therefore as logically unsound.) By her account this *reconstruction* involves adding into the biblical material one or even both *missing* premises and sometimes even also the conclusion, in order to turn the biblical expression into a *modus tollens* argument. It seems to this author that her addition of the conditional premise is often forced because it is not at all clear that the speakers have a conditional proposition in mind at all, often it seems more likely that their thinking amounts to an implied equality, i.e. A=B. Because Moshavi's examples could just as well be "reconstructed" in other logically simpler and more primitive ways that capture the thinking involved, they should not be seen as suggesting that the Torah reflects biblical characters engaged in *modus tollens* reasoning. In contrast to Moshavi's examples from the Torah see 1 Corinthians 15:12, 13, 20 for a bona fide case of *modus tollens* reasoning in the New Testament.

Conclusions

The following questions were put forth early in this Appendix II:

Did the Tannaim have the sort of ordinary reasoning that the Stoics investigated and succeeded in clarifying and formalizing by means of the discovery of *modus tollens*? That is, did the Tannaim argue in a manner resembling the *reductio ad absurdum*?

I turned to Louis Jacobs' Studies in Talmudic Logic to examine the examples he gives of *reductio ad absurdum* in tannaitic literature. I found that the most serious way in which Jacobs' tannaitic examples fell short of being robust examples of simple *reductio ad absurdum* is that the inferences involved closely related propositions. So in inferring from a proposition A to a proposition B there was hardly any need to argue that B would follow from A.

Unlike those that Jacobs cites from the Mishnah and Tosefta, there are examples of tannaitic *reductio ad absurdum*, where A and B are not so obviously conceptually or practically related. Such arguments more closely approach a simple Greek *reductio ad absurdum* argument. One such example that I presented is found in T. Pesahim, chap.4, halakha 6.

Turning to Jacobs' examples of *reductio ad absurdum* arguments from the amoraic period I found that unlike the tannaitic examples he presented, there are many arguments where there is a conceptual leap between the initial claim A and the consequence B with B recognized as clearly impossible. These arguments are therefore more robust examples of intentional *reductio ad absurdum* reasoning. I presented one of Jacobs' examples and followed it with a particularly strong example of my own from B. Bava Batra 11a-b.

Thus there are many amoraic examples of arguably robust simple *reductio ad absurdum* arguments. Simple in the sense that each involves one inference from a proposition A to another proposition B rather than resembling the Socratic examples in Plato's dialogues that involve a chain of inferences concluding with an impossibility (I explained that the absence at least in tannaitic literature of this more complex form of *reductio ad absurdum* with a chain of inferences, may be due to the sort of careful position to avoid *lamed min ha-lamed,* למד מן הלמד.[274])

My answer to the questions posed is that there do not seem to be many real examples of r*eductio ad absurdum* in tannaitic literature.
There are though, good examples of the simple sort in amoraic literature.

I presented an example of *modus tollens* reasoning that I discovered on B. Bava Kamma 29a. I believe this is the first *bona fide* example to ever appear in a publication.[275]

Witnesses to simple *reductio ad absurdum* reasoning in amoraic literature and an example of *modus tollens* reasoning do not imply that the Amoraim could be expected to be reliably accurate in the use of such reasoning. (As shown in Chapters Seven and Eight, the Bavli was oblivious to the logical shortcomings of the tannaitic *o'kheiluf* argument that were laid out in Chapter Five, including ignorance of the logically necessary way (that what is) a *modus tollens* argument must conclude irrespective of its semantic content. In Chapter Eight, the reader saw that Rava did not recognize how his qal v'homer argument divided up into premises and a conclusion and that in committing to the conclusion he was also committing to the premises.) As explained at the start of this appendix, it is the nature of logical discoveries that they uncover the rules of the correct reasoning that people have been using and distinguish it from logical fallacies. Logic formalizes the valid reasoning that people have been using without thinking about the underlying form of their reasoning. Without the benefit of the knowledge of these discoveries the rabbis

---

[274] See footnotes 94, 100.
[275] See footnote 272 for discussion of how Luzzatto's examples are either weak or contrived.

458

could not commit arguments to the sort of analysis conducted by the Stoic philosopher in Chapter Five to determine whether the arguments were valid and to determine precisely what was problematic about them.

Bibliography

Rabbinic Sources

Mekhilta de-Rabbi Ishmael. Edited by Haim Shaul Horovitz and Israel
    Rabin. Jerusalem: Bamberger and Wahrman, 1960.
Sifre Numbers. Edited by Haim Shaul Horovitz. Leipzig, 1917.
    Reprint, Jerusalem: Shalem. 1992.
Sifre de-Be Rav. Edited by Meir Friedmann. Vienna: J. Holzwarth,
    1864. Reprint, Jerusalem, 1978.
Sifre on Numbers: An Annotated Edition. Edited by Menahem I.
    Kahana. Jerusalem: Magnes, 2011 [Hebrew].
Sifre: Bamidbar, Devarim, im perush ha-meyuhas leha-Rabad (and
    with the Vilna Gaon's text version of the Sifre). The recently
    recovered commentary attributed to the Rabad, Abraham ben
    David of Posquieres, approximately 1125-1198, was edited by
    Hebert Basser. Edited by Ralbag, Eli'ezer Dan ben Aryeh
    Leyb, Israel: Mechon Sofrim, 2009.
Sifra: Commentar zu Leviticus. Edited by I. H. Weiss. Vienna:
    Schlossberg, 1862.
Sifra with the Commentary of Rabbenu Hillel. Shachne
    Koleditzky,(editor). Jerusalem, 1992.
Siphre ad Deuteronomium. Edited by Louis Finkelstein. New York:
    Jewish Theological Seminary of America, 1993.
Sifre Zutta. Edited by H. S. Horovitz. Leipzig: Gustav Fock, 1917.
    Reprint, Jerusalem: Shalem, 1992.

English Translations of Rabbinic Sources

Mekilta de-Rabbi Ishmael, Vol I-III. Translated by Jacob Z.
    Lauterbach. New York: Jewish Publication Society of
    America,1933. Reprint 1976.
Hammer, Reuven. *Sifre: A Tannaitic Commentary on the Book of
    Deuteronomy*, translated from the Hebrew, Yale University
    Press: New Haven and London, 1987.
Sefaria online translation of the *Mekhilta, Sifre Bamidbar, Sifra, and
    Sifre Deuteronomy*
Talmud Bavli: Pesachim Volume II, Artscroll Schottenstein Edition,
    Mesorah Publications, 2001, translation into English with
    notes.

--------- *Bava Batra*

--------*Avodah Zarah*

Schottenstein Talmud Yerushalmi: Tractate Pesachim 2, Mesorah
Publications, 2011, translation into English with notes.

Neusner, Jacob. *Sifra: An Analytic Translation*. Atlanta: Scholars
Press, 1988.

Neusner, Jacob. *Sifre to Numbers: An American Translation*. Atlanta:
Scholars Press, 1986.

Non-rabbinic Ancient Sources

Barnes, Jonathan (editor). *The Complete Works of Aristotle*, the
revised Oxford Translation. Princeton University Press, 1984.

Johnson, C.B. (Series Editor). *Dialogues of Plato*. Simon & Schuster
Paperbacks, 2010.

Reinhardt, Tobias (editor). *Cicero's Topica,* New York and Oxford:
Oxford   University   Press,   2003.

Secondary Sources

Abraham, Michael, Dov Gabbay and Uri Schild. *Studies in Talmudic
Logic*, Volume 10. London: College Publications, 2013.

-------- מידות הדרש ההגיוניות כאבני הבסיס להיסקים לא דדוקטיביים: מודל לוגי
(לקל וחומר בניין אב והצד השווה, בתוך: בד"ד 23 (תשע

Berchman, Robert. "Rabbinic Syllogism: The Case of Mishnah-
Tosefta Tohorot." In *Approaches to Ancient Judaism V:
Studies in Judaism and its Greco-Roman Context.*
Edited by
William Scott Green, 81-98. Missoula: Scholars Press, 1985.

Bobzien, Suzanne. "Ancient Logic." In *The Stanford Encyclopedia of
Philosophy* (Summer 2020 Edition). Edited by Edward N.
Zalta.
<https://plato.stanford.edu/archives/sum2020/entries/lo
gic-   ancient/>

---------"Logic. "In *The Cambridge Companion to the Stoics*. Edited by
Brad Inwood, 85-123. Cambridge: Cambridge University
Press, 2006.

Bobzien, Suzanne, with Jonathan Barnes and Mario Mignucci.
"Logic: III The Stoics" in *The Cambridge History of Hellenistic
Philosophy*. Edited by Kiempe Algra, Jonathan Barnes, Jaap
Mansfeld,   and   Malcolm   Schofield,   92-176.   Cambridge:
Cambridge University Press, 2006.

Cohen, David. *Kol HaNivuah*. Jerusalem: Mosad Harav *Kook*, 1969 [Hebrew].

Chernick, Michael. "Internal Constraints on *Gezerah Shawah*'s Applications." *The Jewish Quarterly Review*, LXXX, Nos.3-4 (January-April, 1990), 253-282.

Daube, David. "Rabbinic Methods of Interpretation and Hellenistic Rhetoric." *Hebrew Union College Annual* 22 (1949): 239-264.

Elman, Yaakov. "'It is No Empty Thing': Nahmanides and the Search for Omnisignificance." *The Torah U-Madda Journal* 4 (1993):1-83.

Epstein, Y.N. *Prolegomena to Tannaitic Literature: Mishnah, Tosefta, and Halakhic Midrashim*. Jerusalem: Magnes Press, 1959 [Hebrew].

Gabbay, Dov M. and Karl Schlechta. *A New Perspective on Nonmonotonic Logics*. Switzerland: Springer International Publishing, 2016.

Hammer, Reuven. *Akiva: Life, Legend, Legacy*. Philadelphia: The Jewish Publication Society and University of Nebraska Press, 2015.

Harris, Jay. *How Do We Know This?: Midrash and the Fragmentation of Modern Judaism*. Albany: SUNY Press,1994.

Hayes, Christine. *What's Divine about Divine Law?: Early Perspectives*. Princeton and Oxford: Princeton University Press, 2015.

Heschel, Abraham Joshua. *Heavenly Torah as Refracted Through the Traditions*. Translated by Gordon Tucker with Leonard Levin. New York and London: Continuum, 2007.

Hidary, Richard. *Rabbis and Classical Rhetoric: Sophistic Education and Oratory in the Talmud and Midrash*. Cambridge and New York: Cambridge University Press, 2018.

Hoffman, David. *Zur Einleitung in die halachischen Midraschim*. Berlin, 1888.

Holtz, Barry W. *Rabbi Akiva: Sage of the Talmud*. New Haven and London: Yale University Press, 2017.

Jacobs, Louis. *Studies in Talmudic Logic and Methodology*. London: Vallentine, Mitchell,1961.

———- "The Aristotelean Syllogism and the Qal Wa-Homer." *The Journal of Jewish Studies*, Vol IV. No 4 (1953):154-157.

Janowitz, Naomi and Andrew Lazarus. "Rabbinic Methods of Inference and the Rationality Debate." *The Journal of Religion*, vol 72, no.4 (Oct. 1992):491-511.

Kahana, Menahem. "The Halakhic Midrashim." In *The Literature of the Jewish People in the Period of the Second Temple and the Talmud, Volume III: The Literature of the Sages.* Edited by Shmuel Safrai, Ze'ev Safrai, Joshua J. Schwartz, and Peter Tomson, 83-87. Leiden: Brill, 2006.

Kanarfogel, Ephraim. *The Intellectual History and Rabbinic Culture of Medieval Ashkenaz.* Wayne State University Press, 2012.

Kneale, William Calvert and Martha Kneale.*The Development of Logic*, New York: Oxford University Press, 1971.

Kraemer, David. *The Mind of the Talmud: An Intellectual History of the Bavli.* New York: Oxford University Press, 1990.

Kunst, Arnold. "An Overlooked Type of Inference." *Bulletin of the School of Oriental and African Studies*, vol. X, Part 4 (1942): 976-991.

Lachs, S. *A Rabbinic Commentary on the New Testament: The Gospels of Matthew, Mark and Luke*, Ktav Publishing, New York 1987.

Lieberman, Saul. *Hellenism in Jewish Palestine*, New York: The Jewish Theological Seminary of America, 1962.

Long, Anthony A. *Stoic Studies.* Cambridge: Cambridge University Press, 1996.

Luzzatto, Moshe Hayyim, 1707-1742, author. *Sefer Ha'Higayon.* Jerusalem and Bnei Brak: HaMesorah, 1985 [Hebrew].

------ *The Book of Logic*, a translation of *Sefer Ha'Higayon* by Sackton, D. and Tscholkowsky, C., Jerusalem: Feldheim Publishers, 1995.

-------- *Derekh Tevunot, 1742.*
The Ways of Reason, a translation of *Derekh Tevunot* by Sackton, D. and Tscholkowsky, C., Jerusalem: Feldheim Publishers, 1997.

Maccoby, Hyam. *Early Rabbinic Writings.* Cambridge and New York: Cambridge University Press, 1988.

------ *The Mythmaker: Paul and the Invention of Christianity.* New York: Barnes & Noble Publishing, 1998.

Mates, Benson. *Stoic Logic.* Berkeley: University of California Press,1953.

Moshavi, Adina. "Two Types of Argumentation Involving Rhetorical Questions in Biblical Hebrew Dialogues", *Biblical Studies on the Web*, Vol 90 (2009), 32-46.

Novick,Tzvi. "Rhetorical Markers in *A Fortiori* Argumentation in Biblical and Post-biblical Hebrew Period." In *The Reconfiguration of Hebrew in the Hellenistic Period.*

Edited by J. Joosten, D. Machiela, and J-S Rey, 173-188.
Leiden: Brill, Studies on the Texts of the Desert of Judah,
2012.

Rosen-Zvi, Ishay. התנאית בספרות קריאה :למדרש משנה בין (Raanana:
Open University), 2020.

Rubenstein, Jeffrey L. *The Culture of the Babylonian Talmud*.
Baltimore and London:The John Hopkins University Press,
2003.

Russell, Bertrand. "On Denoting." *Mind,* Vol 14. No. 56 (Oct. 1905):
479–493.

Samely, Alexander. *Rabbinic Interpretation of Scripture in the
Mishnah*. New York and Oxford: Oxford University Press,
2002.

Schiffman, Lawrence H. *From Text to Tradition: A History of
Second Temple and Rabbinic* Judaism. Hoboken: Ktav, 1991.

Schwarz, Adolf. Der Hermeneutische Syllogismus in der
*Talmudischen Litteratur, Eln Beitrag Zur Geschichte Der Logik
Morgenlande, Karlsruhe*, 1901. as cited in Jacobs, 154.

Shenefelt, Michael and Heidi White. *If A, then B: How Logic Shaped
the World*. New York: Columbia University Press, 2013

Spivak, Amelia. "How are Scripture and Reason Related in the
Midrash Halakhah? Refutation of Neusner's Influential View
and its Serious Consequences." Submitted for publication.

Strack, Hermann L. and Gunter Stemberger. *Introduction to the
Talmud and Midrash*. Minneapolis:Fortress Press, 1996.

Tilly, Michael and Burton Visotzky(editors). *Judaism II*. Translated by
David E. Orton, Blandford Forum, Dorset, England. :Stuttgart:
Kohlhammer, 2021.

Vidas, Moulie. "Greek Wisdom in Babylonia." In *Envisioning Judaism,
Studies in Honor of Peter Schafer on the Occasion of his
Seventieth Birthday*. Tubingen:Mohr Siebeck, 2013.

------- Tradition and the *Formation of the Talmud*. Princeton and
Oxford: Princeton University Press, 2014.

Vidyabhusana, S.C. *A History of Indian Logic*. Calcutta:The Baptist
Mission Press, 1921.

Vilna Gaon's version of the *Sifre Bamidar* and the *Sifre
Deuteronomy*.

Weiss Halivni, David. *Peshat and Derash, Plain and Applied Meaning
in Rabbinic Exegesi*s. New York and Oxford: Oxford University
Press, 1991.

------- *The Formation of the Babylonian Talmud*. New York:00

Oxford University Press, 2013.

Wiseman, Allen. "A Contemporary Examination of the A Fortiori Argument Involving Jewish Traditions." 2010 Ph.D. Dissertation, University of Waterloo, Ontario, Canada

Yadin, Azzan. *Logos as Scripture: Rabbi Ishmael and the Origins of Midrash*. Philadelphia: University of Pennsylvania Press, 2004.

Yadin-Israel, Azzan. *Scripture and Tradition: Rabbi Akiva and the Triumph of Midrash*. Philadelphia: University of Pennsylvania Press, 2015.

General Index

Index of Primary Sources

Printed in the USA
CPSIA information can be obtained
at www.ICGtesting.com
LVHW022052281023
762411LV00004B/5